CO-ALJ-132

FLORIDA STATE
UNIVERSITY LIBRARIES

SEP   1995

Tallahassee, Florida

Portrait of
an Unknown Man

Portrait of an Unknown Man

Manuel Azaña and Modern Spain

Cipriano de Rivas Cherif

Translated and Edited by Paul Stewart

With an Introduction by Enrique de Rivas

Madison • Teaneck
Fairleigh Dickinson University Press
London: Associated University Presses

© 1995 by Associated University Presses, Inc.

All rights reserved. Authorization to photocopy items for internal or personal use, or the internal or personal use of specific clients, is granted by the copyright owner, provided that a base fee of $10.00, plus eight cents per page per copy is paid directly to the Copyright Clearance Center, 222 Rosewood Drive, Danvers, Massachusetts 01923. [0-8386-3584-9/95 $10.00 + 8¢ pp, pc.]

Associated University Presses
440 Forsgate Drive
Cranbury, NJ 08512

Associated University Presses
25 Sicilian Avenue
London WC1A 2QH, England

Associated University Presses
P.O. Box 338, Port Credit
Mississauga, Ontario
Canada L5G 4L8

The paper used in this publication meets the requirements
of the American National Standard for Permanence of Paper
for Printed Library Materials Z39.48-1984.

Library of Congress Cataloging-in-Publication Data

Rivas Cherif, Cipriano de, 1891–1967.
    [Retrato de un desconocido.   English]
    Portrait of an unknown man : Manuel Azaña and modern Spain /
Cipriano de Rivas Cherif ; translated and edited by Paul Stewart ;
with an introduction by Enrique de Rivas.
        p.   cm.
    Includes bibliographical references and index.
    ISBN 0-8386-3584-9 (alk. paper)
        1. Azaña, Manuel, 1880–1940. 2. Presidents—Spain—Biography.
3. Spain—Politics and government—1931–1939. I. Stewart, Paul,
1929– . II. Rivas, Enrique de, 1931– . III. Title.
DP268.R513   1995
946.081′092—dc20
    [B]   94-42956
                                                                                      CIP

PRINTED IN THE UNITED STATES OF AMERICA

This translation is dedicated
to Doña Dolores de Rivas Cherif de Azaña
1904–1993

Contents

1931

1933–1940

Epilogue

Translator's Preface

When the Spanish civil war broke out in 1936 John Gunther described Manuel Azaña, then at the height of his fame, as a man of mystery whom nobody really knew.[1] Yet, though Cipriano de Rivas Cherif titled his biography of Azaña *Portrait of an Unknown Man,* the book demonstrates that he knew his protagonist as well as any person can know another. Rivas Cherif remains constant in his admiration; but he writes with candor, and his biases are too ingenuously honest to mislead any reader. Indeed, Rivas Cherif's praises of his friend and brother-in-law provide a healthy corrective to counteract the scurrilous personal attacks by Azaña's political enemies, most of them completely unjustified, that have filtered into accounts by writers trying to be objective by including negative rumors.

This book's focus on one moderate political leader makes it a useful guide through the labyrinthine politics of Spain in the 1930s, whose complexity has sometimes been aggravated by efforts of historians to explain every nuance or to give voice to all of their varying sources. Certainly Rivas Cherif's approach provides a healthy corrective to the simplistic emphasis on Communist influence that commentators have used from the 1930s onward as a red herring or as a *deus ex machina* to explain the republic's failures and defeat. As an example, Rivas Cherif does not treat his hero as a great wartime leader, but he shows as no one else has done how significant a role Azaña did play throughout the civil war period. Other leaders, Francisco Largo Caballero and Indalecio Prieto, disappeared from the political scene in the course of the conflict; Juan Negrín rose to power during the war from relative obscurity. Only Azaña endured as a major leader, the predominant statesman, as he had through the decade.

The author chose not to use Azaña's name in this book. Instead he used various titles tracing Azaña's career: secretary of the Ateneo, candidate for office, premier, prisoner, president. In the Spanish text this sometimes causes confusion with other premiers and presidents and so forth. The difficulty disappears through capitalization of these terms when they apply to Azaña, but this device is my own and not the author's intention. My text has been the expanded 1979 revision of this book, but I have not included Enrique de Rivas's useful and scholarly footnotes, though they have often helped me in making this translation. That 1979 second revised edition also includes a longer introduction by Mr. Rivas, the author's son, and a generous selection of Azaña–Rivas Cherif correspondence.[2] In Chapter 44 I have quoted Azaña's 18 July 1938 speech at length, using the version in his *Complete Works.*[3]

A few explanations may help the uninitiated reader to understand better the world portrayed in this book. The *sereno* was a traditional night watchman who opened street doors of Spanish apartment buildings after lockup time. Obviously *serenos* also served as auxiliary policemen, and, just as obviously, many apartment dwellers retained their own keys as Azaña did for 23 calle de Hermosilla. A *tertulia* is an informal gathering of friends with no fixed membership but meeting with regularity of time and place. As with Dr. Samuel Johnson's circle at the Turk's Head in eighteenth-century London, *tertulias* in Azaña's day were exclusively masculine. *Tertulias* sometimes met very late at night. With evening meals served from 9:00 P.M. onwards, and evening theatrical performances beginning at 11:00, cafés stayed open until 2:00 A.M. or so to accommodate the after-theater crowd.

I thank Mrs. Azaña for permitting me to translate this book. Enrique de Rivas has provided encouragement at every step. He has read the manuscript carefully, and his suggestions have greatly improved the accuracy of the translation besides contributing information from his own knowledge and that of others whom he has consulted. My wife has also read the manuscript, and her suggestions have made all the difference on many pages that follow. Editors of Associated University Presses have clarified virtually every page of the text by their care and skill. A Fulbright scholarship in 1960–61, based on a different project, made it possible for us to live for eight months in Azaña's old neighborhood in Madrid, and that has helped me to get this translation right. I am also grateful for the sabbatical leave granted me by Southern Connecticut State University during which the translation was completed.

Enrique de Rivas has graciously provided a genealogy of the Rivas Cherif and Azaña Díaz clans to clarify relationships. They represent a professional-intellectual class that played a key role in the development of European republicanism and liberalism in the nineteenth and twentieth centuries. Everywhere he goes the author runs into family members, family friends, and members of his friends' families. Lawyers, writers, civil servants—professionals—they had a political orientation clearly different from that of the military, church, and business factions. Their efforts culminated in the Second Spanish Republic; their special tradition ended with its fall and the forty-year Franco regime that followed. Family connections with professional military officers, quite common for this class in Spain, gives Azaña's story special poignancy during the civil war.

Notes

1. John Gunther, *Inside Europe* (New York: Harper and Brothers, 1936), p. 163.
2. Cipriano de Rivas Cherif, *Retrato de un desconocido* (Mexico City: Ediciones

Grijalbo, 1979). The earlier edition (Mexico City: Editorial Oasis, 1961) was considerably shorter.

3. Manuel Azaña, *Obras completas,* ed. Juan Marichal, 4 vols. (Mexico City: Editorial Oasis, 1966–68), 3:378. A recent book reproducing civil war posters includes one showing Azaña's picture, which it identifies as the president of the republic, and a quotation from one of his speeches. The caption identifies both picture and speech as Juan Negrín's—a good example of English-language ignorance of Azaña's wartime role.

ENRIQUE DE RIVAS

Introduction

Azaña, Founder of Spanish Freedom

Manuel Azaña (1880–1940) emerged as the most forceful political and intellectual personality of the Second Spanish Republic (1931–1939). His brilliance and innovations as premier (October 1931–September 1933), his high ideals of statesmanship as leader of the parliamentary opposition (1934–35), and his service as president during the civil war (1936–39) made him a "symbol of the republic" at that time. He showed Spain's people a democratic way of escaping their miserable living standards and achieving a position of dignity for the first time in their history. In one of his famous speeches, Azaña said, "Liberty does not make men happy; it merely makes them men." On another occasion he asserted that he wanted to guide the country "by persuasion and votes." Those two phrases epitomize his humanitarian ideal and his political ideal for Spain. He wanted nothing more and nothing less than for our people to achieve the democratic aspirations that had constituted the western world's essential political dream through the centuries.

Fifty years have passed since Azaña's death in November 1940 when the forces of darkness eclipsed Europe's freedom. After thirty-six years of suffocating and bloody military dictatorship in Spain, and after the restoration of a democratic regime there with the establishment of a new constitution in 1978, he remains the "symbol of the republic"—both for those whose hopes lie in the democracy of his political ideals and for those who execrate those ideals. He also remains the central figure for those historians and other writers about this period who, in the words of the great Italian philosopher Benedetto Croce, believe in liberty as "history's eternal moving force."[1] Azaña appears in history as one of those men whose struggles for liberty became glorified by tragedy, the tragedy of his own people with whom he so closely identified and whose martyrdom during the civil war he shared.[2]

The political and historical figure of Azaña has, however, largely overshadowed the man himself, and his combination of extraordinary gifts of intelligence, culture, and sensitivity—rare in Spanish politicians—has caused many commentators to treat his personality as "enigmatic," "complex," and so forth. In fact Azaña's personality does not conform to any stereotype. Similarly, the motivation behind his political actions and his vocation as statesman does not fit the patterns of the rise to power of European politicians of his era, and Spanish politicians in particular. I believe that much of the fascination Azaña continues to exercise comes from this nonconformity. How could a man with no previous political office, a mere writer and not widely known, a private individual with neither great wealth nor pressure groups behind him emerge in a few months and by strictly democratic means as the major political figure in Spain? How, having come to power in this way, did he escape power's corruption? Why did this man without political ambition dedicate himself to politics to the point of sacrificing his life for it? In what kind of society, in what kind of ambience did all of this happen?

The answer to these questions constitutes the matter of this book the reader holds in his hands. Of more than fifty books dedicated to Azaña, only this one stands as a personal witness covering the most important twenty-five years of his career. The close friendship between Azaña and its author, Cipriano de Rivas Cherif (1891–1967), developed from their literary collaboration and common cultural interests. Family bonds strengthened their friendship when in 1929 Azaña married Rivas Cherif's younger sister. The title *Portrait of an Unknown Man* alludes to the fact that Azaña's real personality remained a mystery to most of the public. The book stands as a tribute to the concept of friendship in the purest Spanish Senecan tradition. Spaniards through the ages have valued friendship highly from the time of Seneca who wrote, "Look for a friend for whom you can sacrifice yourself." Thus Cipriano de Rivas Cherif suffered six years in Franco's prisons for the crime of his friendship and kinship with Manuel Azaña. The book itself comes as an indirect consequence of Franco's repression because Rivas Cherif wrote it during his imprisonment. It goes far beyond all that, however; it presents a lively and impassioned picture of the Spain in which its author lived between 1914 and 1940.

Cipriano de Rivas Cherif

Born in Madrid in 1891, son of a lawyer, Rivas Cherif dedicated himself from the age of seventeen to literature, especially to the theater as a stage director—a profession that did not even exist in the Spanish theater at the beginning of this century. A major renewal of Spain's theatrical scene occurred during the decade 1920–30 through the establishment of four "theaters of the vanguard." Because of his reputation as a director, beginning in 1929 he served with several professional companies. From 1930 to 1936 he worked with the company of Spain's most famous actress of the twentieth century, the great Catalan Margarita Xirgu. Rivas Cherif's theatrical work brought a revival of the classical Spanish repertory, the introduction of mod-

ern stage production, and the presentation of our theaters of works by modern authors, Spanish and foreign, like O'Neill, Schnitzler, Ghéon, Pirandello,
Alejandro Casona, and García Lorca.[3]

In July 1936 Rivas Cherif, then on a theatrical tour of Cuba and Mexico
with Margarita Xirgu's company, decided to return to Spain. Soon after his
arrival in a Madrid shaken by civil war, the government named him Spain's
consul general in Geneva, a post he held until May 1938 when he was named
Introducer of Ambassadors, a protocolary position attached to the Presidency of the Republic. He left Spain with Azaña and his party on 5 February
1939, a few kilometers ahead of Franco's troops. From that time Azaña and
his wife lived together with Rivas Cherif and his wife and their four children
in French exile until the occupation of France by Hitler's troops separated
them.

Chapter 51 of the book describes how Franco's police and the Gestapo
arrested Rivas Cherif in his home near Bordeaux. He was taken to Spain
and condemned to death, a sentence commuted to thirty-years imprisonment. His release after six years in prison has special interest for readers
in the United States because it came through intervention by Claude G.
Bowers, their former ambassador to the Spanish republic and a great admirer
of Azaña. Through his influence President Franklin D. Roosevelt interceded
in Rivas's interest and gained a pardon. In 1945 Bowers, then ambassador
in Chile, wrote to the wife of Rivas Cherif as follows:

> I hope that when he [Rivas Cherif] is out and has rejoined you and Mrs. Azaña
> you will let him know that the last thing Roosevelt did before his death and within
> two hours of his death was to give instructions that our Embassy should express
> interest and do all possible to secure the release. Rivas Cherif will have reason to
> be proud of that.[4]

An indomitable spirit, Rivas Cherif had continued his career in prison
through the formation of a theatrical school for fellow prisoners, and after
receiving permission they performed various classics of the Spanish theater.
Also during this period he wrote several plays, a novel, kept a diary, and,
most important for us, he wrote *Portrait of an Unknown Man*. The title has
several levels of meaning.

The Manuscript and Title

The manuscript consists of ten small notebooks of poor quality, grayish
paper, written on both sides with no margins. Excepting the first, all volumes
are in my father's handwriting. The story of that first volume nicely reflects
that of its author. After having written the first nine chapters, which filled
two notebooks, he suspected that the authorities would confiscate his papers, and as a precaution he asked his cellmate to copy out these first

notebooks into a single notebook. When, in fact, the sequestration of his papers came, prison officials did not take the notebook copied by that anonymous scribe, and it survives.

This episode would have no great importance in the story of this book except that it explains the author's determination not to use its protagonist's name. Not using Azaña's name served to emphasize the message of the book's title, but it also represented a precaution not to provide a pretext for its confiscation. During the years 1939–45 the Franco government forbade any mention of Azaña's name in Spain except for vilification.[5]

Testimony and Memorial

Rivas Cherif wrote *Portrait of an Unknown Man* between 3 November 1941, the first anniversary of Manuel Azaña's death, and 3 November 1943. Incarcerated in Santa María Prison (Cádiz) when he began it, he finished it in the Dueso Prison (Santander). He set down these events, then, when they remained fresh in people's minds. The period after World War I belonged to the recent past; the vicissitudes of the Second Spanish Republic were still very recent, and the civil war had hardly ended since executions continued and more than a half million political prisoners remained in their cells. In these circumstances, my father wrote this book entirely from memory, with his sorrow about the death of his great friend and brother-in-law still raw, the wounds of his own experience still unhealed, and facing a future as dark as his present, since the forces of international Nazism and Fascism seemed triumphant in Europe, Africa, and Asia.

In spite of all that, or perhaps because of it, Rivas Cherif decided to write his testimony about Azaña. In doing it, he fully realized that his friend had written his own testimony about his political activities in *Memoirs of Politics and War*. This great work of Azaña, however, deals almost exclusively with the events that occurred while he occupied government office (July 1931 to September 1933, February 1936, and May 1937 to January 1939). Rivas Cherif intended, above all, to fill in any gaps in Azaña's own record, the years before he achieved prominence in letters and politics, the period 1934–35 when he held no cabinet position, and the last twenty months of his life in 1939–40. For all of these reasons, Rivas Cherif's book varies in the tone and depth with which it covers events. He conceived of his book as complementary to Azaña's *Memoirs of Politics and War,* and that consideration governed his focus as he told his story. Destiny defied his intentions and ruled otherwise. The first, abridged edition of my father's book came out in Mexico in 1961, seven years before the first edition of Azaña's *Memoirs,* also published in Mexico. Rivas Cherif died in 1967. The second edition of Azaña's *Memoirs* was published in Spain in 1978, and publication of the complete version of *Portrait of an Unknown Man* came only at the end of

1979, almost perfectly coinciding with the fortieth anniversary of Azaña's death.

Cipriano de Rivas Cherif as Historian

Along with his unquenchable passion for the theater, Rivas Cherif wrote prolific criticism of literature, theater, ballet, and films. Altogether he contributed some twelve hundred articles to leading journals in Madrid and Mexico. This activity helps to explain his painstaking approach to making his *Portrait* an accurate narrative. Rivas Cherif did not intend to write history as an academician or a specialist. As he said, "that approach is always difficult, and it becomes impossible when you don't have the perspective of time." He did want to infuse his work with a sense of reality through immediate impressions, giving it "the color that the scholar's careful investigations lose, since he must keep to his documents and so loses the life that lies behind them."

One sees this concept of the biographer's role, modified by the natural selection of the author's memory, throughout *Portrait of an Unknown Man,* especially in the last part of the book, which treats the most recent period. This, then, was the conceptual ground from which he approached the writing of history. Rivas Cherif also struck an independent course in rejecting the current conventions of fictionalized biography. He refused to seek commercial success by adopting the patterns and style used by authors like Stefan Zweig, whose books had great popularity in the 1930s. Rivas Cherif agreed to add the subtitle *Life of Manuel Azaña* only at the insistence of his Mexican publisher who had a natural preoccupation with sales. He continued to emphasize that he had not written a *life* of Manuel Azaña; he had merely drawn a portrait. Some challenged that a portrait implied a life, that since Saint Ildefonso of Toledo's *De viris illustribus* (Lives of Famous Men) in the seventh century authors have called *lives* accounts that merely narrated the manifestations of human existence. Rivas Cherif, always passionate in his Pirandellian antinomies, would answer that you cannot put a life into a book; at most you can capture a *persona* in the Greek sense—that is, a mask. He, on the contrary, intended to show the real man behind the mask.

Azaña's own thinking also influenced Rivas Cherif about a biographer's limitations in dealing with his material. Azaña wrote a *Life of Don Juan Valera,* the famous nineteenth-century writer and diplomat, which won the National Prize for Literature in 1926. In writing it Azaña had wrestled with the impossibility of fully exposing a personality, and he admitted that he could "only explore a part of his [Valera's] interior garden with uncertain limits, and some landscapes he could only glimpse." Again, he lamented the impossibility of capturing the "essence" of a personality and said, "What remains to us of a person after we can no longer hear the inflections of his voice?"[6]

Rivas Cherif had advantages that Azaña did not in writing about Valera. He had known his subject very well. He could even reproduce conversations, almost transcribe them; comparisons of passages in the book with surviving letters between the two men show that. Apart from his acute sensitivity to the "living word," which developed from his daily theatrical activities, Rivas Cherif had an extraordinary memory.[7] In spite of all that, perhaps we must finally agree with Azaña that "each man remains an impenetrable mystery both in life and in death." Yet Rivas Cherif's eyewitness familiarity with his subject over a twenty-five-year span renders Azaña, if still mysterious in terms of his ultimate destiny, at least unusually accessible in his lifetime. Curiously, this book may even contribute to realizing a wish Azaña expressed in 1912 at the age of thirty-two. "I believe that a man of merit will not seek admiration from others. He would prefer to have them understand him—to have his life, for want of a better word, shared."[8]

Involvement in History

His own sense of participation provided Rivas Cherif with a special understanding of the history he wrote. He did sometimes play a significant role as protagonist, and he was often a privileged witness of these events. This shows up in his chronicle in his fondness for detail and wanting his reader to participate as he had in events and scenes that he describes. In this he shares the vision of historians like Saint-Simon in the eighteenth century. Furthermore, in the tradition of French and Spanish medieval chroniclers, Rivas Cherif tries to derive a moral or spiritual meaning from the events he describes.[9] The book also reflects a certain personal pride in having taken part in memorable events, like the pride shown by Bernal Díaz del Castillo, that simple soldier of Hernán Cortés in the sixteenth century. Indignant at "fabrications" in histories of the conquest of Mexico in which he had participated, Bernal Díaz called his the *true history*.

Portrait of an Unknown Man also belongs to another rich literary genre which appears throughout Spanish history: prison literature. Many Spanish writers have suffered imprisonment or exile, beginning with Miguel de Cervantes and including Saint John of the Cross, Quevedo, Fray Luis de León, Jovellanos, and in more recent times Buero Vallejo, José Hierro, and Miguel Hernández who died in prison. If this stands as an undoubted sign of Spanish society's intolerance, the works that took shape in their creators' minds in such circumstances remain as proof of man's power to transcend the environment by his indomitable spirit and interior freedom.

Notes

1. Benedetto Croce, *Le Storia come pensiero e come azione* (Bari: Latorza e Figle, 1938), p. 35. [The English title is *History as the Story of Liberty*.] Also see Enrique de Rivas, "Hacia una Bibliografía de Obras sobre Manuel Azaña," *Azaña* (Madrid: Ministerio de Cultura, 1991), pp. 343–73; Enrique de Rivas, "Obras de Manuel Azaña," *Comentarios y Notas a "Apuntes de Memoria" de Manuel Azaña y a las Cartas de 1938, 1939 y 1940* (Valencia: Pre-Textos, 1990), pp. 187–244.

2. "I recognize that the continuous presence of Spain in my mind has influenced me in very diverse ways. . . . It is undoubtedly the greatest influence in my moral life, the predominant element in my aesthetic education, my link with the past, my orientation towards the future. . . . I feel that I live in Spain, am expressed by it, and, if I can say such a thing, am at one with it. . . . One truth grieves my soul: impelled by barbarism Spain has returned to the depths of her misery. The class struggle analysis makes absolutely no sense here: that some persons have fallen so that other persons can stand. The decline has terribly crushed the whole population, as if an avalanche had hit it." Manuel Azaña, *Memorias políticas y de guerra* in *Obras completas,* ed. Juan Marichal, 4 vols. (Mexico City: Editorial Oasis, 1966–68), 4:628–29.

3. The Madrid theatrical monthly *El Público* dedicated its entire December 1989 issue to Rivas Cherif's theatrical career.

4. Letter of Claude G. Bowers, 1945, Archivo de Cipriano de Rivas Cherif, Mexico City.

5. Exaggerated censorship went to the point of requiring the inking out of Azaña's printed name at the end of the introduction to a book published in 1929.

6. Manuel Azaña, "*Asclepigenia* y la experiencia amatoria de Don Juan Valera," *Obras completas,* 1:1062.

7. The following example illustrates Rivas Cherif's mnemonic capacity. On 13 July 1940 he was imprisoned in an unlighted cell in the basement of Central Police Headquarters in the heart of Madrid. He remained incommunicado for a hundred days. During this time he occupied his mind by composing in his memory four thousand verses and two verse plays. Twenty-five years later he could still recite them. On the other hand, he had trouble remembering dates.

8. Manuel Azaña, "Cuadernillo de apuntes, Paris, 1912," *Obras completas,* 3:796.

9. The forty books Rivas Cherif translated include three books of memoirs: those of Casanova, the duke of La Rochefoucauld, and Mlle. de Lespinasse.

Portrait of
an Unknown Man

1914–17

1

Secretary of the Ateneo

He remembered details of our first encounter better than I did. Actually we merely glanced at each other. Having recently returned after taking my doctorate in law at Bologna, one fine May afternoon I went to look up old friends at Madrid's Ateneo.

I entered the lower lobby, celebrated in House annals as "the Crock Shop." Old-timers called it that because of some decorative pottery, part of its former adornment. My generation called those ceramics "chamber pots." Pedro Salinas, who came in with me, was showing off recent redecoration of "the Learned House." A few years would pass before he published his first poems. Years later, even toward the end of his life, the new Secretary of the Ateneo remembered with a smile our first unfortunate, chance encounter. It seems that I asked Salinas somewhat impertinently, "Who's responsible for this mess?" According to the Secretary, whose memory was as accurate as his foresight, Salinas gestured to warn me of his proximity. Deep in conversation with a group near us, he seemed not to notice my impudence, but he did.

Trying to reconstruct my first impression from later ones, I see him corpulent, more than just heavy; a double chin stretching from ear to ear rounded off his massive head. That head rested so solidly on his shoulders that he could hardly raise it above them even by stretching his neck. He had a pale complexion and blondish hair that appeared redder in his crisp, full moustache, its ends now trimmed, though in the past he had twisted them up as fashion decreed. Absentminded, relaxed, maybe he was smoking a cigarette, nervously flicking its ash and, by way of contrast, tranquilly watching the rising smoke. He leaned back in an easy chair, one leg crossed over the other. He wore a brown suit, or maybe gray. Habitual carelessness spoiled the effect of his good clothes, the impeccable work of an English tailor he had patronized for several years. To tell the truth, at first glance those suits didn't look like much.

I soon observed that the Ateneo's new visible elegance involved more basic reforms. For the new Secretary responsible for that elegance, these reforms had two dimensions. A year before that spring of 1914 he had joined Melquíades Álvarez's Reformist Republicans, a new party in the tradition of Emilio Castelar's Possibilists. Their specific purpose was to bring Spain's monarchy up to current European standards of democracy and freedom. At the same time mandated elections for a new governing junta at the Ateneo had established him as its Secretary. He had only very recently emerged as an active member to fight against a campaign to discredit Segismundo Moret, the society's former president. For this the Secretary had abandoned his refuge in a *tertulia* whose members jokingly referred to themselves as "the vital forces" because they did nothing but kill time.

He had never spoken in public; then one afternoon in the course of a discussion he rose in the meeting hall to defend the Ateneo's previous administration. My friends described it as a revelation. He had warned that behind the unjustified campaign to expel former leaders there lurked antiliberal reaction against the Ateneo's distinctive spirit. A society without peer and without model, it transcended the limits of a mere association or recreational *tertulia* through its involvement in academy, church, and tribunal. I need not mention its famous public library. Thus it exactly assumed the role played by clubs that had developed in France in the past century.

From curiosity I attended a regular monthly meeting of members. A band of unconditional admirers and a solid majority of supporters backed the new Secretary. From his side of the presidential table he listened unperturbed, with a kind of cunning seriousness, to interpellations and quibbles about rules that mimicked debates in the Cortes. Finally he intervened with persuasive eloquence—and a relentless logic whose conclusiveness almost seemed irritating. In the subsequent vote he easily defeated his opponents. His special antagonist, Sandalio Tendero, an amateur lawyer, had annoyed both sides in the discussion by his minute examination of the society's financial records.

At that time Rafael Sánchez Ocaña moved in a circle of youths whom we judged likely to succeed in politics. Still a young man, though older than my age group, his short stature, his vivacity, loquacity, and boyish congeniality made him seem more of our generation than his own, and we called him "Rafaelito." One night he insisted that I join him and other friends to attend some kind of rally or public meeting that the Ateneo's new Secretary had scheduled at the Peristyle on the calle de Villanueva near the corner of Velázquez. Its name reflected a former grandeur; it had become a skating rink.

At first I decided not to go. With little interest in politics and less in the Reformist party's activities, I felt indifferent, though not hostile, toward the new party. Finally I did decide to go with some other Ateneo members to hear the Secretary in this, his second venture in his special vocation. Somewhat earlier he had participated in a rally in Alcalá de Henares, his hometown, with Enrique de Mesa, a former Ateneo secretary and a recognized poet of ten years standing. He, too, was trying out professional politics at that time but did not persist in it.

I have forgotten none of the details, though they must have seemed insignificant, trifling. Their persistence in my memory demonstrates an importance I did not appreciate at the time. I don't mean that the occasion itself proved notable, except that it awakened a liking from which our lifelong friendship grew. A few listeners gathered in a small theater next to the ice-covered rink. At that hour some resolute skaters still raced around and cut figures, and the whirring of their skates echoing from the skylight distracted our attention. The Ateneo's new Secretary appeared on the stage and advanced toward unlit footlights and a prompter's box without a prompter. He approached the proscenium with a forced smile, walking rather too fast for the occasion's seriousness but with a diffidence that encouraged our confidence. Now unprotected by table or glass of water, he faced that scanty audience of comrades converted into spectators, all of them his supporters, so close that he could see their faces and their reactions. He shrugged his shoulders at the inanity of the situation. Wrinkles in his trousers shortened them noticeably. He adjusted his glasses, holding them with two fingers and not really looking at them before he replaced them. He did this as deliberately as he might have done it leaning back in a wicker chair in a circle of friends at the foot of the Ateneo's stairway.

To finish off his deficiencies, the choir did not measure up to the music; his voice didn't suit his corpulence. Not so high-pitched as to sound ridiculous, still it did not fulfill expectations raised by his imposing presence. Though the vivacity of his manner and his authoritative eloquence indicated youthfulness, his careless propensity to fatness and his baldness somewhat lessened that impression. Still, his words flowed in a chain of rigorous logic, and his speech proved entirely persuasive. I found his choice of words notable: concrete yet lofty, sonorous, and precise. Neither the situation nor the occasion suited grandiloquence. I did not feel obliged to offer exaggerated congratulations on the speech.

My literary and theatrical interests attracted me to youthful *tertulias,* and I began by attending one not connected with the Ateneo. Afterwards, however, a *tertulia* of Ateneo members took its place. With no particular common interest, six or eight of us faithful night owls would meet with the new Secretary around a table at the Granja El Henar on the calle de Alcalá very late, when theaters got out. Others would join us from time to time, but we soon settled down to a few regulars. Enrique Amado, a wonderful Galician boy and a writer died from a horrible general paralysis a few years later. Juan Serrano was a highway engineer. Juanito Lafora requited his father's lucrative antiques business through his own dedication to a university career specializing in history. Angelito Tomás Cuesta, son of a wealthy cloth manufacturer, had entered a mistaken vocation in diplomacy to avoid working in the family business to which he eventually returned. Pedro Salinas, another of us, did not stay up really late, so Antonio García Herreros, whom we called "Tonino," and I offered the only real competition to the

Secretary of the Ateneo in never going to bed early. García Herreros, Juan Serrano's colleague, had recently completed a long-extended course of study. We had no other purpose, I repeat, than to talk about our day's activities. The Secretary sometimes complained, though with no real grievance, about having to go in every morning to his job at the Registry Office of the Ministry of Justice.

The Henar *tertulias* had less political or literary pretension than those that met at the Ateneo. We joked about everything human and divine, and we respected no authority, however prestigious. Still, we did not think of ourselves as iconoclasts; we just had trouble accepting or recognizing the presidency or leadership of any party or group. Our friendship with the Secretary—taking him as the most significant member then, and of course later—did not involve his assuming any kind of leadership or dominion over us. Certainly we had no aspirations toward becoming a political faction. So far nobody thought of the new Secretary as unconsciously developing in the Ateneo's meeting hall oratorical or polemical skills he might use in campaigning for election to the Cortes.

At first impression the new Secretary seemed somewhat reserved, and he had a reputation for having a bad temper because of his sharp responses at Ateneo meetings and his inflexibility in ending corruption in its administration. Certainly he surpassed fellow *tertulia* members in his disdain for pedantry, which we all hated, and he neither pontificated nor assumed a professorial air. He seemed a man who had outgrown youth's carefree illusions; he asked for nothing but peace to read books and friends with whom he could talk. "How happy I was," he liked to say offhandedly, "when I had nothing to worry about but professors and whores!" He spoke the Castilian language with clarity and precision. Even his ordinary conversation had exceptional charm because he embellished it with popular phrases and classical allusions from his university past and books in his library, quite casually but with instinctive rightness.

He bragged about his seniority. When I teased him about it he told me to respect my elders. Another Ateneo member, Fernando Durán, irreverent disciple of Dr. Simarro, nicknamed him "the Colonel" as a friendly joke referring to the authoritarianism with which his opponents charged him.

In the middle of that summer war broke out between Austria-Hungary and Serbia; it later deteriorated into a general European conflagration. With neutral Spain divided into two bitterly hostile parties, the Secretary of the Ateneo quickly emerged as clear leader of the House's Francophile faction. To us the Allies' cause against the Central Powers seemed preeminently represented by the French republic.

2

His Hometown and Its Laudable Countryside

Along with everything else going on at the Ateneo, strictly literary sessions continued. This remained one of the most notable activities of its members. The Literary Section organized a series of lectures similar to the elegant "Spanish Self-Portraits" some writers and artists had presented in the past century. This new series, however, did not focus on persons typical of a region, profession, or office but on Spain's towns and cities, their atmosphere, their native spirit, in a word, their life. It surprised many people when the Secretary undertook to give a lecture evoking the spiritual panorama of Alcalá de Henares his hometown.

As far as anyone knew, the Secretary had neither written poetry nor published turn-of-the-century-style articles or literary essays in the fashion of Azorín (I mean debased imitations by some of his provincial admirers). He had not taken part in literary contests; he had not contributed to *Los Lunes del Imparcial* or to little magazines edited by Villaespesa or Martínez Sierra, certainly not to Acebal's *La Lectura*. Thus members took the announcement of his lecture as a tribute by organizers to his reputation within the Ateneo where men who did not recognize his other talents did acknowledge his administrative skills.

His discourse proved exemplary. He read it in a manner suited to the occasion and its theme. In beautifully structured sentences he evoked for his listeners illustrious monuments of the Laudable Countryside that had itself been a monument in Spanish history since the Romans founded Compluto on the banks of the Henares. However, he gave us more that afternoon than a survey of archeology and notable buildings, a collation of dates, or a tribute to Cervantes. He gave us a lyrical description of an autobiographical environment, the terrain in which he, as a child, had first looked at the world. His lyricism did not drift into romanticism, certainly not into that degenerate sentimentalism that has done so much, along with a decline of good taste, to corrupt the purity of our Castilian language. What I say about that lecture also applies to the personality of the man who read it and wrote it. His pen's grace, giving that word its exact meaning, did not pour out "the fullness of his heart." He expressed himself with restraint, in succinct, clear concepts—solid substance tempered by delicacy of nuance and the smoothness of his finishing glaze.

I had joined a cluster of enthusiasts around him after the conference when our mutual friend Don Francisco A. de Icaza, a distinguished Mexican who had lived in Madrid for many years, extended his hand, his surprise emphasized by the special ardor of his native accent. "How secretive you have been about yourself! Obviously you are an accomplished literary man." The Secretary expressed thanks for praises and encomiums with an appropriate smile. "And you, haven't you anything to say to me?" He shot that in my direction. I answered, "To tell you the truth, it hasn't surprised me." Later, after I had made innumerable encouraging comments about his writing, he remembered that first conference and asked me to tell him, frankly, the reason for my candid response on that occasion. Why had I not been surprised by his success and the quality of that essay? I never could explain it. It just did not surprise me; I already knew what others had just discovered.

That afternoon's lecture also gave me a clearer insight into the true nature of his spirit and revealed an undoubted sympathy with my own hypersensitivity. Through all the jokes in Ateneo corridors and over café tables, I had glimpsed the depths of that formidable man. Disenchanted with commonplace illusions and ascetically free from ambition, he also had a sensibility similar to my own. Perhaps I was more open to it because the closest friend of my youth had recently died.

"What did you like best?" Again he insisted to me. "The part about the Laudable Countryside," I answered without hesitation. Some words have their own evocative power to which discursive development cannot add much. With all of his color, his blending of historical learning and Alcalá's rustic charm, the Secretary of the Ateneo had best expressed the heart and feeling of the landscape setting of that worthy archive of native wealth by simply repeating *el Campo Laudable,* the august name given by its Roman founders. Actually they gave the name to the flat land surrounding his illustrious hometown. The Secretary had lived there as an innocent child; only later did he fully appreciate it: the crystalline light of spring mornings, golds in autumn's west wind, midday winter brightness, the seething embers of summer. He had considered "Elegy on the Laudable Countryside" as a title, using its Horatian name to express the vigor of that ancient land through centuries. "That's what they call it," he repeated, "the Laudable Countryside"; he wanted no credit for a poetic invention bequeathed by an ancient and refined culture.

We agreed to visit Alcalá de Henares together; I did not know it in spite of that city's proximity to my native Madrid. It took us a long time to realize our intention. For some years he had only returned to his hometown sporadically and briefly to see his married sister who lived in their family home.

Needless to say, his own countrymen still refused to honor him as a prophet, in accordance with the proverb. He told me laughing good-naturedly of an incident during a recent visit. He had met an old acquaintance on the street, who had asked quite casually, "And you, have you finished your degree yet?" That man did not realize that the Secretary had been a doctor of the law at twenty, twelve or thirteen years before. No, most of his fellow citizens did not highly esteem him. Excepting those who really knew him, they did not recognize talents and qualities of character that made him greatly worthy of their admiration. Some did appreciate him, though, even in the days of our early acquaintance. He had two friends among his countrymen, one shrewd with peasant wisdom, the other with some pretension to small-town family distinction. Both worked as archivists there, and the Secretary regarded both with benevolent esteem, especially Vicario. The elder of his two friends, Vicario, was about my Friend's age but appeared older. He treasured Vicario as a living memory of his own young manhood in Alcalá, a period of his life that he now hated.

He also hated the carelessness, negligence, and decadence the "sons of Alcalá" had allowed to prevail in their city. Citizens called themselves that, and he parodied them, sad at the way these over-praised grandees boasted in contemplating the ruin they had caused. He grieved about the deterioration of culture, reflecting the natives' provincial backwardness, about sounds of spurs echoing from the plaza's arches—the contribution of a new population of cavalry soldiers, about the inordinate ambitions of those officers and their female relations, about the proximity of a horrible women's prison or penitentiary. For him the city seemed a cemetery for the living where past fame lay buried, but his elegiac sarcasm spared the Poor Bernardine nuns and the Reformed Oratorians. Echoes from steps of solitary passersby sounded from walls of many convents along those streets; only their walls elicited sympathetic comment in the general disgust of his patriotic spirit.

He missed a bygone dignity lost in houses that had passed into hands of newly rich or vulgarly rich owners. Neither group had any sense of the kind of life wealth should provide, the comfort of security and the pleasure of living nobly. His melancholy focused on his own family's ruin. He had refused to spend his lifetime in sad contemplation of a yesterday that had dissolved, though vestiges of its greatness remained. Nor would he mortgage his freedom in a futile attempt, doomed to failure, to restore the past. Instead he settled as an independent youth in Madrid and forever turned his back on the listless life of his Alcalá.

I learned the most important details of my Friend's earlier life during that visit we had promised ourselves. He told me about it as events arose in his memory or as some incident in our conversation triggered other memories. Sometimes he himself played a role in a story involving family or friends; sometimes he had merely stood by as an always curious observer. Thus I came to know that, born in 1880, he was younger than he looked at first sight and eleven years older than I.

As a very small boy he had lost his mother and his father, the one soon after the other. Reared by his paternal grandmother, he finished his preliminary schooling at the College of María Cristina, commonly called the University of the Escorial. He took his licentiate in law at the University of Zaragoza. Then, after going through the doctoral program at the Central University [in Madrid], he received his doctor-of-law degree in 1900. Notably, he had attended classes of Don Francisco Giner. After that he turned to an easy life made possible by his family's well-to-do situation, though he did work as an assistant in the eminent Madrid firm of Díaz Cobeña, the most famous lawyer of his day in Spain.

By his own account, he later had a notion to play the farmer and work his own estate, but he lost money at it. After that his elder brother, not much older, invested almost all of their family fortune in an electric-light power plant. People's cruel indifference in witnessing, even abetting, the ruin of that enterprise contributed much to the Secretary's negative feelings toward his heedless countrymen. He identified envy as the characteristic quality of their decadence, something that applied to our national scene with broader significance. Proud, though without vanity, he and his brother made it up to their younger sister of whom they were very fond. They gave her the family house on calle de la Imagen and a fine orchard on the riverbank. Only the house, orchard, and sufficient money for one person to live on remained of their inheritance. His elder brother, also a lawyer and very able in the Secretary's opinion, turned to a legal career; he himself preferred Madrid and the Registry Office of the Ministry of Justice. When I knew him, he had advanced to the position of department head, and, though the least bureaucratic person in the world, he performed his duties very competently.

I went to Alcalá to visit him, then, in the middle of the European war's third summer, which we expected would be its last.

After an excursion we had made together to the north of Spain, he had gone home for a few days to the house on the calle de la Imagen, recalling vacations ten or fifteen years before that he could not recapture. Bored to the point of distraction, weighed down by summer's suffocation, he found some relief from both in writing to me from a shadowed office his sister kept for him on the ground floor. With no other respite from his reading but afternoon walks in the company of his two friends, he wrote that he missed a sense of escape, nightfall on the outskirts under the sparkling light of that same evening star, breathing in heat and with it fragrance from grain on threshing floors and mown straw ready for harvest. At the time of my first visit, drowsing Alcalá enjoyed an unusual amount of activity. In normal times the lives of its inhabitants were rarely disturbed even by the visit of a commercial traveler or a passing tourist. This change had come because of the presence of a large group of refugees from Germany's colony of Cameroon who had sought asylum in our territory of Guinea at the war's outbreak and who were later permanently interned in Alcalá. They became an unstable nucleus implanted in the soporifically placid life of the old university. Ending its calm and silence, they had made it a noisy center of disturbance in the city's life.

With him I roamed ancient streets. I looked in at the archives and the university, at Santa María and San Justo—a remnant of true greatness. I contemplated the font where they had baptized Cervantes and the tomb of Cisneros—a monument truly worthy of the man it commemorated, which a fratricidal bomb damaged twenty years after our visit.

Two indelible memories remain of my first visit to Alcalá: a plaza with trees, where, he told me, he used to go alone as a very small boy "to relish his own sadness," and a nighttime walk through El Chorrillo, an urban park his father had created when he served as mayor. A few remnants had survived of woods separating the park from railroad tracks, but the natives' rampant barbarism had replaced most of those trees with flowering acacias. Flowering acacias and dwarf palms shared the declared enmity of the Secretary of the Ateneo. Oaks, live oaks, chestnuts, black poplars, white poplars, and elms shared his favor with willows, but the cypress ranked first.

On the afternoon when I arrived we inspected the arches of the calle Mayor and the plaza; we sat at a table in front of the Salinas Confectionary; we strolled through deserted streets. Here he pointed out the site of the first school he had attended as a little child, and he recalled his first day as a scholar when nobody could get him out from under his brother's desk. There he showed me a grilled window behind which lived two unmarried sisters, one of them the object of his first platonic love. Farther along came another street-level window with a more recent memory of his daring boy's first wild oats. He had had the complicity of the *sereno* and, needless to say, of his lady-love who facilitated his entry under cover of night.

After eating at my lodging, we went to the Chorrillo, now taken over by pleasant shadows that, for him, belonged to the past. The singing of cicadas filled the silence of that heavy August night; a shrieking train whistle broke in from time to time. "Those can't be cicadas," he said, laughing. "Cicadas all wear out by the Day of Santiago. We town-bred boys know things like that which you city boys miss."

His voice softened as a memory arose. In some connection I happened to mention the Holy Children [Saints Justo and Pastor]—patrons of Alcalá, as he had told me when we passed near their church. "I am living proof of their miracles," he said. Telling me about it, an element of sentimentality tinged his irony. As a small boy, a toddler, some kind of malady had confined him to his carriage, his legs covered with pimples. On the Day of the Holy Children his mother returned from Mass and found him running around entirely cured. "So you see. What can I say! As I later lost my mother, I don't make fun of it."

He did laugh, though, about difficulties he made for his family and neigh-

bors when they wanted to give him a purgative. If they finally did force him
to swallow it, his fits of temper and choking largely undercut the medicine's
effectiveness.

His sense of being an orphan became more acute as time passed. Very
circumspect in matters of family feeling, he waited a long time to tell me
that his grandmother had arranged a second marriage for his father. Seeing
him ill with flu in the 1885 epidemic, she feared that his death would ultimately leave her grandchildren quite alone. She chose a middle-aged lady
with whom the bridegroom had not had any previous relationship, however
useful prior acquaintance might have seemed. The fiancée cared only about
herself. When in due course he told me about it, the Secretary merely repeated what he had heard from his Uncle Félix, his mother's brother, who
considered this second marriage invalid because the bridegroom had entered
it on the point of death. "The Case" had lasted many years until the woman
finally gave it up and settled for a lifelong pension.

The Secretary had real affection for his Uncle Félix, a cultivated, sensible
man from whom his nephew inherited much of his caustic spirit. The uncle
had portrayed in verse his fellow citizens' concept of their town as hub of
the universe:

> Never did their imagination
> Stray a moment from Alcalá.
> They would claim that the wind in Russia
> Blew from the Pico Ocejón.

"He had a mania for collecting timepieces. In their youth my nieces and
nephew finished off what remained of his collection." The Secretary's remembering an insignificant detail like that showed his affection for his uncle.

Beyond the Chorrillo and its little plaza came open fields, then lying
fallow, and a building standing by itself. He told me that it had been an inn,
a famous hangout for bandits when they inhabited the Alcarria Mountains.
In that very place bullets of the Civil Guard had cut down the last of a
famous band in an ambush. A local bandit, El Batanero, had more than once
come to his grandfather's law office, and on one occasion the old man had
permitted him to present a gift to the Secretary's elder brother.

My Friend remembered afternoon rides as a very small child with his
grandfather. They would go only as far as the vineyard so they could get
back in time to watch the short line from Guadalajara go by. It got to be a
kind of race between the train puffing asthmatically along and the little mule
that pulled their cart. The boy's healthy, ravenous appetite amused the old
man. One time after he had eaten a big lunch at home he called on his
grandfather. The latter asked, "Would you like some kind of a snack?" The
boy answered, as if he meant it, "A whole fried mule!"

Childhood memories alternated with melancholy thoughts and vague

2: His Hometown and Its Laudable Countryside

hopes about our friendship. Up to then it had represented little more than a mutual enjoyment of loafing, but it was becoming something more solid.

At daybreak I went back to rest at my lodging place. He felt extremely sorry not to offer me accommodation in his home. Unfortunately his sister's husband was suffering one of his chronic attacks of epilepsy that periodically upset the general felicity of her marriage. The next day the Secretary introduced me to his house with touching simplicity. We crossed the vestibule and went into a big ground floor salon where his father's portrait presided. I could not miss the resemblance, not so much in physiognomy as in the set of his head, somewhat stiff between broad shoulders, and in a frank, open expression. From there we went into his office, filled with tall bookshelves and pleasant summer shadows. I got an impression of some special fragrance, perceptible only to my imagination. He had spoken of a room that he could not enter without being assaulted by a painful sense of fragrance, flowers surrounding the bier of his brother's child. For no reason, I identified this as the room. The Secretary's other brother had also died in early adolescence, and he retained an affectionate memory of that dawning fraternity. Many years later, when I wanted a name for my third son, he casually suggested, "Why don't you call him Carlos; it's a nice name. My brother who died was Carlos."

We ate in the town's club, which looked like a print portraying an assemblage of off-duty soldiers. We went to the orchard, but we left almost as soon as we entered it. Careless maintenance of a property he had shared in happier times put him in a bad mood.

Later we drove out with his two friends to eat some wonderful melons in the melon patch, "as it should be done." He boasted again that he could handle any challenge so far as food was concerned. The appetite of his youth had continued. He jokingly exaggerated my moderation, parodying Shakespeare, "These pale young men who drink no wine."

Looking toward the mountains that crown Alcalá, dominating the ancient Compluto and blessing its Laudable Countryside, he remembered hunting expeditions when, "as a *señorito*," he had joined friends in leasing a mountain from the marquess of Ibarra.

Seeing me off at the station, he left me with "La Mantoncito," a charming little lady in a shawl. Formerly the model of a famous artist and the mother of his daughters, she had now separated from him. She acted very much the lady and looked more handsome than ever in the Madrid-style fringed shawl to which she owed her nickname. She told us that she had become engaged to marry one of those Germans confined in Alcalá. Of course she didn't marry him, and fortunately. More than one or two desperate women of that city did marry those foreigners. Their husbands forgot all about them when the war ended and they returned to their own country.

Leaning out of the window of the train taking me back to Madrid, I saw my cousin, a young cavalry lieutenant. We had shared childhood vacations in my grandfather's village in Valladolid Province. He had moved to Alcalá with his family. His elder brother, a priest and chaplain at the women's prison, had some local fame as a preacher and even as a mystic. He was a man free from the worldliness of many clergymen, especially in our big cities. The Secretary of the Ateneo knew something of these relations of mine through his own friends and family.

Taking advantage of my Friend's going off to speak to somebody, my cousin the lieutenant said to me, in a tone of protective warning, "I don't like to see you in his company." When I made a gesture which left no doubt that I would not agree with anything he might say, he insisted, "He comes from a very fine family, but he himself. . . ."

3

Diversions [Consuelos] and Renunciations

My cousin's advice did not influence me or change my intentions; I habitually dismissed other people's opinions that conflicted with mine. At that point I did not comprehend the influence of unjustified malice. To my own cost, it took years for me to realize the power of gratuitous malevolence. Today I cannot say that those accusations against the Secretary of the Ateneo had no explanation. Then I simply passed them off as the natural human tendency to be jealous or to react negatively toward someone with superior intelligence. To a greater or lesser degree, persons gifted with above-average talents do experience this envy from their fellows; but, though it may bring them injury and denigration, it also contributes to their exaltation. Afterwards when the course of my Friend's life elevated him to a position where the great mass of Spaniards knew him as a public figure, I fully recognized the larger historical significance of petty spitefulness. The meaning that his name and person came to have—as a kind of political myth—seemed an excuse to persons of a certain social class for propagating this kind of thing. At that later date my cousin the cavalry lieutenant, despite his anonymous ordinariness, personified this class; before that he spread this calumny quite ingenuously.

I don't think that we spoke of that futile warning when we saw each other in Madrid early in the following autumn. I do remember that my Friend and I talked of my traveling companion, La Mantoncito. Her little hat and ladylike airs, the graceful good looks and simple winsomeness of that painter's model revived in him thoughts of youthful pleasures. He had shared these with me more through allusion than in so many words. I'm not sure, either, of the exact day or hour when, drifting along Recoletos, we nearly bumped into a woman, nothing special at first sight but actually charming, and if no longer a girl still quite attractive. We had already passed her when they both turned back at the same time, and with an unmistakable impulse of curiosity they decided to speak.

"Well, kiddo, you're getting fat."

"Do I look old?" he asked, smiling, a shade of teasing regret in his eyes behind the glasses. "You haven't changed a bit."

"Well, I'm no spring chicken. I can't lie to you about that."

"How is your father?"

"Just the same, kiddo. A bolt of lightning wouldn't change him."

Their conversation ended abruptly. They didn't know what to say next. She glanced at me, and not recognizing me as one of their mutual acquaintances, she assumed an air of indifferent reserve.

"Well, I'm off. See you around, pal."

"Call me some time."

"O.K., I'll call you."

"I bet you won't."

"Sure I will, man, I'll do that. I can't get over your being so fat. Can I call you at the Ateneo?"

"Or at home. You know where I live?" He gave her his address.

After they had said their goodbyes, he calmed down and said to me, "She's not going to call. Her call me!" "Then you call her," I answered, sure of catching his passing fancy. "Come on, man," he protested. I understood that the fleeting moment had passed. "Well, now you have seen Consuelito," he finished. "I figured that out, but she seems quite young," I went on. "From what you said, I expected some old bag." "She must be thirty now," he answered, "past her prime. I knew her at sixteen. You should have seen her then. And very sharp; she has gone way ahead of me in the world. She has settled down as a morganatic duchess, so to speak."

My Friend and Consuelito had met at a masked ball, in the turn-of-the-century style. At first he used to visit her at the so-called bawdyhouse where she worked. He laughed with delight remembering a night when they were together and he heard the arrival of two Ateneo friends who considered themselves very sophisticated and who asked the madam for Consuelito.

With characteristic capriciousness Consuelito showed a kind of predilection for my Friend. He left the pension where he lived and rented a flat on a little downtown street between the Plaza del Callao and the Plaza de Santo Domingo, and they set up housekeeping. One day some meddling friend from Alcalá came to call in his absence; Consuelito received their visitor with such politeness, so unembarrassed and naturally bright, that he went home singing her praises to the town. My Friend relished that memory, taking pleasure in a kind of protectiveness toward the woman who had offered him her first love. Having undertaken to live out a Galdós novel, they never again achieved another incident so perfectly matching Don Benito's best inventions.

Though Consuelito came from Segovia, not Madrid, she adjusted very readily to big-city ways. He enjoyed giving her gifts and making her happy. Not inclined to bragging, he did not talk about his liaison to Joaquín Eugenio Creagh, then a member of his Ateneo *tertulia,* and like himself rich, carefree, and from an old Alcalá family. Creagh also had greater literary gifts than he had yet demonstrated. Years later, when I first knew the Secretary, he shared a flat with this friend.

Consuelito had a rascally and picturesque father who tolerated his daughter's life-style with a certain dignity. She did not retain many friends from the old days of her shameful life. She enjoyed housekeeping, as is often the case with those whom Spaniards wrongly call "women of dissolute life," or just "the life." Perhaps her ambitions went no further.

The ruin of his family fortune ended the carefree delight of these lovers. Neither of them had a particularly sentimental nature; their liaison did not really go deeper than satisfaction of their sensuality. One sad day he realized that he could not count on one penny from his father's estate. He faced up to facts and prepared for a civil service exam that would provide him with the means to live independently. As a start, he had to end an amorous extravagance he could no longer afford. He explained the situation to Consuelito. They would have to part. In telling about the crisis he delighted in remembering Consuelo. In the past he had freely given things to her with happy abandon; now she came to him without her fashionable hat, wrapped once more in her fringed Madrid shawl with a bundle of bank notes in her hand. By pawning and selling her trousseau she hoped to remedy the cause of their separation. She probably did not realize how perfect a Galdosian ending she gave their story.

He resisted that temptation. Perhaps in turning down the pleasant option incarnate in the charms of his lady-love he pretended indifference to cover his inclination to yield to an unacceptable desire. Soon after that he turned his entire willpower to a task both concrete and immediate. He went to spend the summer in Alcalá, and he refused to allow Consuelito to weep over scruples that now separated them and that she thought excessive. Very possibly his instinct for self-preservation helped him to break from a commitment that would certainly have ended his independence and coarsened his life.

He shut himself up in that house on the calle de la Imagen and thought of nothing but preparing himself for a scheduled examination for appointment to the Registry Office, something made extremely difficult because of the short time left. He told me about it; he had treated it like any educational task. "I figured up the days remaining and the assigned topics indicated in the published announcement. First with a pile of books I worked out each answer exactly in writing. Then I went over these drafts until I could repeat them perfectly. To have let my thoughts stray to my private affairs would have meant failure. Finally I knew all the topics—there were X number (he recalled the number exactly), and I could answer the questions in any order, taken at random from a bowl as in an oral exam. It involved, after all, the whole of the law on mortgages."

He laughed, noticing my real horror. He had no helpful personal recommendation from anyone. He took second place. It did not require years of service to disillusion him about the usefulness of bureaucratic life; he had no illusions about it from the start. Nonetheless, he performed his duties in a highly skillful way. When he became famous, it amused him to read ridiculous stories in more than one newspaper or to hear foolish chatter about his modest and humble service in public administration; sometimes they even intended praise. His work did not seem extraordinary to him, but he found it worthwhile even compared to more distinguished careers in state service. Besides, it seemed to him preferable for an intellectual, who in Spain often could not entirely devote himself to his scientific or literary work, to have a government salary rather than to turn to the slavery of journalism, or to let commerce and the tastes of the general public control his work.

After an interval of fleeting and mercenary amorous encounters, entirely without sentiment—like a student's, he lived for a while in a mezzanine on the Plaza Santa Ana with another woman. She also became famous later, and somewhat notorious, but at that time she had just begun her career and had not become a chanteuse. They both liked jokes, and, uncharacteristically for him, they enjoyed youthful escapades. He remembered with ingenuous bragging an occasion when he took her dressed in one of his suits to a beerhall to join a party of good friends. He mentioned the event to demonstrate his thinness in those days and to explain Consuelito's surprise at seeing his girth ten years later. This other Consuelito, who curiously had the same name though she never used it professionally, left him with a less tender memory, and a sadder one; she cured him of further infatuations.

He pretended not to recognize her afterward when in the frequent chances of Madrid's Vanity Fair, smaller then than now, they would meet at a theater, a café, or on a streetcar in the Salamanca District where he moved after he became Secretary of the Ateneo. The last time they saw each other she had to make way for him as Spain's premier at a theater where she had considerable importance as associate manager. He had by then had time to slake the excesses of a healthy sensuality that he satisfied fully, not only when he felt that he needed to have a woman to sleep with but at mealtimes when he showed that same childish appetite, ready to eat "a whole fried mule."

A few months after we got to know each other, a slight inflammation of my groin (inguinal infarct), the consequence of a shoe chafing my foot, kept me at home and away from the Ateneo for a few days. He wrote to me jokingly attributing my absence to "excesses of intemperance" and inquiring about my health. In response to his thoughtfulness I went for the first time to his home on the calle de Hermosilla accompanied by Tonino García Herreros. We found him in his simply furnished study—a table, two upholstered chairs, and a bookcase with green glass doors—partaking of a large cup of coffee and milk with bread and lots of butter. For years afterward we kidded about his brief, lukewarm offer to give us something to eat.

I went back alone on another occasion, and that time I asked him to show me something that he had written. "What if I haven't written anything?" he asked, smoothing his moustache, with the smile of a man who, apart from his talent, doesn't bother to write because others have already said everything worth saying. I insisted. He didn't fool me. A novice did not write that lecture on Alcalá for the Ateneo. He finally took a folder from the bookshelf, pretending that he had trouble finding it. From it he took a sheaf of papers, already yellowing, part of an unfinished novel. "Read it. Here. If you think it worth the effort." I read it that same afternoon with both curiosity and pleasure, and I had no trouble in convincing him of the sincerity of my reaction. He finally said, "I don't know. I hardly even remember. It seems to me like something written by an apprentice of Galdós." It had a lot of Galdós, mainly its setting in turn-of-the century Madrid where he had lived with such youthful abandon. Also a feeling of autobiography, transposing his own experiences into novelistic form.

I reproached him affectionately, "Do you want to tell me why you haven't continued the novel or gone on writing?" It didn't take much effort to get him to explain the problem. He had Guillermo Pedregal as his special friend in the "vital forces" *tertulia* that met in the Ateneo's hall opposite to the Crock Shop, protected by a folding screen from less exclusive circles. Guillermo's father, a minister of the First Republic, had become famous for "Who is Pedregal?"—the malicious response of a hostile faction to his nomination. My Friend described young Pedregal as a man of very exacting taste, developed by careful reading, and with the same acute critical spirit that later characterized the Secretary. Juan Uña, a less wise member of that *tertulia,* also had a notable republican father, a friend of my grandfather and a model of honesty and virtue in the tradition of the classical Roman ideal. Juan Uña's friends continued to call him Juanito into middle age. In this period he showed great promise among those marked out by their training at the Free Institute of Education in the more or less practical and rising field of sociology. More exactly, he benefited from the first grants to study abroad. Though my new Friend did not hold as high an opinion of him as of Pedregal, Uña's frankness made an undoubted impression when, after reading those same first two chapters of the novel, he advised him to spend his time on something other than writing.

I protested vehemently against that opinion, challenging Juan Uña's judgment as subject to appeal and his taste itself as debatable. I even dared to question whether the Secretary's exaggerated praise of Guillermo Pedregal corresponded to objective reality. Perhaps the sad circumstance of his friend's premature death, a little before, fostered his homage. I protested against a spirit of criticism whose contagious skepticism might well nip in the bud the temperament of a writer as fastidious about his own work as my Friend.

Keeping at him about returning to his project, I suggested a title sure to stimulate the will of the remiss author. "Yes, quite clearly," I said to him, "you should call this novel 'Passion and Death.'" He liked it well enough, but my eager interest as a reader pleased him more. Still, he did not feel that he could go back to a theme whose feeling he had now lost.

Instead he looked around for something else to write about. In the process he took out some clippings titled "Correspondence from Spain"; he had written these dispatches during his stay in Paris three or four years earlier. Very few people knew, and not many cared later, that the Secretary of the Ateneo had written those articles published under the pseudonym of Martín Piñol, Spanish incarnation of the medieval devil. Yet through these articles Joaquín Álvarez Pastor came to know him as a writer and to appreciate the excellence of his work. A casual acquaintance in Paris, he eventually became a professor and a valued friend. The Secretary also fondly remembered other young Spaniards he had known there at that time. Daniel Alarcón was the Benjamin of three brothers, one of them a writer and all of them show-offs; at that time they were fairly well-known in Ateneo *tertulias* and café coteries. Dr. Pascual, from Cartagena, then pursuing his experiments in Paris laboratories, would play an outstanding role of dramatic importance in the advent of our republic. Among others, Juan Pujol, later a well-known journalist, assumed the role of mediator in their disputes. From what others have said, however, it seems that he never participated with complete frankness or camaraderie.

A professor from Spain's Graduate Training School for Teachers [Luis de Hoyos Sainz] played the role of dean in this small group transplanted from Madrid to the Latin Quarter in 1911–1912. Older than they, he seemed much older as he had aged prematurely. He and his wife, a very handsome and amiable lady, had five daughters, all of them pretty and bright. The eldest of them had reached that delightfully difficult age between girlhood and womanhood. Later, back in Madrid, the professor became an active member of the Ateneo, and my Friend took me out to his house. The family received me with the same informal cordiality they showed to my Friend, but he himself seemed reticent when I alluded to his youthful adventures in Paris. One of the little girls took me for his nephew; no doubt kinship explained to her our mutual affection and casual friendship. Certainly we didn't resemble each other physically.

It didn't take much shrewdness to recognize some kind of serious feeling in the continuous kidding that went on between the eldest daughter and my Friend, calling each other "Uncle" and "Miss." What I perceived as a spark turned out to be embers. The first time I ventured a suggestion about it, he rejected it absolutely. This did not lessen my concern, and I brought it up casually, but privately, with the mother as better able than her husband to distinguish between coquetry and the household's honorable freedom.

Finally she agreed to tell me, not about something going on then, but about what had happened back in Paris—or, better, what might have happened. With no son, the father depended on his bored, adolescent daughter to act as assistant in his ethnographical research. Absorbed and short-sighted, he failed to realize that his daughter had hardly any source of distraction apart from members of the *tertulia* who came to his home. Though some of them considered themselves good-looking and lady-killers, she chose the Secretary to approach one day to weep out her romantic desperation and her family's lack of understanding. He tried to console her by playing down her vaporous passion as resulting from her monotonous duties, but he sought the mother's assistance to do something about her daughter's sentimental obsession. The mother, more moved than her child, confessed to him that it would make her very happy to see her daughter married to a man like himself.

Again he had no difficulty in controlling his appetite, especially for so tender a fruit. He did not want to assume responsibilities beyond his material resources, and he could not afford to support a family, especially with a fifteen-year-old wife. To some extent unconcerned about his future, he found sufficient compensation in freedom for his solitary life. The matter went no further. When I first knew the family, Merceditas had a military suitor, much to her father's annoyance, as he hoped for a better match. She married him some years later. My Friend retained a kind of affection towards her.

Before that, another sweetheart, to whom he had declared his love, married someone else. Some years later he courted his cousin with nighttime conversations through a grill or under a balcony in the Argüelles District where she lived, and she responded in a casual kind of way. Separated from her by circumstances, he always retained a sincere feeling for her that she did not reciprocate. She married a military man who rose to the generalship; my Friend asked her to serve as matron of honor at his wedding. A terrible fate would destroy this relationship both cruelly and definitively with the outbreak of our war.

4

The Reasons for Germanophilia
(Variations on a Theme)

At the outbreak of the 1914 war liberals favored France more on the basis of instinct than because of reasoning or politics. Quite naturally, then, not adventitiously, Madrid's Ateneo adopted the positive and optimistic position that victory comes from having a just cause, in contrast to the negative argument that it comes solely from having superior military forces. On the basis of this orientation Rightists and Leftists became respectively Germanophiles or Francophiles.

If, after all these years, some curious soul still cares about reasons for Spanish neutrality, he will find no more succinct or pertinent explanation than one given by our Friend the Ateneo's Secretary at a meeting in the course of the confused, larger debate. In it he explained the feelings of those of us who shared the Francophile attitude. His title revealed his purpose, *The Reasons for Germanophilia*. He found Germanophilia, quite simply, a negation of everything French and English culture meant to us in Spain and everywhere in the civilized world. We identified this culture with the liberal viewpoint toward life. That lecture and the discussions which followed, spreading from the tribune to members in the conference hall, established the Secretary in a terrain accessible to the general public, much as his purely literary address on Alcalá had established him within the Ateneo.

Many intellectuals from belligerent countries, men and women, came to Madrid concerned to proclaim in neutral countries the moral basis of their struggle. In a move to reciprocate for our hospitality and to follow through on that propaganda, France's government invited several distinguished Spaniards to visit the war front. The French ambassador and diplomatic secretaries, themselves mostly limited to the world of protocol and so-called high society, turned for advice in choosing this delegation to professors of the French Lycée, long established in Madrid, as persons in touch with Spanish intellectual life. Any delegation had to include the Secretary of the Ateneo. The duke of Alba headed this mission as the great exception to our aristocracy's prevalent Germanophilia. Through his descent from the Bastard of England [James Fitz James, son of the future James II of England and Arabella Churchill] he also held the title duke of Berwick, and, as my

Friend told me after returning from the trip, Frenchmen called him "Your Highness." The duke always signed his name "Fitz-James Stuart," though Don Juan Valera, in writing about this Alba's father, had established "Estuardo" as the standard Spanish spelling of his name. Some academicians, including Don Ramón Menéndez Pidal and Don Jacinto Octavio Picón, also traveled in this stellar company, as did some Catalonian writers and journalists who went directly from Barcelona. Characteristically they made a show of their separatism from Madrid and Castile.

War actually seen, not merely imagined, proved sad indeed. Besides predictable photographs of ruins and a formal portrait of the inevitable convivial celebration shared by our delegation and their French companions, the Secretary of the Ateneo brought back from the front a curious portrait of himself. It showed him wearing a helmet, then in fashion again after many years, and high boots, contemplating the results of a bombardment on Pont-á-Mousson. Twenty years later, serving as consul in Geneva, I used that photograph as a comparison to others of terrible German-Italian bombardments of Madrid, Barcelona, and Guernica. My public exhibition showed what attacks by aviation and artillery against civilian populations had become in the world war then beginning in Spain.

The sadness of war in France did not, however, overwhelm his more heroic impressions: the "great mutilation" of cathedrals and the French soldiers' stubborn defense of their soil, literally burying themselves in it. If *The Reasons for Germanophilia* stands as a logical antecedent of that journey, the few pages of *Rheims and Verdun,* an address he read to the Ateneo on his return and published as a pamphlet, came as its result. In it his tight-knit thought reaches heights of lyrical prose.

During that trip he also made an obligatory visit to general headquarters of the English expeditionary forces established in a castle. Years later he still commented on that organization, well-stocked with provisions that matched in a gastronomical way the British soldiers' athletic appearance. One of those officers surprised him with the information that the best Spanish guitars come from Cuidad Real. Another officer, of higher rank, asked him, quite ingenuously, "Are you Spaniards governed, as we English are, by mediocre men?"

President Poincaré of the French republic also entertained them with a banquet. The Secretary of the Ateneo often recalled the president's elegant finesse in answering one of his table companions who, admiring some crystal wineglasses or porcelain tableware, said that he would like to take a piece home as a souvenir. Poincaré had answered, "Take all of it; that way you won't spoil the set."

The Italians, not wanting to do less, in their turn invited a group of Spanish intellectuals to visit the Carso front. The Office of Propaganda, where I worked, got involved in preparations for this journey, but my low rank kept me, again, at home despite efforts by count Ponzone, who had charge of the expedition, to enable me to go with my friends. Besides the Secretary of the Ateneo, delegates included the philologist Américo Castro, the journalist and liberal deputy Luis Bello, and, most famous of them, Santiago Rusiñol and Unamuno. My friend's lively descriptions of that journey's minor vicissitudes, a frequent theme in his conversation, always afforded delight.

Bello left later than the others and missed his connection at the frontier. Not finding a representative of Italy's government waiting to assist him, he telegraphed in garbled Italian to the delight of his companions who had already crossed: *"niente d'ufficiale"* (nothing official). Afterward the Secretary of the Ateneo always called our mutual friend "L'Onorévole Bello" (the Honorable Bello), recalling the title Italians invariably gave him, following their practice with parliamentary deputies. The guide called Don Miguel Unamuno *"Professore* Uñamucco," but the Secretary never reminded that perpetually bad-tempered rector of Salamanca about it. The rector proved worse-tempered than usual on this excursion, judging from my Friend's recollections of his childish obstinacy. He refused to drink anything but water at the railroad stations of the Côte d'Azur, where they did not sell it as they do in Spain; he preferred to burn with thirst rather than to try any of the plentiful refreshments available. He argued with French traveling companions, casual acquaintances, exaggerating to them the virtues of the Italians, which they lacked; and he recited to them verses of Carducci and Leopardi, which they did not understand. By way of compensation, which did no good for the Frenchmen who had departed and could not hear him, in Italy he started to praise France and quote verses of Lamartine, Victor Hugo, and Baudelaire whether they pertained to the conversation or not.

Altogether it seemed that Unamuno had undertaken this expedition for the sole purpose of discussing philology with Américo Castro, at that time wearing his black beard and looking exactly like a foreigner's conception of a typical Spaniard. Unamuno refused to make a moonlight tour of Venice, the city completely blacked out because of wartime regulations. Monstrously disfigured by sandbags covering the marvelous decoration of San Marco and its square, the Palace of the Doges, and even the Colleoni statue, it made an overwhelming impression on my Friend. Nor could they get Don Miguel to interrupt his endless philological polemic to look at Milan's cathedral. Rusiñol, in contrast, remained always open to the scenery's sensual nuances and to easy comradeship. He slept in a cloud of heavy tobacco smoke. For luggage he brought only a little broken comb, with which he kept his beautiful white hair neatly combed. At lodging places he merely splashed himself with water from the lavabo, and yet his personal cleanliness did not seem to suffer from it.

As the Secretary of the Ateneo related it, the incongruity of this disparate commission reached its climax during their visit to L'Isola Bella in Lake Maggiore. The Borromeo princes, its owners, wanted to entertain the distinguished Spaniards for an entire afternoon. My Friend blushed at the elegant reception given them and their own boorishness. Liveried servants lined up on the pier, from which one entered the palace directly. The young couple, holding one of Italy's oldest titles, met their visitors at the threshold; their children and the dowager princess were waiting in a salon. Unamuno, unwilling to adapt his appearance and his independence to courtly manners, had agreed only to put on a clean collar over his high black vest. At first sight he looked like a Protestant minister. After visiting the gardens, when the hour came for them to meet to have tea with the princesses, nobody could find Unamuno or Rusiñol; they had gotten lost.

"Still," my Friend urged, "Rusiñol's personal charm and bohemian aura compensated for his lack of manners. He ended up entertaining everyone with his chatter and truly irresistible good nature. But honest Unamuno! Those ladies, waiting with bated breath to hear what the wise professor might have to say, hardly heard the sound of his voice. When the princess asked whether he would like a cup of tea, he shrugged his shoulders with a characteristic gesture and answered 'Pchs." Nobody could tell whether he wanted it or not. To top it all off, while those ladies strived to communicate with their guests, to make the general conversation as pleasant as possible, he paid no attention at all and, putting the little princesses on his lap, concentrated on shaping paper birds for them. What do you think of that!"

Unamuno had great skill at this kind of paper folding, a complete mystery for me. He even wrote a treatise explaining *cocotología* (origami) the word he uses for it.

In Milan my Friend went up in an airplane for the first time. Unamuno, as his only comment on this experience, and eloquently enough, blessed the earth when he got back down—with a theatricality he would have despised in D'Annunzio. The Secretary of the Ateneo must also have felt unhappy about his first experience. He only went up three times in his life, and one of those times in the face of danger more pressing than the risks of flight.

They all much admired Italy's frontier entrenchments within Austrian territory. Some stories promised by my Friend to the newspaper *El Liberal* had already arrived in Madrid when news came of the Caporetto disaster, which invalidated his prophetic gifts. A layman could not hope for more than a problematic judgment on the basis of one visit to encampments and military installations. Certainly neither that first account nor any other of the Secretary's Italian journey ever appeared in print. He always retained from it a supreme memory of Pavia's Carthusian monastery in the magnificent Lombard plain where vineyards grow as garlands among trees and where only the Alps on the horizon distinguish earth from heaven.

5

The Throne of Philip II and
the Friars' Garden

I had only gone back to the Escorial once since my graduation from its secondary school operated by Augustinian monks. I believe that the Secretary of the Ateneo had also not often returned after finishing his course of study at the Royal College of María Cristina at the Escorial, commonly known as the University though its curriculum never really justified that title—especially back then. We wanted to visit together this site of our respective schools. However much our experiences there caused us both to hate Augustinian pedagogy, my Friend's ill will did not equal mine, which even included the famous building. He had succeeded in sorting out his memories as time passed, getting beyond personal feelings to an understanding of Herrera's magnificent architecture and an appreciation of the countryside that provided its setting.

He did not have nightmares, as I did, about the terrible north winds that swept into the cloister and even about the spring breezes carrying sensuous perfume from roses blooming luxuriantly on a facade opposite the window of his college room. On that excursion I came to understand his affection for the place. He felt roots here in the heart of a Spain that he could never call his own. He belonged to Spain more than it ever belonged to him.

We went at the beginning of summer. We tried to avoid contact with early vacationers idiotically bunched together on the calle de Floridablanca. We wanted to get away by ourselves to contemplate the monastery in its natural setting, blending into that severe and magnificent countryside. A night at the Victoria Hotel, not yet filled with guests as it would be in August, gave us a delightful sense of tourist's detachment.

We spent our morning in the solemn basilica, in the royal pantheon's funereal inanity, and in the pictorial splendor of the capitular galleries. Hearing my Friend explain the artistic majesty of that immense monument enabled me to appreciate it much better than I could have just by looking at it. That doesn't mean that with me or anyone else he spoke oratorically, except on the public rostrum. He always spoke quite naturally and without pedantry. Still, he spoke so well that it was a delight to hear his explanations, whether of nature's varied spectacle or man's artistic achievements.

How many times had I crossed the Patio of Kings? Only now, as we entered the basilica's porch and atrium, did I recognize how its various elements added up to majestic harmony. We passed a loquacious guide showing off his erudition to yokels in his charge standing before the drunken Peleus. With just a few insightful words my Friend turned my thoughts from schoolboy memories to an understanding and appreciation of the artistry of that monument before us. I had been blind. Without overdoing it, he showed me the perfection of that architecture. Suddenly it all seemed new to me. He hardly needed to solicit my admiration; he had given me an appreciation, if not an extravagant appreciation, of the Escorial's measured grandeur.

We crossed the church itself, fortunately still deserted, without a disturbing tourist hubbub. Just three or four praying women unconsciously complemented the building; the gracious modesty of their position and their comparative smallness emphasized the nave's vastness, crowned by its dome's daring clerestory. My Friend's dislike of pretentiousness—in himself as in others—caused him to check any tendency of our conversation to become overly erudite. Thus he turned to recollections of his student experiences as an acolyte in that illustrious temple. He especially remembered Holy Week services, Tenebrae Wednesdays and Holy Saturdays, which he considered the most beautiful and inspirational of the Catholic liturgy. Smiling, singing in a low voice, he repeated to me a refrain sung in the choir and repeated by the people down below when the three celebrants prostrated themselves before the altar. Later with the Gloria of the Mass, the lighting of the candles revealed that purple Lenten veils had been removed.

We stood under that pulpit where we had so often listened unmoved to the falsetto tremolos, accompanied by flapping black sleeves characteristic of Augustinian preaching. He confessed to me his old wish to preach a really good sermon, something he afterwards repeated in the same joking tone— which did not exclude sincerity. Maybe he felt a need to restore this religious art because all the priestly orators we had heard seemed insipid, routine performers, unworthy of their signal opportunities.

Surely our adverse commentary on the gloomy royal sepulcher included counting up sarcophaguses and noting that space remained for only one more king. Everybody notices that. We did not linger in this pantheon. A suggestive touch added to the ugly gloominess of those marble and bronze coffins for the monarchs and the banal white ones for royal children. A short stairway led from those showy coffins to the little doorway of the *Pudridero* (Rotting Place). That horrible name always aroused a loathing in my Friend. We went up to the capitular museum.

Entering the *Sancta Sanctorum* of Escorial paintings, we did not stop at the famous, coldly academic *Holy Family* by Claudio Coello. I wanted to take him straight to Tintoretto's painting with the dog that always looks straight at viewers, the only thing the blessed brothers point out to students in one of that great Venetian's most beautiful canvases. How differently I now approached it with my Friend, trying to share with him my recent discoveries in the marvelous Italy of Robusti, Veronese, and Titian! After that he led me to the supreme master of that collection, Tintoretto's direct heir in Spain, peerless El Greco. His brush combined the Byzantine formalism of his origins, the noble mastery of his calling that he learned in Venice, and the spirit of his extraordinary creations that he found in his adopted Toledo. I never could discover my Friend's preference between the *Burial of count Orgaz* in Toledo and the *Centurion* in the Escorial. In the latter he delighted in unique yellows and blues that combine with the protagonist's elongated body to give a spiritual effect.

Crossing the Patio of the Evangelists we recalled the fragrance of its carpet of broom, thyme, and spring flowers laid down for Palm Sunday processions.

Next we went on to the palace where tapestries woven from Goya's designs decorate pervasively cold walls with Bourbon luxury. We went on to Philip II's rooms, and at the guard's orders peeped, as everyone must, through a little window down into the chancel of the basilica. Afterwards my Friend's eyes turned to the grilled window of another room contiguous to the royal bedroom. It opened onto a corner of the Friars' Garden called the Prior's Garden. The view from that window, a delightful vista protected by a wall but extending all the way to Madrid on the horizon, gives a better understanding than the view into the chancel of the concept of Catholicism held by that son of Charles V.

In the monastery library my Friend spent more time before Pantoja's portrait of Philip II than before the glass cases displaying precious manuscripts. As a boy I had challenged my teachers' admiring words by finding that portrait repulsive. My anticlericalism easily countered their epithet "the Prudent King" with the Protestant "Demon of the South." This contrast of commonplaces did not satisfy my Companion on that excursion as an explanation of this complex royal personality. I think it was while looking at the Pantoja portrait that I first heard him say, "How German this king seems whom we take as the Spanish prototype."

We barely entered my school. He offered no opposition to my unwillingness to walk again those chilly hallways, or to see the desolate assembly hall, or look into a gallery next to the refectory heavy with the smells of conventual cooking and the burping of generations of students caused by those flatulent meals. We went out into the fields.

We began to climb. We hadn't known about the Abantos highway. He protested that it desecrated the austere countryside. Only hewn stones and slate, perfectly combined by an architect of genius, could possibly justify altering that landscape's perfection. Furthermore the highway had promoted construction of a colony, Escorial de Arriba, whose cheap-looking houses swarm up the mountain and spoil the monastery's overall appearance. As we climbed he stopped to catch his breath and to enjoy an ever-widening view. It brought back college "field days," including, inevitably, memories of a healthy boyhood appetite for succulent tortillas and breaded cutlets, the principal nourishment of such holidays.

Picking our way along a difficult path, a shortcut down to "The Pines," he fell headlong. Perhaps I overreacted and laughed too much in relief that he had not hurt himself; anyhow, he became indignant to the point where our mutual enjoyment of our holiday almost ended right there. He recovered, and we both proceeded more carefully; I disguised the fact that I found the path easier, being lighter. We paused in the "La Herrería" woods.

He relaxed body and soul, surrendering to the blessings of light, fragrance, and the murmur of those rustic surroundings overflowing with the atmosphere of his early adolescence. I have rarely seen anyone enjoy himself so fully, and at the same time savor each minute detail of the "feelings awakened by country life." Suitably, at the beginning of his rambles he would often absentmindedly whistle the evocative theme from Beethoven's *Pastoral* Symphony. Once again the sight of his contentment, his serene exhilaration, caused memories of my unhappy schooldays to give way to a new and pleasant mood. We hardly even spoke that afternoon. We drifted in an atmosphere drenched with country perfumes toward the Arenitas Basin. Why was I so determined to get to the Throne of Philip II?

When we came to the bottom of its rocky hillock, he seemed unwilling to make the ascent. With no real purpose, I insisted stubbornly and succeeded in getting him to make that short climb to the very place where, legend tells us, the Catholic King liked to sit contemplating the construction of the masterwork of his own tomb, a kind of competition with these mountains which provided its building stone. What hidden feeling, what unconscious modesty caused my Friend to resist my suggestion that we climb up and rest from our long walk? He finally sat down and gave himself up totally to contemplating the monument. Unless we grant Philip II intelligence equal to his willfulness, Herrera must himself have chosen that site as the best long-distance viewpoint of his creation, standing out as the centerpiece in a vast panorama.

Somewhat vacuously, now reacting against the diatribes of Ortega y Rubio, my history professor at the Central University, I suggested a measure of real greatness in that king. He had, after all, considered a chair at the back of that basilica among Jeronymite monks singing the Te Deum as the best throne on which to receive the news of our Lepanto victory, "the greatest event seen by the centuries." My Friend did not go along with my dithyramb, but I never heard him denounce the historical phenomenon of our imperial monarchy. He considered it both effective in its time and impossible to recreate.

He silently contemplated that completely realized architectural phenomenon standing before our eyes, a consummation in stone transcending nature in a supreme artistic statement: the Monastery of the Escorial. He mused over the always unfinished undertakings of Spaniards, concentrating on architecture, which he considered an art possibly superior to music. He could not think of one truncated tower, unfinished palace, symmetrical plaza, nor any example of stone resting on stone in our vast Spanish heritage that did not demonstrate the frustrated Spaniard's yearning for the absolute or else the destructive cancer that gnaws at Spanish souls, making them either infertile or mothers of abortions. Only the Escorial stood as a finished work and the product of one single inspiration, the only one on our soil.

Returning from our walk we paid a brief visit to the university. His hand's eager pressure on my arm as he pointed out a window, his student room, clearly showed his emotion, though, as always when his feelings rose to the surface, he tried to hide them. Entering the patio he noted changes that had improved it in practical ways but that disfigured his college memories. He had passed so many times through that lower cloister, now glassed in but then open to the full blast of those horrible winters with snow driven by blizzard winds. As at my College of Alfonso XII we left very quickly, fleeing from our own unhappy shadows. We looked out over the Alamillos parapet and went into the Friars' Garden.

Pereda is not one of my favorite novelists, but rarely have I experienced so strong an emotion in my reading as from a passage in his *Up in the Mountains*. The author interrupts his novel with a cross, signifying the unhappy moment when his son's death interrupted his pen. I put another cross here as I recall my Friend in the peace of the Friars' Garden. He gave that title to one of his best works, and it still remains in print. I do not want to falsify my memory of that day by flattering my vanity with the suggestion that his inspiration came from that moment.

Cross and elipsis.

6

Other Landscapes as Background for the Portrait

Along with other less desirable forms of cosmopolitanism, the war brought an artistic revolution to Madrid.

The Russian Ballet had already had a tremendous vogue in Europe for several years when the Spanish court's wartime neutrality gave us an opportunity to view it. The Secretary of the Ateneo had seen this ballet company in Paris and retained a dazzling memory of its performance, which the rest of us now saw at the Royal Theater. Our cobwebbed stage finally witnessed that resplendent display with which the nineteenth-century theater of grand spectacles expired so beautifully.

At one of these performances of the Russian Ballet there occurred in that royal playhouse what literary historians call the first spark of antimonarchism. People in the topmost gallery, which they call "Paradise" at the Royal, made obvious gestures of hostility toward Their Majesties as they withdrew from the royal box where they customarily presided for our most brilliant entertainments. My Friend and I had seats that night in that highest balcony, in accordance with our practice of attending all new shows we could afford. Annoyance among military men about the king's favoritism and involvement in military affairs had aggravated the quarrel between Germanophiles and supporters of the Allies. This annoyance resulted in the formation of Juntas for Defense headed by Colonel Márquez, very famous at that time. His projected plans included the sort of reform undertaken by the Young Turks in Constantinople. These juntas made no pretense of republicanism, but at that time authentically liberal Spaniards were increasingly disillusioned with the parties and factions which called themselves republicans in the service of the monarchy.

The Ateneo's Secretary did not share the general enthusiasm, even among Reformist party members, for these juntas. He saw them as a kind of echo of nineteenth-century, Isabelline-era army revolts representing nothing more than the traditional dispute within the military class between the privileged and those who considered themselves neglected. They had no real plans for solving our nation's problems.

In spite of Spain's neutrality, the contingencies of the European war influenced this developing crisis, as did the contemptuous attitude of our king and his premiers toward parliament. As a result an Assembly of Parliamentarians met, first in Barcelona and then at Madrid's Ateneo under the presidency of Senator Abadal, a Catalanist conservative. Don Francisco Cambó, recognized leader of the regionalist Catalonian *Lliga,* took a very active part, but after a speech condemning the established power, he left the meeting never to return. Summoned to the Palace for consultation about the crisis, the next day he became a minister in a coalition cabinet headed by Don Antonio Maura.

Melquíades Álvarez did not want to become a member of this cabinet. The Secretary of the Ateneo, a member of Melquíades's Reformist party, confided to me the argument he had expressed in party councils against his leader's holding back at so decisive a moment in Spanish politics. Melquíades Álvarez had answered by positing constitutional reform as the essential condition for his participation. This stood as the publicly declared fundamental principle, the *sine qua non,* for Reformist collaboration either with another opposition party or within the coalition supporting His Majesty. Melquíades also believed it more opportune just to wait for an easily foreseeable breakdown of that patchwork ministry. The other political parties would not be able to restructure the ministry because Maura had included all of their leaders in his cabinet. Thus the Reformists would inevitably come to power with their entire program intact, or so thought Melquíades.

The Secretary of the Ateneo believed, on the other hand, that no other opportunity would arise so favorable as the present one for intervening in our nation's government. Furthermore he argued that if this hybrid ministry headed by Maura collapsed, once it had exhausted its parliamentary options, some other faction might take control. Another possible development of this impasse was to be feared. The king might succeed in broadening his military camarilla by personally recruiting young officers to his cause. Alfonso XIII had begun to adopt a policy of satisfying the limited ambitions of these men by promotions based on sham battles in Morocco or misrepresentation of Pyrrhic victories as defeats of the Riff. Thus the Ateneo's Secretary believed in sacrificing principle now for the sake of efficacious political activity. The sacrifice was not insignificant since the Reformist party would give up a republican national constitution, and the king would not have to make any explicit promises. Still, becoming part of the cabinet might prove a breach through which to take power in a legal way afterward and offer both monarchy and country a change in national precepts that might prevent the latent revolution.

Early in the summer of 1917 the illusory Kerensky republic seemingly controlled the Russian revolution; we did not foresee any imminent expansion of revolutionary activity. Then, however, signs appeared of the first counterproductive effects of that revolution on Russia's war effort. Easing of pressure on the eastern front facilitated a new German offensive in

France. Then, too, French resistance weakened, eroded by the tremendous mortality of their counteroffensives and by defeatist propaganda and espionage behind the lines. At this point, in August, conditions in Spain became exceedingly complicated by the declaration of a general strike by the Socialist party and the General Confederation of Labor (*Unión General de Trabajadores* or UGT).

This strike failed to achieve its immediate objectives, but it made clear the strength of the organized working class. Now for the first time our bourgeoisie reacted with protofascist demonstrations against the workers. "Pioneers" from General Miguel Primo de Rivera's Patriotic Union and even Falangist "Legionnaires," young conservatives and others who tried to appear young, established themselves as "honorary policemen." The government under Premier Eduardo Dato cruelly repressed trifling excesses by some highly circumspect leftist revolutionaries, and this seemed intolerable. They arrested the entire strike committee—Besteiro, Largo Caballero, Anguiano, and Saborit—and threatened them with execution by firing squad—much to the fear or hope of contending factions.

My Friend and I used to take nighttime walks on the heights of the Castellana or under the trees along Florida or Moncloa boulevards, hoping to catch a gasping breath in the blast-furnace atmosphere of Madrid's summer. These walks helped to alleviate the natural propensities of my youth, aggravated by lovesickness, and they became a kind of mania for me. My Friend helped me to get over my moods, appeasing my melancholy without trying either to change my mind or to temper my foolish anxieties with the voice of his experience. Public unrest increased our personal restlessness: the instability of the political scene, a general spirit of nervousness and uneasiness caused by the strike, and even the spectacle of Spain's stupid, ignorant isolation from the tremendous wartime dangers facing the rest of a world where she had played a central role in past centuries. We found refuge in thoughts of consecrating ourselves to art and literature, retreating from the uninspired vulgarity of our surroundings. Even in writing, though, we didn't see much future for ourselves. Despite my slight interest in politics, I got caught up more than he did in its illusions. His skepticism had deeper roots than my feelings; where I tended to yield to enthusiasm, he always remained controlled by reason. Indeed, an instinctive caution normally controlled his thinking.

We had to interrupt our nightly roving into the suburbs because of military regulations, though the curfew imposed by the state of war had not proved very effective. We were not personally involved, but we could hardly escape the general excitement, and did not break our usual habits to the extent of returning home before midnight. Early closing of cafés cut off our usual opportunities for exchanging impressions, so we took to wandering through the streets in a vain attempt to understand events merely by looking around.

It made some sense, but, of course, what we saw depended on what we chose to look at.

One August night after meandering through the Salamanca District, talking in our habitual way, to each other but in a kind of monologue, we ended up at his place at daybreak. Echoes of occasional distant shots added dramatic excitement to the oppressive heat. The battle of Cuatro Caminos between strikers and armed forces was coming to an end, and we didn't feel sleepy. Though we had nothing more to say, we went over again what had happened and what might happen next.

We looked out from his balcony; its elevation and a slight depression toward the Castellana and Serrano afforded a view over houses and through the Milky Way to a starry sky. We looked toward the Chamberi heights trying to make out the glare of explosions on a brightening horizon. I watched him lighting a cigarette, another of I don't know how many during that vigil. Maybe the crisis had caused him to break an abstention from smoking that he imposed on himself from time to time when stomach troubles or loss of memory "warned him," as he used to say. Then he would take it up again, and coffee, when he needed a stimulant for writing. In this pattern he restrained or yielded to his appetite.

"Can it be," he said after a pause that the night's sorrows seemed to impose on our random thoughts, "is it possible that they will execute Besteiro?" Quite naturally our protest against the terrible fate threatening this professor and his three companions focused with special concern on the Secretary's friend. I knew Besteiro only through mutual friends of a few years' standing from the Free Institute of Education, whereas he knew him as a close friend.

Then he said something in a few simple words I cannot now exactly repeat about "respect for life" as a fundamental responsibility for a civilized society. He blamed on war the subversion of moral values characteristic of liberal progress. Fond of reviving in current usage the original meanings of words, he suggested that Cervantes in describing as "liberal" the generous lover in one of his *Exemplary Novels* had come closer to its basic meaning than the modern usage describing a political position that has existed since the Restoration era.

Before the war—the Great War of 1914—incidents like the torture of anarchists in Montjuich Prison or the execution of Ferrer had scandalized Europe. Among his, then recent, memories of his beloved Paris, he liked to recall attending a rally in support of Armenians in connection with one of many massacres by their Turkish oppressors. Manifestly a transient element in the population of the City of Light, those refugees had even spoken in their own language, which nobody understood. Yet they had attracted a crowd, and he himself had added a modest donation to a collection with which their rally ended. He smiled ironically, philosophically confident in a skepticism that could not accept great truths as incontrovertible merely because they had come down from one or more generations, but that daily affirmed his faith in a morality inherent in one's own conscience.

With the subversive movement overcome and Socialist leaders merely condemned to prison, we all breathed more freely. We felt sure that amnesty would soon restore their freedom, and so it happened. Of course that interval did not seem short to the prisoners.

We ourselves returned to our nonchalance about all political events. An indelible memory remained, however, of Melquíades Álvarez speaking to a rally at a Workers' Club, Socialist headquarters, in support of Asturian miners during the general strike. "I have said it in the king's courts'" and my Friend, the Secretary of the Ateneo, laughed at my imitation of his party chieftain's grandiloquent style. He, in turn, parodied the exaggerated tone and Asturian accent of another party member who had lauded Melquíades Álvarez's speech. "It makes me weep buckets; it makes me slobber." From his own circumspect and moderate position that reaction seemed excessive, especially coming from a man who boasted of being a member of the soft-spoken Free Institute of Education.

While my Friend had no high opinion of his chief's strictly discursive skills, he did admire his natural oratorical talents, especially the magnificent strong voice. "How would you, as a listener, characterize it?" he asked, joking. "Baritone?" "Dramatic tenor," I answered, picking up his implication and correcting his appraisal. He also liked Melquíades's correct pronunciation and fluent use of Castilian, but he noticed a shallowness in his pointless digressions and a poverty of examples. Melquíades Álvarez lacked good literary judgment, something that constituted an important element in my Friend's talent. Still, the Secretary's sincere horror of garrulousness did not stop his determination to use his own voice in support of the people's cause.

We went on, then, enjoying golden autumnal afternoons in Retiro Park. He used to protest vehemently against a famous gardener's brutal pruning; the city government had appointed him, and nobody spoke up for the martyred trees. A particularly splendid moment comes when the sun sets behind the arch of the Puerta de Alcalá and, for a moment, turns our sky a magnificent bloody red. Many times we paused to contemplate this celestial spectacle and then walked down the street to buy roasted chestnuts at a stand next to the main post office on La Cibeles. He walked with a light step, buttoned into his greenish blue overcoat, hands thrust into its pockets. Though he held his head high, his gaze upward, his coat collar completely covered his neck. He had now shaved off his moustache, the glory of his youth.

"How strange!" he used to say every year at the beginning of October, "I dreamed again that I was back at the Escorial. It has happened ever since I left that school." Sometimes that season also evoked for him the picturesque affectations of Madrid at the turn of the century. I remember him once saying "Leaves . . . ," and he twisted his face into an expression of comic sentimentality as he kicked some of them that had blown into our way. "Leaves . . .! That's how young men talked the days when we wore fitted overcoats, frock coats."

Frequently we would take Streetcar 11 as far as Rosales, preferably on weekdays to avoid the Sunday crowd and the dust they stirred up shuffling along. The view over the Casa del Campo and mountain cheered him up. He later wrote of it as *Paseante en Corte* ("Strolling Cavalier"). He admired the Pardo's classical severity, softened by the silvery greens and grays of that Velázquez countryside, clear-cut contours with details blending in; and the massive Royal Palace standing out on the hill above the river, sharply defined in that clear atmosphere. A few years later they built the Seminary, an oppressive abortion that matched the Palace and flattened a silhouette that Goya's painting still preserves. We frequently went on through the Western Park, careful to keep trees—grown so fast in a few years—between us and that abominable monument that has survived in spite of lightning, thunderbolts, and bombs sent down by an unjust heaven and stupid mankind. Good walkers, we would go down through Moncloa's ancient and fragrant pines, now pitilessly and unnecessarily cut down by the tasteless planners of University City. Next we would cross the little square in front of the Pardo Palace and climb the stairs through those delightful little gardens to the Florida boulevard and catch our streetcar at the stop near the Chapel of San Antonio. They had not yet built the second matching chapel or, still worse, set up that big-headed monstrosity created by a sculptor who had shown talent in other minor works. Certainly he did not evoke the Goya who had painted the frescoes in that chapel.

As we walked along the Florida boulevard my Friend always complained about the barbarism of the agricultural engineers who had established there the experimental fields for their school. If they had used the ample space available east of the capital they would have preserved Florida's woods and gardens, of which only remnants now survived. "You see how it goes, and I have seen so much more. The same thing happened at Aranjuez," he said.

I also enjoyed the special delights of the Aranjuez gardens with the Secretary of the Ateneo, as I had previously shared them with a friend, a sweetheart, in a budding love affair. That royal seat provides a background suitable for friendship, courtship and pleasure. Where I preferred the melancholy, isolated Prince's Garden, he liked the better-groomed Island Garden. We agreed with everyone else that Versailles had inspired the gardens' design. Yet La Granja and Aranjuez no more reproduce Versailles than Philip V and Charles III equaled the Sun King at his highest ascendant. My Friend laughed at the modernist predisposition, noxious in most people though winning in Rubén Darío, to reject Versailles's highly cultivated woods in favor of the Petit Trianon of mock shepherdesses, with its clipped labyrinth and its charming hemmed-in meadows.

1918–20

7

His First Electoral Campaign

Someone in the Reformist party's governing council spoke in favor of assigning my Friend a place among its candidates in the elections the Liberal cabinet finally scheduled after a series of crises. His designation for Puente del Arzobispo in Toledo Province, however, did not mean electoral victory. Don César de la Mora, currently the district's representative and for a long time the cacique who controlled its parliamentary representation, was a very rich man and kinsman of former premier Antonio Maura. Both his supporters and his adversaries regarded him as invincible. No electoral pact the Reformists might register with the minister of the interior could neutralize this man's omnipotence in that district. Nobody, least of all my Friend, conceived of his campaign as anything but a blank cartridge.

The Secretary did help his chances of election by joining a coalition in the *turno* system, at that point coming to its end. Under this system two or three large parties with roughly the same viewpoint grouped together under a common label. Nonetheless, the regime's vicious corruption prevented any opposition party from having real strength among the voting populace. When the government called for elections, the minister of the interior, in consultation with party leaders, assigned candidates to play out a constitutional farce. Rarely did anyone get chosen on the basis of honest votes, and there was small likelihood of surprises. Especially in rural districts, electoral campaigns became a matter of intrigue, soliciting, and bribery rather than presenting a platform. Still, even in a congress selected in this way, a deputy had some personal initiative in discussion of laws. Parliament offered a tribune that echoed louder in our nation than the Ateneo did.

Admirers of the Secretary hoped for this; their expectations went no further, and he fully realized his slight chance of getting elected. Close friends and clients of old-timers made up much of the government's majority, and they controlled politics as a kind of shameless patriciate based on strict seniority. Nobody dared to tamper with its norms, a system that had little to do with its own supposed model or with normative parliamentary practices.

My Friend might have saved himself a lot of trouble by planning his political career along traditional lines after he finished his university career. The marquess of Ibarra, a great landowner in the Alcarria district near

Alcalá, often dispensed support and favors just for the asking. Furthermore, the Secretary's elder brother, when he took over their family estate, had some inclination toward the conservative politics that suited their strictly family interests. However, this *señorito*'s capricious approach to politics had no appeal for either brother, though both were then *señoritos* themselves. They felt unwilling to sacrifice independence, to accept discipline from someone else, in return for the privilege of waiting in line for political favors. During his first stay in Paris, the spectacle of French public life had stimulated my Friend's thoughts about the satisfactions of public service. He had come back to Spain not so much with political ambitions as with a craving for the intrinsic democratic satisfaction of holding public office. Incapable of queuing up in ministerial antechambers for favors or of joining the coterie of some petty political boss in the congressional conference hall, he now proved amenable to suggestions from persons who recognized the Ateneo Polemicist as a born politician. Maybe seeing his party chief pay less attention to his opinions than to those of others moved him, against his natural indolence, to accept this opportunity offered him in Puente del Arzobispo. Certainly he recognized beforehand the election's inevitable result.

He could not begin to compete with his opponent's monetary expenditures. His family's ruin put him out of the running for that, and, anyhow, that approach contradicted his conception of the political profession. Up to then and for a long time afterward, he had no opportunity to think much about the aims of government or even about his own political purposes. He just went on enjoying the means without considering the ends, with a vocation opposite to that of the Jesuits, according to the common view that attributes to Jesuitism the justification of means by ends.

He did need some money for essential campaign costs, and he did not have it. His salary went for personal expenditures and to pay the usurious interest on a loan he had taken out at the time of the loss of his family fortune. He never clearly understood who in his party provided the pesetas necessary to present his candidacy. This involved nothing more than making contact with Toledo Province's few Reformists. He would have wasted his time campaigning in the strongholds of the deputy currently in office, who had support from rural caciques and through them controlled the town governments. Local Reformists arranged necessary election propaganda. A friend, a professor at the Graduate Training School for Teachers, accompanied him. This good gentleman, a fellow party member who knew the district, had worked at the Institute in Toledo when Besteiro did. He had also repeatedly tried without success to represent Santander in the Cortes. My Friend long afterwards joked about their excursion together and especially about a trip they made from town to town by burro. He described this professorial candidate's efforts to persuade his asinine mount, by reason more than by whip or stick, that he should keep to the middle of the road, where it would find "the shortest distance between two points." The animal did not seem very sensible to his words, and the professor laughed at himself. Portraying the backwardness and poverty of an inn or tavern at the edge of some sorry village, my Friend repeated what they said to him when he asked what they had to eat, "whatever you have brought with you." In another hamlet in the mountain region people lighted their homes with torches—like cavemen.

A proprietor in those lands, another young Ateneo member, died at the dawning of the republic. Let it stand as his monument that he discovered, and revealed to others, the Secretary as a politician. I had just discovered him as a great writer, and our friendship developed from that. Martí Jara gave him the opportunity to become a public man. This man provided my Friend with votes of his own friends in a town where he had some influence. Among them he counted the peerless Cristeta. A fairly prosperous villager, my Friend esteemed her because of her good grace and tact, her generosity expressed by succulent gifts on special occasions, and her native good sense developed through political experiences. In short, he saw in her the discretion that characterizes Spain's people. He recognized these as unmistakable underlying personality traits clearly shared by all our people in spite of their many differences in the various regions that make up our nation.

The Secretary was essentially Castilian himself and thus a pure Spaniard. He liked the plains of the Duero, the Tagus, the Ebro, the Henares, and the Jarama—the heartland of this basic national type—and he liked the simple people who worked those plains. He loved as an obsession every inch of the territory stretching from Toldeo's Sagra Range to the Gredos foothills and from Oropesa to the frontiers of Estremadura and Portugal. This region sounded the depths of his imagination, and his thoughts always returned to it. In that first visit to his district, which never really became his, he discovered the La Jara region, the undoubted source of our friend Martí's surname, where La Cristeta maintained a kind of archetypal matriarchy.

I could not go with him on that first electoral campaign. He consoled me by exaggerating its annoyances and playing down the good times. Besides, the opportunity it presented somewhat deviated from the horoscope I had cast for him. To a zealous advocate of his devotion to literature, this political inclination seemed an interruption of that sacred idleness which fosters artistic creativity.

As with his wartime journeys to the front, his reports had to suffice for things we could not otherwise share. His habitual comment was, "At least it gives us something to talk about." Later he applied it to our various misfortunes. While I have always formed my own opinions of things independent of what other people say, his accounts seemed a boon. Though he tried to describe reality, not to exaggerate it, his descriptions seemed works of art to me. He, on the other hand, laughed at my narratives and, years later, at my sister's; he said that she exaggerated as much as I did. "You don't know how to talk; you have to act things out."

He wrote about his acquaintance with my namesake, Mr. Cipriano, and later spoke of him. He told of this shepherd's rustic clothing and undyed sheepskin jacket that, through his countryman's ingenuity, he kept perfectly white. This Cipriano and his fellows seemed to my Friend reincarnations of characters he enjoyed in Cervantes's *Novels* and *Don Quijote,* books he kept rereading. These men seemed to preserve the charm of an earlier age. He greatly valued their friendship, far more than they in their dignified modesty could believe. Another proprietor, far more influential than La Cristeta or Mr. Cipriano, proved particularly helpful and solicitous and dug into his capital to help with election costs. Still, his influence did not suffice to counterbalance that of César de la Mora's principal political agent, a Galdo-sian personage even in his name, Platón Páramo. He had made most of the fortune local gossip attributed to him by buying antiques under the guise of being an amateur collector and then selling them at outrageous prices. He also loaned out money as a pawnbroker, charging the highest possible interest.

The Secretary of the Ateneo lost his election, but he returned to Madrid having had an experience that left an indelible mark on his later political career. Reformists counted for little in that district, and Republicans still less, in spite of the brief revolutionary history of neighboring Talavera *de la Libertad,* as they had called themselves at the fall of Isabella II. During our republic they called themselves, more simply and more suitably, Tala-vera del Tago. Socialist organizations had already become important. The class struggle, or more exactly the battle between private property and com-munal property, manifested itself in a secular court case in Oropesa, the Socialist party headquarters and a more important city than the district capital. Litigation dated back to the eighteenth century involving extensive lands identified with the ancient Frías family; it concerned the rights of tenants-by-custom to property belonging to members of the Common Coun-cil. These tenants now made a claim with the city government asserting rights threatened by the sale of this property. The expert Employee of the Registry Office had no doubts: justice lay entirely on the people's side. His recognition of the validity of their claims later helped to establish a closer bond between the Candidate and his aggrieved electors. Like him, they knew that victory needn't come in the first round or even in the second. They supported him unconditionally.

My Friend did not, however, get carried away by the enthusiasm his jour-ney aroused in people who had seen him or come to hear him. Everything remained to be done. Good will alone did not suffice.

8

On the Road

Don Rafael Altamira, distinguished Hispanic-American professor of history, called the Secretary of the Ateneo to ask him to recommend a discreet young man to help out one of his colleagues. This colleague, a professor from the United States then passing through Spain on his way to Italy, planned to give a series of lectures in our northern cities later that summer. He needed someone to arrange his tour in terms of locations, dates, and probable audiences. The United States Embassy had offered to pay expenses and lodging in those cities for someone who would make these arrangements. I could lose nothing by undertaking the commission. My Friend proposed to come along as my traveling companion for a short summer trip if the ministry would advance his vacation a little. We departed like students on a holiday. It pleased me that by accepting this assignment I could provide my Friend with an excuse to refresh his spirits. They always sagged a bit when he spent several successive months doing office work.

We went first to La Coruña. That beautiful city gave us a happy reception, with the amiable bustle of its calle Real and sunshine reflecting from its smiling bay onto thousands of windowpanes. We had letters of introduction to the mayor, apparently a republican, and to other important persons who might help us in making arrangements and help the professor afterwards. Between calls we got acquainted with the city through leisurely walks and after-dinner *tertulias* near a kiosk at the wharf. People gathered there, half-anticipating summer rains. Sometimes, indeed, a downpour obliged us to take refuge in some café.

Very soon my Mentor pointed out to me how much closer La Coruña seemed to Havana or even to Buenos Aires than to Madrid. One continually heard people speak of these American capitals with no sense of distance, referring to relatives or friends whom everyone had on the other side of "the pond" as if that represented nothing more than the bay lying before us. On "packet days" (members of our *tertulia* used this sailor's term for the mail boat from the Antilles or South America) and on the first of the month when "the check" came in from overseas, a long line formed at the Banca Pastor doorway. Mostly women from villages, they waited to cash the welcome bank draft by which the emigrant supported and fed the hopes of his family remaining behind to take care of their cow and the poor soil of their fields.

After we had arranged publicity for the American professor we went on to our next stop at Santiago de Campostela. At Órdenes our bus passed a procession of poor people; only Valle Inclán's dream world has captured this harsh reality. The city's imposing architecture struck my Friend more than its picturesque ambience which attracts casual tourists. We both had to yield, though, to the power of a scene that we might have thought staged for visitors if it had not occurred quite spontaneously and with no other spectators than ourselves. Crazily climbing a hill next to the cathedral came a funeral procession. I say crazily because behind the cadaver and priests came friends, grieving because of their loss, and others, possibly hired for ritual mourning, everybody stumbling and bumping along that uneven pavement.

When our bus stopped at Pontevedra on our way to Vigo, he pointed out signs of a canal to the sea on which local political bosses had spent millions in hopes of creating a port; obviously a failure, it remained unfinished. Passing through Marín we saw Lourizán, the estate of "Monteiro," as my Friend called the old politician Montero Ríos. We also saw the ironclad ship *Carlos V* anchored in an estuary, perfectly reflected in its still water, and a house called "Maricel" standing among pine trees. Here for the first time I heard my Friend speak of a wish he would repeat through the years in other places: he would like to settle down in retirement somewhere alone with nature, someplace where he could devote himself to idle work—not a paradox. Two desires attracted him that finally pointed in the same direction: to tear down and to rebuild on the site where he had destroyed. At his family home in Alcalá, at the Ateneo, or sitting on a boulder by the side of the road, he would hardly pause to contemplate an oasis or a moor, a ruin or a building in good repair, before he started thinking of ways to alter anything but a tree. Wall up a doorway or make an opening in a wall, knock down a mansion or rebuild a ruined tower. It fulfilled his need for active contemplation.

Arriving in León we went at once to its dimly lit Plaza de la Catedral. Neither the Gothic cathedral nor the Renaissance facade of San Marcos gave us a real sense of the historic kingdom of León. That came at San Isidro. In this Romanesque pantheon of León's kings, more severe than the pantheon of our Austrian and Bourbon kings at the Escorial, my Friend felt infused by a feeling for Spain's age-old monarchy. Here we saw the foundation of the great Spanish republic on both sides of the Atlantic that survives in the Castilian language.

After I had made arrangements for the professor's lecture in Gijón, we took a quick trip through Asturias. My Comrade felt a predilection for its deep, damp valleys. He said that they consoled him. A gray mist softened and tempered the deep green panorama. This compensated for the absence of the tableland's implacable clear sky, its plowed fields and yellow stubble.

We went on to Covadonga where phony religious-patriotic piety has diminished those mountains' epic grandeur with a gaudy basilica and a panoramic cave. In this cave, where they say Pelayo took refuge from Arab invaders, we left calling cards in accordance with a ridiculous custom. We had no time to tour the mining district, but he took me to San Esteban de Pravia, one of his favorite stops. After returning to Oviedo, we went on to Santander. We found nothing there to interest us beyond the basic purpose of our trip.

From Santander we took off on an adventure. We traveled to the Picos de Europa by way of San Vicente de la Barquera and Unquera and the Hermida Gorge, a region of mines and a lake. We made part of the ascent on horseback, and he overflowed with happiness during these diversions. On the way back we stopped at Santillana. The beauty of its cathedral church aroused his indignation against the garrulous inanity of a novel fortuitously set in that locale. That book had some ephemeral fame, and it had brought its author, Ricardo León, a reputation beyond his merits. We entered the Cave of Altamira. The Secretary of the Ateneo enthused to me about the perfection of its paintings apart from any archeological considerations; he compared them to masterworks of the greatest periods in history.

We went on to Bilbao, where we found new friends who gave us banquets more succulent than those of Oviedo. The estuary, with its industrial banks, impressed my Friend more than the old city so dear to the hearts of Vizcayan nationalists. In passing he boasted of having one Basque grandmother and one Catalonian, but his own clear Castilianism explained his feeling for Spanish unity. By unity he did not mean the Bourbons' limited concept, which had degenerated into sentimental royalist identification with the king. He meant another French idea, this one coming from their revolution: a people can achieve true individual liberty only through common devotion to national unity. San Sebastián marked the end of our excursion.

The closed-in valleys of Vizcaya and Guipúzcoa pleased him less than the wider, deeper ones in Asturias and Galicia or the sunnier ones in the Montaña region around Santander. The Valley of Loyola, so peaceful, interested him less than the characteristic towns of Azpeitia and Azcoitia, with their typical resistance to change. "Look," he said to me, stopping in front of a mansion decorated with a shield that seemed medieval. "In Castilian towns they built that way in the fourteenth century, but those buildings date from the seventeenth century. They lagged that far behind."

His friend and housemate Creagh had studied in Oñate, seat of an ancient university, precursor of those at Deusto and the Escorial, and also the site of the Pretender Don Carlos's ephemeral court. Creagh had known Galdós in some connection or other, and the author of *National Episodes* had asked him to send a careful description of city streets, buildings, and other details. Thus the novelist gave a very true impression of that place in *From Oñate to La Granja,* which seemed written by a spectator or participant in the historical events it related.

We climbed Aránzazu, a real challenge, to enjoy a broad panoramic view of sunrise over the valley. That hike proved instructive; we found a girl at a roadside inn who was at least ten years old but did not know one word of Castilian. This launched my Friend into a discussion about the need for a unified national school system to impose the learning of a basic language to link our nation together. Still, his linguistic imperialism did not extend to what he considered the error of some great philologists like Don Ramón Menéndez Pidal. Menéndez Pidal had supervised publication of the *Dictionary of the Spanish Language,* more accurately titled *Dictionary of the Castilian Language* in earlier editions. The Secretary of the Ateneo felt that all the peninsula's languages were Spanish languages, including Portuguese, but he did not limit his conception of Hispanism to language. Hispanism had existed before the Catholic Monarchs achieved political unification. He strongly insisted that "Iberian," commonly and erroneously used today as the broader, inclusive term, represents only one element, however basic, of Hispanism.

In the monastery of Aránzazu we heard vespers sung in the Gregorian style that those Franciscan brothers take pride in preserving accurately. The next morning, again very early, we climbed Aizgorri accompanied by a guide who usually tended goats on those cliffs. My Friend got this goatherd to tell stories of the legendary lady, of witches and demons, and the boy firmly believed all of them.

Our first glimpse of plains came at Vitoria. Once again a suggestion of open fields in the transition between Basque mountains and Castilian Rioja gave my Friend an exultant, clear sense of his ancestral roots.

After we returned to Madrid, our journey had a brief postscript in two escapes, to Ávila and Segovia. My memory of our visit to Saint Teresa's city culminates in our contemplation of the tomb of Prince Don Juan where the supreme enterprise of the Catholic Monarchs met its untimely end. In believing this, the Secretary of the Ateneo followed the opinions of other wise men who deem this a fatal loss for Spain's destiny. With the death of this male heir, the monarchy's clearly Spanish personality ended. The problem of the succession of Doña Isabel and Don Fernando remained an inexhaustible theme in my Friend's thought, clearly worked out, though he never put it down concretely in a historical essay.

If Ávila is silvery gray, Segovia is unmistakably golden, except for its aqueduct, magnificent over the Azoguejo, which changes colors constantly at the early-morning market hour. I retain a memory of a magnificently autumnal Segovia on that trip. We stood on the Parral road, on the Eresma's bank, its water bubbling with crystalline foam, and above us the Alcázar dominating the city. The ruins of the monastery of El Parral bothered my Friend even more than those of the monastery of El Paular. For him the justice of ending mortmain did not justify neglectful abandonment of these relics which that change had deprived of necessary support. As always when facing a ruin, my Comrade thought about restoring its fallen walls and scattered stones.

Seated on the terrace of a café in Segovia's plaza, rather chilly in the late afternoon shade, but with yellow reflections from the nearby cathedral, we saw a newsboy running with a local paper. He was hoarse from shouting his sensational report: the Germans, defeated by General Foch, had asked for an armistice.

Tears of happiness came to my eyes. My Friend smiled, "Good," he said to me, "we have won the war!"

9

Paris on Our Side

Besides the familiar Madrid newspapers that existed at the turn of the century and *Sol,* which originated during the 1914 European war, some ephemeral dailies emerged, among them *Fígaro.* I don't recall just how the Secretary of the Ateneo came to know its editor. Somebody got an idea that my Friend should make a trip to victorious France, as he had to the wartime front, thus recognizing the validity of his Ateneo campaign supporting the Allies. He would report on Alsace and Lorraine, now returned to France; his pretext would be attending a ceremony restoring the French University at Strasbourg on the anniversary of the armistice.

His salary as a correspondent did not suffice to permit him to take me along as his secretary. He wouldn't have done it anyhow. Neither then nor later did he want to assign me a subordinate position that fell short of my talents. When I later gave myself the title "stage director" to define my theatrical work, he smilingly acknowledged that the appellation exactly suited the influence of my friendship on his own undertakings. He did, however, ask me to go along with him. I had saved up a few pesetas, payment for some translations, and so to Paris we went, pooling our scanty means. We intended to stay two or three months and return to Madrid for Christmas.

At San Sebastián we took window seats so as not to miss our crossing of the International Bridge after Irún. "Now you are in France!" and he squeezed my arm to share his excitement, a characteristic gesture when his usual constraint gave way. At that moment we had passed a frontier marker in the middle of that bridge over the Bidasoa. I don't know what vague presentiment made that simple passing of the frontier seem to us an anticipation of some fatal event in our lives. The trip, short-term and purely recreational, could have no significance beyond what we gave it.

We woke up the next morning already on the Île-de-France. A Spaniard's first impression of the French countryside might go no further than noting the apparent monotony of its complete cultivation. My Friend, delighting in those green plains through which we were speeding, tried to make me recognize it as man's efforts complementing nature. "France is a garden," he said.

"Of course, they have a countryside as flat as the palm of your hand, blessed with broad, smooth-flowing rivers."

Railroad tracks with intricate patterns on the outskirts of Paris contributed to the feeling of a great city that pulsated in the air. My naive, excited anticipation exhilarated my Friend; seeing my first enthusiasm renewed his own from the past. My uncertainty and surprise about stepping onto an escalator to come up from the subway at the Quai d'Orsay amused him, like someone guiding a child or a country cousin. If he could have, my Comrade would have blindfolded me so that I would first see his Paris from the vantage point of the river and the leafy Tuileries Garden, unspoiled by any other impression. It really did seem like his city, the way he did the honors.

"Wait and see! Just you wait and see!" he kept repeating as our cab approached the hotel. He tried to avoid my absorbing some impression he wanted to save for later. Close to the station, on the Quai Voltaire, our hotel was famous because Oscar Wilde had lived there during his last stay in Paris. Its outward aspect and its clientele dissipated any doubts about its character. In the lobby, which looked like that of a second-class country inn, we happened to see His Excellency, the Bishop of Angers arriving at the very moment we did.

We lost no time in getting out into the streets again. In spite of a steady breeze it seemed considerably more humid than Madrid; and, though the trees still had their leaves, autumn had already brought them to that magnificence, that last glory which comes before winter's bareness. A slight mist softened the blue of the sky.

We crossed a bridge toward the Louvre. In the place du Carrousel my Friend pointed out to me the Arc de Triomphe, its rosy grace both Pompeian and Napoleonic. Then he made me turn to the right toward the palace wall, and then in the opposite direction toward the Tuileries Garden. "Look!" He pointed towards the Arc de l'Étoile up the Champs-Elysées. He was right; no perspective anywhere compares to this one in its blend of grandeur and grace. "Notice the perfection of the proportion, so that your eye doesn't reach beyond the arch. The rise of the slope is so gradual that you don't notice it."

Then, probably, I first heard him say something that he often repeated afterward to stress his point: Paris satisfies the mind because it was built for the normal human perspective. He suggested that one of the city's greatest enchantments came from passing down its customs from generation to generation so that its pleasures continue. Thus a visitor who returns after an absence finds intact the scene that his mind has tried to preserve, and he enjoys again his earlier feelings. There stood the Café Napolitain, and my Friend remembered its red plush booths and mirrors that still gave back the same distorted reflections. He particularly liked its unforgettable brioches but found them considerably more expensive than on his first visit to Paris.

My Friend measured the world's center by the boulevard des Italiens, the boulevard de la Madeleine, the rue Royale, and the rue de Rivoli, with the river for background. Returning to our lodging that first night he pointed out to me a pleasing contrast between the boulevard's hubbub and modernity and the silence and modest provincial air of the neighborhood on our side of the Seine. I say our side from a Spanish perspective, the Left Bank, *la rive gauche*.

Notre Dame and the Sainte-Chapelle attracted us from both sides of the river to the medieval peace of the Île Saint-Louis. With the Louvre so close at hand, we soon visited its treasures, alternating these visits with window-shopping as we wandered through the streets. First we went rapidly through the Louvre's halls and galleries without pausing, not wanting our archetypal experience spoiled by a chronological approach, but we found it hard to resist the temptations offered by so many renowned masterpieces. He calculated which of the corridors converging on that supreme exhibit would give the best effect, and we approached it gradually, seeing the Venus de Milo emerging in its clarity from surrounding shadows. Then he took me to the foot of a staircase where the anchored Winged Victory of Samothrace flew. Last we went to the Salon Carré filled with the light of Italy's Renaissance by Veronese's *Marriage at Cana*. After the resplendence of that masterpiece came two Titians which always reminded us of visits to the Prado Museum in Madrid, the *Portrait of Francis I* and *Young Man with a Glove* in whose elegance he saw the summation of several generations of breeding.

My Friend did not follow intellectual fashions of the moment but concentrated on masterpieces in all kinds of art, giving special attention to less celebrated ones that offered a kind of virginity for a viewer to discover something new through his own close observation. He liked to decide for himself about great works and what constituted their greatness. This doesn't mean, though, that he paid no attention to other works whose interest lay merely in exquisite detail or anecdotal charm. Many times he called me "the Indifferent," referring to the attitude and protagonist in Watteau's painting, a benevolent reproach for my bad habit of exaggerated youthful nonchalance.

As much as to the Louvre, we went back day after day to pictures in the Salon d'Automne of the Grand Palais, and up and down stairways of the Printemps and Galeries Lafayette department stores, to great national theaters, and to *chansons cabarettes*. My Friend especially extolled the variety of pleasure that characteristic French freedom made available to both foreigners and natives not merely as something guaranteed by law but actually practiced. He also noted a change in the attitude and conduct of many French people caused by the war in which they had sacrificed a generation of young men. They no longer showed that happy accepting sympathy toward foreigners he had noticed during his first stay in Paris. He thought he sensed a certain reserve, if not hostility, toward citizens of neutral nations now returning to the pleasant country they had not acted to defend. For me, unable to make comparisons, this seemed less evident.

Certainly we both noticed the weather turning cold. Coming out from a Colonne Orchestra concert on November 1, we saw a lowering black sky whose contrast with recently fallen snow on tile roofs suggested a superb etching. The chiaroscuro with which its atmosphere had decorated the city's most illustrious monuments provided romantic grace notes that my Friend admired in the formal severity of Parisian architecture. Violet patches on columns of the Madeleine, the Odéon, and the Chamber of Deputies building culminated in the burnished splendor of the Louvre's anterior facade. Only Sacré Coeur's inexpressive whiteness, its smiling Jesuitism, varies the grayish harmony of the city accumulated at the foot of the hill during passing centuries. Yet he came to believe that the mysterious infallibility of Parisian taste showed up in that basilica's striking appearance when a pale sun broke through mist in the Seine's autumnal mornings. Then one saw it there shining through haze at the end of a street leading up the little hill from the boulevards.

My Comrade frequently spoke of how monuments had blended into the visual continuity of Paris. As an example, he pointed to the Eiffel Tower's more vulgar and up-to-date silhouette, airy by its nature and penetrated by idealizing river vapors. Yet defenders of the city's harmonious symmetry had at first refused to accept it as a legitimate part of the characteristic panorama, the grandiose harmony of stones and trees in Gallo-Roman style consolidated by Napoleon III. Who would now question the beauty of that monument erected for a world's fair as an exhibit of scientific construction but then entirely alien to current norms of artistic taste?

My Friend felt the same inclusive fondness for the Eiffel Tower as for the place des Vosges or the gilded dome of Les Invalides. His affection also extended beyond outstanding monuments, true milestones on the highway of French civilization. He loved the streets and squares of an earlier age, the picturesque corners, the anachronistic houses (formerly palaces) standing between courtyard and garden in the faubourg Saint-Germain, and the little shops in the rue Saints-Pères, and also the rue Bargue, which recalls an ancient passage that crossed the river there from one bank to the other. In the course of our first walks by the wharves, where parapets along the river serve an additional purpose with their row of stalls for dealers in secondhand books and prints, he pointed out a little street. It was as narrow as any in Seville or Toledo, shadowed by ancient eaves and corbels, shut in by the convex walls of its venerable houses. All of this made him an unofficial citizen of that great fatherland which Napoleon had claimed for himself with all the burdens of its history.

One day, casually crossing the Invalides esplanade, we witnessed a spectacle of grieving patriotism. It proved a foretaste of our imminent trip to Alsace and Lorraine to fulfill my Friend's journalistic assignment. It also seemed a kind of hyphen connecting us to his recent memories of the wartime front. We saw people congregating behind some military musicians, and we joined them from curiosity to observe a ceremony that occurred frequently in those days. I had never seen a Victory Funeral. In the center of that great square participants assembled around a flag. Some general representing the Ministry of War presented medals to widows and orphans filing past in deep mourning dress, mothers with black plumes in their hats in memory of their family sacrifice on the fatherland's bloody altar.

"*La guerre est triste* (war is sad)," my comrade and Mentor said to me as those troops marched away to the music of the "Marseillaise." Despite its heroic lyrics this peerless hymn sounded melancholy.

It turned very cold.

10

Journey to the Eastern Front

In 1919 train trips in France were adventures, with services still disorganized from the war and an enormous number of travelers on account of demobilization. It cost us a considerable effort even to get two seats in an empty coach near the front of a very long train. At nightfall, after many delays, we pulled out of the station on our way to Metz.

An excited party of soldiers soon took our first-class compartment by storm; they had found all second-class and third-class compartments filled. One of them, apparently a peasant, made excuses for the others; we could hardly refuse their company, and we did not regret it. Later we accepted a drink of local *pinard*. In the trenches they had used this word for wine, and survivors of that tremendous camaraderie continued to use it. When an officer appeared at the door to order those soldiers to move out, we told him that we would gladly have them stay if this call to duty came from concern about our comfort. We found their company worth a little crowding.

My Friend started a conversation with the most talkative soldier, a man who had already asked us where we came from and our destination. He and his comrades were heading for the Rhine to mount guard. He spoke very well, with a peasant's openness—not quite the same thing as candor. Our conversation turned quite naturally to the war and the peace. That soldier made telling points in blaming us for our neutrality. True, countries that had not taken part in the battle of Europe had preserved a whole generation that France had sacrificed; but perhaps in the long run a neutral nation was not better off. Though a pacifist, he had no doubts about the necessity of his current military mission. He came from a southern village that did not face continuous danger from the *Boches* as northerners did, especially in the East Mark. (No Frenchman of any class or condition called the Germans anything but *Boches*.) Nevertheless he understood very clearly and said unequivocally that, whether fighting from a trench or mounting guard on the Rhine (which France would never abandon), he defended not merely a concept, an abstraction, or a mere idea of the fatherland, but France's soil, land he and his family worked. And by his family he did not mean ancestors, by his land he did not mean territory marked on the map by a tricolor flag. No, he meant those who had given him life and their own plot of earth.

75

Besides, he stood behind the administrative concepts represented by the national government France had set up first in the Revolution and later in the Third Republic after Germany defeated the Second Empire in 1870. This government protected every Frenchman's freedom.

"You see," my Comrade said, commenting on my surprise at this countrified soldier's sound thinking, "that comes from the elementary school. And normal schools provide teachers for elementary schools."

Metz received us with bitter cold, aggravated by a sleet that froze as soon as it hit the ground. We hurried through streets and squares and soon arrived at the great main plaza. My Friend recalled ironically the fair held there and in adjacent arcades. "Azorín admired the little tents, the booths, the color."

Afterward an equestrian statue of Louis XIV in another square, with its clearly French monumental character, moved him to repeat his unchangeable view about the legitimate connection of Lorraine with France. He did not, however, subscribe to Maurice Barrés's rigidly nationalist theories. We had begun to read Barrés's recent novel about Colette Baudoche. My Friend recognized the author as a great writer, but he felt repelled by his murky doctrine linking the fate of a land with those who had died there in a kind of inescapable destiny.

With all of its fascination as a frontier outpost that had resisted germanization for forty-eight years, we found Metz, if not dead, at least a sleeping city. Many times our footsteps echoed on its flagstone pavements as in a tomb. At the doorway of its cathedral we noticed among the modern statues of saints, one famous as a portrait of Kaiser William II. If that kind of commemoration showed abominable taste, the new municipal government had surpassed it. To satisfy a perverted whim of the populace, French authorities had hung heavy convict's chains on the wrists of that statue's praying hands. "These Frenchmen are incorrigible!" my Comrade said to me. His appreciation of their many good qualities did not blind him to their national faults.

We got lost looking for a man to whom we had a letter of introduction, but we finally found his printing shop at the end of a very long street, almost in the suburbs. A wartime atmosphere lingered in spite of the time that had passed since French troops had arrived. The servant of this printer received us with extreme caution; at first he pretended not to know where we might find the person whose correspondence with Madrid's *Fígaro* had brought us there. That spoke more clearly about the distrust in which Lorrainers had lived and their fears about the future than all the paeans of victory and the diatribes against their defeated German oppressors. The personage we wanted to see, editor of a regional periodical, had maintained the sacred flame of French spirit through years of German domination. He also had forgotten that we were coming to see him. We had already seen enough of the situation in Metz to satisfy my Friend. As soon as we ate supper, at seven in the evening, with an excellent Moselle wine, we went straight to bed. We felt very cold and very tired, and the cafés, considerably less congenial than in Paris, offered very little attraction.

From Metz we went to stay for less than twenty-four hours at the Hotel of the Black Lamb in Alsatian Mulhouse, now restored from its German name, Mülhausen. Coming direct from the station we checked into that inn and found it both typical and inhospitable. Then we went to visit Mr. Grumbach, the city's prewar Socialist deputy to the Reichstag who had sided with France from the outbreak of fighting. He lived modestly with a large family, including some small children, all in one very big room. In the center of that room stood a large tile stove, and members of the household crowded around to enjoy its warmth. Grumbach himself opened the door for us, and he talked with us on a wooden bench against the wall. Now my Friend got an interview on the Alsatian problem.

"No, it's not exactly the same," he answered me afterward in response to the parallel I immediately suggested between our problem with Catalonia and the reincorporation of Alsace and Lorraine into France. "No, not the same. In the first place, without a doubt, Lorraine remains entirely and absolutely French: geographically, historically, and, most important, culturally. Alsace poses another question. It has its own personality as a crossroads of European civilization. Certainly it isn't German either. I don't know whether the French will find it as French as they want. They will have trouble incorporating it into the rigidity of their centralized administration.

"Catalonia differs from Alsace because Catalonia is as Spanish as the Basque provinces or Castile. Let the Catalans speak Catalan all they like, but they remain as Spanish as the rest of us. The reason for using Castilian as our national language seems obvious. Tarrasa businessmen with sales mainly in the rest of Spain and America do not raise the question of language. The reasons for political unity are more complicated."

On the other hand, he considered Catalonian separatists no more foolish than Castilians who can accept Portugal as an independent nation in the Iberian peninsula but treat the concept of a separate Catalonia as insanity, suicidal for both Castile and Catalonia. Unwilling to consider the possibility of recognizing her separate identity, these people treat separation as a punishment Spain might impose on Catalonia. The *Fígaro* Correspondent inclined to accept Napoleon's political unitarianism. Possibly this was the only real contribution his empire had made in Spain to our revolutionary heritage: unity for the sake of liberty and achieved through liberty—the fundamental principle of France's republic. My Friend regarded the principle of local autonomy as regressive; it degenerated into rule by council or mayor or even into feudal anarchy. The Spaniard's propensity for anarchism makes this especially true in our country.

Mulhouse hadn't much to offer, and we did not see the little it might have had. Mr. Grumbach added nothing to what the Correspondent already knew. Thus in hopes of finding better accommodations we went on to Strasbourg.

We found its limpid blue sky no more clement than the leaden black sky of Metz. "You have this kind of cold in Valladolid," he said to me. "The wind seems to throw rocks in your face. Worse than the porch at the Escorial." All of that meant that I should not open the window any further that first morning when we woke up in Alsace's capital. It didn't matter. Years of German domination had not at all lessened that ancient city's characteristic loveliness. German efficiency had contributed a lively quality we had not found in Metz, in spite of its importance as a manufacturing center. Strasbourg immediately won us as we walked through its modern streets. If the circling river constricts it, visitors find compensation in innumerable little bridges, both decorative and convenient.

We climbed its cathedral's famous tower, and at each vertiginous embrasure in our ascent he pointed out the country at our feet and the bold metallic bridge crossing Father Rhine. The war had advanced France's eastern frontier that far. In the museum we saw, among other pictures, notably some fine Spanish canvasses, a lovely portrait by Zurbarán similar to his Saint Catherine in the Prado in its portrayal of womanly beauty in a purely pictorial way. I mean feminine delicacy and elegance with no mixture of disgusting bloody mysticism, or the contortions or distortions of asceticism that foreigners customarily take as the most characteristic Spanish idea.

We went to Kehl, "so you can say that you have occupied German soil." He said that to me with the air of a conqueror. Kehl, the first town on Germany's side of the Rhine, is one of many summer resorts. We saw very few people in its silent streets, and these people seemed more suspicious than curious about us. The place had more a feeling of a field than of a garden. A flock of geese, apparently untended, enhanced the enchantment of that idyllic village scene. The cathedral tower stood out as an unmistakable landmark in Strasbourg's panorama on the opposite bank.

I remember neither the name nor the position of a Strasbourg government official whom my Friend questioned about the problem of education; they don't matter, anyhow. The Germans had strictly imposed their language and educational methods in Alsace. That had brought organized resistance to preserve the French language and heritage. This official had no doubts about his responsibility as a French Alsatian to make the government in Paris understand that they must not repeat this capital error. On the other hand, how far did his duty allow him to permit more or less surreptitious supplanting of French by the Alsatian mother tongue? Realistically, a bilingual approach made sense. My Friend believed that the religious question might pose an even more serious problem. Separation of church and state seemed definitely established in the rest of France. This had revitalized Catholic feeling and observance and the role of the monastic orders. Lay governments had effectively prevented a retrograde clerical influence in politics and shown a tendency to amnesty once the Church had withdrawn to its own precinct. My Friend believed that a clearly republican and national central administration could well make concessions to a tradition that withdrew from the larger political scene, once its zealous adherents had reconciled themselves to not crossing the bounds.

Our stay in Strasbourg ended with the ceremony for which we had come: the inauguration of the French University on the site where imperial Germany had established its ambitious curriculum in buildings worthy of their intentions. French banners decorating the auditorium disguised its coldly modern, severely Protestant style. At the appointed time President Poincaré made his entry; short and chubby, he looked like my neighbor on the calle de Atocha in Madrid, and even more like a lawyer than my neighbor. Accompanying the president and still serving as interim governor of Alsace, came M. Millerand. Formerly a Socialist, he had for many years served in the Chamber of Deputies as representative of the extreme right wing of the republican Radicals.

My Friend had explained to me French political developments since the Dreyfus Case better than any books or newspapers, so now he could assume some knowledge on my part. He relived it all enthusiastically, very much admiring the system despite its vices. He never confused the defects of its deviations with the virtues and efficacy of its norms. For instance, it occurred to me as an impulse and from ignorance to lament the French people's ingratitude toward Clemenceau, the famous "Tiger." This man headed France's government during the wartime crisis in national morale, and he had galvanized the patriotic spirit that had carried so many unknown soldiers to victory under Foch. My Friend, on the other hand, explained this as an example showing the advantages of a democratic regime. Clemenceau, like a good Jacobin dictator, had ruled as man of the hour. After his hour had passed, however, Frenchmen would have erred in following his policy of intransigent Radical republicanism, something purely and exclusively French, in drawing up a peace settlement that must reach beyond the borders of Paris and the fertile fields of France. Clemenceau also had to leave office for other reasons. The whole French population had won the war, not just one class, and it had cost much in men and treasure. Like it or not, they could not restore their damaged patrimony on the basis of the narrow vision and single viewpoint of a middle-class, bourgeois party. My Friend, while recognizing the merits of Poincaré—Clemenceau's irreconcilable enemy in everything but the war effort—thought that France's first postwar elections would show a decided shift away from his position and to the Left.

During that academic inauguration, standing beside my Comrade, I especially recall my spirits stirred by the "Marseillaise" that accompanied the procession into the auditorium. Frenchmen had created the archetypal national hymn to accompany their prototypical national revolution. We heard a baritone voice singing its first stanza slowly and seriously from a high gallery behind us. Then a thrill ran up our backs as those on the platform joined in the chorus, president, ministers, and professors wearing colored hoods of their various faculties.

Aux armes citoyens;
Armez vos bataillons;
Marchons, marchons!

Afterwards we felt saddened watching the review at the university gate on that cold, dull morning. First came the corporations dressed up in comical costumes and hats or grouped behind their standards and emblems, parading before the authorities. Then came the victorious troops whose ill-disguised poverty my Friend pointed out to me as indicated by the small, shaggy horses supplied to cavalrymen because of the terrible wartime carnage of the imposing mounts of the past.

11

The Right Bank

Translation work we had undertaken for a Spanish publisher provided us the wherewithal to prolong our stay in Paris, so we decided to change our lodgings. Memories of the past attracted my Mentor to the Latin Quarter. As it turned out, we had trouble recapturing that past, frustrated by overcrowded hotels, rooming houses, and pensions filled by a multitude of students and nonstudents who lived like them. After looking around for some time, we moved into what they advertised as an "English boardinghouse," facing Monceau Park, but it turned out to be only a family style *pot-au-feu* without the advantages of the new British mode. In that moment of victory everyone in France tended to exalt the alliance. Though American aid may have helped as much as British aid, or more, French people preferred fashions that came from across the channel to those that came from across the ocean.

The casualness of Yankee ways clashed with the discipline that obsesses Frenchmen. A Parisian writer, Abel Hermant, years before had portrayed a New York family's discovery of Paris in his comic novel *Americans Abroad,* which he himself had adapted for the stage. My Friend and I translated it, believing that it might interest some producer in Madrid. We didn't even get anyone to read our manuscript. The insurmountable division this play and book portray develops from personalities their author created to represent the two worlds. "When you speak of the Left Bank," an American character says to a Parisian, "you refer to the Seine; we immediately think of the Atlantic."

Much as my Friend enjoyed the temperateness of French middle-class life, we did not seek out the contacts which he, more than I, might easily have made. We deliberately lived apart from the social scene. He did make inescapable courtesy calls on this or that professor whom he had known in his travels as a Francophile member of the Ateneo. I did not press him to accompany me in my ventures into pseudoliterary and artistic circles, with their vague flavor of the salons of past times. "The last salon where they sewed *(el último salón donde se cose),*" he punned, referring to the manifest decline of the traditional salon with a bad Spanish translation of the phrase "the last salon where they conversed *(dernier salon où l'on cause)*." Sometimes we looked up Ventura García Calderón, the Peruvian writer and diplomat then living in Paris. I don't know whether we met with Corpus Barga, correspondent of Madrid's *Sol,* other than one night when he invited us to the Théâtre des Arts to see the Pitoëff Company, acclaimed from that season onward, perform one of Lenormand's first works with an incomprehensible show of empty-headed modernism.

We carried on as simple, curious spectators, sampling the sights of Paris, enjoying the *cabarets-chantants* that had replaced the old *cafés concerts,* except for the Bobino in Montparnasse. It made my Friend feel like a Parisian to share the innocent mischief of typical satire directed at ministers and other prominent figures in the capital's political, literary, and artistic life. One night we especially enjoyed a joke made by one of these singers about "The Inauguration of M. Raymond." It told, comically, how the president and his wife came very early on March 21 to attend the official events announced in the program for his Inauguration Day: inauguration of an exhibit of plants and flowers, inauguration of a statue of The Unknown Mayor, inauguration of a neighborhood judicial system, inauguration of a program of Indo-Chinese studies, inauguration of a new customs post. M. and Mme. Poincaré eventually fell asleep. The president woke up about midnight, and his wife, feeling him stir, asked, "Shall we inaugurate springtime?" "Can you imagine that kind of joking in Spain?" my Friend commented. "What wouldn't they say back there about respect for elected officials?"

He felt that the French regime could allow this kind of harmless lampoon because of its basic strength. This type of humor, called *frondeur* when it became more or less explicit and subversive political protest, peppered newspapers and electoral campaigns. At some rallies we attended in the height of the electoral campaign, I heard terrible insults directed against the National Tiger, heroic Clemenceau, including references to his private life. What impressed me more than anything else—even more than the revolutionary flavor of neighborhood public gatherings—was the obstreperous hissing during a speech by President Poincaré given in a riding academy, with most of the crowd standing. A majority seemed opposed to the speaker. "Well, what did you expect," my Mentor asked, "that Mr. García Prieto controlled elections here?" In spite of inevitable excesses, this full recognition of a citizen's rights of free expression, not mere tolerance, solidified the republic's foundation. In this way hostile opinion expressed itself peacefully in party struggles that maintained the democratic political system.

Opposing the strong Socialist propaganda, exaggerated by the large working-class population of Paris, the reactionary Right launched their own propaganda campaign raising a specter of bolshevism. They issued an effective campaign poster that became famous. It personified the communist danger by the enlarged head of a terrifying Soviet revolutionary, a knife between his teeth to kill the bourgeoisie.

I feared from my reading of major Paris newspapers that the election would bring a rightist triumph. My Friend reassured me that in spite of this clear opinion in the conservative press—and that adjective never had the pejorative sense we gave it in connection with the Spanish press—Paris was not the entire French republic. The departments counted; they decided elections, especially the votes of peasants. France's republic had roots deep in her soil; the ideal of liberty drew nourishment from rural proprietorship. Even in Paris, the large population of workers in the industrial districts counted for more than Rightist youth of the *Camelots du Roi*. He explained my fears and calmed them by suggesting that a Spaniard, accustomed to thinking about politics as a world apart from the country's real life, found it hard to comprehend the bond between French institutions and French society. That bond gave tremendous vitality to parliamentary life, the most characteristic part of the system. He took me to the Chamber one day, and we witnessed an emotional session in which one Lenoir, accused of treason, had to speak before the deputies. He later paid the supreme penalty after a trial that the newspapers turned into a kind of deplorable circus.

We did not remain long in the boardinghouse facing Monceau Park. From there we moved into a French *pension de famille* on the Avenue Victor Hugo near the Étoile. Run by a widow, Mme. Verdin, it did have a family atmosphere, and we chose places at the central table rather than at one of the three or four little tables set apart for less sociable guests. The proprietress had a very beautiful and disdainful daughter who hardly spoke to guests, partly because of her involvement—in the fullest sense of that term—with a young Persian. The articulate maid who took care of our room called him "a very able young man." Through her we also learned that the landlady's daughter studied sculpture. This well-informed maid looked over our books and gave us her literary opinions. On Sundays, dressed up in her stylish coat, which she probably bought at a department store, and her little hat, she appeared no different from any other young lady. This leveling of appearances to a decent middle ground and the practice of calling both the newspaper vendor and the president's wife simply "madame" seemed to my Friend admirable manifestations of republican equality and human dignity.

We had trouble getting tickets for the Russian Ballet's premier of Manuel de Falla's *The Three-Cornered Hat,* and I turned for help to our old acquaintance, the composer. Falla found us seats in the proscenium mezzanine just as that brilliant performance was about to begin. Our happenstance companion that night was a former Ateneo member, friend of several writers and artists from the Canary Islands whom we knew. At that time he worked in our embassy's secretariat, thanks to help from his countryman, the ambassador, Quiñones de León. We very much enjoyed attending the theater in Paris. My Friend's beautiful translation of Mérimée's *The Carriage of the Holy Sacrament* resulted from a performance at the Vieux Colombier. He took childish delight in the circus, and we went to the Medrano Circus on the hill of Montmartre. We climbed up there more than once, besides, just to look at the immensity of Paris at our feet.

After the war art dealers moved their shops down from Montmartre. In this they followed a migration of cubist painters who had cornered the market in Picasso's wake. A little old lady, knowledgeable about this branch of artistic commerce, explained to us the success of this new style of painting. In her little shop we saw many canvasses by Juan Gris, whom I had known in his early bohemian days in Madrid, and many others by Frenchmen like André Lothe, then just beginning to establish reputations. When my Friend asked her why Lothe's paintings cost more, since all of them seemed much the same, she answered without hesitation, "Ah! because he writes!" M. Lothe, in fact, had become an art critic at that time.

For a contrasting approach, my Friend took me to look at the romantic-realist Courbet's painting of his studio in which, like Velázquez in *The Maids of Honor,* he painted himself, palette in hand, with his models and his easels. Perhaps he looked like that on the famous day when some professional critics, discussing art, turned to him for his professional opinion. He answered, simply, "It all just seems easy to me," and turned back to his work.

From the Courbet and the Manets in the Louvre's modern galleries we went to the Luxembourg Palace where Manet's *Olympia* and Courbet's *The Balcony* demonstrate Goya's contribution to the European patrimony of his century. But at the Luxembourg my Friend preferred the exhibition dedicated to the splendors of Impressionism. In Madrid he liked to compare the natural scenery with the backgrounds of Velázquez's paintings in the Prado. Now in Paris he took me from the bridge above the Saint Lazare Station with its chimerical atmosphere of gray smoke to its masterly reproduction by Monet in the museum. And so innumerable Corot's, in whose foliage dwells the ineffable spirit of Paris environs, sent us out to Fontainebleau or Saint-Germain to compare the countryside represented by his brush with actual scenes. Up and down the river we viewed the landscape from Saint-Cloud's terraces or in the midst of Compiègne's forest. Gardens and forests of the Crown of France perfectly illustrate the definition of Rusiñol, our poet of the countryside, "A garden is nature put into verse." This is alexandrine verse, broad as a spreading tree, sung by Versailles fountains, not some merely graceful rondel or quatrain. The prospect from the Palace of Versailles to the Great Basin provides an example worthy of this majestic concept of gardening as an architectural art. My Friend highly praised it to me as symbolizing Louis XIV's grandiose concept of royal power. It far surpassed the pretty decoration, labyrinths, and Petits Trianons that the Versailles style means to persons unable to see the truth with their own eyes.

Spring brought us, along with windy March rains, or *giboulets,* the first clear skies. My Friend laughed remembering my fear of drowning as we stood jammed in a crowd watching some highly vulgar mid-Lent parade. The lower classes suited me better, at the Villette, a cabaret in the district of the apaches in northeastern Paris. Here still water by wharves evokes the allure of a seaport, and this infects its adjacent suburb. At that time Jules Romains was reading his unanimist poetry at the Villette. In those ineffable April twilights the river's humidity produced a blue atmosphere that blended the fragrance of gasoline exhaust and the pavement's asphalt. Our own times have added this perfume to Paris, a city transcending the centuries.

12
La Pluma [The Pen]

Unwittingly M. Deschanel bade us goodbye on behalf of France as he mechanically doffed his hat. A few days before our departure for Madrid curiosity led us to join an unenthusiastic crowd in front of the Grand Aumont Mansion to watch the French republic's newly elected president ride by in a landau on his way to City Hall. The hat he doffed was, of course, a top hat.

During our stay in Paris I had written a few stories, including my postwar impressions, for *La Libertad,* a daily which had split off from *El Liberal. Fígaro,* in whose service my Friend had undertaken his journalistic mission in France, had died in the bud. We brought home with us translations we had made for the Calpe publishers. My Friend had very much enjoyed his work on *Pathetic Simon* by Jean Giraudoux, then becoming famous. The literary bureaucrats who made decisions about publication apparently did not enjoy it so much or appreciate the Translator's beautiful style, very close to the original. I don't know what circumstances prevented it; no ill will seemed involved, but, after dragging on for some time, they decided against it. I suppose that text must have disappeared forever; it remains a mere footnote in the history of a writer later called to his destiny by the skill of his pen.

From that period, too, comes our Castilian version of *Memoirs of Mlle. Lespinasse* the only book we did together. He suggested other projects. Perhaps no author with such natural gifts and solid preparation ever rated his own work so low or remained so little satisfied with it. What do I mean by "satisfied"? Uncertain of his abilities in a field where he had so much to feel confident about, he always remained far from the highway that leads to Vanity Fair. He thought more about my development as a writer than about his own. I, on the other hand, recognized clearly enough that my inferiority as a writer would make me a deadweight in his development. However, though my collaboration would prove counterproductive, I could still play a useful role by encouraging him to continue with his own work.

Now my attention turned seriously to the theater. From childhood I had admired this supreme art. My family and friends discouraged me, fearing that I would waste my time in the inanity of our contemporary theatrical world. My experiences in Paris renewed my vocation. I had witnessed there the theatrical revival sweeping Europe, based on minimalist staging and highly refined productions in contrast to the vacuous splendor of nineteenth-century productions. My Friend, without actually arguing against my wishes, did point out difficulties that might frustrate my hopes in an environment like Madrid, so alien to the Parisian passion for novelty. I might lose time and work better spent on something else, however dazzling immediate material rewards and glamour might seem. I could end up selling my soul to a devil of bad taste whose influence was so apparent in the sloppy productions of the degenerate Spanish theater.

In the end we founded a monthly literary review. Our friend Amós Salvador, who for some reason had come through Paris during our stay there, liked the idea and offered us a subsidy of five hundred pesetas, his salary as a legislator. The son of a former minister, Amós belonged to his father's faction of the Liberal party. With Amós's money we bought enough paper to guarantee the life of *La Pluma* for a trial run; wartime shortages had sharply increased the cost of paper, so this purchase seemed vital. My Colleague thought up that title, and he found our motto among the classical sentences in the archive of his memory: "The pen sustains castles, crowns, and kings—and upholds laws." He also worked out the general design and internal layout, the arrangement of titles and pages, and, above all, he provided the humorous viewpoint, that touch of irony which enlivened our publication's literary seriousness.

Spaniards do not react kindly to teasing. Our friends wrongly attributed *La Pluma's* casual humor—which had no serious intent—to me. They made the same mistake in seeing malice in my *tertulia* gossip. From the first issue our joking brought us contemptuous frowns and even malevolence from persons who took offense. We lacked sufficient capital to pay the kind of contributors we hoped to attract and so depended on gratis contributions. Some came from highly respected authors like Valle Inclán, Unamuno, and Juan Ramón Jiménez; others came from literary newcomers like Enrique Díez-Canedo and our Mexican friend Alfonso Reyes who lived in Madrid at that time. We considered the latter two almost partners in this venture. With no malicious intent, I repeat, we wanted to indicate in our first issue the flavor that would differentiate *La Pluma* from similar publications. Accordingly, instead of just publishing the usual list of contributors and editorial staff at the beginning, we included a brief comic note at the end listing persons we felt certain would not write for our review. Thus we would get the jump on them for their anticipated contempt. They included, principally, Pío Baroja, Ortega y Gasset, and Eugenio d'Ors. At least to these men we very circumspectly granted the title "Don." With no commentary, we mixed in their names with other important persons, but persons who occupied a different kind of literary position like Countess Emilia Pardo Bazán. Except for the eminent countess, who never even noticed our offering to the shrinking population of lovers of true literature, that little joke upset those persons to whom we referred so innocently, and they could not hide their pique. They never forgave our impudence and lack of respect.

My own primary concern was that my Friend continue his writing. To this end I sacrificed my personal whims. If I had turned to the theater at that point, he would not have had the encouragement for his writing entailed in our collaboration on *La Pluma*. Because of this, he dedicated *The Friars' Garden* to me when it appeared as a book.

For some time he had kept coming back to an idea, and, like all good inspirations, the muse did not whisper it into his ear all at once. Anyhow, he didn't operate from sudden inspirations. The French say, "genius is a matter of great patience," and his literary genius came from much creative loafing. We could only laugh at the panegyrist, possibly an enemy, who later, with good or bad intentions, described him as a grind. Unamuno has said more than once (and he wrote down every one of his ideas at least three times and said them a thousand and one times in those running monologues he called conversations) that work of an essentially poetic nature comes as the product of leisure. Still, in his later years, malice prevented Unamuno from recognizing this in a man he should never had considered his adversary. Denying his own insight, Unamuno called my Friend intellectually lazy. Indeed, the Author of *The Friars' Garden* considered himself a loafer, and none of his writing came from workaholism. As with the conception of a human being, leisure, through love, led to artistic creation.

He found it hard to sit down to write. When he did get to it, impelled by some task he had set for himself, he never did it with regularity, at a fixed time, and he always wrote by hand. His pen followed his thoughts. He never put a thing on paper until previous rumination had fixed what he wanted to say in its precise form; hence he wrote somewhat slowly, and his manuscript pages have few corrections. This did not come from lack of facility. Still less did it come from an effort to achieve unusual effects; that would have run counter to his clear concept of literary art. Rather, it came from his determination to express himself with perfect clarity and to achieve a perfect blend of thought and expression. He sought for the exact word, the clear-cut phrase, the linking musical turn that suited what he wanted to say. He intended his ideas to flow smoothly and clearly, free from ornamentation. In short, he sought for a style that provided a due measure of feeling but avoided anything overly effusive, always controlled by that ethical concern usually called good taste. Characteristically, he just called it taste.

I cannot point to a specific moment in our conversations about his youthful years at the Escorial, so rich in suggestions of a rite of passage, when he may have felt the first real impulse that led to his novel. I like to think that the vital moment came during our excursion to that monastery and its fields. I mean something apart from all practical considerations, not his book's basic motivation—that lived on in his conscious memory of his college life. I mean some unconscious enthusiasm about an incident from his past that came into focus when circumstances prompted inspiration. It pleases me very much to think that I deserved the dedication of his book because of my insistence that he write it. It pleases me still more that this insistence came from what he shared with me of his remembrances of the Escorial as they arose in our mutual digressions, more often walking through public streets than in the privacy of his home. These he later transcribed and revived as a work of fiction.

The essence of his skill lay not so much in invention as in discovery. In this case he discovered his own life, not as one looks in a mirror that reflects the actuality of the moment, but as one remembers through a distance of time and space.

Many have mistakenly viewed *The Friars' Garden* as the autobiography of his youth. Some of them praised it when it first came out—and it did not have the tinselly bookstore success of some shorter-lived books. Later the insanity of political passion led adversaries to ruthlessly denigrate it. It irritated him, perhaps exaggeratedly, that readers took literally the grammatical first person of his protagonist just because he did not provide a novelistic name to emphasize the fictitiousness. He assumed enough literary sophistication in his readers not to make a prior explanation, but to sustain an element of uncertainty in a composition that involved frankness as well as modesty. Could the Author remain candid and still present himself as that person remembering his own school days with the Augustinian fathers at the Escorial? No more than his sensitive reader could fail to appreciate his book as something of a confession, the secret interior of a budding man, along with a feeling for the atmosphere of life in the monastery, a transcendent perfume of garden and field.

I knew from our earliest serious conversations that as a youth he had read Rousseau's *Confessions* with ardent sympathy. He never told anyone his impressions when he first read this book at an age susceptible to its spell, so it remains problematical whether he then found a spiritual forebear in Rousseau, especially given his own struggle against sentimentalism. Yet to me Rousseau's influence on him seems unmistakable. His own serenity and rigorous control over any sentimentalism in himself did not mean that he despised feelings usually called romantic. When, in the last days of his life, he heard me criticizing *The New Heloise,* which was not part of the literary education of my generation and which I had no curiosity to read, he urged me to read it, emphasizing its charm. Besides that, when in my random, though not foolish, reading in Paris I discovered Max Stirner's *The Ego and His Own* and, a little later, Sorel's *Reflections on Violence,* he checked my ingenuous enthusiasm about these books, my propensity to discover the obvious, by referring me to Rousseau's masterpiece, *The Social Contract.* Though not a fanatic about that book, he believed it, as compared with the others, decisively important in the development of European political thinking since the Declaration of the Rights of Man. Like the Author of *The*

Friars' Garden, I preferred the *Confessions,* their exaggerated sentimentalism notwithstanding.

During those days of *La Pluma* he showed me a photograph that he had found among his family pictures in Alcalá. It dated not from his student days but from childhood and showed him mounted on a hobbyhorse. In this portrait, taken out of doors in the country, he seems to be gesturing as if talking to someone not in the photo, somewhere in front of him, possibly the photographer. His profile in that picture clearly demonstrates the continuity of the personality whom I eventually came to know. With his arm raised, reaching somewhat backward, already robust, he showed a clear propensity to fatness; of course he grew taller and more corpulent later, but his head sat strongly on his shoulders just as it did afterwards. Later I saw another photograph from his student days, an enlargement showing just his head and shoulders. It confirmed the exactitude with which the Author of *The Friars' Garden* had patterned his moving portrait of the student at María Cristina, his discretion and the protestations of his unblemished modesty notwithstanding. His refined face, later given premature seriousness by his double chin, his clear gaze, blurred by myopia and only restored to natural strength by optical lenses—his whole expression shows that special charm melancholy adds to the faces of some young dreamers. His eyebrows had the same characteristic quality of pointing at each other. Time would give them a disdainful tilt; in this photography they add sensitivity.

Still, all things considered, the Author of *The Friars' Garden* was correct in denying that he had written an autobiography. Along with recollections of the Escorial's stone walls viewed from the window of his room looking out toward the Alamillos, he had looked inward at himself after a passage of time, with natural human narcissism, and he had discovered a person he had not known until he wrote down feelings he could not have expressed in his youth. This person became his discovery, his invention. The book's modernity lies in the Author's suggesting, insinuating, exploring, and penetrating his own feelings rather than describing or narrating his story. If difficult to achieve, this approach bears ripe and fragrant fruit, and his achievement compared with the best of subtle intellectual explorations of universal human emotions by writers of the interwar generation. This chiaroscuro, animating apparently trivial, everyday events with the protagonist's personal lyricism, is presented by someone who knows the royal seat well. In this environment the character emerges through revelation of his feelings, a real person, not a personification of some idea or a caricature, neither a creation of the Author's intellect nor a flash of inspiration. In describing the Convalescent's Gallery, arches open to southern sunshine, flooded by the Escorial's intense springtime light, but protected by the cloister's welcome shade, its Author catches the special viewpoint of *The Friars' Garden.*

Deadlines established for *La Pluma* kept him at his task until he finished his book. Before we published each issue, with no excuses, he had to complete a requisite number of pages in segments we judged suited to our reader's curiosity. This stimulated him more and better than I could have by my urging. My special task consisted in utilizing his respect for my literary discernment to convince him that we, and especially he in this particular case, were not such superior creatures that we could have no audience among the general mass of readers. Both of us found repugnant the idea of a few demigods living on Mount Olympus as sole arbiters of literary excellence. We believed that a sufficiently large readership in the middle ground would keep our enterprise alive; we did not hope for more than that. Two hundred subscribers gave us a good start; we distributed other copies of that first issue on commission through bookstores in Madrid and the provinces, and we sent the rest to America by way of advertising. We never printed more than two thousand copies, but we later cut back to one thousand, since we did not get the growth in subscriptions that our initial success promised. We gave my Colleague's home on the calle de Hermosilla as the address of our editorial offices. I went there every day after dinner unless we met somewhere for a walk. We spent afternoons writing until the hour before the evening meal when we met our friends.

Luis García Bilbao unfailingly presided over these gatherings at the Regina. An extremely shy person, though a writer and an investor in the unstable weekly *España,* he literally drowned his talent in alcoholism. Ashamed of it, he worsened his condition by constantly drinking coffee, apparently his only food. These habits, combined with his disinclination for exercise, seemed to indicate that he accepted his wasted talent. Others regularly joined that *tertulia:* Díez-Canedo, Valle Inclán when he came to Madrid, Luis Bello, Ricardo Gutiérrez—better known as Juan de la Encina from the pen name he used as an art critic, the painter Juan Echevarría, Luis Araquistáin who later deserted because of Canedo's criticism of his playwriting, and the architect Gregorio Marañón whom we nicknamed "the Good" to distinguish him from his cousin the doctor. Sindulfo de la Fuente also attended our nightly *tertulia* at the Henar, which we had now revived. We regulars met there after our evening meal. Julito Lafuente joined us then, at that point a fledgling lawyer serving his apprenticeship in the office of Don Ángel Ossorio where he boasted of his friendship with us. The Mexican Martín Luis Guzmán also came, descended from conquistadors, the kind of person with whom Spanish America rewards us after so many centuries. Several others joined us from time to time, especially at the Henar, but Amós Salvador always turned up at the Regina before dinner to give us daily political gossip.

The Sáez brothers press, behind the Noviciado movie theater, printed *La Pluma* for us. Natives of Madrid, these amiable brothers both owned and worked the press; the younger died of tuberculosis a few years later. They went on doing our work carefully, and before long they suggested that we buy up the machinery and become partners in their firm. My Colleague liked the idea and went so far as to suggest it to Amós Salvador. He, however, showed no interest in going beyond the limited and gratis help he was already giving us. Later, seeing the prosperity of that excellent press, my Collaborator on *La Pluma* reminded me of his foresight.

We scrupulously corrected proofs, he much more carefully than I, and we unfailingly received each issue from the printers on the first of the month. There remained the chores of wrapping each copy separately and bundling them all together to carry to the post office. As we tied up the bundles, he always noted my lack of manual dexterity.

Of course he contributed more to *La Pluma* than his monthly installments of *The Friars' Garden.* Alternatively he signed his work with one of two pseudonyms. One came from Cervantes, and as the quixotic Cardenio he often showed his highly romantic side. Writing as an observer of Madrid's passing scene, he signed himself *Paseante en Corte* (Strolling Cavalier), and he proved a worthy successor to Mesonero Romanos and, better, to Larra. Indeed, he might have considered himself their heir except that minor playwrights and fifth-rate journalists had greatly debased the profession of gossip columnist since the days of the *Curioso Parlante* (Indiscreet Witness) and the suicidal Fígaro. He later collected in *Words and Sketches (Plumas y Palabras)* much of what he had written as Cardenio and Strolling Cavalier. The file of *La Pluma* contains much precious evidence of his caustic wit. His initials identified his book reviews and articles, but our casual acquaintances almost invariably attributed his sharp, unsigned banter to me.

13

Death Opens the Door to My Home

Of ten children born to my parents, five survived, three of us considerably older than the others; I was the eldest. A few months after I returned from Paris, Ramón, seventeen, the handsomest and apparently the most robust of us, had to stay in bed for a few days because of a fever our doctor diagnosed as paratyphoid. He recovered very quickly and soon returned to outings in the Guadarrama Mountains, which he had always enjoyed. In mid-January, I think, with my father away from Madrid on his professional legal business, my brother began to vomit blood. It was already too late, even to move him to the country where we hoped that he might find a cure. Instead, we fitted up one of the best rooms in our apartment as a sickroom, as isolated as we could manage. By mid-March we began to give up hope as his condition steadily deteriorated. My youngest sister, extremely fond of him and only a year his junior, insisted on seeing him one last time before he died, coming home for at least one day from our aunt's home where they had sent her to avoid serious danger of tubercular contagion. As soon as she entered his sickroom, she fainted.

The Carlist Vázquez Mella lived in an apartment near ours on the Paseo del Prado. The two youngsters had gotten along well with him, as he had nobody in his household but a big dog that the porter took care of. The former Secretary of the Ateneo had readily joined us in teasing my young sister about that old bachelor's innocent fondness for her. Still, my Friend felt somewhat uneasy with my family.

Now all our usual fun turned to tears and anguish. I could not hide our misfortune during hours devoted to *La Pluma*. This new affliction renewed my parents' sorrow about another sister's death some years earlier; I had taken that especially hard because of her strong resemblance to me. Now I rebelled against the unfairness of life and the stupidity of the men we relied on for healing. I fell into the common practice of blaming our doctor, a family friend, because he had not made the right diagnosis in time. My desperate protest so much impressed my Friend that twenty years later in his last hopeless illness he feared that I would lash out at the diagnosis of the doctors treating him.

Now he came more frequently to my home than before, to inquire about the invalid and to share our sad company. Highly sensitive, he was greatly moved by the story of my little sister's last visit to Ramón when she found her brother unrecognizable after not seeing him since his first hemorrhage months before. One night as my Friend and I sat silent in a large study next to the sickroom, my mother entered, heartbroken, and she sobbed out her despair. During her continuous attendance at Ramón's bedside, with immense strain, she controlled herself, acted natural, and kept smiling. Now she embraced me, saying, "I can't stand it any longer! I can't stand it!" My Friend had withdrawn to the doorway, and he watched, trembling, moved by her sorrow. When my mother became aware of his presence, she excused herself for breaking down. He wanted to leave, but she said to him, "No, no, don't leave. You are part of the family." Unwittingly, with those words she sealed a pact of mutual fidelity.

From that point onward, my Friend no longer felt an orphan. Since his family's financial misfortune, he had lived mostly apart from them because of disagreements about that ruin, even between siblings fond of each other. Though not hostile toward his family, he had little to do with them. His elder brother, twice widowed, the second time with five children, had married again in the Audalusian town where he served as a judge. He had said nothing about it to my Friend, knowing that he would not approve of the marriage, simply because it had to represent a complication, not a solution. Our family grief made him feel closer to us. He made me see the shallowness of egoism by his wish to share our sadness instead of trying to distract me from family sorrow. He later treated this subject with great acuity in one of his best *La Pluma* essays, emphasizing the happiness that comes from losing oneself in family feeling, even in its bitter tears. In his earliest years he had lost this warmth. He had a clear concept of filial love, but his mother's death had deprived him of it in early childhood. My mother's words sounded a distant echo in his heart.

My brother died in the spring of the year and of his life. We decided to change our residence, as the doctor advised us that we could best avoid another tragedy by living as much as possible in open air. Particularly concerned about my little sister, I took to the streets at once in search of a new home, regardless of the conventions of mourning. My Friend almost always accompanied me in that peremptory duty. I decided that we should move to a villa, one of the first built in the Prosperidad District a few years before when it was still open country. My family soon caught my fervor to take precautions before it again became too late, regretting that we had not taken them earlier. Concern for my younger sister, Lola [Dolores], inspired all of us. We continued to think of her as a little girl, exaggerating her youthfulness.

After we moved, the family decided to go on a real country vacation to our home in the castle of Villalba de los Alcores in Valladolid Province. Breaking a tradition of my grandfather's time, we had not gone back after my sister María died there eight years before. I wrote to my Friend to join us for a few days, and my father endorsed my invitation. He wrote in verse speaking for "our little girl," no longer so young or so innocent as he visualized her. This recovery of our father's characteristic good spirits after our tragedy was welcome, but my sister did not find his humor amusing. My Friend accepted in a poem addressed to her. This surprised me more than anyone, not because he took up the joke, but I had never known him to write verse, even in jest. He had, though, assured me that he admired those who wrote verse, even badly. My sister also did not expect this poetic reply, and she kept it. The poetry itself did not astonish her, but up to then, in spite of my assertions, she had not believed him capable of the joking wit his letter demonstrated.

He arrived in excellent spirits. After briefly settling in, he came downstairs from his room to join us in the great vestibule or entry hall where we usually gathered. Seeing another guest, my sister Adela's friend, he smiled. "You see," he said to her, "I am not displaying anything from *La Pluma* on any part of my body." She was furious at me, realizing that I had told him of her comment, "Watch he will have some advertisement for *La Pluma* pinned to his belly." He soon convinced her of his good humor and that he did not mind them calling him fat.

His days with us helped to assuage our grief, and he greatly enjoyed them. He immediately started to plan a restoration of the castle my grandfather had bought—along with the town walls to prevent natives from making a quarry of those historic stones. My Friend planned this work as though we would begin it the next day. We spent mornings in excursions in a mule-drawn coach or else in reading and writing without accomplishing much. After our meal we waited for the mail, and we always had our afternoon snack in the Esperanza, a vineyard embellished with fruit trees and small vegetable and fruit gardens my grandfather had designed. Town roads, in effect walkways, cut through it leading to a little hill overgrown with wild grapevines that belonged to a communal park, most of which the municipality had unwisely sold a few years before to a rich man from Santander.

Returning one day, as usual at sundown, in our family carriage, we noticed a man in a gamekeeper's uniform following us on horseback. My little sister asked in one of her whimsical sallies, "Can it be a bandit?" This so amused my Friend that he remembered it the rest of his life. Often afterwards he recalled my sister Lola, in a Pamela-style straw hat, imagining herself pursued by a highwayman. She seemed to be playing out some romantic whimsy about the countess of Teba who became Empress Eugénie of the French! Pushing this theme further, I used to say to the Secretary when his Ateneo friends reproached him for some kind of air of caesarean authoritarianism, "That's how Napoleon III began." In fact, the bandit in question turned out to be someone delivering a thank-you note to our house.

My Friend prided himself on speaking simply and clearly, and the custom among badly educated young ladies of talking contemptuously of the Castilian language irritated him. He took it as a treat to share the company and conversation of Uncle Rufino, a household servant who performed the duties of coachman and cellarer with more dignity than efficiency. My Friend liked to ride with him on the driving seat, even taking the reins, to hear that old man's dignified, fitting discourse calling each thing by its right name, which few people do. According to my Friend, Uncle Rufino understood very well what he talked about, and he had common sense, something not always true of persons who consider themselves learned. His folklore charmed our Guest. Most people wrongly think of folklore as a collection of proverbs, but it is more, a whole tradition, a people's usages and customs, their transcendent worldly experience. Certainly you can't learn it in a college education. Besides, after a long spell of urban bustle, my Friend felt the country's attraction. In some ways he even preferred the distilled life of a hamlet or village to that of our great provincial capitals. One time he said to me, "Cities don't really amount to much until their population reaches two million." Experience had taught him to dislike places standing between big cities and small towns.

One afternoon he almost had a crippling accident during a visit to the ancient monastery of Matallana in the run-down settlement of Valdebusto, a property of my father's sister. My Friend came in for a share of her fragmented inheritance when he married into our family. As we passed the gateway of a fenced-in threshing floor a mule ran through it and pulled the threshing harrow over his foot. Because the harrow hit against a rock it gave him only a glancing blow, but this experience gave us all a bad scare. Almost as frightening, one time when he was driving our coach down a small hill, mules not broken in to the harness refused to respond to the reins. Treating it as a joke after our danger had passed, none of us could guess what future perils we would face together under his guidance.

Visiting neighboring castles we went to Medina de Rioseco's five magnificent churches, its only glory. We went from there to our relations the Cuadrilleros to hunt on their preserve in Zamora Province near Villalpando where uncultivated land affords a panoramic view extending from the thickets and poplar groves on the Cea's banks to the blue hills of León. I had never forgotten my first and only experience as a hunter years before when I almost shot a guard, and refused even to carry a rifle. Still, I enjoyed hiking all day through that shrubby countryside typical of New Castile. It pleased me to see my Friend's healthy enjoyment of walking with a clear objective. When I remarked that it seemed like our other walks, he answered, no. Not being a hunter I could not appreciate the pleasure of the chase. He added that he missed this noble passion he had enjoyed so much in his days as a *señorito*.

On that trip we visited Valladolid's provincial museum, very badly housed until the republican government set it up in surroundings worthy of its sculptural richness. My Friend found much to admire in Berruguete's work here and in Rioseco, but he never felt the enthusiasm for it that he had for Spanish painting, culminating for him with Velázquez, or our literary achievement, which Cervantes brought to its supreme triumph. These he thought could stand beside the archetypes of the classical world or the Renaissance, or Rodin, or Beethoven's nine symphonies. As we went through the then unpleasant Valladolid museum, with disagreeable guards wrenching stuck shutter bolts to let in light and trying out various big keys in doors, it seemed to me that the sculpture's striking realism pleased him by its artistry, but that its bloody subject matter disgusted him though our artists had found a typically Spanish fulfillment in it. In Valladolid he liked best the Renaissance patio of San Gregorio; it evoked for him a patio in Alcalá, not so much by its actual appearance as by our echoing footsteps. I remembered waiting in this same Valladolid patio years before, uncertain about the outcome of my examinations for the law degree.

After returning to Madrid he continued work on *The Friars' Garden,* but he also found inspiration in our Moroccan war for some very clever articles still preserved in the bound volumes of *La Pluma.* A devotee of chronicles and histories, he saw surprising parallels between the accounts of past centuries and newspaper stories about current events. Both demonstrated a persistent error in our concept of national continuity; in fact, our national continuity existed only in terms of this erroneous conception. Hurtado de Mendoza's *The War against the Moriscos of Granada* provided him with many examples of these parallels that defied all argument. He saw our current war against the Riff as a clear continuation of the seesaw guerrilla activity that had lasted for eight hundred years—until the Catholic Monarchs decided to declare it ended. Very late in the day historians began to call this warfare the Reconquest. Reconquest of what? My Friend had hazarded more than once the idea that the term *Spaniard* applied as much to Arabs in Spain as to Hispanicized Iberians, Celts, Carthaginians, Romans, Vandals, and Visigoths who had invaded before the Arabs. Beyond this, unquestionably, the same Berber race inhabited both sides of the straits, and Moroccan Berbers regarded Arabs from the east as foreigners just as Spaniards did. From this viewpoint the Reconquest became nothing more than a collection of innumerable civil wars that had contested control of the peninsula. The triumphant empire of the Catholic monarchy had achieved no more than earlier conquests, which had, indeed, built on a far more imperial base by incorporating all three national religions.

My Friend believed that the Europeans had failed in their most recent opportunity to establish a common Spanish fatherland, in what we call our War for Independence. English historians—he pointed this out to me on several occasions—call it the Peninsular War. They name it for the duke of Wellington's expedition. In articulating these fundamental themes of the realities of Spanish politics he never assumed professional airs. At that point his speculations involved no governmental responsibility whatsoever. Later they became a part of his committed political thinking as a statesman. Finally they contributed to the hopeless serenity of one who had been overcome in his turn.

In those days of 1921, unlucky for our military efforts in Morocco, it amused him to copy out passages from other centuries to read to me and to print in *La Pluma*. As he read each pertinent discovery then, he did not have to take off his glasses to see better; in later years, when he exchanged his pince-nez for common spectacles, he would take them off to read.

14

Military Policy in France and
The Bible in Spain

My Friend gave a series of lectures at the Ateneo, and the Calleja Publishers printed them as a book, *Military Policy in France*. He intended this as part of a larger work, "Studies in Contemporary French Policy," but he never completed it. My Friend had little to do in preparing that book beyond compiling the carefully reasoned texts of his lectures. His regular readers hadn't much to learn here, especially those familiar with his political thought.

In these pages he formulated basic concepts about republican government, though he never specifically addressed the Spanish situation, which he would later be called to restructure. Still, he always thought in terms of practical application, to the point where he defined philosophy as "the way to conduct oneself in life." Thus he could never treat "public affairs" in abstract terms, apart from historical time and a given state. He had chosen the example of France's republic partly because of his clear understanding of its problems and their resolution, and partly because of their clear similarity to our own problems. After all, the debate between the two camps about our wartime neutrality had centered on a contrast between German force and the supposed French lack of discipline that Germanophiles believed would certainly cause the Third Republic's defeat. Above all he wanted to establish for his listeners and his readers the argument, based on irrefutable facts and fundamental principles, that Germany's clear superiority in the 1870 war against France came solely from the perfection of her tactical and strategic methods. It did not, for instance, demonstrate a need to subject national education to discipline suitable to barracks but incompatible with freedom.

Spain's basic military problem, aggravated since the loss of our colonies, related to the disastrous consequences of an excessive proportion of our national budget devoted to military expenditures. The military class, favored by our king for its maintenance of public order, had lost much prestige as the result of African campaigns between 1909 and 1921. Now a retrograde law had stifled antimilitarism by giving jurisdiction in crimes against the army, here newly defined, to military tribunals with their own law code.

Consequently, a subversive spirit with no effectual outlet had grown among our people, no longer able to openly criticize the military.

The French example provided clear guidelines for our situation. Obviously, due allowance had to be made for differences of time, place, and culture, and for the different characteristics of Spaniards and Frenchmen. A famous trial had served to clarify the conflict between army and state in France once and for all, and that clarification had provided the Third Republic with its stable foundation. My Friend considered the Dreyfus Case, the famous *Affaire,* as the neuralgic center of the French republic's climactic crisis. Politics in our neighboring country had centered on it from the end of the last century to our own time. So long as the Dreyfus Affair lasted, it divided France in a truly civil struggle, truly *civil* because it remained bloodless and never degenerated into fratricidal warfare. Against Dreyfus—a surprised propitiatory victim—stood forces of reaction that favored monarchy and empire: the regular clergy and persons who identified patriotism with ideas that had collapsed in the great Revolution and that various reincarnations of revolution had repeatedly decapitated during the nineteenth century. My Friend undertook to show that Minister of War André's purge of the French army had culminated a struggle against caudillismo going back many years. Also he pointed out that French caudillismo included no less a man than the modern world's one epic figure, Napoleon.

A few years after he had definitively set down his lectures in this book, my Friend argued against someone's suggestion that they provided a pattern for his military reforms under the Provisional Government of the Spanish Republic of April 14. As that republic's first Minister of War, he did not base his policies on those of the Third French Republic, something impossible in any case. Nonetheless, his basic governing principle, the basic concept underlying his reforms, was, indeed, to reshape the army to match our new regime, not to remake it. The reforms intended to remove military men from politics, to restrict them to their purely professional duties. This much does seem an implicit translation of the French experience that my Friend explained in his book. More basically, however, his policy represented something characteristically republican, with universal relevance far transcending a particularly French context.

In speaking of *translation* here, I refer to ideas that did not come from any existing foreign text, to something put together by the Author of *Military Policy in France.* He did, nevertheless, like to do actual translation, and in doing it he exercised his gifts as a writer. I don't know what circumstance caused our friend Alberto Jiménez, director of the Students' Residence and editor of the Granada series of Spanish and foreign books, to ask him to translate *The Bible in Spain.* It did occur by accident, quite casually. In this valuable account, its author, Mr. George Borrow, agent of The Bible Society, told of his journey through our land during the past century when Mendizábal served as premier. People called Borrow *Don Jorgito el inglés* (Georgie the Englishman), and he accepted it as he went about proselytizing, trying to sell the New Testament. This delightful account was the principal result of Borrow's travels through Estremadura, part of Andalusia—and he intended to go on to Galicia.

Of the many foreigners who have applied their literary talents to the endless rediscovery of Spain, this Englishman seems the most accurate, the most sensitive to the Spanish panorama and especially to our people. The Translator responded to his author's pleasure in the people, his affinity, and the translation preserves an enthusiasm found in Borrow's always picturesque and judicious pages. Later my Friend undertook to translate Borrow's book about Gypsies, less interesting because it included too much minute detail. Certainly in the latter book Borrow seems highly selective in choosing material to suit his philosophic and ethnographic scientism.

Writing of Seville in *The Bible in Spain,* Borrow mentions an *oidor,* what we would now call a judge, grandson of an emperor of Morocco and son of a convert to Christianity, notable as a prince with an ultimate claim to his ancestral throne. Borrow makes little of the conversion itself, a remarkable event during Ferdinand VI's reign, but my maternal surname descended from it. The Moorish prince in question became my great-great-grandfather, and he converted to Catholicism, at least as an immediate cause, in order to marry my great-great-grandmother, a lady of Granada. This cherifian prince and convert had three sons: one of them became a friar of the Brothers of Sacro-Monte in Granada, another died gloriously fighting against French invaders in the Battle of Bailén. Of the third son, the *oidor* who served in Seville at the time of his visit, Don Jorgito says very little more than that he had lost much of his regal dignity. It much amused my Friend that my mother should seriously protest that Englishman's casual acceptance of her grandfather's bad reputation, something not uncommon for administrators of justice. She had not known her grandfather and up to then knew nothing about him.

Though an interested observer, the missionary did not forget his journey's purpose in his enjoyment of Spain. The Translator took particular interest in Borrow's interview with Mendizábal, the revolutionary liberal who ended mortmain and in whose government this evangelist placed great hopes. I do not recall whether Borrow says anywhere what I heard from his Translator, in connection with *The Bible in Spain* and many other times, that Spain has still to be Christianized. This conversion seemed overdue to my Friend, especially in regions like the Basque country and Galicia, which had resisted the romanization that has left an indelible stamp of that civilization and brought most of the Spanish nation into the mainstream. When Borrow visited Mendizábal he urged that supporting his mission and the English influence it represented would serve the liberal regime the premier was trying to establish. The premier replied, as Borrow himself tells, that he needed more from England than Bibles; they should send him cannon to win his war against the Carlists. In many ways, apart from this suggestive page from history, my Colleague on *La Pluma* noted the good sense of this statesman whom he could consider his predecessor and model in working for reform on a solid foundation of private ownership of capital goods.

On some valuable page of Don Benito Pérez Galdós's *National Episodes,* I don't remember where, he describes a pronunciamento and a consequent battle right in Madrid's Puerta del Sol. The Translator of *The Bible in Spain,* a book unknown to Spaniards until he made it available to them in some of his best prose writing, pointed out to me the identity of the novelist's scene with an earlier description of that pronunciamento in Borrow's text.

As often happens with a people like ours who don't read much, Don Jorgito became popular as a personality, even though his book did not really catch on and he failed to convert the Spaniards to Protestantism. That seems the only explanation for how, a century after his journey, I was able to buy for his Translator a small painting of no artistic value but of great anecdotal interest. It showed a character with the ridiculous appearance Andalusians give to the English, his good Bible under his arm, clearly bargaining with Gypsies about the price of a mule. Fat Meléndez, as we his fellow *tertulia* members at the Ateneo called him, sold it to me in his bookshop on the calle de Cadaceros at the corner of Arlabán. I think that he had found it in the Rastro.

15

Puente del Arzobispo

In the spring of 1923 García Prieto's Liberal government asked our king to dissolve the Cortes and hold new elections. The Reformist party's executive committee proposed that my Colleague again run as their candidate in Puente del Arzobispo. At first it seemed that the principal financial backing for his campaign came from a blond, bearded marquess whom my Friend knew better than I did. I may, possibly, have exchanged a few words with this man in Ateneo hallways. Even my Friend did not know him well, though, nor had he seemed so great an admirer of the Secretary of the Ateneo as to explain such generous expenditure, especially as he did not have a lot of money. The Candidate soon learned that, in fact, the principal donation came from a Bilbao millionaire, apparently a shipowner, whose republicanism we heard praised by prominent members of the Free Institute of Education. My Friend could accept that money only because the donor's anonymity guaranteed his own personal independence against any kind of political sycophancy; he would never have agreed to that.

The sum by no means equaled the extensive resources available to his opponent. It did, however, enable the Reformist Candidate to arrange for basic protections (such as election supervisors, canvassers, and notaries) against illegalities practiced by city hall officials and Don Platón Páramo, dealer in secondhand goods.

This time I could accompany him. The campaign took place in two stages, first the customary electioneering and appeal to voters, then the election itself on its appointed day. To me it all seemed like recreation and an adventure given zest by my Friend's growing success with his partisans, which even led me to believe that he would win. He always felt less certain of it than I did. Native skepticism made him "doubting," as he liked to say with rustic canniness; his deliberate, ironic solecism emphasized his touching self-protection against any pitfall with which vanity might confront him. As clear landmarks of that first trip to Oropesa, I remember the castle of Maqueda standing high above the highway and a simple inn at Talavera where we stopped for gas.

At nightfall we got to the house of a Reformist representative who had courageously offered us lodging. In making that offer to a candidate opposed to the cacique, that good man risked his family's well-being. His business was already in trouble, and things soon got worse because of the winner's political ill will; his later misfortunes confirmed the real danger involved. A middle-aged couple, their children, including a charming young woman, and a meddlesome grandmother made up the family. Contrary to general practice, the women joined us at dinner. Elsewhere during that trip, following the old Castilian custom, we rarely met even mistresses of houses where we stayed.

In this house in Oropesa, they had prepared for us a very large bedroom. The natural dampness and small windows of a ground-floor room facing the street combined with a high ceiling to make it very chilly. Immediately we noticed a huge urinal at the foot of one of the beds, what they call a chamber pot, a useful convenience anticipating a guest's need for a nocturnal excursion. My Friend exploded with laughter.

He told me of difficulties on the first night of his previous sojourn. Lacking an opportunity before bedtime to inquire discreetly of his host that piece of information most necessary in an unfamiliar house, he had waited until everybody went to bed and then tried to search out on his own the needed facility. He did not expect that it would prove so difficult and complicated. First his footsteps echoed noisily on the entrance hall stairs; then the door's bolt proved stubborn. Next came a vigilant voice in the darkness and then the light of a candle. After that there soon appeared an excited procession, with each family member from grandmother to youngest child offering his own explanation, exhortation, and opinion about the Candidate's ill-concealed needs. Then there seemed to come an answering family chorus clarifying and emphasizing the situation. Like it or not, he had to allow himself to be guided through patios, corridors, and fenced-in yards until, finally, at the back fence, next to fields, and after an aroused watchdog had calmed down, they arrived at the privy. After negotiating some wobbly stairs he found himself in a very dark shack with facilities far in excess of his need, a wooden board with three seats carved out in it. "I assumed that they arranged things so that they could hold a session of the town council there," he said. I believe, in fact, that our amiable host did serve on the council.

A cow, paraded through the streets, heralded our arrival in the district; the Reformist party promised its holocaust as a kind of reward to tempt greedy electors with a triumphal feast. The victim announced its own sacrifice with a placard reading "Long Live Candidates of the Left" attached to its tail.

A few days later we crossed the superb Tagus River over a magnificent bridge that gives the district its name [Archbishop's Bridge] and memorializes that dignitary of the Church of Toledo who had it built long before. In the district's titular city we stayed in a pharmacist's house. His dwelling proclaimed him a wealthy man, but the large size of its rooms seemed to us to aggravate the coldness that you always find in houses standing by themselves, separated from their neighbors. The Avila sierra acts as a protecting wall against north winds for these fields and the very pleasant countryside. It was the Candidate's preferred landscape: level fields, with trees, and a mountain range to provide limits and height. When he had no immediate duties to perform in connection with his campaign he relaxed and enjoyed scenery as we traveled from town to town along the highway.

Our preliminary trip culminated in the town of Navamorales, principal seat of the House of Pacho. This constituted a large estate whose administration involved a related business in usurious loans, the usual basis of rural caciquism. Pacho's widow, owner in his name of that property, headed the House. We supposed from her deep mourning dress that she was recently widowed, but later learned that by local custom one turned more and more to black garments as years passed after a bereavement. For many years the House of Pacho had remained faithful to a pact that had assured Don César de la Mora of electoral victory with very little effort. Now the House appeared propitious to shifting the votes of its servants and clients to the Reformist Candidate. The House of Pacho does it *this way*—and everyone from Oropesa to Navamorales accompanied those words with an impudent gesture emptying out his jacket pocket into his hand to weigh imaginary coin. The House of Pacho does it *this way,* and that said it all.

The House manifested itself to us in the widow's rustic artfulness. Circumspect and discreet, she interspersed her few words with more or less furtive glances toward her agent. She listened to the Candidate's explanation of his intentions; he modified what the electioneers had told him to say, adding what seemed important. This lady began by disclaiming the usefulness of any open pressure on her clients; she ended by saying that, in any case, she would have to recover from him any expenses the election cost her. Her agent spoke more specifically about just what each vote would cost. The House of Pacho does it *this way*—with the Candidate's money.

Those of the populace who got involved in the election behaved even less circumspectly. Our campaign workers judged that in places entirely corrupted by demoralizing custom they had to adopt our opponent's traditional bribery. We had to buy votes. Accompanied by the honorable secretary of the Socialist Workers' Club and our assigned host, so unlike our honest host in Oropesa, I went to the houses they pointed out in the poorest neighborhoods. Usually my attendants could convince even the most reluctant with a few words and a five peseta coin. The Workers' Club in Navamorales, however, refused to accept, even in the name of a gift to their common fund, one peseta beyond strictly legal election expenses. I think that all the Socialist organizations in the district did the same.

On election day I took up my vigil in Calera, where we did not feel we had to worry about "muscle"—a term the Candidate picked up from his local supporters. Here voters would presumably decide on the basis of their own preferences. Our friend Francisco Vighi accompanied me; more interested in poetry than in engineering, he lived a student's irregular life in Madrid centering on café *tertulias*. He had enlisted Ciria Escalante to bring him in his car to monitor the Secretary of the Ateneo's election. Ciria, also a poet from the latest batch of Ateneo members, and a very nice, bright kid, came from a rich family.

By midmorning an unexpectedly small number of votes for our Candidate made clear the influence of barefaced pressure and threats from " muscle" under orders from Don Platón and Candidate de la Mora. Ciria went to check with our Friend at his headquarters in Puente del Arzobispo. Ciria returned with orders that at twelve o'clock sharp we should break open glass panels of our opponent's ballot boxes crammed with "sausages" (politicians' jargon for fraudulent votes put into the urns all bundled together). We soon carried out our assignment, but as that afternoon progressed and the time for closing the polls approached we lost hope that it had done any good because nobody paid any attention to our complaints. Then Vighi distracted the Civil Guard commander on duty, and the sound of breaking glass became general as we punched in ballot boxes on other tables.

That Sunday night after the election we pondered that total abuse of the law by supporters of the government's candidate. As reports had come in from district towns it became clear that town hall secretaries linked to the cacique had falsified returns in any place where intimidation and bribery had not produced the necessary votes. We headed back to Madrid full of the bitterness of defeat. Alone, the Candidate and I talked about the inanity of spending so much effort in vain, and indignation brought tears to my eyes. Once again wretched circumstances had denied him an opportunity to develop his talents within the framework of Spanish political life. "We must concentrate on our writing," he said with a disillusioned smile.

I could not accept it just like that. Certainly I tended to exalt him because of my own enthusiasm, but clearly the public had also felt that way about him; and defeated voters of Puente del Arzobispo had voted for him to represent them. I expressed my protest vehemently. No, the situation became intolerable when a protected yet lawless member of the government perverted, falsified, an election, when, by refusing to recognize the people's will, he made it impossible for them to express themselves. My Friend said, "Maybe we have to think of some other way." "What way?" I interrupted, anxious for an immediate solution to correct an injustice that seemed insufferable for even one more day. "How do I know?" he continued calmly. "Some other system. This kind of election is good for nothing." Quite clearly his evolutionary reformism, as we called it, had made no headway against existing forces. Inevitably our thoughts turned to expedients that looked to more radical change.

Abuses in connection with this election resulted in a court case in accordance with our election law. It took place in the Palace of the Council on the calle Mayor; the courts met there during the restoration of their building on the Plaza de las Salesas, which a famous fire had nearly destroyed some years earlier. The defeated Candidate challenged his opponent with so much evidence that he would have succeeded if evidence had decided the case. Félix de Lequerica, a Maurist deputy who defended the infamously proclaimed candidate, had lectured at the Ateneo a few years earlier and later acted cynically but intelligently in defense of the interests of Bilbao's plutocracy. Now he spoke against the Secretary of the Ateneo with such violence and lack of manners that his attack seemed motivated by personal animosity. Representing the elected candidate, this brazen lawyer attributed to his Opponent all the outrages, forgeries, and violence that Don César and his local caciques had themselves perpetrated in the district of Puente del Arzobispo.

The lifelong republican Don Gumersindo Azcárate was also defeated in those elections after many years of representing León in the Congress. Some sanctimonious Ateneo members joined with a liberal newspaper in foolishly and pedantically awarding him a compensatory title "President of the Congress of Morality." My Friend laughed and turned down a similar post in that Areopagus. He did not think of politics as some kind of ideal or abstraction. One could choose to get involved or not, but once involved one had to accept the evidence of defeat.

Through mutual friends, Don Ángel Ossorio did console him. Commenting on the defeat of the Secretary of the Ateneo and other more famous candidates, he apparently said, "This Cortes will never assemble." He had in mind General Picasso's famous investigative commission that, in fact, covered up military responsibility for the disastrous defeat of Spanish troops at Anual two years earlier.

16

Govern or Let the People Govern

In June 1923 we suspended *La Pluma* after exactly three years of publication. Luis García Bilbao had provided money to found the weekly *España* in homage to the genius of Ortega y Gasset. When Ortega deserted it, Araquistáin became its editor, and in that post he made his name as a polemicist during the 1914 war. Now it faced extinction unless someone came to the assistance of its debt-ridden publishers. When they approached Amós Salvador he suggested that we take it over as Editor and secretary to continue it as a weekly concentrating on politics where it had an undoubted influence on public opinion. My Colleague felt less sure and hesitated longer than I. Though continuing to think of him mainly as a man "consecrated" to writing, I did not want him to give up politics, and it seemed that *España* offered a good foundation to build on after two electoral defeats. In the end we decided that since *La Pluma* had not grown after its initial momentum, we risked seeing it die gradually, and so we decided in favor of *España*, with its greater monetary compensation and other inducements.

We finished off *La Pluma* with a special issue devoted to Valle-Inclán, in recognition of his invaluable contribution to our journal. Distinguished writers from among the companions of Don Ramón's literary youth supplied material for this issue honoring him. We could find no one we knew who could sum up his contribution to contemporary Spanish letters so well as my Friend. Though not an unconditional admirer of the author of the *Sonatas,* his friendly criticism astutely pointed out, above all other artistic considerations, Valle-Inclán's typically Galician native sensitivity and an underlying humanity that he disguised in his own life. The picturesque character hid a real man.

My Colleague and I had begun to settle into our new weekly routine with *España* when General Primo de Rivera's coup d'état brought a new stage in the monarchy's breakdown. The Editor of *España*, though unaware of the trap destiny had set for him, had a clear understanding of what that event portended for Spain. He could not for a moment accept the premises behind the military takeover. Nobody opposed more than he the vicious practices that had created the illusory parliaments of our public life. Few felt as disdainful as he did toward its political usages and those persons who

108

personified them with their inveterate clienteles of family and cronies. An abyss lay between that, however, and accepting the insurrectionist general's proclaimed housecleaning, or accepting his pretense that he represented a new brand of politics. Vague suggestions about our adopting something like the fascism that had triumphed in Italy under Mussolini did not convince my Friend. He saw no similarity. It seemed iniquitous to him, even stupid, to accept Primo's pronunciamento—in which he had risked even less than the nineteenth-century caudillos. What else did Primo, himself, represent but "the old politics"? To what else did he owe his successful career, with no significant military achievements, but to the blatant politicism and politicking he now pretended to despise?

Above all, though, my Friend refused to reject our political system merely because some persons misused it. He could not under any circumstances accept the establishment of military discipline as the norm for civil order. Division of powers must underlie any democratic administration of national power, but legislature, executive, and judiciary remain nothing more than emanations of a unitary authority delegated by the people. The army has a clear and limited function: to defend national territory against enemies, to make war. A defeated army seeking revenge against fellow citizens who had delegated to it their defense seemed monstrous, an abomination that could lead only to disorder and the state's destruction and disappearance.

For just a moment my Friend hoped that Melquíades Álvarez would rally common sense and democratic feeling in defense of popular government after Premier García Prieto's prompt surrender at the rebel general's command and following the king's complacent whim. Melquíades Álvarez, chosen president of the Congress of Deputies when it assembled a few months earlier, seemed to have only one possible course: defense of the constitution that Alfonso XIII had abandoned, apparently yielding to Primo de Rivera's force. Yet Primo would never have risked his coup without previous royal consent. What better opportunity for Melquíades Álvarez to reverse the decision by which he had led the flower of Spanish youth clearly and legitimately into the monarchical orbit?

"Govern or let the people govern." The most zealous defender of royal prerogatives might have said those words as a last warning. Coming from the mouth of Don Antonio Maura they might have seemed a kind of expiation. Melquíades Álvarez did not make even that kind of mild protest, not even as a warning. In the past he had adjusted his basic political principles to conform to the monarchical regime to avoid violence in Spain's historic crisis. Up to now some hope had remained of preserving the monarchy, though less with each succeeding crisis. It had seemed justifiable in the name of exhausting all reasonable possibilities to sustain hopes about the Crown's true feelings, though inevitably public confidence in the king had eroded. Now, however, did Melquíades Álvarez have any choice but to reassert his own freedom of action and that of Reformists by returning to pure republicanism? He did not do this.

The defeated Candidate for Puente del Arzobispo wrote a letter to his former chief resigning from the Reformist party. His earlier suggestions for military reform, laid out in a kind of programmed manifesto, stood as a clear warning of the step he now took. He believed that any comprehensive reform of the state must necessarily begin with military reform. This new course did not mean that he was turning to politics and away from the literary work in which I took such pleasure. In fact, he now withdrew from making speeches and from debates at the Ateneo. He lacked both means and a propitious climate for revolutionary conspiracy; besides he had no vocation for it. Anyhow, he had spoken in public more from a kind of physical need than from any wish to attract proselytes. In the meantime censorship stopped any real effort to criticize the policies of Primo's dictatorship. *España,* of course, fell victim to the rigors of the red pencil. Readers of that embattled weekly had to feel let down when we shifted to a literary emphasis—with no clear satirical thrust. They found it as hard to read between the lines as we did to write without complete freedom.

My Friend's disinterest in opposing or overthrowing the dictatorship in its early days did not come merely from its leaders' inanity. The people it governed also seemed inane to him. Perhaps they had the kind of government they deserved. He remained constant in his clear-sighted opinion about the "lay of the land" for the dictatorship. He used this popular expression in making predictions about persons and events in a political essay published in several installments in December 1923 in the French review *Europe* and, in its original Castilian, in *Nosotros* of Buenos Aires. Here he explained the previous decline of constitutional liberalism by its obvious incompatibility with the dynasty, and, most notably, he explained our present Military Directory and Government of the Dictatorship as the death agony of Spain's monarchy. In no sense did the new regime represent a dawning or a renewal. Still, he did not believe that it had accelerated the monarchy's breakdown. He predicted the steps by which the military class would show its incapacity to resolve Spain's fundamental problems. He, personally, was settling down to prepare for the long run; he did not share the optimism of those who believed that our new regime would collapse by itself.

17

Republican Action

Now the theater called me again, like a siren awaking from a nap in the prompter's box. When *España* followed *La Pluma* into the grave my own attachments went with them. My vocation as a writer had never progressed beyond emulating my Friend. Now my arguments in favor of the theater found support in a promise of greater emolument than literature or journalism had provided. The husband and manager of a well-known Italian actress [Mimi Aguglia] sought my assistance as adviser and publicist for a series of performances by his wife throughout our peninsula. She would perform in Castilian with a Spanish company, and they planned a subsequent tour of Spanish America. My Comrade and Mentor could find no valid reason for me to stay in his vicinity, though he pointed out the dangers of a precipitous decision. He agreed with me that a preliminary tour of Spain and Portugal would be all right, but that I should leave unsettled the question of going to America. It remained under consideration, but with the condition of a guaranteed return ticket. Adventuring in our former viceroyalties did not seem very attractive to my Friend. He did not believe in El Dorado, always placing his faith in more tangible things. Though he did not require physical involvement, he was, after all, a sensualist. His highly acute understanding came through his senses, the straightest road.

Perhaps he thought that I did not appreciate his political inclinations, or, rather, that I feared his dispersing his talents on politics, neglecting the literary genius I had awakened in him and that required all his attention. Certainly it pleased me to see him enthusiastic about many things, though he complained about precisely this tendency in me. I expected that, left alone in peaceful idleness, with nobody to push him, he would fall back into that stagnation of indifference he had complained about at the time of our first acquaintance.

During my first absence from Madrid with the theatrical company, he began going to Dr. Giral's pharmacy on the calle de Atocha, near the Church of San Sebastián. Martí Jara took him there; the sincere admiration of this fellow Ateneo member explained his new venture into politics after his two defeats in Puente del Arzobispo. The doctor had his laboratory in the mezzanine over his shop. The first of a new generation of republicans met there.

Several dedicated young men, disenchanted with reform like my Friend, looked toward the next stage. Hardly any old republican patriarchs of 1873 remained alive. Don Gumersindo Azcárate, though widely respected, had no reputation as a revolutionary. The very old and infirm Don José Fernando González, confined to his armchair, had taken no part in politics for many years. A few ephemeral federalists still survived. Rodrigo Soriano, of the race of crusading journalists, had a certain popularity based on the coarse humor of his work in *España Nueva* and on his challenges in Congress during his service as a deputy. Roberto Castrovido, a man whose reputation did not do him justice, had largely wasted his great potential. Long the editor of *País*, devotedly republican, and a superior journalist, his honor had increased in adversity when others had foundered.

Lerroux headed the only republican organization in Spain that had survived from the days when his "Young Barbarians" had taken to the streets with supreme insolence, renewing a spirit of protest, revolt, and noisy opposition against the monarchy. Unquestionably their hooliganism had been effective. In spite of this, Lerroux's immorality remained an insuperable obstacle. Nobody stood so far from the classical republican virtues represented in Spain by Castelar, Pi y Margall, and Salmerón. Indeed, many years before, the Jovian Don Nicolás Salmerón had hurled Olympian thunderbolts at him. More recently Azcárate and Pablo Iglesias had denounced Lerroux before the Congress. With our hopes of Reformism gone, with no republican god on Mount Sinai, those of us who had never heard the voice of Castelar but could remember the lion's roar of Grau or, better, Costa, had to find someone to unite us, to galvanize our spirits, united in our hopes in spite of individual differences. Unamuno was a symbol, not a leader. Blasco Ibáñez, despite his sorties into the wider world and his increasing fame in America as a novelist, did not pass muster with his political cohorts in Valencia.

Our theatrical tour began in Valencia. The Italian nationality of our leading lady pleased members of the local press corps whose names I had been given. Azzati, an Italian settled in our country, edited *El Pueblo*. A group of editors, reporters, and their hangers-on, along with Sigfrido Blasco, the famous novelist's son, welcomed me at the Café de la Democracia, whose house pianist had to play the "Marseillaise" several times a day by popular request. I found them all stirred up about the printing and clandestine distribution of a pamphlet, *For Spain and Against the King,* that Blasco Ibáñez had written in France and that his secretary, Carlos Esplá, had sent from Paris. It pleased them very much when I offered to hide many copies of it in our company's luggage to distribute in places we passed through.

After several months of traveling, I met my Friend in Bilbao, where he had gone in connection with his duties as judge for the Notary Examination. In his free time, mostly at night, we socialized with my actors and more frequently with friends we had met seven years before. The most diligent of them were Mourlane Michelena and Joaquín Zugazagoitia a pharmacist with literary pretensions who seemed to value our friendship highly.

I parted with the Italian actress's company and returned to Madrid invalided by an attack of rheumatic neuritis. The nervous symptoms of my malady became so obvious that Doctors Lafora and Sacristán had no trouble in diagnosing it, and they cured me more by friendly advice than by professional treatment. Doctor Luis Fortún, a fellow director with Sacristán of an insane asylum at Ciempozuelos, was the brother of my university friend Fernando who had shared my first literary efforts. His premature death ten years earlier had stamped my youth with grief.

Now my Friend and I went to visit the asylum, moved by natural curiosity and by Lafora's publicity campaign for reform of that kind of sanatorium. My Friend told me that his Aunt Rosaura had lived in confinement at Ciempozuelos for many years. He found her at the end of a hallway, trailing her hospital gown with regal dignity. She seemed like an actress performing the role of an insane person in a play. She lived a happy, illusory existence, mistaking the institution for a palace and its doctors and guards for her faithful servants. She couldn't remember anything and did not recognize her nephew.

Another patient, a nun, affected my Friend more than his aunt. As attendants had predicted, she no sooner saw us than she began to pack her trousseau into a suitcase, and by preference she approached my Friend and asked him to take her away from there at once. That "little nun from Azorín" moved him to unspeakable sadness. No, we did not laugh at her insane urging, her hunger for freedom. No sooner would her witless hopes subside than some new impertinent observer would turn up at her door to revive them in a pathetic cycle.

Back in Madrid, I did not find my Friend prodigal with confidences about his conspiracies. First, he did not want to present one more temptation to my natural propensity to waste time by getting involved in many unproductive activities. He did not consider idleness itself a loss of time, but he objected to trivial fussing around. Besides, part of his fond friendship involved some strong instinct that I still do not understand, some groundless concern to protect me from any risk. In spite of this protectiveness, he did mention to me once some difficulties about circulating another of Blasco Ibáñez's pamphlets. Soon after that I conceived a ruse for receiving a shipment from émigré conspirators in France—one of them José Sánchez Guerra, a Conservative party leader, had fallen victim to the dictator's enmity, for practicing "the old politics." It occurred to me that they might send two or three boxes of pamphlets from Paris to Amós Salvador in care of the secretary of cultural affairs at the Ministry of State. Amós, an architect and a member of the bureaucracy, would arouse no suspicion. No sooner said than done, and it worked perfectly. Afterwards we apportioned these manifestoes among many households for further distribution.

In this connection my Friend came more frequently to my home than ever before. My mother and sisters graciously cooperated in wrapping and stamping that mountain of papers, and we mailed Blasco Ibáñez's pamphlets as we had once mailed *La Pluma*. It appeared to be a simply commercial product. Only my little sister protested, complaining to me about my Friend, that gentleman who caused us so much nuisance with his political activities. He continued to tease her about her Carlist leanings, whose evidence he pretended to see in her friendship with our former neighbor Vázquez Mella.

For the moment the political activities of the fledgling Conspirator of Giral's shop did not go beyond that. People who met there did not form a party. They did not have to prove their republicanism by subscribing to some formal creed. Hopes for the republic depended more on a blueprint for government than on unpublished statements of their beliefs. They needed to *act*. Well, if in the beginning was the Word, they had first to formulate a parameter of their possible action. That group meeting with Giral, though not yet a party, came to embody the renovating impulse of the imperishable republican ideal. Later, under the name Republican Action, they launched Spain's new republic.

18

Fresdelval

In the summer of 1926 my Friend went to Burgos to participate as judge in another examination. We met there again for a few days. As in the past, I sought consolation in his company for the absence of love. More precisely, I was on my way back from a quick trip to France to see my fiancée off at Boulogne on her voyage to the United States. As usual we made fun of our sorrows, and he returned to an old joke, comparing me to the "Knight of the Greeks," an outlandish but not uncommon translation of "Chevalier des Grieux" in *Manon Lescaut.* He meant the tenor protagonist in Massenet's opera, not the original character in Abbé Prévost's novel which he considered one of the best of its sort in French. Remembering subscriptions he and friends had in his youth for a box in the Royal Theater, he went on to suggest amusing situations resulting from mistranslations of opera librettos. "Vasco da Gama appears, and, seeing him, everyone freezes," from *L'Africana.* Or *Manon's* first scene set "on a dusty street in the Harbor of Grace." "And you will end up," he said to me, referring to dilemmas of my courtship, "going to New Orleans and dying on a plush rug." In fact, the scenery of the King's Playhouse simulated in just that way green turf at the foot of a tree in the culminating scene of *Manon Lescaut,* a lyric history of two exemplary lovers—which does not necessarily mean that they should be imitated. In our theaters Anselmi and La Storchio or La Vix portrayed them.

He met me, then, in the Castilian capital and told me about having to move from his first lodging. As in Zumárraga and San Sebastián nine years before, and last year in Bilbao, he had been cruelly attacked by fleas and bedbugs which he could not stand—creatures bred in Spanish walls through centuries of neglect. He told me how after midnight on his arrival he had gone through Burgos from *sereno* to *sereno* trying to find better accommodations than those offered to the passing traveler. During his first days there he had run into Pedro Salinas, then teaching a summer course for foreigners. Now our only friend in the vicinity was Amós Salvador, vacationing with his wife and two daughters in his nearby house at La Vega.

As I had no business to pursue, when he finished his we went several times to the cathedral partially renovated by Lampérez. My Friend missed the effect of romantic slovenliness contributed in both France and Spain by neighborhoods which had grown up around cathedrals during the slow process of their construction. Freeing the Gothic cathedrals from those structures clustering around their walls had clearly diminished them. Certainly we gain perspective with the openness, but we also lose something. Congestion obliged a viewer to elevate his gaze and his spirit to the pointing towers and the sky.

While we walked through its naves, he hazarded observations about the special and distinctive features of Burgos's principal church as compared to those in León, Toledo, or Seville. He did not approach it from the vantage point of its construction but from its artistic style. He did base his arguments on the architecture, but he did not limit himself to terms used by architects and builders. He tried to begin with the feelings an object, natural or artistic, aroused in him in order to avoid confusing data that came from his observations with what he had read or heard. He used his intelligence in an inductive way to correlate and rank his impressions. This process occurred so naturally with him—I don't mean to call the process common or ordinary—that you never got an impression of a tiresome professor constantly lecturing; rather, he always seemed a friend with trustworthy opinions. Beneath the vaults and before the tombs of Burgos, I faced no risk of a garrulous academic disquisition. However much such academic explanations attempt to stir up enthusiasm, they always have an opposite effect.

We visited the Carthusian monastery of Miraflores and the convent of Las Huelgas. The convent is famous and also highly regarded among monastic communities for the aristocratic excellence and dignified tradition maintained by those who profess there. As it turned out, our illusions collapsed at the sight through the grill of a procession of its inferior choir. Those ladies had no more gravity or distinction than the sorry choristers in *Lohengrin's* Wedding Scene as sung at the Royal. I use that performance to make my point as it was a notorious example of theatrical shoddiness.

On Burgos' outskirts we visited the ruins of a palace that had belonged to the princess of Éboli; even today natives call it "the house of the king's whore." My Friend delighted in repeating these words, so clear and precise. Here as on other occasions he praised, not just the precision but the musicality of a common expression that had emerged from an insult, "son of a whore." Cervantes graciously dignified it for posterity by putting it into Sancho's mouth, but my Friend meant not *hi de puta* (whore's son), as Sancho says it, but the full measure *hijo de puta*. He repeated it, taking pleasure in its euphony. "It is a complete phrase, with all the vowels and none repeated. Also it does not have too many consonants, but exactly as many as the vowels. The Castilian language has few phrases so perfectly clear." Then he returned to the origin of his brief disquisition. "What a good sound! The house of the king's whore! The whore! 'The desired' *(querida)*. Not 'the beloved' *(amante)*, which has unfortunately become our common term."

I don't mean to suggest that my Friend was profane like so many Spanish men today, especially natives of Rioja and Navarre. Sometimes he swore in joking with me, or when he got angry, or to strengthen the force of something he was saying. Never, even by accident, did he swear in the presence of women.

Our friend Amós spent summers in a house at La Vega, part of an estate of the kind they call "boundaried farms" *(cotos redondos)* in Old Castile. Fields surrounded the house and farm buildings, with a grove of old trees and even a scenic river watering its meadows, where, according to season, pasturage for a good flock of sheep alternated with stubble. Once again my Friend felt somewhat attracted by the possibility of a similar retreat for himself. Only "somewhat," however, because village life soon bored him. A typical Spaniard, he could not enjoy country pleasures without missing city conveniences.

On the day we had dinner with our friend Amós, some titled young ladies appeared there for an afternoon visit. Though distant relatives of my Friend, they refused to acknowledge the connection, and I believe that they really did not know of their kinship. Belonging to a Madrid family famous for its wealth, they also regularly came to the Burgos region for summer vacations. The sight of their "family car," a near-omnibus in which these relations drove up, caused my Friend to react in a way that recalled other occasions when he had denounced a class of Spaniards who seemed incapable of enjoying a simple life. By custom the local gentry did not even use their carriages in summertime, except on feast days when they might spare a couple of mules from the harrow to pull them.

Somehow in our random conversation we expressed regret for a not-so-distant past and concern about an uncertain future, contrasting yesterday's security and tomorrow's chanciness. One of those young ladies ventured a suggestion, nothing more, in connection with bolshevism and the memory of Russia's revolution, then quite recent. "And afterwards . . . that poor family!" Her lament, referring to the last czar of Holy Russia, had an element of aristocratic commiseration with an equal, like a common sorrow shared around the table of a modest *tertulia*. In any case, it was ridiculous.

My Friend never had to explain to me why he kept away from the kind of society in which his odd relations figured prominently. Henceforth, however, we always thought of them in terms of their skinniness, exaggerated by the typical Spanish black of their clothing that emphasized their complete lack of femininity, dried-up inside and outside, stiff in their unmerited vanity. They barricaded themselves behind their ignorance against the wave, the monster, what my Friend laughingly called the "specter" of revolution. Sweeping through the world, it suddenly threatened the social order they represented, based solely on money and apart from any consideration about its source.

Our brief stay in Burgos culminated in another visit involving just the two of us and some stones. It had no pretext other than looking at a monumental ruin. Amós Salvador had told us that we should not miss Fresdelval.

My Friend did not belong to the school of romantics with a predilection for the ruined wall covered with ivy, something perennial and indifferent to its own survival. Seeing any ruin disturbed him, the scattered stones of some spoiled masterwork sent him into despair. Inevitably, then, our visit to Fresdelval evoked a characteristic plaint I had heard before, a diatribe against decadent Spaniards. By "decadence" he didn't mean the usual scholar's concept, lamentation for our lost imperial grandeur. His feeling had little or nothing to do with rhetoric. Here, as always, he spoke precisely, using words carefully, with their exact meaning, like a man who understands language as the means by which a whole nation expresses its nature. For him decadence meant collapse with no hope of protection or maintenance. Of course he recognized the inexorable effect of time on all human building. He did not find a ruin itself insupportable, but for him a ruin told the defeat of the heroic force, virility, creativity in a society that had created the original building, and he could not bear that.

He found no satisfaction in restorations, touch-ups, or other cosmetic treatments that gave a false sense of continuity. He found less satisfaction in something made brand-new for the mere sake of novelty, unless novelty fulfilled the essential nature of the original model, maintaining its tradition and contributing some inevitable element to it. This, of course, precluded mere decoration. He liked preservation of an original structure; when a building had survived intact, having outlived its original purpose and transcended into the realm of the purely artistic, when church or palace no longer represented anything beyond its own structural essence, then, in his eyes, it had achieved its full significance.

My Friend's alert and sensitive spirit could grasp at first glance the transcendent significance of a solitary village church, an ancient convent presiding over a valley, a castle guarding some former frontier; he instinctively understood the need that had created these buildings centuries ago. It grieved his soul to see the ruins of battlements and towers, cloistered patios, vaults, and bell towers—not so much those brought down by war, fire, or lightning, as those abandoned through indifference, through a break in continuity in the changing rhythms of Spanish life from one era to another.

However much one tries to ignore them, monasteries erected on the natural highways of our history stand as centers of gravity in any Spanish landscape. Their stones mark points of civilization contrasting with uncut stone in nearby quarries. Few sights that we viewed on our excursions from Madrid proved so rewarding as what we saw in Sigüenza, which I had visited twice in my youth. This typical frontier fortress between New Castile and Aragon not only marked a natural frontier; it also marked a very clear transition in style between medieval and Renaissance tastes. Its cathedral showed both styles—a notable building combining fortress, temple, mausoleum, and palace all in one. In that massive cathedral, perhaps a statue of a page most impressed my Friend. It seemed an archetypal tomb sculpture, as though the sculptor's chisel had summed up the essence of his whole work in one exemplary creation. He did not portray that young man as dead, but reclining with a little book in his hand. My Friend believed, as he said to me, that the spirit of this sculptural masterwork compared to the poetry of Jorge Manrique's *Verses on the Death of the Master, His Father*. This elegy also remains unique in its perfection from a century when Spain uttered its dramatic prose through the mouth of La Celestina.

Even so, Sigüenza endures, finally, as a monumental hodgepodge, its surviving stonework defying time with the same assurance as the mountains that shadow its walls. The monastery of Sobrado de los Monjes in Lugo Province represents something quite different. My Friend had discovered it on another of the professional trips he now combined with political proselytizing—the harbinger of his fatal vocation. These ruins provided new and stirring matter for his general elegiac lament on the collapse into barbarism of a culture whose fallen vault, surviving column, or isolated arch brought tears to his eyes. In his enthusiasm, he called Sobrado de los Monjes a Galician Escorial, built in a lofty balanced style in that enchanted abode, home of witches and sprites, goblins and crowned demons, where primitive Celtic paganism resists all outside influence. He later acquired magnificent photographs of it that he kept to the end. This monastery, part of the same expansion of papal power that had achieved the first great architecture at Campostela, may have collapsed with the mild revolutionary gust of Mendizábal's disamortization of ecclesiastical property ninety years before. That connection really upset my Friend's philosophical equanimity, usually so adaptable to tricks of fortune. Nearer to Madrid, the ruins of El Paular and El Parral did not represent irreplaceable greatness, and they made him fully appreciate the monastery of Saint Lawrence of the Escorial, whose sovereign balance of intellect and feeling gave him a sense of fulfillment and thus of tranquility.

That day in Burgos Province my Companion's enthusiastic reminiscences about all these things he had seen made a far greater impression on me than our visit to the ruined cloister of Fresdelval. It still stands in the shadowed valley indicated by its name. He, however, had an almost physical reaction to that monastic ruin. He always felt this anguish when confronted with an airy Gothic ogive or fragile column, a carved flower or labyrinthine gargoyles, and finials of fantastic animals and leaves. They brought home to him the certain ruin of all works the lyric flights of intrepid architects will ever erect on earth. Oh how the water trembles that undermines the foundations of Venice! But our delight in that ruin on that lazy summer afternoon caused my Companion to forget his usual lamentations, and we surrendered to its spell. By their very commonness our few words regained their primal worth. Had we been conventional romantics, that natural theater would

certainly have called forth expressions of purest rapture. In spite of the
evocative setting, though, we did not feel moved to speak; we just gave in
to the feeling of the place.

On the next day, for months later, and through the passing years, the
name Fresdelval continued to provide real enchantment for my Friend.
Nonetheless, later he resolved to drop an "l" because "Fresdeval" sounded
better to him. It became the title of a novel, interrupted several times by
circumstances and finally cut off by death, like the cloister of that monastic
ruin in the Burgos countryside.

19

Preparations for Saint John's Day

Republican Action gradually put together a definite program. The former Secretary's friends whose sure instinct had caused them to ask him to join their cause did not ask me to join them. Certainly they did not consider me an antagonist. They did, however, consider me overly involved with literature and the arts in general, including "good society" in the most frivolous sense of that term. I seemed incapable of a real vocation for politics, something that requires suspension of critical thinking about oneself and everything else. Perhaps when they considered it they also feared that my influence, great or small, on my Friend's thinking might turn him from that strict devotion to public affairs required of members on a party committee. We had, after all, shared a somewhat exclusive friendship. They did not realize how much they had me as their ally when they involved him in activities that happened to be republican and that provided him an opportunity to develop his talents—mainly oratorical in this case. Of course I regarded these political activities as useful in a different way than they did.

More skeptical than I, my Friend also did not want me to get involved in his new activities. In fact, these never represented his primary interest, nor did he get involved for the sake of ambition. He sacrificed his own private projects to the public interest, primarily so as not to yield to the temptation of disinterest or detachment that overtakes persons who, from lack of ambition, accept defeat without a struggle. On the other hand, he feared that I would waste my time as an amateur politician, trailing along in his wake from lawyer's office, to editing a journal, to trying for a seat as deputy. Thus he never asked me to accompany him to the conspiratorial meeting held in the back room of Dr. Giral's pharmacy. Certainly a term as apprentice conspirator would have amused me more than it did him.

Like all profoundly serious persons, he had a propensity for sarcasm and irony. If not as openly as I did, he laughed skeptically at the closeness of party rituals to the most solemn rites of worship. Like almost all republicans and many of the Reformists whom he had abandoned, most of his new friends were Masons. I don't know whether they had already asked him to enter Freemasonry at this point. Where curiosity, arguably unwholesome but certainly innocent, inclined me to seek initiation at this time, he, on the contrary, anticipated it with the annoyance he felt for all fraternal organizations. In due course he did agree to membership, though minimal, as he passed directly from his initiation to a state of dormancy through his abstention from further participation in the ritual. He never gave the slightest encouragement to my casual hints that I might like to join. He knew well enough my habitual flippancy toward pedants, however well established as masters of their own disciplines. Indeed, my aversion to pedantry had provided a basic element of our friendship.

After his completion of *The Friars' Garden,* which he dedicated to me, and the suspension of *La Pluma,* my Friend still found time for other literary work of some importance. This provided relief from the boredom political chores often entailed. Not long before, I had met and had some dealings with Doña Carmen Valera, daughter of the distinguished author of *Pepita Jiménez.* As my Friend had agreed to write an introduction and notes for a new edition of this novel in the *Clásicos Castellanos* series, he got permission to go through Don Juan's letters—and the most important and revelatory parts of those letters still remain unpublished. My Comrade found in them a suggestive chronicle of the nineteenth century that shed unexpected light on more than one aspect of the life of that great novelist and critic, and he reread that amiable genius with new understanding.

Soon after he finished his own novel, *The Friars' Garden,* my Friend undertook to write a life of Don Juan Valera. He turned to this work with such energy and enthusiasm that he finished it in time to enter it, still unpublished, for the National Prize for Literature. He won it. This prize carried no responsibilities about publication, and only the chapters "Valera in Italy" and "The Novel about Pepita Jiménez" appeared in print, and separately. Though among the best, these chapters do not compensate for the loss of the larger book. He kept on trying to improve it, which was impossible for his prizewinning manuscript was already a finished work. Unfortunately, some quality of personality caused him to strive for a consummate perfection in terms of research and style. In the dreadful crisis at the end his life all papers connected with "The Life of Don Juan Valera" disappeared, probably stolen with most of his later political papers, but possibly just lost, to everybody's loss. His introduction to the *Clásicos Castellanos* edition of *Pepita Jiménez* survives as a long and valuable summary of his work on Valera's masterpiece.

Though he appreciated filial love as Doña Carmen's motive in her attitude about the publication of her father's works and the preservation of his unpublished papers, the defenselessness of that archive disturbed him. It lay at the mercy of heirs or rights-holders who might not even care about preservation of the documents that had come to them, to say nothing of valuable historical light those documents shed on the author's work. He kept urging Doña Carmen, since she did not consider it proper at that time to publish many events and opinions involving persons still alive in the memories of close family members and old friends of the Valera family, to at least act to safeguard her father's autograph letters from vicissitudes that might endanger them. She might, for instance, turn these papers over to the Biblioteca Nacional with an express stipulation to withhold them from the public for whatever period she considered fitting for proprieties of social intercourse. In this he followed the thought of the author himself.

Doña Carmen Valera's husband, quarreling with her at this point, had already done irreparable damage to those letters—an act inconceivable from a person with the background and culture presumed in a career diplomat. My Friend had held in his hand the original of a letter written by Don Juan Valera as secretary of our embassy in Saint Petersburg that his son-in-law had barbarously mutilated to suppress information that he judged should not appear in the *Complete Works*. No doubt this had saved him the trouble of copying out what he considered should go to the printer. The daughter objected to relinquishing the correspondence at that point because of the letters' personal and private interest. Her father's loyal Biographer disagreed with that, and, furthermore, he said that it went against the intentions of Don Juan himself, who had sometimes even made two copies of his letters. In this way he had preserved an exchange with Estébanez Calderón *(El Solitario)*, highly amusing precisely because of its licentiousness. Clearly he intended posterity to read and enjoy the delightful literary backbiting at the courts of Naples and Brazil or among his friends and even family members in Madrid—matters that scandalized his hypocritical contemporaries.

Combining the responsibilities of his position at the Registry Office of the Ministry of Grace and Justice with those involved in his more recent political vocation in the cause of the republic, my Friend traveled to Valladolid. He had again to act as judge for the Notary Exam there, and he held several meetings similar to those in the pharmacy on the calle de Atocha. Now, however, the meetings concerned an upcoming coup, planned in agreement with the military, to overturn Primo de Rivera's dictatorship. Little time remained; they had agreed on the date of June 24 [Saint John's Day], and in its honor they called the event *la Sanjuanada*. Don José Sánchez Guerra, staunch Conservative leader then in Paris, figured prominently among the conspirators; the dictator had exiled him. Another conspirator in France, Santiago Alba, a former Liberal minister, had also fallen victim to the swaggering general's first moral shots. I say "moral shots" because, with the king's connivance and with the submission of the premier and the president of the Cortes, Primo had not had to fire actual shots to end the simulcrum of democracy and liberalism with which Spain's Bourbon dynasty had camouflaged itself.

Republicans of the Action also counted on assistance from the prestigious artillery. Its officers felt disgusted with the dictator because he undervalued their branch by basing promotions on wartime performance while they supported a system of promotion based on seniority. Several infantry officers had also become involved, headed by General Aguilera, a man from La Mancha, who was both completely trustworthy and charmingly uncultured. He spoke the language of the people, fluent in picturesque expressions and lewd barbarisms out of keeping with his personal code of ethics and his rank.

In the past Santiago Alba had ruled Valladolid as a political fief. My father had never supported him with the electoral influence he could wield as proprietor of the nearby castle of Villalba de los Alcores. Now, however, my father openly offered to support Alba; his student days at the Segovia military academy had left him antimilitaristic. Besides, he did not like Primo de Rivera's infamous harassment of Alba. Given the dictator's misuse of the law against Alba, and Alba's bad reputation that partly justified Primo, this support counted for quite a lot.

In Valladolid my Friend had occasion to deal with some sincere republicans and with others neither so democratic nor so liberal as Republican Action sought, men whose support for popular government came only from their opposition to the prevailing tyranny. A journalist among the latter had pretensions as a writer and a shrewd affectation of gentility. On the basis of his moralism he never forgave the former Secretary for a casual insolence at a café table toward the Queen Mother of Alfonso XIII. The people had called her "Doña Virtudes" in sarcastic reference to her bigotry.

The *Sanjuanada* failed because of poor preparation and because of the unreadiness of popular opinion and the general ambience. A boat bringing Sánchez Guerra from France to participate in the rising in Valencia turned back after coming in sight of that city. (He continued his work in the subversive movement.) They had mistakenly believed that Castro Girona, captain general of Valencia, had joined the insurrectionist cause.

From this period dated my Friend's acquaintance with Don Juan Hernández Saravia, his first adjutant, later a major and today a general of the republic. Also at that time he came to know Arturo Menéndez, then a fine aviator, who eventually shared the misfortunes and fate of the Second Spanish Republic.

1928

20
A Masked Ball

We had never been friends with Pío or Ricardo Baroja, but the latter's late marriage to a North American lady with a Catalonian name and background brought my Friend and me into rather close relations with them. The new bride wanted to cut a figure as hostess for an exclusive literary and artistic circle, and she established a weekly salon after dinner in the dining room of her home on the calle de Mendizábal. Several regulars of the Café Regina and Café Henar *tertulias* attended these pleasant gatherings, including Valle Inclán, an old friend of Ricardo and his fellow member in a famous group of painters that met at the Café de Levante. Ricardo and his wife occupied the lower floor of the Baroja family house. Other members lived upstairs, the mother, Pío, his sister Carmen, her husband the publisher Caro Raggio, and their two sons, children at that point. Pío, unsociable and full of his own importance, did not usually join us, but Caro's wife often did. We never had more than six or eight participants in those after-dinner discussions.

Ricardo had some pretensions as a Renaissance man, even through his Italian second surname, Nessi; he was an amateur etcher, painter, novelist, and dramatist, though he never had really striven for professional success along any of these lines. On the threshold of old age, his wife's innocent enthusiasm had pushed him into emulatory competition with his brother, the famous novelist, whose celebrity had not caused any envy up to then. Ricardo's reading to us of an essay his wife had written on the drama prompted me to suggest that we organize a little theater in that very place. We called it "Theater of the White Raven" as a parody of the "Bats," "Blue Parrots," and "Golden Cockerels," exotic companies from Germany and Russia that had some fame at that time touring through Europe. We ourselves had some renown if only for exclusivity, since the apartment's size limited our audience, often to an author's own family. Most of us, and especially the masters of the house, acted as interpreters of our own works. We did it for fun with no other purpose.

These performances, in which my Friend participated only as a spectator, brought my family into the Baroja circle. Intimacy grew when my father graciously undertook, as a lawyer, to resolve details of a case involving

Ricardo's wife against the widow of one of her brothers about a paternal inheritance.

As the carnival season of 1928 approached, Doña Carmen Monné Baroja decided to further enliven the amusements of "The White Raven" with a masked ball for participants and spectators of that little theater. She absolutely insisted that everyone come in costume or not at all. My Friend's supposed seriousness made him the sole exception. He might come unmasked if he chose, or he could remain at home, as he promised to do. He said that his stern presence might disturb the foolish amusements of the young and those who, if not so young, felt that way. He might intimidate them in their tardy expansions. Thus nobody expected him that night. Nor did I. In fact, I agreed with the lady of the house that her exception in his favor would not overcome his inhibitions. It surprised me when he asked me, in complete secrecy, to find someone among my theatrical acquaintances who would lend him a costume that would completely hide his identity. Since no one suspected him of trying to trick our hosts because of his supposed seriousness and disdain for that kind of joke, he felt that his party costume would prove the more indecipherable. And so it did.

My little sister decided to dress up in old family brocade as a young lady of the Second French Empire, much in the style of the Spaniard Eugenia de Montijo. Of course, it also surprised my family when my Friend came to our home to get dressed as a cardinal in the clothing and beard of Niño de Guevara, lent by Don Fernando Díaz de Mendoza. Díaz de Mendoza was both starring in this role and directing Ardavín's *Lady with an Ermine* with Doña María Guerrero at the Princess Theater. My elder sister, not interested in parties or amusements at that point because of our mourning, decided at the last minute to join us, also in costume, and she brought along a friend whom the Barojas hardly knew. This friend, also wearing ecclesiastical dress, came as the cardinal's attendant, and, carrying his train, presented a graceful contrast of stature. I dressed up in a very different way from what I had planned, and, with my brother having hideously disfigured his face, we added up to a very disparate troop accompanying the Cardinal with the Second Empire Lady on his arm. Nobody knew us when we entered, and they absolutely could not guess my Friend's identity until he chose to reveal himself well into the evening.

The lady of the house understood better than I—no doubt through woman's intuition—my Friend's secret, his intention on that unusual occasion. Mrs. Baroja rightly guessed the underlying purpose behind the bold cardinal's costume at her ball. In that disguise as a gentleman-escort my Friend found a device to overcome the timid resistance of my youthful sister. Thus he called her to a shining destiny.

21

Word and Deed

"I'm going to write a play!" he said to me suddenly one day while we wandered through Madrid's streets. I read into those exuberant words a kind of challenge to my own avocation, my squandered enthusiasm for the theater that had not yet resulted in any actual creative work. No doubt, in springing his idea on me as a sudden inspiration, he was really making a commitment to himself. His words revealed a deeper impulse that he had merely pondered up to then. No sooner said than done; working steadily, he finished his project bit by bit.

He assured me that his intention had preceded any concrete ideas about the work, even its plot. He had, as you might say, imposed a sort of academic task on himself to try something he had never done. Since he had a novel, *The Friar's Garden,* and "essays in the literary style of our time," *Words and Sketches* and "The Life of Don Juan Valera," now he wanted to write a play. Even in the confidence of our unreserved friendship, he would not proudly declare his intention of turning out a masterpiece each time and in a different literary genre.

Rereading the works of Galdós for a study he wrote later, but for which he had already taken many notes, my Friend found that author somewhat careless and disorderly as a novelist because of his discursiveness. On the other hand, he rated Galdós higher as a dramatist than earlier critics who tended to emphasize details of production rather than the plays themselves. As a rule my Friend preferred to base his judgments on a longer perspective, on a play's intrinsic merit, rather than on popular reaction to its performance. It goes without saying that he did not intend to imitate the Galdosian theater. Nourished by deep reading, he always took the greatest classics as his models. I do not mean that he indulged in pseudoclassical language; indeed he sometimes laughingly parodied the "pure" style of some modern writers, "a stile whycche was ne'er spoke in Castylle."

"I have started my first scene," he said, "not knowing what will happen to my characters. I don't know whether that is the way to do it. I have imagined a scene and a critical situation for the protagonists. From that I will develop whatever action fate imposes, taking each step in logical progression."

The fledgling Dramatist narrated to me the beginning of his first act. A woman dressed as a man and her traveling companion, passing through rugged mountain country, come to a dying campfire with some supposed shepherds sleeping around it. Immediately I noticed and commented on his intentional suggestion of Rosaura's entrance in Calderón's *Life is a Dream*. Nevertheless, this influence did not diminish his own achievement. After seeing *The Crown,* my Friend's play, staged, a mutual friend, Álvarez Pastor the philosopher, pointed out Schiller's influence. The Dramatist himself took pleasure in calling attention to Musset's influence in an episodic scene in the third act. These influences merely affirmed the Playwright's own personality; he approached the theater with a mind steeped in the best dramatic literature of modern times. He had never really acquired a taste for Greek drama, which he could read only in translation.

For the reader and theatergoer, as for the Author, the story, developed through dialogue, comes wonderfully to life as it follows through from the event which begins his play. I do not remember in *La Celestina*'s magnificence, in the most illustrious flights of Lope, Tirso, and Calderón, not even in Shakespeare's sublimation of the natural passions of men and women, a scene which so perfectly presents loving ardor as the beginning of *The Crown*. An astonishing scene, its dialogue suggests not merely the feeling but the very action of the ineffable pleasure of two personalities interacting. His travelers fall to the ground with a mound for their pillow, finally united in an embrace, lulled by night murmurs that appear from the dialogue more than from stage devices. The public finds itself transported by poetry, the most authentic representation of passion in my memory of the theater. A cock's crow finally interrupts them, then the sinister cawing of a crow, then soldiers burst in—the false shepherds. They reveal the fugitive young man as the royal princess of Lys.

When he summarized the plot prior to reading me his second act, I commented that it somewhat resembled Sardou's *La Tosca*. The Dramatist did not take this as a joke, but I didn't intend to degrade his play to the level of a well-crafted melodrama. Incidents in Sardou's play seem trivial and adventitious; here, as in the best tragicomic tradition of Shakespeare and *La Celestina,* each incident develops the emotions and the inevitable logic of each scene.

Like all really dramatic work, *The Crown* stands on its own and needs no analysis. Its actions do not connote some abstruse meaning. Its French translators wanted to call their still unpublished version "Word and Deed,"—merely, I think, because of another play called "The Crown" already registered. My Friend protested angrily against what he considered their unnecessary redundancy and mistaken understanding of the dramatic confrontation. He had no intention of posing a political or moral thesis. He had undertaken to write a play about love; that sufficed.

He was, in fact, expressing a state of mind comparable to the greatest emanations that have ever inspired poetic creativity. My absolute proof lies in his simple dedication of the printed version of *The Crown:* "D. R. Ch." My Friend had fallen in love, though neither so late nor so resignedly as the famous subject of his biography. Don Juan Valera, old and blind, had kissed unseeing the braids of a young woman who killed herself for his sake not many years later. I did not even suspect it. I believed him safe at his age from the disillusionment that must follow unrequited love late in life or a marriage of convenience.

One fine day he surprised me, then, with the least likely confidence I could have expected from him, given the skepticism with which he protected himself from the pitfalls of chance and self-deception. He asked me quite casually and in the street, just as he had told me that he intended to write a play, what I thought about the possibility of his marrying. I could tell that he was not joking in spite of the smile that covered the seriousness of his feelings. I answered in my usual way, asking whether the object of his affection might be an attractive, well-provided widow, recommended to him by that mother of good-looking girls, among them his very youthful sweetheart. This really amused him; my mistake once again revealed my unawareness of what went on around me, something he frequently talked about in affectionate reproach of my bewilderment. It knocked me for a loop, as they say, when he finally told me that he wanted to make my youngest sister his wife. Thirteen years younger than I, and twenty-four years younger than he, if no longer the girl we always considered her, she seemed in no way the kind of woman who might suit him. His suddenness in confiding this to me, involving me in his decision, somehow balanced his years of deliberation during his contact with my family that had contributed so much to our friendship.

I could hardly refrain from telling him my real thoughts, but did not. I had never dared to hope for something so well-suited to our friendship, that he, free to direct his life in so many ways, would make such a decision, overwhelming both prudence and experience. Now I had to disillusion him, put him on guard against an anticipated and almost certain refusal from the interested party. I hastened to exaggerate the disadvantages he might incur, the need to control one's whims, the incongruities involved. I meant incongruities in the exact sense of that word, the disparity of their ages, tastes, inclinations. There were also differences of temperament and character because my sister, like many pampered young ladies, had been coddled by her parents. She looked very much like my mother, whose exquisite sensibility had aroused a kind of filial affection in my Friend. This, however, pertained to my mother; to persist on that basis alone might represent what, in another order of things, and slightly modifying a metaphor, is the common veneration of a saint for the sake of her statue.

He continued to smile at my comparison and my earnest insistence on showing him the difficulties of his plan. My deprecating my sister's merits, including her obvious physical attractiveness that had played a very im-

portant part in catching his attention, I hoped to temper his unhappiness in
the certain disappointment of his hopes. Quite obviously "the little one," as
my father still liked to call her, felt secure in her other suitors, young men,
after all, and more suitable to her in tastes and years. In fact, speaking quite
sincerely, I considered my Friend a truly superior man. In spite of her
intuition and native intelligence, and though she now better understood my
Friend's nature, it did not seem that she would really appreciate him. Of
course, as a conscientious lover, he pointed out qualities in the young woman
that we, her family, may not have fully appreciated. Perhaps because she
had retained her charming innocence, we still treated her too much as the
girl we remembered. He saw her as a living statue whom he would shape
by the power of his love.

My mother and I discussed the situation confidentially. We had not wanted
to speak of it, but had no choice. As I expected, she shared my concern,
and not merely because she felt, as I did, that Lola would respond to my
Friend's unmistakable ardor with a crushing refusal. (Indeed, my sister
seemed to be trying to avoid his increasingly frequent visits.) My mother's
concern also came from the profound effect this refusal would have on our
whole family. My parents thought of him as one of us, and that made things
more delicate as they had no objections to the marriage apart from the great
age difference between Fiancé and fiancée.

Thus the Author of *The Crown* wrote into his drama an autobiographical
sketch far more valid than that which some critics had perceived in *The
Friars' Garden*. If the supposed portrayal of his own youth in the protagonist
of the Escorial novel does actually include certain things from his boyhood,
it does not really portray his state of mind. Even if he had used past feelings
for autobiographical purposes, they could only have appeared as translated
by memory after a long interval and always as shaped by his present
thoughts as he wrote down those feelings after so many years. On the other
hand, though *The Crown*'s plot has nothing to do with events in its Author's
life, each and every one of the characters represented his present mood.
Especially with the two initial protagonists, the Poet's own loving disposition
guided his pen, consciously or unconsciously. He fulfilled the inescapable
duty of any creator in giving life to each of his fictional characters by lending
them the actual voice of his own thoughts.

My Friend first met Margarita Xirgu at the Fontalba Theater in the autumn
of 1928 when García Lorca asked us to hear a reading of *Mariana Pineda*,
then about to be staged. Margarita, to whose dressing room I later took him
once or twice, called him "the Republican Gentleman" in admiration of his
natural eloquence. Her epithet foreshadowed the more suitable "Man of the
Republic" bestowed by popular favor some years later. I gave her the completed manuscript of *The Crown* to read, and she praised its merits as particularly suited to a serious reader. Nevertheless, unworthily of her
exceptional talent, she reacted in a way typical of that era. She found the

play too long and too slow-paced for success with the audiences of our theaters. In spite of that, following my suggestions, my Friend agreed to shorten his play by cutting parts not essential to its dramatic development. He found this difficult because his work had no wastage. Even the modified version did not interest the actress. It also failed to interest Irene López Heredia, who the next year entrusted me with the stage direction of her company in a tour of Argentina.

Published as a book, *The Crown* had signal success. In the major journals theater critics gave it unusual attention for a play that remained unproduced. Enrique Díez-Canedo, Melchor Fernández Almagro, and Luis Calvo all gave it excellent notices. The latter deserted *ABC* later, after the proclamation of the republic, and he remained a friend of its Minister of War. Then, when the real testing came, he deserted us.

1929–30

22

The Pact of San Sebastián

Of all our friends only Mrs. Baroja had perceived both the Cardinal's interest in the Second Empire Lady and her reciprocation, something far from obvious to our family. Though not famous for her discretion, this time the gracious Maecenas of "The White Raven" kept her secret. Only the Interested Party knew of her reliable woman's intuition about the certain success of his secret hopes.

With the pretext of fulfilling his social obligations to Mrs. Baroja and the women of my family, my Friend invited her and my mother and sisters, with no other men, to one of the tearooms then fashionable in Madrid. The pleasure with which the ladies of my household responded to this invitation and the host's obvious happiness, amused at seeing my confusion about it, made me realize our misinterpretation of my sister's shy retreats. What we had taken as repudiation of my Friend meant no more than the innocent timidity of a girl in love. No doubt my Friend's first advance did not dispose her to his society, in spite of his honorable behavior. At first sight his imperturbable masculinity hid his affectionate character and that tenderness which, once discovered, overcame all resistance, whether in a young woman or in a multitude. There, precisely, lay the secret of his ability to charm on any occasion; after the judicious man's clever discourse there followed a flow of human feeling, whether political or amatory.

A few months after the formal engagement they were married in that same Church of Saint Jerome where Alfonso XIII got married. If the occasion lacked the full pomp of a royal wedding, it still involved all the trappings of "good society" at which we had scoffed when they concerned others. In the past when he had asserted his confirmed bachelorhood, I used to tease him, little guessing the truth of my prediction, that he would tie the knot to the tune of Mendelssohn's Wedding March. It turned out that way as a tribute to his fiancée's ingenuous wish to shine in a dress of white tulle, and the Fiancé's willingness to go along with anything that did not conflict with the limitations imposed by his own strict conscience. The unrestrained happiness of my mother and, if possible, even more of my father, replaced their first uncertainty and concern about the age difference. In any case, the now resplendent wife would never have made the decision if her parents, or her brother, or sister had raised objections.

They married in February of 1929 and went to Paris, which my sister enjoyed with an enthusiasm similar to mine years before with that same guide. During their honeymoon I too got married, deciding a fate years in negotiation through the window of my Friend's apartment on the calle de Hermosilla, which opened onto the garden of my Juliet; we used no ladders. Shortly after they returned to Madrid, my wife and I left for Buenos Aires; now for the first time I was directing a theatrical company. We returned at the end of December with our first son, born in Buenos Aires two months before. It saddened us not to have been present at the deathbeds of my mother and of my wife's father, Enrique de Mesa, the poet and a good friend of myself and my new Brother.

During 1930 I pursued my theatrical labors in the provinces, returning to Madrid well into the spring. My Brother-in-Law attended to his duties in the Registry Office and to his political activities in shaping a conspiracy against the monarchy. The fall of Dictator Primo de Rivera and his subsequent death in Paris in February had encouraged them. In Barcelona that June, in connection with my direction of the company of a young actress, Isabel Barrón, I renewed my friendship with Margarita Xirgu. From that came my contract to serve as director of her company at the Español in Madrid that fall. In the interim, we spent our summer at the ancient Carthusian monastery of El Paular in the Guadarrama Range, and my sister and her Husband spent theirs in Fuenterrabía. They went there in connection with a famous meeting in San Sebastián of representatives from Republican and Socialist parties, later identified with the Pact of San Sebastián, the immediate origin of Spain's Second Republic.

At that time he told me few details of what they had done at San Sebastián. It sufficed for me to understand, as everyone did later, that, against my Brother-in-Law's prudent judgment, they had, in fact, taken a decisive preparatory step toward establishing the republic. They had succeeded, in the first place, in gaining the adherence of Catalonian republicans. My Brother-in-Law, as an intellectual and Secretary of the Ateneo, had already made essential contacts in Barcelona a little earlier. In toasts given at a banquet there, his personality emerged as exceptionally honest and perceptive, though the *Revista de Occidente* correspondent and "Olympus" of the *Sol* editorial staff gave greater prominence to others. My Friend's political vision appeared especially in what he said about possibilities for reconciling Catalonia's aspirations for autonomy within the framework of a new Spanish state. So far they weren't considering Basque nationalism. On the other hand, though a representative from the Socialist party had attended that San Sebastián meeting, the General Confederation of Labor (UGT) had not sent a delegate. Strictly speaking, the party represented the union, but its numerous affiliates retained independence to the point where they almost seemed syndicalist. They did not have to subscribe to an agreement for revolution merely because the party did or because the party had sent a representative to that meeting. Finally, at San Sebastián the new political force of the Action had consolidated its alliance with the old and numerous committees identifying with Lerroux.

No real pact emerged from that meeting; later events greatly magnified the occasion's importance. Ultimately more important, however, was that it did demonstrate the willingness of those in attendance to fulfill the Spanish people's desire, until then unsubstantial, to regenerate our nation's government by taking it into their own hands. The flower of our middle class now rallied to the cause of democracy in Spain.

Don Niceto Alcalá Zamora emerged in those San Sebastián talks as the potential president. A turncoat Alfonsine Liberal, he had a real appreciation of the dangers of military caciquism from his previous service as minister of war, and he had the backing of a hegemony of conservatives. Miguel Maura strongly supported him—a man who owed his influence among the republicans to his father, Don Antonio Maura. Until a few years before Don Antonio had bridged the gap in the bitter division between Right and Left, a division that broke out again in civil war seven years later, the cruelest of the many wars over generations and centuries in which Spaniard has killed Spaniard.

At San Sebastián my Brother-in-Law formed his first impressions of several persons whom he had known only slightly or not at all. Circumstances and events in the following years did not much alter these impressions. From that time dated his liking for Miguel Maura, though they differed on many issues. My Brother-in-Law never hid his friendly feeling in spite of some annoying incidents provoked by his colleague's intemperance. Here, too, lay the roots of his political friendship with Indalecio Prieto, which became both personal and sincere on the part of my Brother-in-Law. Later he suffered considerable disillusionment in this friendship when he found himself defeated and with very few friends beyond his wife and family and my own family. He died without knowing the full measure of Prieto's perfidy.

My new Kinsman and his wife returned from San Sebastián at the beginning of Madrid's golden autumn. He said little about what had happened. Apparently nothing had modified his own skepticism, though some reformers had already begun to assign the meeting considerable premature fame. I often played devil's advocate with my Friend, giving full reign to my propensity for optimism in the face of what most people call the reality of things. I pointed out that at least circumstances seemed developing for him to address a larger audience than "his" public at the Ateneo. These opportunities were about to expand as never before.

23

The Four Horsemen of the Apocalypse

Preparations began in mid-September for a republican rally in Madrid's bullring, a public demonstration supporting the pact agreed to in San Sebastián by the coalition of representatives of antidynastic parties. When the great day arrived, less well-known orators representing various parties and factions alternated at the rostrum with Alcalá Zamora and Lerroux.

Cárceles, very old, the famous Cantonalist from Cartagena, spoke for survivors of the 1873 republic and Federalists. At that point a mere relic of the past, he seemed an enigma to most persons attending that rally. Those who did know what he stood for, and some who shared the platform with him like my new Brother, dismissed concerns about the antipathy Cárceles's presence might bring them from persons who blamed federalism for the First Republic's collapse. Though little or no support remained now for federalism in the historical tradition, the explicit acceptance of Catalonian nationalism at San Sebastián implied similar promises later to Basques and Galicians. That would cause great concern to persons ill-disposed to giving up our highly centralized government.

The Secretary's faithful friends, and I first among them, believed that the republic could have no better spokesman than himself. After an interval, my Brother-in-Law had again become Secretary of the Ateneo. Yet none of us, however much we might have wished it, guessed that his speech that day would prove the main event of this first rally. From then on people called him "the revelation of the republic," something that became even clearer a year later. Martí Jara, his most determined backer, did not live to enjoy this clamorous success. A sudden illness snatched Martí away from the few incredulous friends sweltering with him in Madrid's summer while delegates met in San Sebastián. The Secretary's triumph brought us joy in spite of that loss, and no one rejoiced as I did. All at once he revealed himself; the larger public found in him their perfect spokesman.

At first his voice seemed somewhat inadequate for the sharpness of his thought, the seriousness of his bearing, and the impressiveness of his figure. Later it gained volume, became fuller as his reasoning deepened; sometimes it went high with irony, other times it deepened with the severity of admonition. The words of that man ended once and for all the years—even centuries—of historical hopelessness that had weighed on Spain's people. With irrefutable logic, in which contempt for all chicanery furnished the best justification for his audience's enthusiasm, he fed the faith of a multitude prepared for serious action.

"But who is that man?" a surprised murmur passed from person to person during his speech. Even before the final applause and acclamation, there came an enormous outburst when the newly discovered Orator with one phrase finished off the vacillating Bourbon monarchy's prestige, signaling the end of its long domination in Spain.

For some months a few prominent politicians had worked to restore public freedom within the context of the constitution, dismantling Primo de Rivera's regime. In fact, General Berenguer, the premier, had no mission beyond a gradual restoration of the government that had existed before Primo's coup as defined by the constitution. Some old Liberal leaders stood as direct heirs of the political system established by Cánovas and Sagasta—some of them had close personal ties with the latter. They, too, were struggling to restore the precarious constitutional balance that Primo had upset with royal acquiescence. Actual membership of this so-called Constitutionalist faction hardly extended beyond its visible leaders. Melquíades Álvarez, first among them, had offered no resistance to Primo's attack on his position as president of the Congress of Deputies. At his side stood other former presidents of the Congress: Villanueva, an old Sagastan Liberal; Santiago Alba; and Burgos Mazo, another discredited cacique.

The Orator, saint and symbol of the republic, destroyed this team with one phrase soon after he came to the rostrum. "Caricatures of the Four Horsemen of the Apocalypse" he called them sarcastically, slightly raising his eyebrows, somewhat in the manner of the dead Canalejas. That whole plaza shook with a unanimous outburst of laughter. He fully deserved it; he had provided a suitable epitaph for the pseudo-liberal policy that the hapless regime had followed for a quarter of a century.

Still, he had also that day to affirm republican indivisibility against any effort to sustain the tottering throne. Compromise with our king had become impossible; the hour had passed for accepting constitutional revision under the king's old collaborators or the Reformists. Only the republic remained as a means to achieve Spain's inevitable social revolution. Thirteen years after its 1917 prorogation, the time had come to reconvene the Assembly of Parliamentarians. Nine years after our military disaster at Anual in the land of the Riff, seven years after the establishment of the army dictatorship, realization had dawned on public consciousness, as it never had on Cortes members, that the king, as principal instigator of our Moroccan campaign, bore a major responsibility for that irremediable national catastrophe. All signs pointed to fundamental change in the regime governing our country.

Nevertheless, things remained far from ready. Like all republicans, I felt a revitalizing enthusiasm, a renewal of that ingenuous faith which moves mountains. My Brother-in-Law, on the other hand, realized that we had more to do than skin the tail. The Socialists were bargaining hard for their adherence to a cause that absolutely depended on them for success. The undisputed Leader of Republican Action shared with me concerns that caused him to insist within the so-called "Revolutionary Committee" on their need for support from the General Confederation of Labor. He believed that clearly bourgeois republicans and organized workers would have to work together to achieve a program of fundamental social readjustment and radical agrarian reform. He feared with good reason that leaders of the workers, completely untutored about our current political scene, would remain locked into a policy of enforced party discipline and refuse to commit themselves to any real compromise with bourgeois capitalists. After all, the Socialist party could gain certain strictly political concessions without even committing the mass of UGT members to the republican cause. Yet the republic needed support from those union members even more than it needed the more or less implicit support of party leaders.

Largo Caballero, the UGT secretary, and Julián Besteiro, a long-standing republican and for many years a Socialist, did not seem very ready to support the Pact of San Sebastián as a means of achieving political revolution in their followers' interest. They had, on the other hand, eagerly and shamefully collaborated with the dictator. Largo had gone so far as to accept a seat in Primo's Council of State. I defended this service in Primo's government, reminding my Brother-in-Law of his own earlier criticism of his former leader, his blaming Melquíades Álvarez for rejecting political opportunism. My Kinsman had no trouble pointing out the difference of that situation. Even with the pretext of placing an agent in the enemy camp, one could not accept a post in a regime that denied a citizen's basic rights and freedom.

The Secretary of the Ateneo continued, of course, as a member of the Revolutionary Committee. Under the unquestioned presidency of Don Niceto Alcalá Zamora, they went on discussing conditions for the development of the Pact of the Republic. Though false reports circulated from time to time and stirred up interest in their meetings, not much actual information leaked out despite the natural curiosity of Ateneo members and the propensity of Madrid's citizens to spread rumors. My Brother-in-Law, committed to silence, did as much as he could to prevent public discussion of the committee's activities. The police kept track of the comings and goings of its members with obvious surveillance. Still, he could not believe that all these meetings and discussions would actually result in Alfonso XIII's dethronement and the establishment of a republic.

Republicans now sought both to strengthen their political alliance and to clarify it. Indeed, they considered this absolutely necessary for the anticipated change of men, methods, and principles in our nation's political life, which promised to be violent. A republic that would shape this monumental revolution—and the change could mean nothing else—had to fix clear points of agreement among its diverse parties. They could not leave the essential bases of our new republic to the chances of competition between rivals.

They agreed, then, that the Provisional Government would immediately establish by decree fundamental laws concerning individual rights which a Constitutional Cortes, subsequently elected by our people, would confirm. The relevant reforms were: separation of church and state; submission of the army to norms of rigorous discipline and absolute obedience to civil authority, its functions strictly limited to military affairs; agrarian reform; and reform of education on all levels. Finally, they would issue a Statute of Labor that clearly stated minimal concessions to the working class as a basis for later social legislation toward building the economic position of Spanish workers to a level on a par with that of the rest of Europe and the wider world.

Regional autonomy posed a harder problem. My Brother-in-Law, a strong supporter of Catalonian autonomy, did not consider it useful to make the same concessions to every Spanish region, except in principle and according to the special circumstances of each case. He saw no possibility of including even Catalonian autonomy in preconstitutional laws as an inevitable part of the republican system. After a republican Cortes had been elected and the time had come to discuss the law on autonomy, then the Provisional Government could present to the Cortes the compromise they had reached; delegates could consider it or modify it for other regions. For now, the presence of Nicolau d'Olwer, a Catalan, in the Revolutionary Committee spoke louder than could any premature decree on this issue.

The presence in the committee of Indalecio Prieto, a Basque, representing the Socialists along with Fernando de los Ríos, involved the economic question with the problem of whether to extend the same or similar administrative and political freedom to Basques as to Catalans. Prieto opposed it absolutely, and the Secretary of the Ateneo shared his opinion. The Basque people did not have so strong a claim as Catalans, in spite of apparent similarity. My Brother-in-Law indicated the difference quite clearly. Catalans thought of their independence in the context of the Spanish republic's inherent goals, while those persons who supported Basque liberation stood fundamentally opposed to republican aims. Thus the two movements for autonomy contrasted. To put it simply, Catalonian nationalists were leftists whereas Basque nationalists were reactionaries. In the Basque provinces Socialists and republicans remained declared opponents of autonomy.

Objection to Alfonsine favoritism had brought some military men into the Committee and made them strong partisans of the republic. From that time dated my Brother-in-Law's low opinion of Major Ramón Franco. This man's transatlantic flight had brought him exaggerated and pernicious fame, and his extremely ambitious family had fully exploited it. At this point I had not heard much from the Secretary about Captain Galán.

In the end, thanks largely to Prieto's efforts, the Socialists, with UGT support, did agree to a revolutionary action to establish a republican provisional government. Unfortunately, the anarcho-syndicalist National Confederation of Labor (*Confederación Nacional del Trabajo* or CNT) did not support the general strike that was to begin the revolution so clearly or so unanimously as the UGT. Further difficulty arose in the discussion of the simultaneous rising of military insurrectionists against the government, scheduled at dawn for the sake of surprise. It seems that a young army man present that afternoon in the Ateneo, impetuous and spirited judging from his words, said that they must not merely arrest General Berenguer and his ministers but assassinate them in their homes, beginning with the premier. The future Minister of War laughed when he told me some time later of Don Niceto's horrified reaction. My Brother-in-Law had pretended to go along with that idea. He had asked the young officer whether he himself would assume a leading role in so important a mission; in particular, which minister would he eliminate? The young man had answered, "Officers don't do this kind of work." Nobody had said anything more about it.

Lerroux did not hide his unhappiness about his designation as minister of foreign affairs in the Provisional Government; he would have preferred the Ministry of the Interior or the Ministry of the Treasury with richer fields to harvest. One November day, Lerroux surprised the Committee by saying that Monsignor Tedeschini had called on him, revealing that, through his Spanish and foreign informants, he knew more about the conspiracy than Spain's government did. Apparently the papal legate knew everything. He had asked the future minister quite plainly whether the republic, if established, would spare the Church official persecution. Lerroux, instigator of convent burning in Barcelona in 1909, communicated to the Committee his response to the nuncio. Speaking officially, if somewhat prematurely, as minister in charge of diplomacy, he had said that, in conformity with a clear agreement on this primordial issue, he could assure His Holiness's representative that the future Provisional Government of the Republic had no significant plans along these lines other than to proclaim ipso facto separation of the Church from the republican state.

All signs pointed, then, to a general conviction about a relatively easy change of regime, without much resistance from those who wrongfully held power at that point. Still, the Revolutionary Committee prepared for an interim period of dictatorship for at least six months after the republic's establishment by a military rising in Madrid and other principal garrisons with all-out support from a general strike. This would ensure orderly functioning of government agencies and allow time to arrange general elections for a constituent Cortes.

Late one afternoon, early in December, as we walked toward our neighborhood, my Brother-in-Law said to me, unexpectedly, but smiling happily—unlike his usual apprehension when he faced uncertainty, "Who knows what the calle de Alcalá will witness during this coming week!" Responding to my surprise and curiosity, he told me, pushing his hands deep in his overcoat pockets and raising that head which rested so solidly on his shoulders. "Yes, this coming Friday. I don't know, I don't know. . . ."

He would go no further with me than that, but I yielded to the wildest imaginings. Still, I could not quite believe in his elevation to power just like that, so soon. Certainly the Four Horsemen parodied in the Newcomer's speech in the bullring would have prepared themselves against a collapse of their world in such an apocalyptic way.

24

We Meet at the Calderón

On December 12 my wife and I had an invitation to dinner at the home of the First Secretary of the United States Embassy. I had already dressed when a telephone call came from my Brother-in-Law asking me to stop at the Ateneo before dinner without fail. He urgently needed to talk with me.

My wife waited in our taxi at the Ateneo doorway. I went right to the Secretary's office. He astounded me with news that he had just learned and that the government had not yet released. Captain Galán, pledged to the anticipated rising—which the Committee had now agreed to postpone—had revolted that morning with the Jaca garrison and had failed completely. My Kinsman would not even let me question the possible inaccuracy of his information. Years passed before we learned that Galán had not received notice of the postponement, but we never understood why. Now, with all possible speed, the Committee had to mitigate any immediate consequences of their revolt's inevitable failure. They had scheduled it for a few days later, and confusion resulting from the premature rising meant further postponement. More immediately, the authorities planned to arrest everyone involved. Certainly they would arrest the movement's leaders; the police already had them under surveillance, and they would end up in jail unless they managed to escape. He had bought tickets for a performance of a Russian opera company that evening at the Calderón Theater.

He planned to attend the opera but not to go back to his home afterwards. He wanted me to go to the theater in time to pick up my sister after the performance while he tried to slip away. He also thought that she would be less upset if they attended the opera as planned. Besides, the police planned to make their arrests early the following morning, when they could expect to find everyone at home, not before. For that reason it would help to behave normally; government agents who always carefully followed him would not suspect his early warning.

I had not visited the United States Secretary's home. His rich and rather eccentric wife had arranged through mutual friends for my wife to give her Spanish language lessons. Furthermore she wanted help in writing a history of Spain, or, more exactly, she apparently wanted to put her name to a book written by my wife. She and her husband seemed interested in meeting me, but I had avoided this encounter two or three times because I had little practice in speaking English and little interest in the couple themselves, judging from what my wife had said about them.

We sat down to dinner late, as the butler kept having to reset the table to remove the places set for frightened guests who called up to cancel out at the last minute. They had heard that a dangerous night lay ahead and that they should take all precautions and keep off the streets. Our host got up two or three times during that meal to receive calls from his informants. As that evening progressed other calls confirmed the failure of the Jaca military insurrection, and we all agreed that it could have no importance since official notices kept saying so. (I found myself obliged to go along with the company to hide my pained reaction.) Our hostess, especially, insisted on the impossibility of any government in Spain not based on Alfonso XIII's monarchy.

My thoughts strayed from the conversation. I had to get to the theater in time to escort my sister. We stayed only a little while after dinner, made our excuses, and—with some difficulty—finally did escape. I dropped my wife at home and went on in the same taxi to the Calderón. We had an old joke at the Ateneo about a saying attributed to the coxcomb Maestro Benedito on the occasion of his first appearance there as a conductor. His musicians paid no attention to him, and consequently, as legend had it, they all played together only after the *calderón,* the sign in the musical score indicating a pause. As my taxi raced along the calle de Atocha, a voice in my head kept insisting, repeating Benedito's supposed words, "We will meet at the *calderón.*" It seemed almost mocking; tonight we would, indeed, meet at the Calderón Theater and also during intermission, a pause in the opera's music. It made no sense; but another breakdown of coordination had plunged me into danger, searching for some solution to a predicament in which the Conspirator found himself.

The box office reported, as I anticipated, that they had no seats available. I asked for admission to a box and went down onto the main floor. Signs of extra precautions appeared everywhere because the queen and infantas were present; with a show of casual elegance, they presided over the brilliant assemblage from a proscenium box. I soon discovered my sister and her Husband in the second row. At the intermission he met me in the aisle while she talked about Queen Victoria's beauty with some friends she had encountered. Her husband teased her about her great admiration for the queen. He recalled other nights at the theater when, as on this one, she talked on and on about a necklace of aquamarines which our sovereign liked to display, "the same color as her eyes."

No sooner had he lit his cigar at the stairway leading to the foyer than some friends gathered around him. They overreacted in their surprise at his pretended calmness. Though more patient than supposed, he finally could not abide their onslaught. "What are you doing here?" Don't you know that they have ordered the arrest of leading republicans?" "This seems highly imprudent!" "Don't you see the policemen have their eyes on you constantly?" They repeated rumors running through the theater. A moment earlier in the parquet boxes Dr. Marañón had spoken with the lawyer Leopoldo Matos until recently General Berenguer's cabinet minister. They had assured each other of the madness of Galán's attempted coup, and they had spoken with exaggerated sarcasm about republicans.

Then it occurred to me to ask my Brother-in-Law to come backstage since he needed some excuse to avoid returning to his seat after the intermission. "Slaviansky," I said to him, "asked about you during the last intermission. He wondered whether you would come to see him." He looked at me confused, not seeing my plan. Up to then we hadn't even known the name Slaviansky, the orchestra conductor that evening. "He asked whether you had forgotten our friendship in Paris." Then he understood that I intended an excuse to break away from that persistent group surrounding us. Seeing him ready to come with me immediately, I suggested that he get the overcoat he had left at his seat so that he wouldn't catch cold in backstage drafts. Now, at last, he fully understood my plan, and we went quickly down to the basement location of the artists' dressing rooms. None of the people milling around there would feel surprised to see me looking around for some acquaintance. I pushed him out through a little hidden door used for bringing in materials to build scenery, into a street running down to the Plaza del Progreso. I returned to the auditorium and to his seat next to my sister in time for the dimming of lights and the beginning of the last act.

When the performance ended, solicitous friends behind us offered to escort my sister, letting me know that they had noted her husband's unexpected absence. Otherwise our ruse proved completely successful. The queen and infantas left first, applauded more enthusiastically than usual by the pseudoaristocratic audience of the main floor and boxes. As the audience left the theater we noticed confusion among the police agents because the bird had flown.

At first I did not know where to find him. Afterwards, when he did tell us about it, he left out many details as it remained unwise to identify persons who had helped him in his chancy wanderings from place to place. He spent that first night near his own home, staying with Martín Luis Guzmán on the calle de Velázquez. Guzmán had repeatedly offered this refuge. The next day he suggested sanctuary in Mexico's legation, anticipating the consent of another of our friends, Dr. González Martínez the poet and at that point minister of his country. The Fugitive, however, prudently judged that he should not remain in Guzmán's home and also felt that he should not take advantage of diplomatic friendships. Very opportunely, he moved to the home of another Regina *tertulia* member, because a few hours later police searched the apartment where he had spent that first night.

One afternoon some time later a man turned up at the Regina asking for Álvarez del Vayo who was supposed to inform Largo Caballero about a republican rising scheduled next day, but Álvarez had gone into hiding earlier to avoid arrest. Not much secrecy remained about this rising. Even I knew that Largo and my Brother-in-Law planned to wait at the Florida Hotel for the mutiny in the morning of troops stationed in the Montaña Barracks. They intended to join those soldiers coming along the calle Preciados and go on with them to assault the Ministry of the Interior. Assuming a simultaneous takeover of the post office and telegraph service, the conspirators expected that Berenguer's government would immediately surrender. They believed the government would not expect another attempt so soon because of their untimely recent failure at Jaca. The messenger at the Regina had come from the Florida Hotel's proprietors. Dedicated republicans, they strongly advised abandonment of this whole plan, never quite solid in any case. Police had appeared and made a search of the hotel, which clearly indicated suspicion.

I offered to go at once to inform Largo at his office in the Workers' Club, though somewhat uneasy about the errand as we did not know each other. First I went to tell my Brother-in-Law and found that he had just heard about the search. Then I went on to Largo. He had no alternative plan for a temporary hiding place apart from the Florida, so, as a stopgap, we went on to the Español Theater. Stagehands could not help staring at their secretary of the UGT, whom they recognized immediately. I hid him briefly in my office and then, so that he would not get bored staying alone, at the rear of a box to watch our matinee performance.

We were putting on *Street Scene,* an interesting play from the United States by Elmer Rice. Largo got so caught up in its story that he often afterwards complained to me about my not having left him alone to see how it came out. Act 3 had not yet begun when an urgent call came from Miguel Maura for me to bring Largo to the Ateneo at once. After all those hiding places and evasions, now the Revolutionary Committee held forth with no more precautions than usual. This provided my Brother-in-Law with another instance to point out to me his comrades' inconsistency in anything requiring prudence. He judged Maura completely irresponsible, and the others did not seem much better. On the other hand, their meeting at Ateneo also highlighted the government's inability to take any corrective action apart from a major retaliation in force. The moral position of the authorities of the established order had fallen that low.

On the following morning, Major Ramón Franco, having recently escaped from confinement in the Military Prison, flew over Madrid. He did not bomb the palace, however, which was his assigned part in the Madrid garrison's rising. He limited his contribution to dropping leaflets that instructed people to remain calm and called on the government to surrender. Apart from that, the insurrection just did not take place. With no military initiative, the unions did not declare a general strike, which, from the viewpoint of our general populace, had to constitute the principal instrument of victory.

Largo tried to reassure me about it that day when I came at his request to a clinical laboratory on the calle de Claudio Coello. Its proprietor, a member of the Ateneo and a great friend of Martí Jara and other promoters of Republican Action, had taken him there after the previous afternoon's meeting. In spite of Largo's assurance to me, streetcar service had not stopped at the stroke of twelve noon, and construction workers had not laid down their tools. I could only tell him that, while my Brother-in-Law and Lerroux remained at large, the police had arrested Don Niceto Alcalá Zamora and Miguel Maura that morning. I put him in contact with the son of Ossorio y Gallardo, to whom the conspirators had given some kind of mission and on whom, somehow, fell the blame for the failure of this coup d'état—they never really cleared the matter up. Only my Brother-in-Law and Lerroux, in fact, did not fall into the hands of government police. Largo Caballero surrendered because of some kind of party consideration, and, sooner or later, other members of the Revolutionary Committee who stayed in Madrid followed him into prison.

My Brother-in-Law did not feel that he should remain in the home of another friend who had taken him in. Following Fernando Salvador's suggestion, he moved into a little private hotel in a new suburb on the Hipódromo heights. It was managed by the sister of a professor from the Free Institute of Education, one of my university friends. We laughed afterward at the Fugitive's tale of Christmas Eve spent among its friendly but disparate boarders. The mistress of the house and her brother kept their new guest's identity a secret even from their own mother. Still, introducing him as a professor from the University of Valladolid on vacation led to a ridiculous contretemps when, at Christmas dinner, he found himself face-to-face with an Ateneo member. The latter, quite naturally, had great difficulty in accepting the amazing resemblance of the supposed visitor from Valladolid to the Ateneo's Secretary, in spite of all their assurances. The Fugitive had to spend most of the day in his room, and when his wife paid him a secret visit she found him bored to the point of desperation by his forced isolation after only two days. Thus he offered no objection to a plan for him to hide in our father's home on the calle de Columela, where he could feel quite safe precisely because of its unlikeliness as a refuge.

This offered the best way for the couple to go on living their life together. Though my sister continued her residence in their flat on the calle de Hermosilla, it could not seem strange to anyone that, in her husband's absence, she should spend most of her time in her paternal home. We had one maid, Juana, trained to the hazards of conspiracy by service in Giral's home and discreet to the point of self-incrimination. We had no fears that she or Enriqueta, our cook, would say a word to anyone about the new member of our household. He moved in one night without anyone seeing him, not even the *sereno,* and he remained there for three months, hardly leaving the two rooms my father had left unused in respect for my mother, who had died in one of them. Thus relations and friends who visited my family did not find it at all surprising to see them closed up. Only my little José Ramón, already babbling some words and with whom his uncle carried on long conversations as childishly as the little boy, more than once almost revealed the hiding place. He always made eager signs of wanting to enter the room when he passed its closed door.

The impolitic execution of Galán and García Hernández after the failure of the republican coup provoked the people instead of quieting them. At the Español Theater I was directing Calderón's *The Great Theater of the World* during that Christmas season. The play's religious significance hardly coincided with public feeling at that point, and there regularly occurred an audience reaction far different from the intent of that very Catholic and very monarchist Golden Age playwright. Audiences invariably applauded some irreverent verses spoken by a peasant commenting on the death of his natural lord and sovereign:

> My barn is full
> And with good weather and no king
> Things will get even better.

Though my Brother-in-Law had no intention of leaving Madrid, it occurred to him that he might usefully create an impression that he had fled abroad. Therefore I wrote a letter to Carlos Esplá, who had remained in Paris since he went there as Blasco Ibáñez's secretary, asking him to send a letter to Spain telling of the Secretary of the Ateneo's arrival in that city. We intended this for the censor, who, in fact, reported it to the minister of the interior. General Marzo, who held this post, passed that information on, confidentially, commenting on the Central Police Department's efficient operation. He believed the news confirmed a complete breakdown of the republican conspiracy. Another rumor circulated among our friends and even family members that my Brother-in-Law had really found refuge from Spanish police surveillance in Pau. According to this hearsay a railroad engineer from the North had given him a ride as far as Burgos, and, somehow, he had gotten from there into France.

He felt that, in allowing themselves to be taken, his comrades of the Revolutionary Committee had chosen an easier course than he and Lerroux. The others had followed Don Niceto in letting the police arrest them, or had surrendered like Largo Caballero to show solidarity with the rest. My Kinsman also believed that the movement's organization, damaged by precipitancy, had suffered an incalculable setback.

Bored in his confinement, he turned to writing the novel inspired two years earlier by the ruined monastery of Fresdelval that provided his book's title.

1931

25

The First Chapter

About a month later he wanted to read me what he had written, the first chapter of his novel *Fresdeval*. He had conceived a setting based partly on his earliest childhood memories and partly on a mixture of his grandparents' recollections and of tales he had heard in their home in Alcalá. Seeing my interest, possibly even greater than in other things he had read to me, he explained his overall plan though he had not worked it out entirely. Beginning his story in the mid-nineteenth century, he would use pictorial realism but not necessarily follow strict chronology in his narrative. He would tell the story of at least three generations of a family, centering on the disamortized property of the monastery of Fresdeval from which his novel took its title. He would present these generations alternately, rather than successively, to serve his artistic purposes in leading the reader's curious attention along highways, through trackless wastes, by footpaths and crossroads of feeling to summits of passion and still waters of nostalgia.

As the Author read me his incipient *Fresdeval,* showing unashamed delight in his work, I noticed that his fictional creations had characteristics of actual models. The Narrator's pen depicted a half-familiar personality, landscape, building, or a real event as part of an imaginary episode. Immediately I recognized a close friend, so close that he almost seemed a family member, in the second Budia who appears early in the book. Somewhat later a bandit appears, partly patterned on the actual Batanero. The Bastard of Anguís clearly speaks for the Author, and to a degree he is recognizably autobiographical. The fictional world in which these characters live provides a vivid picture of Spain in the period following our Carlist wars. Among modern novels only the great works of Tolstoy and Dostoyevski provide so broad a panorama.

Thus on the eve of the Revolutionary Committee's taking power, a moment closer than he realized, my Friend was occupied with creative work of an essentially poetic nature. Surely very few of his political coreligionists, even those most enthusiastic about the Orator whom our masses had discovered in that rally in Madrid's bullring, could understand this as preparation for his leading role as Minister of War in the new government. For him as for me, this poetic disposition, this creative tension, constituted the essence of human sensibility. Here lay the source of our efficacious actions; it was the fountainhead of communication with the segment of humanity that shares our language and nationality; through our nation we relate to the wider world.

One day Amós Salvador turned up at my father's home looking for me; someone had told him that he might find me there. He needed to talk with our Friend. I had made a great effort to avoid this kind of questioning and pleaded ignorance of his whereabouts. It took considerable effort for me to persuade Amós because, except for my Brother-in-Law, people did not have much confidence in my discretion. As it turned out, Amós spoke with such pressing urgency about political needs that, hearing him through the office wall, the Man in question could not resist his insistence. Without further ado, he opened a connecting door and presented himself to the astonished eyes of our literary Maecenas. Amós became terribly frightened because of what he judged our highly imprudent confidence in such a hiding place. He did not feel that our Friend should remain there one day more, at the mercy of some involuntary exposure or some unsuspected hidden enemy. Discovery of the Fugitive would endanger everyone.

Amós suggested another arrangement. He had a vacant flat next to his own office, over his family residence on the calle de Tetuán. Assisted by some reliable person, our Friend could move in right away. Well, a vacant flat would require furniture. First the porter and then curious neighbors, including his own family, would wonder about a mysterious occupant and his servants. Their avoidance of all society would increase this curiosity and surely encourage the very suspicions we wanted to avoid. As a compromise, then, my Brother-in-Law went to stay with Sindulfo de la Fuente, a member of the Regina and Henar *tertulias,* and his Polish wife who had lived in Madrid since the 1914 war. They welcomed him, glad to help. Only my sister knew her Husband's new refuge; she could communicate with him by phone or through his protector.

The most faithful of those of us who continued to attend Ricardo Baroja's *tertulia* received special notice that we should not fail to come on a certain Saturday night. When we arrived we found my Brother-in-Law already there, and quite naturally I assumed that this was his hiding place. I did not ask him about it. We conversed cheerfully about minor events; everything seemed to point to imminent republican success. We broke up, as usual, at midnight. When he left with us I realized my mistake about the Fugitive's sanctuary. Sindulfo joined us heading for a streetcar to continue our *tertulia* in a café with others from the daytime Ateneo contingent. The Conspirator, pulling up his coat collar with a deliberate air of mystery, turned in the opposite direction toward the calle de la Princesa. Though naturally intrigued by this, I held back without saying or doing anything.

Later he returned to my father's place, but he yearned for his own apartment. As police interest appeared to have fallen off, there seemed little or nothing to fear. Public opinion favored those involved with the Revolutionary Committee, and the judge at their trial let them off easy. Thus in March my Brother-in-Law did go home to his wife and shut himself up, turning to the pleasurable effort of writing his novel. It distracted him from less substantial activities. At this time my wife gave birth to our second son, Enrique Manuel, for whom my Kinsman served as godfather. His supposed hiding prevented him from appearing at the baptismal font.

One fine day Miguel Maura, whom I had never met, called me up on the telephone. He had to speak with my Friend, as Amós had before, though now I clearly sensed even greater urgency. Elections for municipal councils throughout Spain were scheduled for Sunday, April 12. In the meanwhile the interim government of Admiral Aznar had replaced that of General Berenguer and had pushed ahead the executions of courageous Captain Galán and his unlucky companion García Hernández. Once more, as with Amós, I assured Maura of my ignorance of my Brother-in-Law's whereabouts, and, again, he did not believe me.

Miguel Maura's amiability and attractiveness immediately made a good impression. My Brother-in-Law admired how he had coolly—and gracefully—absolved himself from identification with his father's politics. On the other hand, he distrusted Maura's contagious optimism, which won over more susceptible minds like my own to any risky suggestion. Maura spoke with so much confidence that people believed him without considering the substance of his few arguments. Now, while I tried to explain Miguel's call as exactly as possible, my Kinsman, with his exaggerated caution about tricks of fate, walked back and forth in his office, waving his hands at its nonsense.

"Miguel says that he must see you at once. After elections on the twelfth, the king will leave Spain on Monday, the thirteenth. Consequently your Committee must meet, and you must prepare to act."

"But don't you see?" he answered me, "That's just Miguel All slap-dash. What nonsense! And he believes it! Besides, I'm sure that he has already told everyone all his plans. The king won't simply pull out the day after the elections! Just like that.

"In the first place, by shooting Galán and García Hernández this government of generals and their stupid hangers-on has turned these elections into nothing but a political protest against the monarchy. We will easily win in the big cities, Madrid, Barcelona, Valencia, Seville, and Bilbao, the capitals. But that leaves the towns, and there secretaries in city halls still control everything. In most towns republicans will lose the elections.

"We will find ourselves obliged to attempt an insurrection under difficult conditions, without the advantage of surprise that would have proved our greatest asset in December but for that premature rising in Jaca. Thus any government will have very little difficulty in shutting us down for quite a long time. Because I assure you that the king knows everything, oh yes, and most of the soldiers in his entourage will continue to defend him. Some people expect the populace to assault the Palace, but that will not occur. Even if things did get to that point, it would suffice for the king to use his halbardiers against us, and he can count on more than halbardiers. In short. . . ."

My Brother-in-Law agreed to meet with Maura in my father's home. It seemed safer than his own in view of what he felt certain would occur. Subsequently Maura felt obliged to defend my Kinsman to various persons who blamed him for fleeing to France. Maura announced to them that the Minister of War, residing in Madrid, was preparing for forthcoming developments in accordance with his duty.

After that meeting with Maura my Kinsman told me about it. "He said the same things to me that he did to you and a little bit more that makes him certain of the king's abdication. Never forget that Miguel is a *señorito,* that he thrives on the kind of gossip and rumors that have always shaped our politics in the corridors of Congress, in newspaper editorial offices, around café tables, in palace antechambers. Miguelito knows, or has heard from someone, that the royal family have already packed their baggage for departure into exile. Always romantic adventures. And they come to nothing." I could think of no arguments against my Brother-in-Law's expectation of disappointment, and, in spite of everything, he agreed to go along with the Committee in their preparations. Still, I felt that same pulsation whose expectant rhythm now moved the spirit of all Spaniards. After all, Maura's zeal appealed more to me than the cautious approach of other friends who also identified themselves as partisans of my Kinsman and Republican Action.

On some occasion after the San Sebastián meeting and during a dangerous automobile trip with Maura driving vertiginously, my Brother-in-Law told me another story. As I understood it, the notorious millionaire smuggler Juan March happened to occupy a table in a Madrid restaurant near the table of some prominent Committee members. Maura had a notion to begin a conversation towards gaining March's support for the republican cause. To his credit, Maura also dismissed that notion. From its founding in 1873, the republic, the *Niña,* had preserved an image of a pure young virgin in Spanish territories, and an alliance with that smuggler would have stained it with immorality. After the republic's proclamation in 1931, Fernando de los Ríos, I think, told me about attending a rally in Toledo with Maura just before the elections. He had actually to pull Maura down by the tails of his jacket to prevent him from promising the crowd that Alfonso XIII would depart in two day's time. Caught up by their enthusiasm, Miguel anticipated what the national will would so unmistakably demand. Before those elections, however, de los Ríos had believed, like my Brother-in-Law, that Maura was moving too fast.

26
Tuesday, April 14

Sunday morning, April 12, I left Cádiz by train for Madrid after a brief theatrical tour. All during our trip, as the day and our train progressed, a spectacle of increasing popular enthusiasm made me surer at every stop of republican success in the municipal elections. At each station we passengers on that express train learned of resounding triumphs of leftist candidates everywhere. I arrived in Madrid at dinner time, and, after our meal, went out into the streets. At the Lyon Café opposite the post office on the calle de Alcalá, I joined friends, among them Josefina Carabias, a young journalist and, at that time, an enthusiastic republican. In those days she was fighting her first campaigns in editorial offices and livening up the Ateneo. Her friend Mercedes, also a member of the Ateneo if not of the world of letters, insisted on giving us a ride in her car, which she drove herself. We went to look up my Brother-in-Law and took him rather clandestinely to a Committee meeting at the house of Don Niceto Alcalá Zamora on the calle de Martínez Campos; we promised to pick him up after the meeting. Everything proved a source of enthusiasm for my two charming companions. They felt very proud of their strong role in the vanguard of the Secretary's coterie at the Ateneo.

After we had dropped our Friend at the future president's house—never dreaming how soon he would come to power—we returned to the Lyon to wait until midnight when he had asked us to come back and pick him up after the meeting. Every newcomer brought some report of streets exploding in a joyous confusion of shouting, singing, and banners. García Lorca came in and regaled us with his story, pretending panic. On his way to the café he had joined in a peaceful but enthusiastic demonstration in the Plaza de la Cibeles. Suddenly, he didn't know why, how, or from where, a troop of Civil Guards came riding roughshod toward them, swinging their sabers. In the tumult Federico had fallen to the ground and had just missed getting crushed by horses' hoofs. From this incident a rumor spread that the government intended to declare a state of war. Some persons, taking word for deed, asserted that they had actually read its proclamation.

Later I drove to Alcalá Zamora's doorway with my obliging *chauffeuse* and her charming companion. While we waited there, we exchanged impressions with other bystanders until the meeting broke up. Those ladies dropped us at the corner of Velázquez and Hermosilla to avoid attracting undue attention. The Inhabitant of 24-B believed that our neighborhood *sereno* still did not know of his return home. He let himself in with the bachelor's key that for many years had enabled him to avoid the careful scrutiny of that nocturnal watchman. Now it helped to throw spies off the scent and just to frustrate curious, casual passersby. We went up to my Brother-in-Law's flat and waited with my sister for Martín Luis Guzmán and his wife.

The Conspirator could not tell us much that we did not already know. Things seemed confused; evidence of electoral success remained unclear. As he had easily predicted, data he considered accurate indicated republican triumphs in the capitals and even in the large towns. Apparently, however, most of the rural population had voted with the caciques who usually controlled the Spanish municipalities. Some signs indicated that the government, which had already begun to confront the natural effusions of popular happiness, intended to counter them with force. Not all committee members agreed with him about how to follow through on the election results. His natural brooding and unwillingness to get carried away by superficial first impressions left him doubtful about the probable outcome of these events.

Perhaps the Guzmáns, Mexicans accustomed to dangers, alarms, anxieties, and hopes of revolutions, understood our feelings in these moments better than others did. He had lived as an emigré in Spain for several years, a fugitive from one of those changes that had sometimes purified, sometimes corrupted the course of his country's political history in our century. His wife, sweet-tempered and a very good friend of my sister, felt great sympathy for her. She remembered her own adventure, and it made a great impression on her to see my sister, childishly earnest, so bravely encouraging her husband. Afterward Mrs. Guzmán fainted while traversing the short distance to her own home, no doubt from the strain of controlling her exhausted nerves, stirred up by excitement and unhappy memories. She had hidden her feelings under a show of affability and exquisite manners characteristic of natives of New Spain, as narrated by the first chroniclers and proved by later experience.

The following day at dinnertime my Brother-in-Law heard of a meeting in Dr. Marañón's home between Alcalá Zamora and the count of Romanones, followed by an interview with General Sanjurjo, commander of the Civil Guard. Both sides had agreed on very precise details, and these had spread so widely that you would have thought everyone in Madrid had witnessed the conversations. Each side, however, reported those agreements differently. At least it seemed clear that the president of the Revolutionary Committee absolutely rejected any suggestion that did not include, pure and simple, Alfonso XIII's abdication. Even in December, Don Niceto had refused to come out of prison to head a cabinet including his companions—a solution suggested through the agency of Sánchez Guerra. As a result of his meetings with Sanjurjo, Romanones, a former premier, advised the king that the Civil Guard seemed unwilling to risk the possibly irreversible unpopularity involved in another bloody repression. The king then agreed to a transmission of power that afternoon legalizing a peaceful change of regime.

The next afternoon, Tuesday, our group at the Henar mingled with other *tertulias* in discussing the latest rumors; everybody had his own prediction. Then Martín Luis Guzmán came in and invited us to come out and see for ourselves, if we didn't believe it, our republican flag flying on the Palace of Communications, dominating the Plaza de la Cibeles. Later we hurried to my Brother-in-Law's home to tell him that the committee, already assembled at Miguel Maura's house, awaited him. "Another month of confinement and I would have finished my novel," he said calmly and with honest annoyance. He gathered up some pages of *Fresdeval* from his desk and put them into a folder with the rest of that manuscript.

Guzmán and I roamed through streets filled with the happy republican excitement of Madrid's people. From the balcony of my father's home we had seen a hostile crowd conducting Leopoldo Matos, unharmed, to a police station. Guzmán wanted my sister to share the indescribable spectacle of general enthusiasm spreading from poorer neighborhoods to the city's center, and we took her in a car to witness this spontaneous, unrestricted outpouring of public rejoicing. My Español company had moved to the little Chelito Theater, then named for an old-time music hall singer and later renamed in honor of Muñoz Seca. The last monarchical Madrid city government disapproved of one of our plays, by Benavente, and they would not let us use the Municipal Coliseum during its run. Margarita met me almost at its doorway, as that theater had very crowded facilities, and she made me say for the first time "Long Live the Republic!" Our corps of actors took up my cheer with theatrical enthusiasm.

In the afternoon we sought out Miguel Maura. We found people jamming his house on the calle del Príncipe de Vergara and also its garden and the sidewalk and road in front of it. We inched our way into the hall, now invaded by a multitude, all strangers to the masters of the house. Maura himself was closeted with his colleagues; his wife had taken refuge in some more secluded room with women friends and family members. Through a doorway we saw some food on a dining room table, no doubt intended for committee members. Afterward many of those who had taken over the house descended upon that meal, following the rural custom at family celebrations and funerals.

Through the closed door of a contiguous office we heard talking on the telephone from time to time. Once we recognized Fernando de los Ríos speaking loudly, apparently to the provinces. Then that door opened and my Brother-in-Law appeared. Smiling, he said to those of us crowded around, "Gentlemen, Colonel Maciá has proclaimed the republic in Barcelona with a shout of 'Long Live Spain!'" Bystander enthusiasm increased markedly.

We still waited impatiently for the formal transmission of power that would legitimatize our hopes once and for all. Then a lady, a member of the household whom we had seen repeatedly crossing the hall, apparently worn out by tiresome errands, came out of another room. In a voice charged with emotion she addressed those of us standing there with such high hopes. "They say on the telephone that the government has postponed its surrender until tomorrow, and that tonight they have declared a state of war to maintain order." Amazement quickly turned into disillusioned indignation. Up to then we had believed in a peaceful resolution of the tremendous confrontation posed by republican electoral victories.

Finally, however, the office door opened, and Miguel Maura emerged buttoning up his jacket with characteristic swagger and immediately followed by his colleagues. More quickly than it takes to tell, they got into cars waiting at the doorway, and we slowly followed in their wake along Príncipe de Vergara and Alcalá toward the Puerta del Sol. I don't know how long it took us to cover the distance. I do know that the stentorian, milling throng who filled that broad street literally threw themselves on those first cars when they recognized committee members grouped in twos and threes, frantic in their desire to embrace them with overflowing republican enthusiasm. Night had fallen when we arrived at the Ministry of the Interior long after the committee. We heard a clamorous ovation as the whole Provisional Government appeared on the main balcony, just as they had arranged it months earlier. Those of us who saw it and felt it found the spectacle magnificent. Newspaper photographs miss its feeling of a thunderous, wild sea spreading over that vast space under the light of that spring evening.

After a lot of effort and squeezing, inching ahead through the crowd, and after much pleading and pounding brought someone to open the Pontejos door, my companions and I succeeded in getting into the Ministry. By now Bernardo Giner had joined us, Fernando de los Ríos's brother-in-law and my old friend from Bologna. (Little did I suspect that ten years later I would enter that building, then converted into General Police Headquarters, as a prisoner destined for an underground cell. They had arrested me in France.) We crossed the vestibule and the first courtyard, clogged with, we supposed, recently arrived official cars. Going up a little hidden stairway next to the elevator, we came to the central reception room, and from there we went into an antechamber next to the minister's office. We were looking for the men whom a democratic vote of the electors and Spanish tradition had already made city officials. In fact proclamation by an open town meeting actually created the Spanish republic.

Ministers of the Provisional Government and their president had retreated to an office connecting with that of the minister of the interior; we interlopers took over the minister's office and the rest of his suite. From time to time one or another of them would join us to look out at the scene in the plaza. At first packed, the multitude gradually dispersed, leaving smaller groups and enthusiastic transients, all enthusiastically expressing their happiness. I went home to eat, so that my family would know that the crowd had not crushed me to death, and returned. Looking out from the Ministry's balcony, we now saw a truck full of obviously drunken soldiers drive into the Puerta del Sol singing out their joyful enthusiasm. The new Minister of War gave benevolent and necessary orders to remove from circulation these innocent transgressors of basic army discipline before their carrousing spread to the barracks and required some kind of punishment.

After eleven my Brother-in-Law decided, in agreement with his colleagues, to take actual possession of his Ministry of War. He went there accompanied by Major Saravia and Captain Arturo Menéndez. I, in my turn, resorted to our usual *tertulia* at the Granja el Henar, directly opposite the Palace of Buenavista, site of his Ministry. Our friends greeted me with acclamations and congratulations, embraces and expressions of mutual satisfaction.

We had chatted awhile about the precipitate events of that historic day we had lived so fully when one of our acquaintances came in beaming with the latest news. He told of a quarter-hour confrontation between the Minister of War and the captain general of Madrid, Federico Berenguer. The new Minister had kept Berenguer standing at attention, not putting him at ease. Apparently His Excellency had insisted on establishing himself at once. His very recently appointed assistants and secretaries and some bystanders watched the scene with delight, and other curious spectators joined them, people who had come through the open street door, up the stairs, and into the minister's office without anyone stopping them. Our informant invited us to check it out for ourselves. My more discreet friends and I did not follow that suggestion, judging that my Brother-in-Law would see our appearance an unsuitable interference in an official act that did not pertain to his fellow *tertulia* members.

Afterwards, when I asked him about that report of his taking possession of his Ministry, he verified its general, if not its entire accuracy. He had, in fact, left the offices of the Ministry of the Interior for those of the Ministry of War uncertain of his reception. He took a company of men ready to assume their new positions, though he had no time to have them confirmed. They had not, however, met with resistance. If the army officers who had occupied the Ministry of War up to then felt a certain natural reserve about the newcomers it had not developed into a confrontation. Federico Berenguer himself had readily made the obligatory formal submission to his bureaucratic superior. My Brother-in-Law did not recall his having exceeded the elemental requirements of military discipline, but the situation did not call for excessive courtesy, not to speak of impertinent camaraderie. The Minister, after all, had not removed him as captain general. He had simply ordered him to cancel the proclamation of a state of war issued by a government that no longer had any authority and to assure order and obedience in the barracks toward the newly established authority. Nothing more and nothing less had happened.

The next day, Wednesday, they arrested Dámaso Berenguer, the former premier and Federico's brother, at his home, and he received all kinds of consideration. My Brother-in-Law had known of the Berenguer family and Federico in particular from the time of his assignment as a cavalry officer in Alcalá. His notorious brother Silvestre, nicknamed "the Savage" by fellow officers, had also served there. We knew another brother, a hopeless drunkard, as an assiduous member of a *tertulia* near ours at the Regina. Federico returned to the Ministry afterward to ask a favor at the time of his brother Dámaso's transfer from a military prison in the old and foul convent of San Francisco in Madrid to one in Segovia's alcázar. His family wanted to provide him with an attendant to treat him for some kind of minor illness. At least at that point my Kinsman said that he knew that the Berenguers felt to some extent grateful to him for granting this.

My sister Lola summed up the great day, throwing in our faces jokes her husband and I had made about her ingenuous expectations and opinions. More than once she had spoken of "when the Republic comes," and we had laughed. Her words suggested the simplistic image of a living being personifying the event and coming right down our street. Now she, in her turn, said to us of its birthday, delighting in making her point, "And you said that the republic *would not* come down the street so that I could see it from my balcony! Well, that's just the way it has come!" Then she joined in our laughter, enchanted by her father's satisfaction in seeing fulfilled his predictions about his Son-in-Law whom he so much esteemed. Even I should not have predicted so much so soon. My sister added ironically, "It is just as well that we married two years ago! If we had done it now everyone would have thought that I married you just to become the wife of the Minister of War."

It made her very happy that her Husband decided, for the present, not to move into the Ministry of War but to continue living in their recently redecorated flat where she felt so contended.

27

Maura Prophesies

The Provisional Government of the republic owed its first popular success to reforms decreed by its Minister of War. Through them he proposed a basic reorganization of our national armed forces. Extremists of all kinds might have preferred the army's dismemberment, reactionaries hoping that this would provoke anarchy and demonstrate the inability of the men of the revolution to achieve peaceful change. Instead my Brother-in-Law undertook to create a republican army, a truly national army. Some persons later wrongly blamed him for trying to destroy the army—something he never intended.

Spain's military problems were closely linked to her political and social problems. The officer corps felt loyalty not so much to the principle of monarchy as to the person of Alfonso XIII, corrupter of all things noble in his mistaken efforts to serve his own interests. These men came from a social class educated by monastic orders and attached to an economic order increasingly at odds with the reality of our national life. On the simplest level, the problem of our army in the monarchy's last years came from an overabundance of officers in proportion to its size. Reducing the army budget, bringing it in line with that of the rest of public administration presented, beyond a doubt, a concern of high priority. It sufficed for a while, as the new Minister understood things, to reduce the officer corps to our army's real needs without imposing economic hardship on individual officers who would have to retire. Forced to abandon their careers without compensation, they would certainly have launched a desperate attack on the new regime. He contrived, then—and this constituted the essence of his decree—their voluntary assignment to the reserves on full salary. Savings, if not immediate, would accrue in the long run.

Other resolutions in that famous decree once and for all recognized "the supremacy of civil power," though I often heard him protest against misunderstandings about that phrase. Confusion came mostly because his former chief Melquíades Álvarez had used it so frequently and freely in his musically garrulous speeches. Newspapers had picked it up and turned it into a catch-phrase. The Minister conceived of public authority as something unitary, not divided; still, his decree established the civil power within it. In place of captains general it substituted simple military commanders without administrative authority in their assigned districts apart from their particular sphere. His decree also suppressed a special Supreme Court for the Army and Navy and incorporated the ancient military orders within the regular military law code, taking away their special privileges.

While the military reforms proposed in that first decree represented the Minister of War's own initiative, research, and writing, they were in line with the Provisional Government's broader plans for general administrative reform. Repeatedly I heard him complain later that his colleagues had not adhered so closely as he had to plans made by the Revolutionary Committee to enact by decree, right away, basic reforms they had judged essential for the foundation of our republican regime. On the other hand, the Minister of War's unswerving decisiveness in fulfilling his pledge to himself and to the nation brought him that special eminence which popular opinion grants to its truly elect. From night to morning after publication of his military reform decree, my Brother-in-Law became the Provisional Government's most notable and most noted member, though other members had longer republican pedigrees and names far better known in national politics. This marked him out for enemy attack and hostility. Just as his public personality emerged with our nascent republic, so reactionaries concentrated their opposition against him, sure that in throwing down the regime's incarnation, so to speak, they would destroy the new order before it became established.

As I recall it, on my first visit to the Ministry of Public Instruction after the republic's proclamation, our friend Carmen Monné de Baroja ran into me at the doorway on the calle de Alcalá. Eagerly, without warning, and as if everything depended on my influence she told me that her husband, Ricardo, must become director of fine arts without delay. I tried unsuccessfully to convince her that this could not depend on me or even on my Kinsman, but did, finally, promise to speak in her husband's interest. In fact the Minister of War answered me as I expected. This nomination did not belong to his department, and it did not seem right for him to make the recommendation to his colleague Marcelino Domingo. The diversity of political parties represented in the new government obliged its members to respect strictly each other's ministerial jurisdiction. Contrary to my expectation that the Baroja claim heralded a competition for jobs among prominent women, nobody else approached me at that time to intervene with my Brother-in-Law. Apparently word got around quickly that he opposed the nepotism that had corrupted Spanish politics up to then.

The marquess de la Viesca had taken over the newspaper *El Sol* from the businessman Urgoiti. He entrusted its management to Manuel Aznar, a lawyer and childhood friend of Amós and Miguel Salvador; I had come to know him through them. Soon after Aznar returned from Cuba to edit *El Sol*, he offered me the position as contributor for which I had been negotiating, though without ever actually approaching the Olympian board of control that supervised the paper. As he has since said, Aznar asked me to act as spokesman for the Minister of War and his Republican Action party. He did not want *El Sol* to go so far as to adopt any specific editorial position, as it had in the past in support of government parties. Instead he wanted to establish a position in regard to the republic comparable to that taken by *ABC* in general support of the monarchy's conservative policies.

Though, again, I anticipated my Brother-in-Law's negative reaction, I passed along Aznar's formal proposal to him. The Minister of War did not consider this arrangement suitable. He felt that the *Gaceta* spoke for him, and he did not agree with me and others that he ought to have either an independent daily paper that would present his views or a newspaper directly under his control. He did not believe that the mere fact that he held a powerful official position justified that. He consented to my writing what I liked on my own account and taking my own risks, but, though he did not actually say it, he made it clear that he didn't much like the idea of my identification with *El Sol*. Since I already had the theater as the focus of my activity, he preferred for me not to expose my pen to temptations that would certainly assail me and endanger his tranquility. An occasion did soon come for me to show my independence; I did not try it twice.

Minister of Foreign Affairs Lerroux found no better undersecretary than a certain Agramonte, a career diplomat. I had seen this man in action in Buenos Aires less than two years before as a member of the staff of Ramiro de Maeztu, Dictator Primo's ambassador. At that time Agramonte was promoting the Patriotic Union (*Unión Patriótica* or UP), which he had founded among Spanish immigrants in Argentina. In that party's journal, a periodical with very limited circulation, he had roundly denigrated republican leaders, with special emphasis on the man he did not suspect would soon become his ministerial chief. Agramonte had turned republican a few months later. According to rumor, his conversion came because the king, whom Mrs. Agramonte had served as a manicurist until her recent marriage, had not obtained a promised promotion for him from the minister of foreign affairs. Also about that same time Ortega y Gasset, the philosopher-journalist, had published an article titled *"Delenda est monarchia"* in *El Sol* easily predicting the monarchy's fall after its execution of Galán and García Hernández. Why had Lerroux promoted Agramonte? It seems that Ortega, a fellow student with Agramonte at the Jesuit college of El Palo in Málaga, had recommended him.

Indignant because this promotion would scandalize those who knew Agramonte's past, I lost no time in denouncing him in one of the first opportunities offered by my association with *El Sol*. They published my article in a special section usually reserved for more famous pens than mine. When the Council of Ministers met that same day, Lerroux passed that newspaper to the Minister of War and asked what he thought of my piece. My Brother-in-Law answered that as I was over the age of consent and responsible for what appeared under my own name, he could not answer for me. Further-more, I did not even belong to his party. Inevitably, a little later, pressure from friends more officious than the Minister himself caused me to enroll in Republican Action. This did not, however, signify my dedication of myself to politics as some persons hoped on the basis of my unfailing personal fondness for its Leader.

One morning in May, hearing reports of mysterious fires breaking out here and there in Madrid, I hurried to see the burning Jesuit Residency on the calle de la Flor. A crowd of people stood watching the flaming walls of that unpopular monastery, doing nothing to help put it out. When some youths joined in a circle of dancers to celebrate the occasion, some promi-nent persons joined them, including the comic poet, my eternally youthful friend and landlord Luis de Tapia. I joined him for a moment in that mocking saraband. When I ingenuously bragged about it to my Brother-in-Law a little later, he answered that my dance may well have cost millions to our minister of the treasury, at that point Indalecio Prieto. Not exactly blaming me per-sonally, my Kinsman pointed out that in our celebration during that popular purgation we shared responsibility for the fall of national securities on the stock exchange. Besides that, some kind of deal with the United States had broken down because of concern about the government's ability to maintain order, and our national economy had suffered. Some people said at the time that the Jesuits had burned their own Residency. At least they had ample time to leave without anyone getting hurt, and afterward we learned that they had sold the building to an Englishman a little before the fire.

Certainly my Brother-in-Law did not share the aroused public feeling against the clergy, and especially the regular clergy, above all Jesuits and Jesuitism—to the point of approving of those fires. The fires undoubtedly had a negative effect in stirring up Catholic fanaticism into revolt after its initial appeasement through the unrestricted freedom allowed to the Church following separation of its administration from that of the state. On the other hand, if you challenged my Kinsman with examples of supposed antireli-gious barbarism, he came out on the people's side. In a famous 1834 incident a mob had murdered some monks because of their supposed poisoning of the public water supply. My Brother-in-Law said that he did not believe that the monks had done it, but if the people insisted that they had, then, for him, that became irrefutable truth. He did not say this just in speaking to me or a circle of friends. He repeated it in at least one speech. He refused, however, to accept my conclusion, deduced from that position. In fact, he seemed to find somewhat pretentious and pedantic my comment that friars always poison the springs of knowledge and clear understanding.

The Vatican's diplomatic representative continued to occupy his post in Madrid, with no break in official relations between the Holy See and the Spanish State. In spite of this, Cardinal Segura, archbishop of Toledo, under-took a course of action that Spain's government judged incompatible with his position, and they obliged him to leave the archdiocese and national territory. Miguel Maura, minister of the interior, brought pressure on the Provisional Government's Catholic president to sign a requisite decree, and that gratified my Brother-in-Law. Precisely because of Alcalá Zamora's Catholicism they needed that signature.

Much against his wishes, the Minister of War consented to his colleagues' decision and left control of our armed forces in military hands, following the liberal monarchy's perverse practice. He issued the relevant decree just a few hours after the state of war ended, demonstrating that for awhile they had no fear of a military challenge. From General Cavalcanti downward, the most prominent representatives of those officers who decided to identify with the new regime, instead of protesting against it or retiring on full pay, appeared in his office to express their loyalty.

When Pérez de Ayala came to express his appreciation for nomination as ambassador in London, he told me something for me to pass on. Juan Ignacio Luca de Tena had spoken to him in confidence about an interview with Alfonso XIII in London. The king had advised military officers who consulted him not to retire into the reserves but to remain in charge of their garrisons and commands. Along these same lines, the duke of Alba, a good personal friend of Pérez de Ayala, had offered to sponsor him in the high English society to which he belonged. We also heard from Sindulfo de la Fuente that he had heard from his friend Javier Ortueta, a hunting companion of Alfonso XIII from boyhood, that the king had written to him expressing admiration for the decisive new Minister of War. The monarch had said that with that kind of counselor he would not have had to leave the country.

Behind the apparently peaceful transition of political power to a new form of government, then, things seemed considerably more complicated. In fact, with great foresight, all members of the Revolutionary Committee had agreed a few months earlier to maintain a dictatorial government until caciques no longer controlled a political organization capable of falsifying elections in their own interest and thus effectively frustrating the people's will. In spite of all this and against the Minister of War's opinion, members of the Provisional Government decided to schedule elections for deputies to a Constituent Cortes. They had begun to criticize him, though still in a friendly way, as tyrannical and bossy, and he had to yield to their opinion. He even became to a degree convinced that advantage would accrue from the Provisional Government's limiting its fundamental legislation to military reforms.

The Minister of War proposed that they change the electoral law by decree, restructuring precincts to avoid or at least limit corrupt practices, which the English call "rotten boroughs" and which infected most of our country. By doing this they largely stopped the buying of control of many districts and the minister of the interior's simply assigning his chosen candidates to districts where victory was sure. These changes helped to achieve an undoubted triumph of public opinion over the Right, including the Right Republican coalition of Miguel Maura, minister of the interior, and Don Niceto Alcalá Zamora, the president. A great majority of electors voted for Socialists, Radical Republicans, and the various parties that made up the Left Republicans. The monarchists shamefully called themselves Agrarians, with the honorable exception of the able count Romanones who made a great show of winning in Guadalajara using his usual monarchist label. Catalans and Basques elected their nationalist tickets.

A few troublemakers from Estremadura worked to undermine our republic from the start. Some army officers who had at first supported the republic joined them. A few of Galán's comrades spoke more or less openly of a double-cross because the Minister of War, concerned to end barrack-room politics, did not simply turn military policy over to them. He tried, without success, to dissuade Ramón Franco from political activity, and, with difficulty, prevented him from creating a feudatory within the ministry's General Aviation Administration. Though Ramón Franco could do nothing about it, he and his restless kindred remained disappointed because his contribution to the revolution had not brought him immediate promotion at the cost of demoting someone else. Indeed, from his first interviews with Spain's most experienced officers the Minister of War got an impression that each man's primary interest lay in his own advancement. His impressions of Sanjurjo, Goded, and Francisco Franco remain highly interesting in retrospect. That parade sickened him; begging and adulation alternated with talebearing, all to gain advantage in promotion or assignment. It seemed that most of the Spanish military cared for nothing else. Of course the sole exceptions pleased him; his secretary Major Saravia and his adjutant Leopoldo Menéndez asked for nothing.

The Constituent Cortes opened with impressive display. What it lacked in the royal pomp of coaches and footmen of the monarchy's last parliamentary sessions a decade earlier it made up in a magnificent expression of popular enthusiasm. I attended that first session, and, having to take my gallery seat hours before it started, could not witness the cabinet ministers' cavalcade from the premier's office on the Plaza de Colón to the Congress building. Descriptions by the Minister of War, in writing and by word-of-mouth, more as eyewitness than as leading actor or protagonist, provided a delightful account of it. Ministers were paired off in cars, and Fernando de los Ríos, riding with him, effusively dispensed honeyed smiles left and right. "Don't be so cold," he said to the Minister of War, unaware of the powerful feeling under his cool dignity. "It's all for you! It's for you!" Ríos insisted when applause noticeably increased as they passed. My Brother-in-Law answered, "They cheered the same way for Primo de Rivera." He sometimes called himself "a man nourished by the people," but now his Alcalá skepticism surfaced. In all that noisy multitude jammed along Recoletos and the Paseo del Prado he noticed only one negative sign, and he remembered it. One independent spirit aggressively waved his arm, flaunted his hostile gesture, above that sea of heads.

Two things stand out in his *Memoirs* about that day: General Queipo de Llano caracoling quixotically on one of the last remaining horses from Alfonso XIII's stables, and the embarrassing jeers with which citizens, before the assembled cabinet, greeted the Civil Guard as it finished up the military parade. Suspension of the inaugural session had enabled ministers to come out and view that parade from the peristyle of the Congress Building's entrance. Many voices called for dissolution of the "Meritorious," the Civil Guard's nickname, and others clearly hinted at it. The Minister believed in approaching this matter gradually; he did not feel that the time had come for dissolution. At least for now he could depend on this corps's disciplined obedience to General Sanjurjo's orders. That allowed time for the development of a substitute, a police organization clearly identifying with our new regime. Possibly the Assault Guards might provide that substitute; Madrid's people called them *galarzas* after the police chief who had organized them.

Burdened by departmental work and Cortes sessions that continued without the usual summer recess, the Minister hardly ever got out for a breath of air except at night. Usually a small group of us met for a walk after dinner, often just himself, Martín Luis Guzmán, and me, followed closely by a highly visible policeman. One hot July night he and I came out later than usual from the Ministry of War, this time without other friends. Not many people frequented the calle de Alcalá in those hours after midnight, and curious citizens might look twice at us, not sure that it was the Minister of War walking along so casually. Still, the freedom of a few months earlier no longer existed for him, and he began to miss it. When we got to the Puerta del Sol the big clock showed 2:00 A.M. "Hombre!" he said cheerfully, looking up at the balcony of the Interior Ministry, "Let's go up and get Maurilla to buy us a cup of chocolate."

No sooner said than done. We found the Ministry's main door closed and entered through one on the calle del Correo. We crossed patios where the minister and his staff now parked their cars, but they still smelled of the Civil Guard's stables. We surprised Maura in a little private room next to his main office, and the Minister of War straightway gave orders to the minister of the interior to provide chocolate and doughnuts. We went into the larger office for our snack. By the time an attendant brought hot chocolate, they had already begun an unforgettable discussion, the principal concern of this chapter.

I was all ears when Miguel said, "Prepare yourself to become Premier." My Brother-in-Law protested with honest indignation, but Maura, unabashed, went on to develop his argument. "Just consider. In a month the Cortes will adopt the constitution. It goes without saying that Don Niceto will become president of our republic. In the natural course of things Lerroux would have taken over as premier. Quite clearly that cannot happen.

He won't do. Instead of bridging differences between parties, the behavior of his Radicals has widened them. He is done for. You stand forth as the most successful minister, revelation of the republic. . . ."

His Comrade of War did not let him finish. One by one, with inflexible logic, he took apart Maura's premises. First, the Cortes would not adopt the constitution in a month. He found absurd their approach to developing the republic's fundamental law. Instead of discussing it in the Cortes, the Provisional Government should draw up a short constitution, something flexible enough that each succeeding administration would not end up modifying it. Furthermore, everyone would henceforth treat each of its long, complicated articles as sancrosanct precisely because the Constituent Cortes had worked them out so carefully to satisfy all parties. No use even to talk about the rest of the prediction. How could Maura even think of such a thing?

My Brother-in-Law believed, unlike his colleague, that the Republican-Socialist coalition that had established our new regime with such unexpected hopes for domestic peace should hold together for a long time. Even after development and adoption of the constitution, the republic's real establishment required complementary laws on which its social structure must rest, especially agrarian reform. Then would come a time for clearly defining the political picture according to different party ideologies. In the meantime Lerroux must head our government as premier. No one had better qualifications, and his great political and historical position put him beyond all judgment. Besides, whatever man served as first premier would soon wear out his welcome because of his innovations necessary to make our young republic function. In future years when things had stabilized, a time would come for the Minister of War to serve the republic as premier.

Maura insisted, "All of that notwithstanding, prepare to become Premier."

"Well, why not?" I asked my Brother-in-Law about that discussion I had witnessed in silence. We had returned to the Buenavista Palace, ordered a car, and were headed home. His gesture left no room for doubt about what he thought of my supporting amiable Maurilla's crazy idea. Neither of us could do anything about it. Time would tell. He did not try to convince me, certain that events would prove him right.

Late in July my wife and I and our two little boys went to spend a month in Zaráuz, combining our vacation with the beginning of the theatrical season and Margarita Xirgu's appearance in San Sebastián. Among the summer beach crowd, some ladies gossiped shamelessly against our republic and its leaders on the basis of Basque-language sermons preached by the parish priest every Sunday. Mindless, ugly criticism, I thought, directed especially against the Minister of War because he had strengthened the new regime with Spain's people. If nothing worse, such talk established a climate for more dangerous challenges.

Sindulfo de la Fuente had also come to San Sebastián at that time as guest of his friend "the rich man." We all called Javier Ortueta that, and he accepted the joke rooted in a notorious disproportion between his wealth and his generosity. Sindulfo came to see me one afternoon in Zaráuz, moved by more than his characteristic amiability. His friend had just passed along an important confidence. It seemed that some aristocrats had asked Ortueta to contribute to a fund destined, beyond a doubt, to finance a rising against the republic. In spite of his own monarchism, he had not subscribed. He knew, of course, that the government would already be more or less well-informed about dangers that threatened it—and especially the Minister of War, whom he liked very much. He did not want to say anything more, and he knew nothing concrete, but Sindulfo gathered that the monarchists presupposed the prior assassination of my Brother-in-Law. The principal reason for Sindulfo's concern came from his host's determined reserve in saying that he did not want to turn informer on persons who had asked for his contributions and counted on his discretion. Sindulfo judged from this that men whom the Minister saw with some frequency numbered among the conspirators.

28

Provisional Premier of a Spain that has Ceased to be Catholic

On October 13 I felt nervous, as on so many occasions since my student days at exam time, because of an unavoidable task that could no longer be postponed. My deadline lay at hand for the National Literary Competition; I had undertaken to enter an essay on "The Theater in Our Century." [The essay won its prize in that 1931 competition.] Thus, though tempted to attend the session of the Constituent Cortes, I stayed home to finish my task. My Brother-in-Law had assured me that he would certainly not speak that afternoon, so it annoyed me to learn that he had not merely spoken but that his speech, his first in the three months since the Provisional Government had taken over, had aroused great enthusiasm and received clamorous applause. Everyone had expected him to defend his ministerial work, the unchallengeable military reforms that the Cortes had not yet considered. Instead he had spoken on the republic's religious policies, then under discussion. Specifically, he had spoken on Article 24 of the constitution.

In telling me about the event, which enthusiasts already called historic, he protested once again against undue praise based on the supposed improvisation of his speech. He did not know how to improvise. He never improvised, unless that meant speaking of things he had mulled over for many years. What had he said? One precise sentence stands as the enduring key to that eloquent blending of clearly reasoned concepts. "Spain has ceased to be Catholic." Of course that proved a challenge to militant Catholics.

Spain had, indeed, ceased to be Catholic, and in repeating what he had heard long before from his professors at the Escorial and what leaders of the Teaching Church continued to say, he had hardly pointed out something new. Didn't bishops complain about a lack of vocations observable in our seminaries? Didn't they write pastoral letters and thunder from their pulpits about the decline of the faith of our ancestors? My Brother-in-Law had, of course, wanted to do more than assert general abandonment of that title which Spanish monarchs had held as the finest jewel in their crown. So far as I know, nobody has ever refuted the simple analysis in that phrase, though the phrase itself drew much attack: Spain had, indeed, ceased to be Catholic. She had abandoned Rome's crusading banner along with the enterprises of her great century, her monumental schemes and adventures; she had withdrawn into herself to live simply. Spain had ceased to be both Catholic and imperial (no colonies, no provinces, no mother country), so that she could become a nation, truly reborn to her own life within the limits imposed on her by geography.

The Minister of Republican Action continued his speech by saying that he had never found his plans as a statesman incompatible with his deep sense of Spanish nationality. The monarchs who had achieved national unity did not quite deserve their reputation as catholic. They had united the nation by exclusion, by expelling many Jewish and Moslem subjects, people as Spanish or more so than those who remained behind under their narrower peninsular rule. Before the attainment of this unity of faith to which the Roman Catholic monarchy had linked its fate, a king with a more truly imperial spirit, Alfonso VII, "the Emperor," had a clear vision of a freer Spain with a sense of nationality more characteristic of modern times. This king had conceived of a union of the three races as one people despite the diversity of their three churches. Jew and Moslem had roots as deep in our soil as the Goth, after whom we still called our best agricultural lands *góticos*. The ancient Berber race, undoubtedly the same on both sides of the straits, had lived in Morocco long before Islamic invaders arrived.

Coming down to more recent history, the Minister of the republic continued by stating that, though a steady defender of Catalonian rights, he remained a convinced supporter of the centralizing policies of Spain's French Bourbon kings. As he saw it, when ministers of Charles III expelled the Jesuits from Spain they acted in accordance with this policy. Obviously my Brother-in-Law did not think in terms of a centralist government based on the person of a king. Rather, he would base it on what we might call the encyclopedic avalanche the French Revolution had forever impressed on the civilized world's political map with its Declaration of the Rights of Man. For him the Third French Republic always served as a mirror, and, while clearly perceiving certain effluvia clouding it, he remained grateful for it. France's republic owed its excellence, its strength, its certain future to the solid principles on which it rested. These were: equitable distribution of landed property; laic education, rigorously controlled by national policy and without participation by the monastic orders; and a national army.

Discussion of Article 24 of our nascent Constitution of the Republic of Workers of All Classes—legislators defined it with deliberate vagueness—marked a critical point in that highly important debate on relations between the state and the Church of Rome. The Minister's arguments easily carried the Chamber; a subsequent vote united Socialists, Radicals, Radical-Socialists, and Catalonia's *Esquerra* in a clear statement about religion.

Not unexpectedly, recalcitrant reactionaries countered this frank anti-clericalism in the new constitution. These persons grasped with outrage his phrase "Spain has ceased to be Catholic." Don Niceto Alcalá Zamora led this angry response. Don Niceto had conceded separation of church and state, with an understanding that the government would not take other measures that might hinder counterrevolutionary activities by Spain's clergy. In fact, though premier of the Provisional Government and candidate for the eventual presidency of the republic, Don Niceto wanted to neutralize our revolution, to check it. The Minister of War intended to guide and direct a revolution he regarded as necessary. Our sovereign people had chosen between them when it elected Left Republicans and Socialists to speak for them in the constitutional debate. Rightists, lacking a majority in the Constituent Cortes, found themselves swamped by opposition votes.

Unexpectedly one day, Alcalá Zamora presented his colleagues with his resignation from the position he had exercised at their head. All parties had accepted his leadership so as to avoid a governmental crisis before the constitution's adoption, though in accepting him some had compromised their own convictions. In his explanatory letter Don Niceto furiously attacked the Minister of War, coming close to calling him a traitor. The Council of Ministers wanted to reject the premier's resignation, hoping that he would change his mind, but he remained adamant and even stopped attending the Cortes. This abdication caused a major crisis; because of the government's anomalous position, it lacked means to resolve even a normal challenge. My Brother-in-Law had said nothing to me about any of this.

The next day I happened to urge him to let me know if he intended to speak, not wanting to miss it again, and, again, he assured me that he would not. He had no reason now. Consequently I used that afternoon to finish up my essay; the contest deadline came that day. An urgent telephone call to my home greatly upset me. Through some intermediary my Brother-in-Law advised me to come to the Congress at once. It seemed serious. What could have happened? Why had he, usually so circumspect, called me with such urgency? I could not even guess. My taxi dropped me at the Floridablanca doorway, normally used by ministers and deputies, and I hurried upstairs without waiting for the elevator. He met me by the telephone room on the corridor to the left of the central hall. Following the custom of foreign parliaments, they called this room "wasted steps" because of the useless, compulsive passage of so many people back and forth to and from it.

In spite of the seriousness his call indicated, he approached me smiling. Only his restless flicking of cigarette ash betrayed his normal appearance of self-controlled serenity. "What's up? What is so important?" I asked. He seemed to reproach me for my anxious question, "Do you think it unimportant that I will have to take over as premier of the Provisional Government?" We went into an office, the anteroom of Besteiro's office, and he told me in a few words what had gone on since the previous night. Don Niceto remained adamant. Besteiro, president of the Cortes and *de facto* head of state, judged that in so uncertain and critical a situation not a day should pass, and he should not dissolve the session after announcing the premier's resignation, without a substitute taking over. Any other procedure would leave the Cortes subject to some act of terrorism. Even now someone might be arranging a coup like that of General Pavía against the First Spanish Republic.

My Brother-in-Law told me about the ministers' preliminary conference. Lerroux had declined his colleagues' offer of the premiership; anyhow, some Socialists had agreed to that offer without enthusiasm. (To what extent did Lerroux's decision come from a majority judgment by his party that his taking this post would mean their party's decapitation?) The Socialists did not want Besteiro to take the position. Lerroux himself had proposed the Minister of War. The smallness of his Republican Action party, compared to the great republican parties—Socialists, Radicals, and Radical-Socialists— meant that his influence would depend on personal prestige more than on the votes of his own supporters. This would guarantee his presidential impartiality and his readiness to compromise. In fact, his position seemed like that of Don Niceto, especially after the Right Republican electoral defeat in June. The Minister of War had only agreed to head the Provisional Government on the conditions that it remain provisional and that its structure remain unchanged, including the men then serving. At that very moment Besteiro was holding final consultations with the heads of various parliamentary factions.

"Well, do you want some kind of job?" he asked, giving his cigarette another flick and looking away to brush off the ash with a nervous movement of his little finger. "Me? Nothing!" I answered impulsively, expressing my own feelings and reflecting his. He did not insist; it seemed right to him. I really didn't want to gain anything from it, and we both felt sensitive about possible charges of my taking advantage of his influence.

I wanted, somehow, to express more fully to my Brother-in-Law how much this promotion pleased me. It pleased him, too, in spite of the burdens it entailed; he could handle it. Before I could say more, however, Besteiro called him to confer formally the premiership Alcalá Zamora had so violently cast aside. Though his Republican Action Party had only a few delegates in parliament, leaders of the majority that unquestionably spoke for our sovereign people were now urging him to take over the reins of our nation. Then the ministers withdrew under their new Premier and Minister of War—he continued to hold that position. Besteiro wanted to present him to the Cortes that same afternoon, without further delay, and the Minister gave his colleagues a verbal summary of a declaration he intended to make to that larger audience.

Public galleries remained jammed. Journalists and curious insiders like myself wandered around impatiently in corridors and conference hall or looked into the canteen, searching out last-minute impressions. Everyone seemed to praise Besteiro, who, as acting president, had assured the smooth functioning of government agencies. With no real norms or clear rules to follow, he had made firm decisions and necessary arrangements. Less than a half hour after the ministers had assembled, movement in the waiting crowd toward the conference hall indicated the new Premier's reappearance. Dignified and erect, he led his colleagues through the crush, his decisiveness magnifying the habitual stiffness of that head placed so solidly on his shoulders. Other ministers were more generous than he with smiles and greetings; he did not pause to answer questions from journalists. As I came up a passageway into the auditorium between the presidential tribune and the blue bench, I heard someone's quick response to an urgent question, apparently about what the Premier might have said in passing. "An interim cabinet until approval of the constitution." Most people probably expected that, including members of parliament.

I squeezed in, among pushing delegates who had not managed to reach their seats and a multitude of interlopers like myself, in time to hear the generous welcome delegates gave the new Premier and ministers. It became unanimous when the cabinet rose in response. The audience gave a clamorous ovation to Don Julián Besteiro after his brief, grave, and dignified explanation of the crisis through which our republic had just passed. Stentorian *vivas* paid homage to that Socialist leader's discretion and civic patriotism in his interpretation of their feeling in confronting and resolving the predicament.

Fresh applause greeted the new Premier when he rose at the head of the ministerial bench. He began as usual, taking a persuasive tone, without emphasis, his voice almost high-pitched. As the Chamber's president had explained with regret Alcalá Zamora's reasons for resigning the presidency of the Provisional Government, his Successor made no special point of it. Neither in that speech nor later did he speak publicly of his predecessor's infamous conduct. He did obtain an enthusiastic round of applause for his colleague Miguel Maura, who had also resigned from his ministry but without any lessening of his support for the common cause. Maura's colleagues appreciated that, especially those who had shared with him the hopes of the recent past and the difficulties of the republic's first hours. The former interior minister had to stand up, moved, as he received the recognition for which the new Premier called.

After a brief pause the Premier and War Minister explained his position. He intended to act as leader of the same Provisional Government that, with the Cortes, constituted our republic; but he saw his position, if in some ways interim, not as transient. He intended to exercise fully the authority his colleagues had assigned him. Conscious of the responsibilities he now assumed as agent of the people's will in completing their common task, he planned to exercise his role as premier so long as he retained the confidence they now bestowed upon him. This did not mean, of course, that he limited himself in any way; malicious persons need not hope to play on his future discouragement to achieve a counterrevolution. He intended that the fruitful situation of the present should continue for some time and anticipated no interruption. The cabinet, though provisional, would require that the Chamber continue the work it had undertaken until it had adopted a constitution, and they would govern as though they intended to continue for many years.

He spoke rapidly, concisely, without hesitation or uncertainty, and with irrefutable logic. The simplicity, decisiveness, and forcefulness of his speech provided its eloquence, yet it was also sonorous and flowing. The whole Chamber burst into clamorous applause when he finished, the deputies unanimously, and spectators in the galleries, breaking strict regulations, joined in. Our eyes filled with tears, our throats tightened with emotion. I relished my happiness in a dream suddenly come true. I had a strong sense of history in the making; it seemed that time stopped for a moment to point to this landmark. Though others shared in the general pleasure, they could not really share my personal satisfaction as, in some sense, the creator of this man whose range so obviously exceeded the norm, this eminent man in all meanings of that word. Others did not realize that I had stood in the vanguard of believers in the new Premier's speedy ascent. The majority of deputies filed past the blue bench with effusive expressions of endorsement and strong support; their number emphasized the fewness of those who did not come forward. Excitement overflowed into the streets. Popular enthusiasm, the real essence of any republic, replaced despair as the feeling of the day. In the Premier's words explaining his actions the public recognized its spokesman, a man marked out by his destiny as a Spaniard to personify our national will, to direct our nation's fate untrammeled by restrictions or reservations.

Meanwhile caricatures of his face, sympathetic or acerbic, became a new element in the annals of Madrid's satiric journalism. Strokes and flourishes created a more or less ugly, false image, multiplying warts on a fleshy face. A missing tooth became his trademark. In the first months of his ministry, bothered by a minor pain, he had sought recourse in a dentist's chair and had allowed, rather than requested, extraction of an incisor. As a result, from then onward cartoonists remembered him that way and disfigured him with a gap in his teeth, almost always to suit the malevolent purposes of their editors, themselves servants of subscribers and stockholders. Some editorial commentators who wrote about him every day followed suit. Spite had not ceased to be Catholic.

29

The Author Onstage and in the Wings

The new Premier judged that it no longer suited his own convenience and the dignity and unavoidable responsibilities of his position to stay in his flat on the calle de Hermosilla. He and his wife moved into Buenavista Palace, traditional site of the Ministry of War. The premier's offices remained in a mansion on the Plaza de Colón. There he established Enrique Ramos as under secretary and, as private secretary, Juan José Domenchina, a very well-known member of the younger generation of poets and our friend from *La Pluma* days. Devoted to my Brother-in-Law and a regular member of the Regina *tertulia,* he fitted in well with that select company.

During continuing parliamentary debates on the constitution, Alcalá Zamora's resignation obliged the council of ministers to consider other candidates for our republic's presidency. Yet, once the former premier had recovered from that untimely pique which had brought our newborn government to the brink of perdition, he had demonstrated fitting contrition to expiate his intemperance. He maintained a prescribed silence, and, when he returned to the Chamber after a brief interval, he behaved discreetly and in a way worthy of the position his governmental colleagues had earlier assigned him. Thus when the moment came for finding a president, with a definitive vote on the constitution at hand, Alcalá Zamora's name came up again. There seemed no better solution for this fundamental problem of the republic.

Leading representatives of the national will found problems involved in the choice of other possible candidates. Unamuno, for instance, who paraded his candidacy before the Cortes and who pointed to his integrity and independence, seemed equivocal apart from those qualities. His group, which included Ortega y Gasset and Pérez de Ayala, called itself rather vaguely "Association for the Service of the Republic," but it lacked any real political support in the country whose destinies it aspired to rule. Similarly, Ossorio y Gallardo, with a solider claim, did not seem quite presidential timber. My Kinsman spoke unequivocally against the concept that independence from any party discipline, by raising a budding president above all civil contention, represented an advantage. He argued that a republican system must develop from party conflicts. For that reason, he also did not really approve of the candidacy of Don Manuel Bartolomé Cossío, though he supported it.

This man was the spiritual heir and actual kinsman of Don Francisco Giner, founder of the Free Institute of Education. Serious illness had confined Cossío to bed for several months, and the Premier had one of his greatest satisfactions in calling on him to inquire about his health and to congratulate him on his deserved offer of the presidency. Devotees at the invalid's bedside seconded my Brother-in-Law in this. Nevertheless, when Cossío declined the offer on grounds of the illness that finally caused his death, my Kinsman admitted to me that he preferred this prudent abstention. Cossío's political inexperience, counterpart to his spiritual orientation, would inevitably have finally diminished his reputation had he become president. The Premier believed that the political profession requires a real vocation and that in politics seniority should not determine leadership. We needed something better than amateurs and theoreticians.

Maybe I imagined that he feared a violent outburst from me when he told me one sad day that they had decided on Alcalá Zamora as the best candidate for our presidency. My Brother-in-Law always regarded me as overly strong in my opinions. In fact I reacted by giving him back his own earlier arguments. Consoling himself for the enormous upheaval caused by his predecessor's resignation, he had said that no wind blew so ill that some good did not come of it. Don Niceto's withdrawal at least avoided an otherwise inevitable clash and serious struggle at the top after adoption of the constitution, when normal political confrontation would begin. Now he responded to my exaggerated arguments against the choice of Don Niceto merely by saying that they could find no one better. The Radicals continued to resist the choice of Lerroux. The Socialists, with Besteiro himself as their spokesman, refused to repeat their discouraging experience in Ebert's Social Democratic Germany under the Weimar constitution. As my few alternatives evaporated, I suggested a candidate with a white beard, Don Rafael Altamira. Newspapers somewhat ambiguously labeled this history professor, born in South America and an outstanding member of the Hague Tribunal, as a "distinguished republican." They labeled many others the same way with as much justification. The Premier seemed just to dismiss my suggestion, but his memoirs indicate that he gave it serious consideration.

He told me that he felt, as he had a month before, that Lerroux remained the best choice for president since his position in the new regime represented a major problem for republicans. They had to recognize him; they might possibly purify what he and his historical contribution to the republic represented, but they could not ignore it. Nevertheless the stigma of this Radical leader's personal immorality and that of his party could destroy our republic in the eyes of the people. They might, then, give Don Alejandro the vainglory and honorable retirement that the presidency represented in most people's opinion—along with a presidential salary of a million a year, which he required.

Though my Brother-in-Law spoke of the presidency in this way in this particular connection, he really had a different concept of it. He believed that those persons erred and misinterpreted our pending constitution when they attributed to the president merely the moderating role of a constitutional king adopted by Spanish monarchs since the restoration of Alfonso XIII's father. In his judgment the responsibilities of the republic's president involved nothing less than effective direction of national policy. Picking up on this, I ventured a suggestion made by M. Herbette, treating it as nothing more than a flattering comment. Since his arrival in Madrid a few months before, this ambassador of the Republic of France had shown himself an admirer of my Kinsman to the point of diplomatic imprudence. He went so far as to express to me, in a chance encounter in the congressional conference hall, his hope and almost certain expectation that the present Minister of War and Premier would soon become our nation's First Magistrate. My Brother-in-Law let that pass. Like *The Crown*'s main character, he remained cautious and without illusions, ever reticent about the future. He never tipped his hand.

At last the day came, or rather the night, and finally the dawn for a final vote on our constitution, and with that the unstable Provisional Government's first stage ended. Because the parties lacked strength to hold their members to defined party positions, we escaped becoming a federal republic by a very narrow voting margin. But if a federal constitution seemed a very serious danger to the Premier, given Spanish propensity to base patriotism on regions or even small localities, he found still more intolerable the concession of the vote to women. That became law unexpectedly and only by a one-vote majority. Perhaps his natural affection for them made him strongly antifeminist. Even if he didn't take the trouble to discuss it, his opinion, and, of course, his feelings, remained firmly against women's political rights and open involvement in public life.

As that nocturnal session of the Constituent Cortes came to its end, with the first hints of dawn evident, I met my friend Luis Araquistáin at the auditorium doorway, and he began to praise my Brother-in-Law's rapid ascent. "Even his party's name corroborates the spirit of his policy," Araquistáin said to me, referring to the qualities that distinguished him among his governmental colleagues as a real man of *action*. I don't remember his exact words, and don't want to force my memory into a false coincidence. It doesn't really matter, anyhow, because he may only have hinted then what he later asked openly, "Why doesn't this man become a Socialist?" "Because he isn't one!" I answered laughing. "So what. Lots of them are not," Araquistáin replied. Certainly he did not say, "Lots of us are not." Few people realized how many of our republic's prominent Socialists had only recently accepted party discipline at the time when the Constituent Cortes assembled.

Araquistáin in his review *Leviatán* published the best article on the Premier's governmental activity at that time. Though my Brother-in-Law's political differences with its author prevented him from entirely accepting that outspoken and favorable judgment about his personality and work, he always appreciated the article's clear-sighted intention, which did largely succeed in presenting his goals. Araquistáin's piece finished up by saying that, given the pressure of circumstances, the Premier must either prepare to preside over Spain's inevitable revolution or find himself swept away by that event. Though my Brother-in-Law, with his characteristic canniness, tried to hide it, another deputy's comparison bothered him more than Araquistáin's prophecy. That man, owner of San Sebastián's *Pueblo Vasco,* predicted, half-jokingly, in the corridors of Congress that he would become Spain's Kerensky.

A short time before or after all that, the former Russian premier, Kerensky, came to Madrid. He impressed my Kinsman during his brief courtesy call at the Ministry of War as a limited, uninteresting man, even as a specimen of an unlucky statesman. Altogether, I have considerable reason to believe that Araquistáin's thoughtful prediction and the passing but opportune augury of his Basque supporter influenced the Premier's thought during the course of future years, even though he himself believed that he paid them no heed. This influence came neither from the words' significance nor because he ruminated over that solid writing and that casual comment. No, it came because, allowing for physical and moral differences in politics and history, these prophecies really did to some degree mark out the fatal course of the events of his life.

The actual presidential election found me away from Madrid, in Barcelona on theatrical business. After taking over the stage direction of Margarita Xirgu's company the year before, I had suggested, of course, that they put on *The Crown.* I remembered her saying that she enjoyed reading its unpublished version and her approval of its Author's readiness to shorten his text, which we found overly wordy and weighty. Now, without really hoping that she would take up my suggestion, I wanted to repeat it through theatrical professionals who might have more influence with Margarita. Thus I took advantage of a necessary visit to the Quintero brothers during their summer holidays in Fuenterrabía and mine at Zaráuz and San Sebastián. My primary interest lay in getting them to write a new comedy for us; but, having heard that they had expressed enthusiasm about *The Crown* to its Author, I asked them to recommend its production to Margarita. It seemed to me that their influence might prove especially strong, as they might in some sense see as a formidable competitor this Man of Letters venturing into the theater without a professional's serious concern about making money. Besides, after all, friendship and kinship with the Author combined with my position in the company to inhibit my freedom in giving advice about this particular matter.

Still, I would have given up my efforts to stage *The Crown* after the rapid series of events that brought its Author such extraordinary political prominence. I esteemed his play too much to have it tested before prejudiced audiences who would not consider it simply as a theatrical work. Now, however, contrary to my expectations, both the Author and his chosen interpreter yielded to the temptation to seize the moment. They decided to present a work worthy of refined, sophisticated audiences to merely curious ones. In consequence, we decided to open our second season at the Español with this spectacular piece. According to a clause in our lease, we had to share the municipal theater with another company that year, so we decided to present our premier performance to Barcelona's public.

Pérez de Ayala had passed through Madrid at the end of the summer, on leave from his recent appointment as ambassador in London. He had asked me to direct, in another theater than the Español, a dramatic version of his old and famous novel *A.M.D.G.*, adapted for theater by a little-known actor with a sure instinct for the moment. I agreed, not wanting to offend him by refusing. His play appeared under my stage direction at the Beatriz, which, like the Victoria and the María Isabel, still preserved its dedication to the queen and the infantas of Spain's last monarchical court. We had a great success, partly due to notoriety, and also a great fight in the theater, clearly inspired by the Jesuits in response to republican attacks against them on all fronts of their vast Spanish domain. With much slapping and punching among spectators in orchestra seats, some blockheads got beaten up. My brother-in-law Diego, son of Enrique de Mesa, and Rafael Sánchez Guerra, the Premier's under secretary until a few days before, led the defense. Angry interruptions of our performance, almost from the curtain's rising, merely emphasized the play's Catholic significance.

During my stay in Barcelona with the Xirgu Company, another troop was performing there that same *A.M.D.G.* which had caused such commotion in Madrid. I had nothing whatsoever to do with that Barcelona production but could not escape the influence of their interpretation of the play on my own theatrical business. The Civil Governor of Barcelona, Anguera de Sojo, summoned me to his office; he felt obliged to explain to me the arrangements he had made in connection with that presentation of Pérez de Ayala's play. The growing political prestige of Anguera de Sojo came from his careful compartmentalization of his strong republicanism and his profoundly Catholic religious beliefs. It seemed that some ladies, speaking for Barcelona society, wounded in some kind of Christian feeling, had asked Anguera to prevent the scandal presupposed by the advertised production of *A.M.D.G.* He had answered that he could not stop a performance beforehand; no law of previous censorship existed for theatrical productions. They should consult either the public prosecutor if they believed the work itself offensive or a judge about suppression of its advertisements. His own authority only covered any decision to cancel the play if, during its performance, he felt that it endangered public order. On hearing this, these ladies exchanged significant looks and thanked him.

Understanding what those looks and thanks might mean, he immediately gave pertinent orders to the police department to stop any disturbance that might occur during the advertised performance. He soon realized the rightness of that action. A few days later those young ladies and their gentlemen escorts attended a Barcelona performance of *A.M.D.G.* intending to create a disturbance and confident in the impunity they mistakenly believed the governor had promised them. They ended up cooling their heels in a neighborhood police station and later at police headquarters then headed by Arturo Menéndez, who subsequently served as police chief of Madrid.

Anguera de Sojo, impeccably Catholic through the influence of his mother, well-known and revered for her piety, had not called me in to tell me that story. It did not concern me anyhow. He wanted to tell me that he had received other communications that did directly involve me. Rumors had come to him anonymously and expressed by word of mouth that the Premier's play insulted good Catholics. He had heard that Margarita Xirgu intended to present the play, under my direction, on December 8, the Feast of the Immaculate Conception—a date when its Author could attend the premiere. According to those preposterous rumors—and Anguera took them as such—this play entitled "Conchita" presented a vulgar burlesque of the dogma with which the Catholic Church has crowned the most pure and worthy Virginity of the Mother of Jesus. I easily calmed the governor's scruples, but had more trouble in calming Margarita's apprehension. She saw these rumors, however absurd, as unmistakable signs that political hostility might spoil our strictly artistic plans. Under this shadow we turned to final preparation of *The Crown*.

Margarita knew the writer Joaquín Montaner better than I did. He had two brothers, one well-known as a follower of Lerroux, the other a Barcelona drama critic. Joaquín Montaner had been very friendly toward me since the republic's advent, and he told me that, like most people, he had great hopes about my Brother-in-Law. He knew Catalonia's people well and counted himself one of them in spite of his origins in Estremadura, and he now had as much influence in the Generalitat's government as he had formerly in that of the Dictatorship.

Joaquín Montaner urged that we should transfer our performance from the Goya Theater that we had engaged. It seemed to him that the Premier deserved Barcelona's best stage; after all, his influence had greatly assisted the political compromise that would soon fulfill Catalonia's desire for autonomy. Only the Liceo, though normally used for opera, seemed worthy of the spectacle we were preparing and the recognition due the Premier. He offered to arrange it, and with my permission—because what he said seemed right to me—he undertook to achieve his plan, now ours. I must admit that Margarita, without opposing our proposal, did not entirely agree with us. Perhaps she foresaw the opposition we would meet because of the negative prejudices of some and the weak support we would get from others who ought to have helped us. Margarita, though a Catalan through all four grandparents, had little sympathy with separatists. As it turned out, members of the Generalitat, now experimenting with provisional autonomy, did not sufficiently counter resistance from those who held boxes at the Liceo. Possibly they did not care to make the effort. Among these patrons figured the great names of the small clearly Catalonian aristocracy who, with numerous newcomers, constituted Barcelona's upper-middle class. Finally, after considerable fruitless negotiation, we all became convinced that we should stay at the Goya.

The play had no defined time or place, and Margarita and I agreed, with its Author's endorsement, that the ambience best suited to its staging was a period identified in Spain with Isabella II and in France with Louis Philippe. I changed my mind, however, after seeing drawings of costumes by Margarita's brother and our set designer Burmann's very stylized sketches. His first scene especially bothered me, where you have to take so much care about orienting your audience correctly. Nevertheless, I hid my concern. It also seemed to me during very late rehearsals in Madrid that our actors' slow pace in interpreting the text did not reflect the Poet's dramatic intention. My greatest disappointment, though I could not mention it then, came from Margarita's unusual lack of understanding of the protagonist's role.

My early discontent with the production threw me off pace in my role as director. Inhibited by some kind of veneration, I did not succeed in making my concerns clear. Somehow my fraternity with its Author interfered in a deep spiritual way with my self-confidence in working with *The Crown*. Margarita, too, as she later told me, felt somehow inhibited, unusual for her, by an unquestionable feeling of inferiority and awe that always struck her in the presence of "the Republican Gentleman." His cordial smile did not give her sufficient confidence to counterbalance this reverence. Her problem lay not so much in the play itself as in the responsibility of interpreting her role as Queen Diana. I realized that she did not feel comfortable or happy in the role when she said once that, like all great Spanish dramatists, he had written a work for actors, not actresses. She meant the preeminence of the masculine characters, as she saw it, in *The Crown* over the one whom she portrayed. She did not realize—and I did not fully realize it until later— how very right she was. She had to portray a pure transposition of the Author's own spirit into a fictitious character—as I have already said. We both turned away from all of this to concentrate on superficial details connected with the Premier's trip to Barcelona.

My father had expressed his wish to attend the Barcelona performance, and we promised him a seat. Some chronicler made the point that this event, less extraordinary than uninitiated persons might suppose, had precedents in the politico-literary annals of Spain's nineteenth century. Martínez de la Rosa, Echegaray as treasury minister (though under a pseudonym), and Don Adelardo López de Ayala as premier in his turn—had all risked their reputations before theatrical audiences, considerably less respectful and well-behaved than mere political antagonists. Though advanced in years and still in mourning for his fairly recent loss of my mother, my father kept his good health and spirits, and my sister wanted to fulfill his wish to attend. She arrived ahead of her husband with our father, secretary Enrique Ramos, and his wife. I missed them at the station and had to go back and wait for them at the Hotel Colón, where Catalonia's government had arranged lodgings for the Premier. They almost got crushed witnessing a magnificent demonstration of cordiality when the presidential express train arrived. Railwaymen crowded onto the roofs of train cars filling the tracks, and an overflowing multitude jammed the platform and joined their stentorian cheers to locomotive whistles in an uproar of unanimous applause.

My father reached our hotel before his Son-in-Law's cortege, and he watched from a balcony with me and my sister, tears of happiness in his eyes. Presently the Premier's open car appeared, entering the Plaza de Cataluña from the Ronda de San Pedro, moving as slowly as a carriage through a cheering multitude. We saw many waving banners proclaiming Catalonia and some for the republic. Nonetheless Enrique Ramos on the balcony with us regretted the bad organization of the arrival. He called to my attention that the crowd did not fill the plaza as it should have. In spite of strong illumination from numerous street lights, shadows mostly hid the gaps Ramos noted; but they remained evident.

We didn't dwell on the reception's inadequacies; after all, the trip was unofficial and that probably explained things. Ramos also attributed the lack of numbers we noted to differences among nationalist factions in Barcelona; certainly its people showed palpable enthusiasm for the Premier. The local branch of Republican Action wanted, in opposition to their leader's advice, to separate from the *Esquerra* on the grounds of maintaining some traditional centralist *fueros* in Catalonia. The *Esquerra* had earlier challenged the older, conservative *Lliga*. Cheering crowds who had accompanied the Premier from the station obliged him to come out repeatedly onto a balcony next to ours to acknowledge their enthusiasm for his mere presence. Though he never let a propitious occasion escape him, that night he would not speak. He had not come to Barcelona for that. My Brother-in-Law wanted to witness *The Crown*'s premier performance as a member of its audience, not from the wings as authors usually do. Thus his box inevitably became a kind of proscenium, and the audience in orchestra seats felt drawn by irresistible curiosity to watch his reactions more than the stage action. Margarita, absolutely rightly, later pointed this out as the main psychological mistake in our arrangements, and at the Madrid premiere we asked him not to repeat an experiment that had proved counterproductive. Certainly the audience did not seem inattentive, cold, or indifferent. They crammed the auditorium and listened to the first act in silence. This dramatically intensified the spiritual flow, the communication between audience and stage that constitutes the essence of theater. A volley of applause came after the first curtain; all main-floor spectators turned toward the box where the Author presided, and those in the gallery leaned over to join in generously hailing him. Still, Margarita said to me several days later, recalling our premiere, that she had the impression, which all of her colleagues shared, of a duality of public interest. Our audience had seemed as intrigued by the presidential box as by onstage action.

Our actors themselves never managed, as they say, to get caught up in the play. Nor had the public gotten caught up in it, in spite of the personal acclamation they gave the Premier's erect figure, repeated after the second act and when that first performance ended. Unmistakably, though, they applauded the Politician, "revelation of the republic," more than the Dramatist. The dramatic Poet had to grieve over that, and he did grieve. He did not hide his unhappiness from me. "You have spoiled my play," he said when we met at the hotel after the show. What did our Madrid friends think of his reaction when they expected a very affectionate moment? Did his ingenuous words make them suddenly realize that they hadn't understood *The Crown* at all? I would have wasted my words in trying to explain to them and did not say to him that his unhappiness came from his native perfectionism. However well we had performed his play, he would have remained convinced that our limited understanding did not plumb its poetic depths, its profundity of human understanding. On the other hand, no performance, however clumsy, could have entirely spoiled for him his play's force and gracefulness.

The Author's unstable reaction at the end of that performance made me fully realize something really significant. After all, two or three years earlier he would have welcomed such a performance—combined with his new position of political power. Did his fervent commitment as a statesman include sufficient capacity for common feeling with our people to follow through on the apparently unrestricted responsibilities with which they seemed to have entrusted him? Or better, did he have enough of this common feeling to carry him in the new, still harder tasks that lay ahead? *The Crown*'s failure with its first audience—and he regarded its Barcelona premier as a failure in spite of all the noisy enthusiasm and the palms awarded him—disillusioned him once again (in spite of my optimistic words) about the possibility of finding in the ambit of Spanish society a really wide circle of truly discreet persons. (He meant "discreet" in the exalted sense it had in our great century.) He hoped for a Spanish artistic ambience in our time comparable to that which made possible the great heritage some pens and inspired brushes have left us. This treasury had resisted all the changes of our imperial fortunes and the sinking, decay, and disparagement of those old American galleons with their cargoes of colonial gold.

Three months later, trying on costumes for the last necessary adjustments before our assault on Madrid, Margarita spoke to me of her alarm. Her dressmaker had spoken of sinister intentions on the part of some aristocrats for *The Crown*'s premiere. This dressmaker, still an attractive woman, worked everywhere, and she had connections with "good society" through her clientele and the father of her only daughter. Her customers seemed ecstatic, according to what she said, about something scheduled to happen in the near future. Knowing of her friendship with La Xirgu and that she usually attended openings at the Español as a guest of the house, they advised her not to come *The Crown*'s first night. They said more with smirks than with words, but that sufficed. Margarita, for her part, repeated her former warnings to me: these people were very bad, and my friends and the government seemed too sure of themselves. Everything indicated that we had much to fear, and she felt that they could not take too many precautions.

The Premier wanted to attend our dress rehearsal before the Madrid opening, though he had not attended others. We had scheduled it for an afternoon as usual, and I ate dinner at the Ministry before accompanying him to the theater. We were about to leave; his car stood waiting at the foot of the stairway, when someone called on the telephone with an urgent message for my Brother-in-Law.

The vehemence of his answers and the annoyance on his face indicated that the call was a warning. "No in that case I had better stay at home and not go at all." He seemed finished, ready to hang up. Then the speaker on the other end apparently changed his tune, since my Brother-in-Law listened a few minutes more and reversed his first, unwilling decision. With an understanding smile, he said, "Good, good, fine! In that case we will leave right away." Putting down the phone, he turned to my question, "Nothing important. Foolishness. Let's go."

He hurried toward the office door and the elevator. As we drove past the Neptune Fountain on the Plaza de Cánovas he said to me, quite casually, "Do you know who called me? Arturo Menéndez. He said that they had heard something. Nothing important! Well, an assassination plot. You know that I am not exactly a coward, but it seemed like tempting fate to go to the rehearsal after someone had warned me. He only wondered whether we could delay it. According to their information three armed persons were 'covering the Español's three doors, the stage door on the Calle de la Visitación, the main entrance on the Plaza de Santa Ana, and the other one on the calle de Echegaray."

I insisted that we should not attend the rehearsal against the police chief's advice, but he stopped my movement to signal the driver and footman in the front compartment.

"Menéndez noticed my annoyance, and he told me that they have already arrested a man waiting with a loaded pistol in a tavern opposite the theater. The other two had no contingency plan; if someone got caught, each man would stick to his own post. Menéndez himself said that we could go. We run no risk of danger now."

Nobody at the theater had heard anything about it, and I said nothing to them. We saw policemen everywhere, though, at the doors, in the aisles, among the boxes, at entries to the upper galleries, in the gridirons and the wings. Margarita, extremely nervous though satisfied with our unaccustomed wealth of protection, told me privately that she had no objection to putting everything off to some later date if we thought that useful. She also said that, though it pleased her to have the Author at our premiere, if his presence raised the least danger of something happening, perhaps he ought not to come. She felt terrified of some disaster in the theater, and who could blame her! I calmed her, joking a little about her exaggerated fears and pointing out that obviously her warnings had resulted in extra precautions. The Author would attend our opening as we had agreed, and backstage in the usual way.

I don't recall anything special about that dress rehearsal, or that my Brother-in-Law had further suggestions to add to a few changes we had made on the basis of his complaints about the Barcelona performance. Perhaps he believed nothing at that point could overcome our production's fundamental, inherent weakness. Instead he behaved amiably and graciously toward his performers, toward the actor Maximino and the veteran Contreras—the former very pleased, as he said, with the honor of his role; the latter, though somewhat melancholy about his graybeard's part, still highly gratified to perform in a drama written by his idol. A staunch republican, he always resorted to hyperbole to show his enthusiastic support for that genius, the one, insuperable, irreplaceable, and I don't know what kind of laudatory epithets he used to express his devotion to the Premier. Good Contreras belonged to a pure, unblemished liberal tradition of the past century, combining a Mason's good-natured innocence with a Wagnerian's rapture. He used to play on the piano from memory choicest themes from the Tetralogy and then throw in a complete transcription of *Tannhäuser*'s overture.

The Author treated Margarita with special kindness, and from then onward he always called her Diana, her role in his play, to show his affection. In his presence she lost much of her characteristic feminine charm, and, aware of it, called herself stupid, afraid that he might think her so. She remained especially grateful to me for making them friends when her respect for him dulled not only her vivacity but even her conversation. One time, a little before or afterward, I don't exactly remember, Margarita said to me, half-serious, half-joking, "How happy the woman you love must be!" "My own!" I interrupted, not knowing where this would lead, but sure that no complications could arise between my leading lady and me to disturb our simple friendship. "Because," she continued, "if you know so well how to surprise a good friend like me, giving her exactly what she most wanted, what would you not do for someone you truly loved?" Those words resulted from an incident during the Holy Week theatrical vacation. My Brother-in-Law and I had gone to the Escorial on our usual ride, and he urged me to come along with him to pay a call on Margarita, who was recovering from one of the many physical crises that threatened her life throughout her career. She attributed to me what in fact resulted from a very characteristic impulse of the Author of *The Crown*.

Among the many spectators wandering around backstage at that Madrid premiere, I recall Doña María Guerrero's sister. She had taken up acting late in life to justify the financial assistance given her by the Díaz de Mendozas, a kind of widow's pension in return for her husband's lifelong service as their business manager. Also a friend of my mother-in-law, Anita Guerrero inevitably became Margarita's close friend and confidant. She attended that night, and, as we let her sit wherever she liked, she chose a seat in the first box where she could observe the illustrious Author in the wings, watching Madrid's public reacting to his play.

Moments before the curtain rose, with our audience already in their seats and my Brother-in-Law and me already moving toward the stage, Jacinto Benavente came into the little reception room's vestibule. "I want to congratulate you ahead of time, before the intermission crowd," that flibberti-gibbet said, holding out his cold, little, white hand, smiling, but, as always, not looking you in the eye. "Thanks a lot," the Premier answered drily as he turned away to smooth the hair of a little girl who charmingly played children's parts for our company. He began to talk with her, taking exaggerated interest in her replies. Old Contreras, dressed in his shepherd's costume, also in the vestibule, witnessed that scene. Of course, Benavente did not return that night, nor did he speak to me, either, for a long time. I had already anticipated that by avoiding him except when we met in Margarita's presence. His conduct deserved nothing else.

Months earlier, right after the republic's proclamation, I both saw and heard of some contemptible letters he had written, apparently to his agent, from Arcachon, where he was finishing up a play we later staged at the Chelito Theater. Afterward he had a notorious quarrel with this man. In those letters, with no reason for personal animosity toward my Brother-in-Law and me, he insulted our fraternal affection, attributing to it feelings of a sort that people used to call unspeakable. Benavente did not always hide such feelings in his own personal life. I never could understand, either, the basis of his attack on Indalecio Prieto about something else. All of it must have come from rabid antirepublicanism and his then liberal-monarchist politics. He later went on to become a sympathizer, at least ideologically, with the wildest antibourgeois political doctrines, though he himself belonged irredeemably to that class.

After the first act the Author had to go out before the curtain to greet his public, though he had wanted to save that until after the entire performance. They applauded him loudly, and this time it seemed to us more clearly because of his drama itself than in Barcelona. "How pale he looks," Anita Guerrero commented. "A theater audience makes you more nervous than anything." The Premier was never ruddy, and it was hard to make the Author of *The Crown* blush. Neither the commentator, an eyewitness, nor I could at that point even guess the fatal significance of that paleness. A tremendous ovation after the third-act curtain demonstrated our performance's success. The Author received their acclaim, coming forward a few steps from our assembled cast. After the curtain's last fall, he agreed to a photograph with Diana and her court. Between acts and after the performance close friends and innumerable merely curious persons came up to shake his hand or to embrace him. Don Niceto came backstage between the second and third acts. He had deigned to attend in the official proscenium box; the rest of the cabinet occupied neighboring boxes.

The little world of first-nighters hailed the show with a unanimity unusual in our times. On the other hand, those same critics who had praised the drama in book form three years earlier now passed it off by repeating their earlier judgments and adding that we had successfully staged it at the Español. As with theatrical works of Galdós, some persons had reservations about *The Crown*'s supposed literary superiority to its more strictly dramatic qualities. The stupid pedant who reviewed for *La Época* reversed his earlier exaggerated benevolence toward Margarita and me and adopted an attitude of incomprehensible hostility. His kindest comment was that he had slept. In fact, both sides felt cheated, some because they could find nothing in the Premier's work to use in a political campaign against the army Reformer and Proponent of Article 26 of the constitution. Others, and among them supporters, wanted to hear the Author speaking from the stage about practical problems the Orator had posed, discussed, and resolved so reasonably and eloquently from the rostrum.

All things considered, our success in Madrid might have exceeded that in Barcelona, but the company returned to a slow pace in their second performance before a half-filled house. Usually actors do let up in the second performance, after the nervousness of opening night has subsided, but they normally regain their pace after the first Sunday matinee when they again have a normal audience.

"No play could have overcome it," he said once more as his only commentary, and he turned his back on that disaster for a long time. The failure wounded him deeply and for nobler reasons than lack of recognition at the ticket window of the Society of Authors. After twenty or thirty performances we took down *The Crown*'s posters. Provincial managers had warned our business manager that their subscribers and regulars would boycott the Premier's drama, so we dropped it from our repertoire. Álvarez de Vayo, our ambassador in Mexico at that point, wanting to demonstrate strong support for the Premier, organized a staging there of *The Crown* with a grant from that country's government. As a tribute to its Author it had as great or greater success than in Spain, but it never became part of any company's repertoire.

I continue to rate it as the best Spanish tragicomedy of our century and on a par with the best of our greatest century.

30

Fireworks on the Eve of Saint Lawrence's Day

Some mornings I would look in on Major Saravia, the Minister of War's under secretary, but rarely saw my Brother-in-Law. Office work and appointments absorbed him until dinnertime. I often stayed to share that meal with him and my sister, usually without prior invitation. My eldest son, José Ramón, always found an even warmer welcome. That world of ushers, chauffeurs, and sentries at the foot of stairways delighted the boy. After eating, in the afternoon, we drove out with the Premier to the Escorial, Alcalá, or the Puerto de Navacerrada. Martín Guzmán regularly joined Sindulfo and us. The child almost always came along because nobody amused his uncle as much as he did.

The Uncle showed his pleasure in the boy's visits by paying him much attention and spoiling him. As M. Herbette, ambassador of France, noted, the Minister of War's nephew felt quite at home at the Ministry. "And who's to blame for that?" my sister asked affectionately about some piece of bread or a cookie that the ambassador might well have spotted on a table and that the Minister had brought along for the child. "Some day you will really make a fool of yourself," she said. He did not see it that way, not even one afternoon when a servant came into one of the private rooms and found His Excellency down on the floor on all fours giving the child a horseback ride. Years before, while serving as Secretary of the Ateneo, he had told me about the pleasant impression made on him by some children during his visit to the count of Romanones, then president of that Learned House. While he waited, they peeked through a doorway, playing mischievously behind curtains. Later the count allowed them to interrupt him, even though he found it somewhat annoying; they were his grandchildren.

During those afternoon drives between office hours and sessions of the Cortes—the first real break in his daily routine—the Minister amused himself by teaching his nephew, who still did not talk plainly, the names of everything they passed: trees, nearby mountains, monuments. The Uncle delighted in hearing the child's struggles to pronounce correctly the *-erre* when he pointed out the *Puerta de Hieggo* [*Puerta de Hierro,* the Iron Gate at the Pardo]. He enjoyed still more José Ramón's reaction when we passed a wooden gateway in a village near Madrid; the boy pertinently called out "Don Quixote came through that gate," remembering pictures his Uncle had showed him and one of the first adventures in Cervantes's masterpiece. "Those are not sheep; it is an army!" he cried, and laughed when the adults picked up his allusion, something exceptional in so young a child. Beyond a doubt the boy's greatest treat came when his Uncle took him after a drive to a stand in Madrid's outskirts for a snack of potato chips. More than once or twice we ran into the French ambassador and his eccentric wife at a stand on the Villalba highway. My Brother-in-Law came to call that place *les Follies Herbettes*. In just such a way, he told me, the *Follies Bergères,* the most famous Parisian variety theater in our time, got its name from eighteenth-century Country Follies where court ladies and their lovers went to transform courtly games into country sports.

The Premier did not believe it necessary to resort to mediocre and vulgar appearances to demonstrate republican modesty and democracy. On the contrary, he believed that, short of the monarchy's stiff gravity and ostentatious luxury, we could enhance national prestige through decorum in public appearances. He had wanted the Provisional Government to buy or build some suitable palace as a residence for the republic's president, since the Royal Palace entailed far more expense than it represented in comfort. At first his initiative prevailed, and the Council of Ministers undertook negotiations to buy Cánovas del Castillo's mansion, "La Huerta," on the Castellana, the property of the marchioness of Argüelles, or the Larios Palace on the corner of Villamagna, its property extending from the Castellana to Serrano. The owners spoiled these deals by jacking up their prices, and both would, besides, have required considerable rehabilitation. Don Niceto opposed this whole approach, and they finally resolved the matter, a minor problem after all, to suit him, in what my Brother-in-Law regarded as the worst possible arrangement. As president of the republic, Don Niceto continued to live in his own small house on the Paseo de Martínez Campos, leaving home every morning like a good civil servant for the Palace where his office windows looked out over the Campo de Moro. From the days of King Amadeo they had called these rooms the apartment of the duke of Genoa. At least they renamed Don Niceto's street suitably to honor Don Francisco Giner de los Ríos, who had lived there for many years in one of the first buildings constructed there, his Free Institute of Education.

Our republican government held its first receptions and official banquets in the salons and state dining room of the Palace, called the National Palace after its abandonment by our fallen monarchs. My Brother-in-Law commented to me about the president's very poor judgment in everything representing excellence or just good taste. He though it stingy and unworthy of our republic to order official dinners from the Florida Hotel just to save the expense of utilizing the palace kitchens. Even worse, Don Niceto made a great show of modesty and disinterestedness by returning every month or trimester part of his budgetary allowance for the presidential household. My Kinsman felt that the president might, as he saw fit, contribute part of his salary to the republic but not by sacrificing the dignity of his position and, finally, injuring some state employee or cutting back on hiring. Why didn't he use that money to buy some pictures or sponsor a chamber orchestra? The Premier wanted our republic's first magistrate to show an interest in noble artistic endeavor in a way the last Bourbons had not. Besides, all this economizing seemed to him hypocritical. He learned from the minister of public works that Don Niceto had tried to make the state pay for a special train he ordered for his first official trip as president. Failing that, he had from then on refused to travel except by automobile or in regular passenger trains.

In the meantime, with all of his concentration on public business, the Minister of War still gave some thought to the appearance of his departmental offices as reflecting republican dignity. He had found the Buenavista Palace horribly furnished by its former tenants, without plan or order and virtually uninhabitable. Its ramshackle appearance came from one minister following another, often after very short tenure. First he took down all portraits in one of the reception rooms; then he put back up those that truly decorated its walls and stored away the ugly and undistinguished ones. He spruced up the rooms contiguous to his office with tapestries and furniture from the royal patrimony, much of it discovered in garrets and lofts of palaces in Madrid and the La Granja Palace after their nationalization. At his first banquet he surprised the diplomatic corps with a meal whose distinction equaled in every way the finest which an accredited ambassador might enjoy at Europe's oldest courts.

As to politics in general, the Premier did not succeed in keeping Lerroux or any representative of his Radical party in the cabinet. "I hope that you will be offering us your collaboration," Don Alejandro had said to me with a significant smile in the corridors of Congress a few days after my Brother-in-Law's accession as Premier of the Provisional Government. When I expressed amazement that he could even think of my becoming a minister, he answered, confirming his previous intention, "Well, then, why not an embassy?" Nonetheless, two months later he himself refused to stay in the cabinet.

"You'll soon see Don Niceto's tricks!" Eugenio Barroso, an old friend from Bologna, said in a chance meeting on the streetcar after our not having seen each other for a long time. He was the son of a former Liberal minister and well-known cacique from Córdoba, and he was also the nephew of Sánchez Guerra, though not on good terms with his cousin Rafael. My friend had seen his own brilliant career as under secretary to Premier García Prieto nipped in the bud when Primo de Rivera destroyed the last remnants of our sham constitutional monarchy eight years earlier. Eugenio and his mother asked me to recommend his brother Antonio for the post of military attaché to Spain's embassy in Paris. Saravia and the Minister of War's closest adjutants had no objections, and his appointment went through. Still there five years later, Antonio, of course, joined the insurrection headed by generals secretly hostile to our republican regime. Eugenio insisted in that brief streetcar conversation, "I don't see how your Brother-in-Law can work with Don Niceto. You'll see, you'll see!" At that point I dismissed his warning as the product of natural enmity between two caciques from the same province. Later, though, I remembered my fellow student's ominous words as a terrible prophecy.

Again and again the president came up with some new trick to impede the Premier's innovations for our country. Though my Brother-in-Law tried not to mention anything he believed might damage the reputations of elected officials, I did gradually learn of these problems. For instance, they disagreed about the Premier's strict interpretation of the constitution in respect to their official relationship. The Prime Minister understood that he had responsibility for matters of general policy so long as votes in the Cortes indicated that he kept its support. He also believed that he spoke to the president for the whole cabinet. In this way he hoped to avoid Don Niceto's adopting our last king's practice of dealing directly with individual ministers to undercut the premier's authority, so indispensable for a ministerial government.

On the other hand, from the beginning Don Niceto sought to build a following among politicians whom he believed susceptible to corruption. Why? Undoubtedly he chose as his motto "Divide and Conquer," following our last monarch's inveterate practice. Thus he supported petty ambitions of restless ministers in opposition to the new Leader of the parliamentary and cabinet coalition. In this way, too, Don Niceto vented his hidden rancor against a Man who had won the game fairly. Voters had deprived the president of an opportunity to preserve unchanged the structure of our nation's society through his own faction, legitimately. He now tried in another way to invalidate the profound and revolutionary changes that the Premier had undertaken to achieve without glaring disturbance of our national life.

Delays in implementing a new agrarian law, drawn up with a sluggishness that made it stillborn, proved the principal cause of unrest to spoil the pacific auspices of April 14. After the government had ended sporadic acts of violence in Madrid and other capitals stemming from those first convent fires, reactionaries turned next to passive resistance and strengthening the caciques in the countryside. This provoked the passions of unjustly dispossessed peasants and raving dreamers. The revolutionary virus infected even the heart of Socialist organizations rapidly expanding into rural districts. Here recruits to the party and resistance societies lacked the political preparation of factory workers, and they abandoned the time-tested methods of older members.

Incidents of rural violence had repeatedly occurred under the last Bourbon, and two of many such incidents under the republic revealed an open wound. In Rioja and Estremadura clashes involving the Civil Guard made compelling a political question the cabinet, and the Premier in particular, had wanted to avoid. Both the Guard and the people suffered deaths and injuries, and parliamentary repercussions followed. The Premier stood firm in his judgment: he must punish a traditional yet terrible abuse of authority; he found it intolerable for the Civil Guard to respond with random shooting to a rock-throwing crowd. On the other hand, he could not accept a tacit impunity for those who fostered street risings directed against the Guard and thus undercut the authority it represented. To that extent Socialists in the cabinet supported him. Did they fully understand the responsibilities implicit in that support?

For the moment the Premier tried to avoid posing this matter in terms he felt misrepresented the events. He did not believe that General Sanjurjo, director of the Civil Guard and not personally involved in these unfortunate incidents, would jeopardize the Guard's prestige by linking it to abuses by his subordinates. This represented a change, as these police had traditionally felt sure of government support right up to the ministerial level for anything they did. My Brother-in-Law had spoken to Sanjurjo on several occasions and had found him very well adapted to the good life our republican government had preserved for him in gratitude for his services on April 14. He felt sure that Sanjurjo would not entertain any proposal against the new republican institutions. After all, nobody seemed to have made contact with the general about joining the the Spanish Military Union (*Unión Militar Española* or UME), a group of early renegades from their sworn loyalty to our fatherland and its tricolor flag. It also included a few more or less coerced volunteers from among those who had retired to the reserves with full pay. He had found Sanjurjo an uncomplicated man and not especially bright. A barbarian, a bully, a womanizer, he typified the past century's usual soldiery. African campaigns had provided him with a fund of barrack-room anecdotes. The Premier understood the general well enough to supply the words he lacked in their conversations with each other.

As Minister of War, then, he defended Sanjurjo, getting through a crisis about his immediate dismissal as best he could. He did replace the general after a suitable interval, when it could no longer seem due to pressure from the least judicious elements of his constituency. When the right time came the Minister provided reasonable satisfaction to all parties, moving Sanjurjo from command of the Civil Guard to command of the customs police. This lucrative post seemed to please Sanjurjo to the point of stammering words that the Minister translated eloquently. They agreed that this represented the best arrangement. With no loss of the prestige that his prudence had won, Sanjurjo could culminate his career in financial ease.

In the meantime the Premier kept a careful watch for his industrious opponents. Casares Quiroga, interior minister, aided by Arturo Menéndez, police chief, kept close track of persons who became increasingly daring in their defiance of the republican regime. In spite of all hostile efforts, however, there developed an increasingly solid national base of support for the government among men of good will. My Brother-in-Law told me nothing about all of that, and I knew very little about things that many people knew because my theatrical activities isolated me from public affairs. My relationship with the world of ministers and under secretaries came entirely from our prior acquaintance; our public and private lives remained entirely separate. I had few dealings with Casares Quiroga when he served as minister of the navy, but well into 1932 we began to meet when he and his amiable and charming wife visited the Ministry of War. We hit it off, of course; his jovial enthusiasm seemed so like my own. No doubt his infectious humor was exaggerated, as with tuberculars, by having to live his life with a happy contempt for death. We laughed a lot together about the Premier's legendary ruthlessness. Seeing him playing in such a carefree way with my little boy, Casares titled him "the Ogre." For a few friends—among whom Don Ángel Ossorio became increasingly important—he remained "the Ogre." Later on we referred to him in that way when changed circumstances prevented us from using his real name.

When summer came, my wife and I and our two little boys made our customary move to quarters at El Paular that my mother-in-law had for many years rented from the Carthusians. The Premier came to visit us there on several afternoons, and occasionally I traveled to Madrid to break my monotonous summer in the country. Preparation for our coming season at the Español provided an obvious pretext. Margarita and I wanted to engage some famous actors to enhance our competition with other municipal theaters for crowds. After negotiations broke down with Francisco Morano, I arranged to come to the city on August 9 for an interview with Ricardo Calvo. My Brother-in-Law did not quite tell me to cancel that appointment; he did insist that I should come immediately afterwards to the Ministry of War where he and other friends would be waiting. I left the Fuencarral Theater, where Calvo had a low-paying engagement, before midnight accompanied by López Silva, an actor, and a friend of his whose name escapes me. We took a taxi to save the people at the Ministry from waiting, and I left my companions at the Puerta del Sol, making excuses for my haste in leaving them—not wanting to show off my access to the Premier's residence.

At that late hour it did not surprise me when a sentry at the gate carefully checked my identity; it did surprise me, though, when the sergeant of the guard accompanied me to the Buenavista Palace doorway. I found the Minister's office, the private secretary's office, and a room used by my sister next to it ablaze with lights. Balcony doors stood open to admit misty air from the garden. It surprised me very much, indeed, to learn suddenly what everyone else already knew only too well. Sanjurjo had disappeared; then he had turned up in Seville heading a rebellion they expected to break out in Madrid at any moment, probably directed against the Ministry. With the Minister-Premier were Saravia and Leopoldo Menéndez, his adjutants, and Enrique Ramos, still his under secretary. A door connecting the secretary's office to my sister's room, almost always closed, now stood wide open. She shared their smiling anticipation of forthcoming events, beginning with my dumbfounded surprise.

The Minister and his assistants took calls coming in from the Police Department, the Ministry of the Interior, and by direct line from military headquarters in Seville, and they immediately informed the rest of us of latest developments. Apparently Sanjurjo planned to march on Madrid, counting on picking up support from garrisons as he advanced; thus the Badajoz garrison had orders to cut him off from the flank. The Minister, more knowledgeable about our highway system than his assistants, did not simply leave things to local authorities. He took off his glasses—which now had replaced the pince-nez fashionable in his youth—because they tired his eyes and in order to better study a map showing possible opportunities to attack the rebels. After a while the Interior Department phoned in a report from the governor of Seville: Sanjurjo's coup had failed completely. They believed that he was fleeing toward Portugal, and they had good hopes of capturing him. The Minister repeated orders to all governors from Seville to the Portuguese frontier to take Sanjurjo without unnecessary violence.

At this point a report came in of the arrest of a core committee in an upstairs apartment or studio on the calle de doña Bárbara de Braganza. Under the pretext of playing some kind of game, they were preparing the insurrectionary movement in Madrid for that night. My sister had served us more than one cup of coffee; she did not want to go to bed, but her husband insisted. There seemed nothing more to wait up for; discovery of these conspirators appeared to end the rebellion in Madrid as completely as the one in Seville. Finally she agreed, and she bade us good night.

A little later Arturo Menéndez came in, his usual grin nearly splitting his face. "Let's see how many caps you have brought with holes in them," the Minister said to him, smiling. Of course, he meant nothing cruel by it, only "let's hit them with all we've got." Facing battle in the streets, his attitude became quite military, and it proved effective enough that very few soldiers risked leaving their barracks to join the insurrection. His spirited words to the republic's faithful servant showed a far different spirit from what his adversaries scurrilously attributed to him on another occasion and in other circumstances. Liars and slanderers using religion as their shield, they claimed that he called on his men to "shoot them in the belly." Though completely out of character for a man who never said anything vulgar, some people accepted this fabrication and propagated it. Arturo Menéndez left, and the rest of us waited for something that came soon enough. The Premier lighted one cigarette after another as he walked back and forth between his office and his secretary's office talking with Leopoldo Menéndez, stopping from time to time to absent-mindedly check the pursuit of Sanjurjo on a map, or to take a telephone message from the telegraph office or from Casares at the Interior.

In less than a half hour a heavy explosion very close to the Ministry shook the night. Anita Guerrero, his curious observer at *The Crown*'s premiere, might have thought that he turned pale, but his lack of natural coloring made any change hard to detect. After those first shots that clearly came from the direction of the calle de Prim behind Buenavista Palace, I had the impression of an attack from all sides. Other bombardments followed with echoes rebounding from the closest houses on the calle de Barquillo; then an exchange of shots indicating terrible fighting came from the direction of Cibeles. "Keep away from the balcony," Enrique Ramos shouted, responding on the basis of some previous experience to my thoughtless impulse. He tried to hide his evident, quite natural fear.

After a noisy quarter hour came silence. "I'm going to check on Lola; she must be scared," I said. "Let her alone," her Husband answered. "She will be all right if you don't say anything." I crossed a large salon, unused except for big receptions, and another office beyond it leading to the Minister's private quarters. I came to her bedroom door and entered cautiously after hearing her stirring inside. "Who's there? Come in, come in," she said at once when she recognized me. In spite of the heat, she had her bedclothes pulled up to her chin. "What's happening?" she asked. "Nothing," I answered with foolish carelessness. "Fireworks for Saint Lawrence's Eve. I came so that you wouldn't worry. Nothing, nothing at all."

The next morning, feigning annoyance, she said, as she has said many times since, that I showed myself the greater fool in believing her such a fool as to accept that kind of explanation. Obedient to her Husband, never wanting to bother him, especially about official business, she had gone to her bedroom, but she had not gone to bed. She felt sure that we had remained in the presidential office because we expected more trouble. That first discharge had surprised her sitting in a chair, and she had gotten hastily into bed when she heard someone coming through the passage. I ought not to have tried to deceive her that way. Her Husband had not wanted to mislead her; he knew well enough that she was not fooled. He had wanted to spare her our worried nervousness, though his own serenity strengthened the rest of us. His strength sustained her also, as it did later in moments more serious than that first hint of future hazards.

By dawn the fighting had calmed down, and our triumph became complete in the course of the day as shooting ceased altogether. I hurried to my father's house; his daughter had already phoned very early that morning about our adventures on the night of the fireworks. After quickly giving him my impressions, I returned to Buenavista. Largo Caballero was in the Ministry anteroom where Saravia remained on duty. Up to then the Premier had not spoken to any of his colleagues except his secretary Carlos Esplá and the minister of the interior, both directly involved the night before. He did not even inform the republic's president until eight in the morning so as not to disturb his night's rest in his summer residence at La Granja. Don Niceto congratulated his Prime Minister and hurried to Madrid. Though the latter assured him that he need not bother to come as the crisis had passed, Alcalá Zamora wanted to pledge formally and in person to my Brother-in-Law that he would never sanction the return of those traitorous soldiers to active duty. Among the first politicians to come to express their support, Ossorio y Gallardo appeared, shaken by that first reactionary threat but always gracious and dignified.

Then I received a telephone call in the secretary's office from my old friend and patron of the Spanish College at the University of Bologna, the duke of Infantado. In an anguished voice he told me that when he got up that morning he had learned that two of his sons had left the family home. Surprised by news of the rising and assuming their involvement without his consent or even his knowledge, he wanted to know whether they had been arrested. I promised to inquire and let him know. Later I could reassure him that the Minister of War would not authorize proceedings against them in spite of their almost certain participation. Also, knowing that their father seemed to have no part in the frustrated rebellion, the Minister continued negotiations for purchase from him of land adjoining his estate at Viñuelas on Madrid's outskirts for the construction of barracks. In due course General Franco would establish his temporary residence there.

An enthusiastic public demonstration of support even reached the Buenavista Palace doorway during the cabinet meeting that day. The Premier usually had a far easier time in the Cortes than in committees, but this time the cabinet readily agreed with him to continue government business in a normal way and to present to the Cortes a special bill. It had just one article. This added to confiscations already foreseen in the agrarian law the confiscation without indemnification of property belonging to nobles when their role in the rising had been proved. The Chamber passed it without discussion and cheered the Premier enthusiastically when, with grave dignity, he reported to them the previous night's events.

They captured General Sanjurjo in his flight to Portugal. The Premier took great care to have him brought to Madrid in a car with all possible precautions and security. He felt certain that the general's motivation had not come merely from personal disgruntlement or from the sense of caste represented by the nascent UME, which had not attracted enough support to launch even that kind of desperate, hopeless insurrection. It became clear later that Franco, as the year before when conspirators first made contact with him, did not want to participate in anything smacking of unlawful opposition to the republic or to a cabinet with such strong popular support. From the first, then, the Premier realized that, though General Goded would support a rising, instigation for Sanjurjo's revolt had come from politicians and from republican ranks.

A little earlier in a speech in the Zaragoza bullring, Lerroux had predicted with assurance imminent events expressing the insecurity of a certain social class. Evidently he sought support from that class through the kind of negative political tricks that had corrupted the constitutional regime of our last monarch. In vain the Minister of War, now Premier, tried to convince parliamentarians that a natural bond united them, as civilians, whatever their political differences. As deputies they owed their positions to popular election, and so, consequently, did ministers responsible to the Chamber and the president of the republic himself. Placing one's trust in the strength of a particular faction, such as the army or a branch of it committed to a given political party, undermined the foundations of a regime he was trying to guide in accordance with the norms and irrefutable principles of republicanism. The Radicals, especially their perverse leader, understood things differently, and from that moment they tried to gain power by corrupting the republican system, flattering elements of the army still unwilling to abide by legitimate ways of effecting change. The Premier could not prove what he suspected, but this involvement by politicians had put a trump card in Sanjurjo's hand to play when he chose.

That August 10 became a day of triumphal euphoria in the Buenavista Palace and all Madrid. Some more, some less, but everyone felt that we had overcome an enemy; we had removed an abscess that we had seen growing and getting worse for a year. My sister celebrated the occasion with family and close friends who called to congratulate her on her husband's success. We already began to see a comic side to the previous night's events in spite of a soldier, wounded in defense of the republic, who patrolled halls, checked windows, and provided an element of tragedy for the servants. Then, as we sat in a room next to the secretary's office talking about damage to the building's facade, an explosion stunned us. "A shot," somebody said. I looked out over the balcony, sure that a tire had blown out on some car waiting on a ramp in front of the doorway, but I saw soldiers and chauffeurs looking up to us on the first floor. "A shot? No!" said my sister, smiling complacently. "Those sound quite different. I have heard them very close and know what they sound like."

We learned a few minutes later that in a house next door Major Riaño, demonstrating use of the pistol to someone, had fired by accident. My sister judged on the basis of rifle fire, her only experience with firearms up to then.

31

Preserving Memories

Whole days passed when the Premier, weighed down by work and appointments, did not leave his residence. It almost got to a point where he did not leave his office. Going over odds and ends of the unsuccessful coup, he told us of his interview with General Cabanellas, who had come to ask for a short leave a little before that event. Cabanellas had replaced Sanjurjo as commander of the Civil Guard, and my Brother-in-Law took his excessive protestation of loyalty at that interview as almost certain evidence that he knew about the plot; he had all but cried. Taking the general's place, his back to the central balcony, the Minister reenacted that scene with an element of ironic parody, mimicking his subordinate's gestures and words. Cabanellas was a republican of long standing, a well-known Mason, and, needless to say, a follower of Lerroux. His white hair and beard gave his face an appearance of kindliness—a sort of mask.

One night about when our old *tertulia* usually broke up, the Premier wanted to get out into the streets for a breath of air. To him a breath of air meant going to a café. After midnight not many people remained at the Lyon, near the post office. Indeed, its limited seating capacity did not admit many; later they expanded it into a neighboring building. This amiable retreat brought back memories of his last days as a leisured bachelor. Soon old friends joined us from other tables. It always surprised people to see the Premier's openness and simplicity in his enjoyment of glimmerings of his former life.

After we had drunk our excellent chocolate—comparing it to the inferior brew of later times—we retraced our steps toward the Ministry. He stopped at the Linares Palace corner to survey the Cibeles plaza, a battlefield a few nights earlier, and somebody pointed out bullet scars on tree trunks and on streetcar signposts. We had gone on foot, as it had not seemed worth the trouble to order a car at that inconvenient hour for so short a distance, so I walked with him as far as the elevator, and there we said goodnight.

Two or three days later, I found him alone in his office for a moment, and he spoke to me with a special smile that I had not seen for a while. "Sit down here," he said, and from a table drawer he took a bulky notebook bound in black with natural-colored leather corners and spine—his most recent writing. He had been keeping a diary. He had not done this before and did not do it afterwards. He wrote about outstanding days of his public life and about other days, less memorable but important to us because of impressions he wished to communicate. Here he addressed an unknown future reader, someone who would have the responsibility of judging us, his predecessors.

32

Catalans, You No Longer Have a King to Make War Against You

The Premier smiled, commenting to me about the birth of a myth concerning him in a newspaper account of the night of August 10 at the Ministry. Ramos, I think, had called my attention to a long ash on my Brother-in-Law's cigarette that night, though neither he nor I had attached any significance to it. After all, he himself did not draw the same implications as the journalist who treated this proof of his steady hand as important news and tried to stir up readers' imaginations with this supposedly irrefutable proof. Ramos and I did begin to ascribe importance to it, though, when the voice of the people echoed that laudatory anecdote. Anyhow, the Protagonist, always avoiding pitfalls of whimsy, believed that there were better signs of his sense of security than his pulse rate.

Even before responsibilities of his ministry absorbed him, in the pleasant idleness of his leisure days, my Kinsmen had often called my attention to the apoplectic "aneurism" in his neck, which sometimes did seem very strong. Also his hand would tremble after he had concentrated too steadily on his writing, had smoked too many cigarettes, or had drunk too much coffee. He felt some apprehension about all of that, and I often laughed to myself about his concern. How curious that popular imagination should have seized on precisely this detail of the cigarette ash as a sign of his calmness and presence of mind, since it did not indicate his real physical condition. Apart from that, he habitually flicked off his cigarette ash, and not always into the ashtrays with which his wife tried in desperation to surround him. But history is written with such details, and they don't lie. Even if this accurate detail about the Premier had not come from authentic recollections of that night, his presence of mind at all times provided an unmistakable guarantee of the authority he represented. The best evidence of my Brother-in-Law's self-control did not come from cigarette ash.

Only one witness can testify to the Premier's heartfelt satisfaction in sparing his enemy's life, apart from all political considerations. He had not wanted General Sanjurjo as his enemy, and he continued to believe that others shared responsibility for Sanjurjo's treason. Still, the letter of the law remains implacable; unavoidably, the court that judged the general would sentence him to death. Many hundreds of telegrams piled up on the secretary's desk; not one of them asked for clemency. All of Spain cried out with the voice of Fuenteovejuna for one expiatory victim. Persons who had condemned the innocent, rejoicing people on April 14 as an unruly mob now rejoiced in the idea of a propitiatory victim for a holocaust they themselves would not have dared to light.

"But where are Their Excellencies the Bishops!" exclaimed the Minister, searching for one single voice in support of the pity to which his own soul inclined. In fact, in Liberalism's pusillanimous days anyone condemned to death, however brutal, however horrible his crime, received at least the minimal pity of a formal petition for clemency from pastors of the Church of Christ. How extraordinary, then, that pacific citizens who rejected the concept of vengeance now demanded it, calling it political justice. They insisted on making a warning of this first uprising against our republic to which the condemned man had so recently sworn loyalty. He had also sworn loyalty to our king. The people's representatives, parliamentary deputies and even some ministers, felt strongly disposed to support the execution of a vindicatory sentence. From the first, the Minister of War felt the need to pardon Sanjurjo. My sister realized that soon, but he did not need to tell me about it either, and I did not ask about it. Once he himself became aware of his impulse, as usual he pondered it.

The Premier certainly did not have a reputation for sensitivity. People who get that reputation normally use it as a mask to cover their lack of intelligence. Acting in a malleable, effeminate way, they treat it as something estimable. On the other hand, persons who admired my Brother-in-Law for his supposed coldness mistook his manly spirit of dignity for lack of sensitivity. He had deep-rooted compassion.

He realized the uselessness of speaking of compassion to comrades who did not feel that way or who repressed this feeling because they thought that implacable justice would strengthen their own positions. Even if he had convinced members of the cabinet, he felt uncertain about whether the Cortes would follow his lead in a vote on this issue. He had become a skillful enough parliamentarian to recognize that much, and he did not want to take chances. Our republic's founding legislators had erred in not making the right of pardon a simple presidential prerogative; the Premier speaking for cabinet, had to propose this pardon for the president's final decision. My Brother-in-Law began by speaking to each minister individually on propitious occasions, using the argument best suited to each. When it came to an open discussion in the cabinet, he approached the matter in political terms rather than in humanitarian terms—we know this from routine records kept at the time. He argued that the phrase "feelings have no place in politics" is one of Machiavelli's more limited concepts, completely missing the broader implications. Intransigent cabinet members who didn't realize his intention ended up saying that he had "guts."

Thus he convinced colleagues that they should support his argument about the practicality of commuting Sanjurjo's death sentence to life imprisonment for purely political reasons. They would achieve nothing by making a martyr of a man who had failed to make himself a hero. The monarchical government had shown weakness in its unwillingness or inability to pardon Galán and García Hernández, in shooting them in strict accordance with the law instead of adjusting to circumstances. With Sanjurjo shot, men who had secretly launched him on his desperate, rash adventure could rest easy. That would silence him forever. The fact that the general had not informed on them yet did not mean that he did not threaten them with future revelations. In fact, an imprisoned rebel general would provide the best guarantee of good behavior on the part of men involved in his coup. The Premier agreed with colleagues who argued that, if they spared Sanjurjo now, he would not remain a prisoner for life. He answered them that amnesty granted by the government at its discretion, after consideration, and through a parliamentary vote would relegate to eternal oblivion a general without a command and without prestige. All things in due course, and no irremediable decisions.

After the trial and Sanjurjo's condemnation, with no legal pretext remaining to delay his execution, the Council of Ministers had to resolve the case. Up to then they had discussed it without the pressure of an immediate decision. That morning they could not put off taking action. My sister knew all this and anxiously awaited her Husband's return to dinner. I had agreed to join them at their meal as on so many other occasions but this time with more interest than usual. Although the council often prolonged its meetings, that day she felt especially impatient. Her Husband did not have everyone on his side. He had not given her the assurances he had on other occasions because things might not go his way. She now saw very clearly something she had imagined as a girl at home, the influence a pious queen or the wife of a minister or president might exercise on a powerful statesman toward achieving commutation of a sentence. When he came into the office where we waited, she greeted him with an anxious question, but he could only answer with a tone of voice and a tired gesture indicating that everything remained uncertain. The council had not reached a decision, and we would do well to say as little as possible, especially to anyone, friends or acquaintances, who asked us about it.

I attended the session of the Cortes with him that afternoon. He said nothing about the sentence there, though everyone had heard of it, and he said nothing of the cabinet meeting. He asked me to join him in his car afterward, and I hardly dared to break the silence of our drive to Alcalá Zamora's house. I waited outside while he pushed through a crowd of newspapermen, paying no heed to their questions, went up a short stairway, and entered the president's home. Before long he came out again, his broad, pale face lit up with a smile as he spoke from the doorway, "Gentlemen, the president of the republic has agreed to sign General Sanjurjo's commutation." Waving aside their applause, he came quickly down to the car, and we drove back to the Ministry while journalists dispersed to spread their story.

"A man's life weighs heavy in your hand!" he said to me when we were alone in the spacious apartment he used as his main office. Magnanimity seemed to shine from his eyes and his whole visage. It filled me with joy that he had saved this special confidence for me. Afterward he went to relieve his wife. He and his colleagues had agreed not to reveal the council's decision in favor of Sanjurjo's pardon until the republic's president had ratified it with his signature. Even a word might arouse public indignation, and they wanted above all to avoid a painful and difficult confrontation in Congress. Thus he had left my sister to her worries, certain of compensating her with a peaceful sleep that night. I shared his pride in the almost neurotic sensitivity which his spouse suffered through those difficult hours when the enemy traitor's life hung in the balance. She and her Husband could have lost their lives that night of the Saint Lawrence's fireworks if well-prepared defenses had failed and the Ministry of War had yielded to its vindictive attackers. It made me proud to have a sister so worthy of him.

The Premier now enjoyed Epiphany, the Day of the Three Magi, more than his own saint's day, January 1, which we celebrated with very little more festivity than we had when it was merely a family occasion. An electric train set sent to my elder boy by the French ambassador figured prominently among the many toys my sons received that year. In this way M. Herbette showed his affection for the boy's uncle. José Ramón, however, did not have sufficient space at his disposal for its circular track in our third floor apartment on Velázquez. The Premier, crawling around on the floor, enjoyed himself far more than my son did in setting up that train and running it in the middle of the Ministry's large salon, now refurbished for holiday receptions. At first his nephew waited impatiently for the engine's circling passages, past the station, lighting up signals, but he soon got bored just watching. This is a game for grown-ups. The ambassador's kindness obliged me to pay a call to thank him, and that led to my wife and me receiving invitations whenever the Premier and my sister honored the embassy table. The ambassador also asked us sometimes without the Premier when he entertained politicians, artists, literary people, and distinguished journalists—recalling his own career as editor of *Temps*. M. Herbette and his wife did not have much social intercourse with Madrid's aristocracy.

Proud of his wife, it pleased my Brother-in-Law to see attention paid to her by the diplomatic community, and he made an effort to reciprocate with simple, dignified receptions and dinner parties. In this way he compensated both for the understandable lack of experience of some of his governmental colleagues and for the excessive ostentation shown by others in their eagerness to make an impression. Moreover, he wanted, as Premier, to continue the friendly intimacy of the *tertulias* of the Ateneo, Henar, and Regina, and he hosted gatherings of those old friends for light refreshment at the Ministry after his usual Sunday drive. He also made a special point of giving literary colleagues the social recognition they deserved. Members of the Ateneo had finally elected him their president, but he had to resign himself never to see fulfilled his long-standing wish to have it moved to the Sánchez Toca Mansion on the Paseo del Prado. The time had long passed when, alienated by the Ateneo's decline, he had considered establishing another literary club called "Recoletos." He could at least show a continuing interest in writers, artists, and chosen representatives from all liberal professions, apart from their political beliefs, by inviting them to the opening of the Ministry's newly decorated main-floor salons.

Everyone rightly praised the Premier for his restoration or, better, innovation in the republican era of an elegance that decadent aristocrats had identified as belonging exclusively to royal courts. Guests admired the sumptuousness of these rooms furnished with pictures, mirrors, tables, armchairs, tapestries and chandeliers salvaged from attics and cellars of royal palaces. They appreciated in these rooms the tasteful use made by the preeminent "Republican Gentleman"—as Margarita Xirgu had called him so ingeniously and exactly—of inherited traditions of dignified opulence that people expect to accompany public power.

In a political regime based on representation, persons who represent the people become their physical incarnation—focusing, unifying, personalizing the masses. Those personifying this authority must also exhibit attendant prestige, including inherited prestige, and they must share that prestige with outstanding representatives of various social groups from literature, the arts, and the sciences. The Premier thought of our new republic very much as a republic of letters. In his plan men of letters would even control the peacetime army. Furthermore, they would not orient our armed forces in old patterns but would look ahead to a new era, toward achieving the blessings of peace.

Resolution of the "Catalonian Problem," as they had called it since the days of the Regency, proved one of the Premier's most difficult and unavoidable tasks in his effort to establish our government on a strong political base. He wanted very much to resolve it by a formula Ortega y Gasset appositely called national "pulling together" (*conllevancia*), the only possible solution apart from tyranny. The Premier had contracted a debt of honor with the most distinguished Catalonian intellectuals before 14 April 1931 to achieve autonomy for Catalonia within the broader framework of our republic. Few Spaniards had so comprehensive a concept as he did of what their nation had been, was, and might become—comprehensive in terms of space and time, history and geography, but strictly defined and concrete within the policies of the Second Republic. This appeared clearly during the parliamentary debate on the autonomy of one of the richest provinces destiny has linked to Spain through the centuries. This innate Parliamentarian spared no effort in persuading a majority that did not share his opinion but that had no other clear alternative to offer. From Philip V to the present, Catalonia had preserved the sacred fire of her inextinguishable separate personality in the agglomeration of our great common fatherland. Underground or proclaiming it to the four winds, she had expressed steadfast faith in her identity, more or less openly, more or less virulently depending on the vicissitudes of the government established in Madrid, the logical and natural seat of Philip II's monarchy.

In the Premier's considered opinion, no mistake could possibly arise about identification of Catalans with other Spaniards. They were as Spanish as anybody. Very Spanish himself, with roots reaching from his home plot in Alcalá to Catalonia and the Basque country, he knew that Spanish unity found nourishment in many diverse peninsular soils and from other branches grafted on. The word *Spain* incorporated a very wide circuit. For instance, it exceeded the political limits assigned to it on maps of the Iberian peninsula because Portugal belonged to it as much as Catalonia did. On the other hand, he identified Spain and Spanish unity more with Cervantes than with the Catholic Monarchs, and like our political tradition, our literary tradition established under the House of Austria accepted, respected, and fomented this natural variety. Despite a truly imperial dispersion of the Castilian language, the word *Spanish* did not pertain exclusively to it. He believed that the Academy of Language had erred in defining Castilian as the exclusive Spanish idiom; he regarded Catalan, Basque, and Galician-Portuguese as equally Spanish languages.

How could the Second Spanish Republic recognize this diverse tradition yet escape the extreme fragmentation and dispersion of power that had characterized our First Republic? He had a question for those who rejected a special regime for Catalonia—not to mention the Basque provinces and Galicia—because of their loyalty to the unitary idea of a highly centralized nation, exemplified by our old monarchical empire. Did they realize that Catalonia had not had to contribute levies of soldiers for armies of those truly imperial kings? On the other hand, he never accepted the national state's disintegration that separatists sought—complete independence for their Catalonian fatherland. Perhaps others did not understand the Premier's pioneer policy of political conciliation so well as I did. Others had not heard his words before reading them, and much more that he could not put into writing. They did not recognize the youthful romantic, passionate reader of Rousseau in today's opportunistic statesman, the man of action, the practical man who meant what he said and said what he thought. *The Social Contract,* so rich in its speculative suggestions had applications to Spain's revolution. The liberty that now united the peninsula's Spanish people in one national domain called *Spain,* replacing monarchical authoritarianism, had its true basis in everyone's voluntary acceptance and sharing of our fatherland's common destiny, not in capricious elections by inconsistent voters.

The Statute of Catalonia stood, then, as a political pact sanctioned and sealed by the republic's government. The statute recognized the Catalans' special autonomous law, with their own customs and language, their regional characteristics, but always as part of the Spanish nation. The spirit, thought, and words of the Head of the Spanish cabinet brooked no misinterpretation; he spoke straightforwardly without subtleties or deception. Any Catalan erred who considered autonomy as a mere step toward separation, or who thought of the statute as a compromise to enable the republic's Cortes to accept an eventual, painful separation. The Premier understood the statute as an integral, complementary part of Spain's republican constitution.

In writing about this I have had to look up his speeches on the Statute of Catalonia in his *Political and Parliamentary Addresses,* published at the end of the first stage of his brief career. I think that he must already have begun at the time of these speeches to complain to friends and family. "I don't know what I will say. I have a headache!" and he would raise his eyebrows as a sign of tiredness and disdainful indifference. Later we came to predict the greatness of forthcoming speeches by whether he had slept badly the night before and whether he had a migraine.

Finally, after many congressional sessions, much heated discussion, and the Premier's magnificent presentation, our Cortes voted in favor of the Catalonian statute. Then the Chamber exploded with an extraordinary burst of enthusiasm and reconciliation. Representatives of the ancient Principality of Catalonia embraced Castilian zealots whom they had hated since the famous Bloody Corpus Christi Day in the seventeenth century. Overwhelmed by the undeniable, large majority vote that swamped Aragonese intransigence, the Premier's old Ateneo friend, Don Antonio Royo Villanova, a fervid anti-Catalanist, offered heartfelt congratulations. He complimented me no less cordially with Aragonese canniness, "This will very much please the King-Father. And well it might, well it might!" He meant the satisfaction the Premier's father-in-law would find in his friendly congratulations and those of others, as proof of popular regard for his Son-in-Law.

After the statute's approval came the Premier's journey to Barcelona for its official presentation to Catalonia's Government of the Generalitat. I received a special invitation to join the official party along with many journalists. Having no assignment to write up, I went just to enjoy myself in that surge of overflowing enthusiasm with which an entire people acknowledged the presence of a man who stood for Spanish brotherhood within our republic's egalitarian freedom. Don Jaume Carner joined other worthy Catalonian supporters traveling with the Premier; as minister of the treasury he had proved a collaborator from beyond the Ebro who measured up to my Brother-in-Law's standards. Nobody would have guessed that a few months later I would also witness the last farewells of those two men. Then the great Catalan, hopelessly condemned by his doctors, grieved only for the republic's future. Like his friend, who was at that point the former Premier, he saw it suddenly, dizzyingly unstable where it had seemed completely secure.

We of the entourage went to bed soon after our train left Madrid, having no doubts that we would soon have to get up again. Even in Mora de Ebro, very early next morning, a heedless crowd—every person in town judging by the noise we heard from the platform—tried to get the Premier to make an appearance. I doubt that anyone even went to suggest it to him. He had already foreseen this situation the evening before, and at dinner and afterward to his closest *contertulianos* he had made it clear that he would not get up early. I had voluntarily withdrawn to the company of journalist friends, secretaries, and lesser personages. Carner and another Catalan did get up, and they calmed down the clamorous enthusiasm as well as they could. If the noise did not bring the Premier forth, it did wake him up and put him in a bad mood. He never did find the grace to get out of bed in the morning in a cheerful mood.

Not yet fully dressed myself, I saw from a window a striking symbol as we pulled out of that station. Two hundred meters from the track, standing on the roof of a house under construction, a Herculean man, his shirtsleeves rolled up, was waving the republican flag with his strong arms. Crowds became truly impressive as we approached the capital. Not only on station platforms but all along the tracks, more and more people waited steadfastly to see the Premier's train pass by; its screaming whistle blended with a cheering human echo, and a long trail of eyes followed in its wake as it sped onward. We didn't take account, didn't even notice, in that rapid exchange of glances how enthusiasm turned to disappointment because the Traveler failed to appear. Never prodigious in showing himself to a curious public, he found an easy excuse in wariness of the fatigue awaiting him in Barcelona during the next two days.

Outpouring of popular enthusiasm for his entrance into Barcelona far exceeded preparations made by city officials and ceremonies arranged by the Government of the Generalitat. The Premier, my sister, and those of us in their party had to wait quite a while before we could even get out of our railroad coach. Premier Maciá, his wife, and their daughter María, whom his own compatriots called "Princess María" as an affectionate joke, waited in the railroad station's reception room. Finally a way was cleared for us through the stentorian crowd that had invaded the France Station. Enthusiastic railwaymen on top of train cars mingled their shouts with locomotive whistles in a general clamor of unending ovation. Our Catalonian hosts wanted to show themselves worthy of Cervantes's immortal praise of their people as "a model of courtesy," possibly to correct Dante's terrible judgment about "the avaricious poverty of Catalans." That welcome took up far

more time than mere politeness required, and it upset a meticulously scheduled procession in the Premier's honor. It certainly demonstrated the Catalonian people's desire to render homage to their great Castilian liberator.
That delirious and sincere enthusiasm expressed by innumerable people
shouting as with one voice won all of us, and we joined in their cheering.
As hoarse voices intensified like a swelling of the sea, our throats choked
up, and our eyes filled with tears in an effusion of mutual happiness.

Somehow I managed to crowd into a car with too many others, including
some official who in the confusion had become separated from where he
belonged. We took off slowly following an automobile carrying those two
premiers, heading for the ancient Generalitat Palace opposite City Hall on
the Plaza de San Jaime in the heart of the city. Though we hadn't far to go,
we found it almost impossible to move at all through that dense crowd;
people were packed so tight that you couldn't distinguish procession from
onlookers. As we passed the Plaza del Palacio, Eduardo Marquina the poet
emphasized his happiness by waving enthusiastically to me from a balcony
of the old Governor's Palace (the City Government Building). Soon I recognized his sister, Mrs. Moles, among Catalonian ladies who, with Mrs. Maciá,
welcomed my sister and settled down to hear her Husband's greeting to
Barcelona's people.

"Catalans!" we heard in a magical silence that followed the first clamorous
greeting when he appeared on a balcony above that multitude. "You no
longer have a king to make war against you!" A new howl of triumph rose
into the heavenly blue morning sky from a crowd that filled the plaza, spilled
into entrances of connecting streets, and extended through the Ramblas and
the Gran Vía Layetana. Loudspeakers broadcast his words throughout the
great city from the Tibidabo to Montjuich. At the end of that brief speech,
so full in its linguistic precision, the grave, dramatic national anthem "Els
Segadors" filled the air, and all of us Castilians recognized a new meaning
in that hymn: defiance seemed gone from it. Those thousands of hearts now
overflowed with fraternal feeling.

Still, I don't know whether others felt on that occasion the lack of a
unifying national hymn to celebrate a truly national pact. I did. In the republic's first days a talented musician, Oscar Esplá, had wanted to compose
such an anthem on his own account and in his own way. The then Minister
of War, a music lover, had noticed Esplá's work some years earlier, and he
sponsored a premier performance of this "Rural Hymn" at the Ateneo. Esplá
rather pedantically called it that, hoping to increase its popularity. On that
occasion the Ateneo audience, after courteously applauding this new work,
had called for the Republican Band to strike up the "Riego Hymn," which
they hummed. Everyone had always accepted it as our republican anthem.
They ended by singing the "Marseillaise," bequeathed to the world by the
French Revolution and symbolizing the universal republic.

On that same supreme day in Barcelona we became aware that the Generalitat's premier had a very different attitude from ours about the new statute. Catalans thought of Colonel Maciá, whom they called "Grandfather," as a kind of patriarch. For many years relegated to the army reserves, he had identified politically with the extreme separatist Esquerra. Traditionally this party had counted for little in Catalonian politics, easily outweighed by the more conservative Lliga, which had accepted collaboration under the autonomy offered by Spanish republicans. Then the April 12 elections had unexpectedly set a course far different from that foreseen in the Pact of San Sebastián. The extreme Left had triumphed; the republican party of Catalonian Action, nicknamed "the Little League," had almost disappeared, and controlling power had passed into Maciá's hands.

It took considerable effort to bring Maciá to reason, to make him see that the best foundation for Catalonian freedom lay in accepting what already existed in law, the status quo. He had accepted the constitutional pact only because he saw that a declaration of complete independence would spell disaster for Catalonia and the rest of Spain and that his country's industry would suffer more from it than Spain's national cause. Right away, then, Maciá had adopted the nationalistic attitude the Premier had tried to overcome by granting the Statute of Catalonia. He constantly manifested reservations about the statute by a series of little incidents through which he took pleasure in provoking the central power. On the other hand, my Brother-in-Law never permitted a shadow of doubt about the supremacy of his own position as representative of the Head of State, and at no time would he accept the least challenge that might establish a precedent indicating an equality of the two governments. The Generalitat's premier did not have authority on the same level as that exercised by the republic's Premier. The one represented the Council of Ministers of the entire united republic; the other represented only the Generalitat of Catalonia, with limited, merely regional responsibilities. The republic was unitary, not a federation of independent states.

The Grandfather adopted the recalcitrant political style of a suspicious peasant, assiduously affecting a spirit of extreme localism, the most reactionary provincialism. He and his followers inevitably felt annoyed when Catalonia's people had expressed themselves so spontaneously, welcoming the Premier as their strongest and most eloquent protector. His triumphant entry into Barcelona gave unmistakable evidence of their support. In consequence, though Maciá had agreed to make no speeches that day after his welcome from the Generalitat's balcony, he now wanted to have the last word and to offer a toast at that evening's banquet. The Premier reluctantly agreed, but with an explicit reservation: he must see the text of Maciá's toast ahead of time so that he could prepare his response. Dressing that night, about to leave for dinner, he felt very impatient because the promised text had not arrived. Finally, after many comings and goings, almost at the time scheduled for the banquet to begin, Ramos arrived at our hotel with the awaited manuscript. My Brother-in-Law's first reading of it so irritated him that he violently yanked out his collar button, tearing the buttonhole, and began to take off his starched shirt. He would not attend the banquet in his honor. It seemed an intolerable affront to try to use such a trick to force him to tolerate the kind of offense he had feared. I no longer recall Maciá's words.

Between myself and Ramos—I suggested the amendment of a phrase or two to make the toast acceptable—we succeeded in getting him to agree to it. Maciá still had to approve these corrections, without which the Premier would not attend that dinner. Eventually, the banquet began—at least a half hour late, but it finally did occur. Having no assigned seat, I went, instead, to the Olympia Theater. Here they treated the official celebration in a popular spirit I would not have found at the elegant Liceo.

The next day, after another meal in the Tibidabo District and a ceremony at the City Government Building, neither of which Maciá attended, we drove in a car to make our departure from Reus. This provided an opportunity for farewells that somewhat modified the bad feelings that had marred the journey's beautiful popular demonstrations. The two premiers appeared together on a Reus town hall balcony, and after my Brother-in-Law said a few words Maciá responded with an embrace less awkward than his earlier verbal contributions. The crowd's delirious ovation continued until our train pulled out for Madrid soon afterward.

That night, when the official party had retired, I stayed up very late eating and dancing in an improvised salon in the dining car with journalist friends including a woman reporter and her girlfriend. How many times afterward have I heard in my mind, like an ironic echo, the Premier's words from that balcony on the Plaza de San Jaime, "Catalans! You no longer have a king to make war against you!"

33
Shoot Them in the Belly

Some people have argued that elemental republicanism, that is, liberalism and individualism, carried to logical extremes becomes in its final doctrinal emanation anarchy or political anarchism. On the other hand, in a natural reaction against doctrinaire revolutionary excesses, republics of our times, since the French Revolution, have concentrated on building a popular social foundation—in effect a socialist base. This also includes republics headed by monarchs. The most farsighted leaders of Spain's Second Republic sought viability in some kind of equilibrium between these two diverging directions taken by the masses who had come to control world governments in the past century and a half.

We know that founders of our new regime had not had cooperation from the National Confederation of Labor (CNT)—an organization of anarchist syndicates. The Socialist party, on the other hand, had participated directly in the Pact of San Sebastián, and afterward the General Confederation of Labor (UGT) had supported the regime with its growing strength. The CNT, preponderant in Catalonia, had finally agreed to support the republican and democratic revolution by voting for Catalonia's Esquerra. The syndicates also had considerable influence among Andalusian workers. Another important branch of syndicalism had its base in La Coruña. The Socialist decision to participate in the first republican cabinet aggravated the natural enmity between the two great fellowships into which Spanish workers had divided according to apparently irreconcilable theories and practices.

From time to time my Brother-in-Law pointed out to me the hostility of Largo Caballero, longstanding secretary of the Socialist party and minister of labor from the republic's inception, toward syndicalist organizations. These organizations impeded—mainly in the Andalusian countryside—labor reforms Largo was trying to achieve during both the Provisional Government and the one that followed it. The Premier himself might on many occasions have preferred to follow a policy of leniency to attract support from any syndicalists who felt ready to cooperate with the republic's government, but he remained faithful to his commitments. He used his personal influence to support policies established by the Council of Ministers over which he presided. After all, in spite of his devotion to republican individual-

217

ism, he had little sympathy for the disorder of anarchist thought and still less for anarchist actions, and he did not much respect CNT leaders.

Even during the Alcalá Zamora era of the Provisional Government, with Miguel Maura serving as minister of the interior, some lamentable incidents occurred in Seville. In an attack on a truck transporting prisoners, a rescue attempt in María Luisa Park, Civil Guards responsible for the transport shot at would-be liberators. That revived a campaign against the so-called "fugitives law" (*ley de fugas*), the practice of shooting escaping prisoners. This practice had typified the worst years of repression at the end of the monarchy when General Martínez Anido, as governor general, and General Arleguí, as police chief, ruled Barcelona. The Minister of War didn't say as much in cabinet meetings about the handling of that incident in the park as he did about another that attracted much public attention to Seville and in which he felt that the minister of the interior had clearly gone too far in reprisal. Maura had ordered destruction by cannon fire of the so-called "House of Cornelius." When my Brother-in-Law criticized this as excessive, Maura merely replied that the house, proved location of clandestine anarchist meetings, was empty when they bombarded it. For once my Kinsman broke his rule and spoke to me of the imprudence of exaggerating this matter by an unnecessary show of force, both wasteful and wrong.

Beside the federalists, naturally attracted to anarchistic decentralization, other republicans sought out the CNT. Of course the Radicals felt ready to emphasize their opposition to the Premier's collaboration with Socialists, even through shameful alliances. Similarly, rightist extremists, declared enemies of the recently installed regime, encouraged leftist subversion in order to justify reactionary violence in reprisal. Both groups aimed finally to impede the republic's regular growth and consolidation. Now with the predominantly military coup d'état of August 10 overcome, those same republicans who had clandestinely aided it continued their efforts to harry the Republican-Socialist cabinet by provoking other conflicts against it; they were backed by the landed and mercantile classes. These so-called "men of order" thought only of preserving their privileged position. Toward this end they stirred up the naturally turbulent spirit of anarchists committed to the illusion of a society governed entirely by the will of each individual person, and this entailed subversion of the existing order by means of coup and violence—including hired gunmen.

In consequence, another far more serious rising occurred in the village of Fígols in Catalonia a year and a half after those incidents in Seville. The cabinet decided to deport some prominent Catalonian syndicalists to Villa-Cisneros in Africa to join the *señoritos* already serving time there for their part in the Saint Lawrence uprising. Thus they attacked the malady by amputation, but it hardly required a medical specialist to realize that these first symptoms of cancer might return. Even a layman could see that.

On another equally important front, officials of the Catholic Church, at

first seemingly responsive to the good relations between the Spanish government and the Holy See, reversed their position. This came in spite of benevolent efforts, especially by the Premier, to alleviate all difficulties in
connection with the law separating church and state. Now church officials
adopted the antirepublican attitude of most religious orders. Led by the
Jesuits, their schools dissolved, they turned to a highly effective propaganda
campaign, working behind the scenes through their favored clients. The
propaganda soon spread from pulpit to confessional, from sacristies and
associations of aristocratic charities, confraternities, and catechists down
to the simplest daily communicant on her knees asking for a miracle before
some image. It traveled through pilgrimages and local Holy Week processions, to confraternities of the Forty Hours and Nocturnal Adoration. From
there it showed up ostentatiously in the gold, jeweled crosses that now appeared in the outfits of great ladies and in the generous décolletages of
music-hall singers and second sopranos. This campaign was further perpetrated by mystery plays that lacked the poetic power of the classics and,
much more commonly, by the coarsest burlesque passing as satire and performed for clienteles in theaters that had usually presented a very chaste
repertoire. And also by three-day and nine-day penitential processions. And
even by apparitions of the Virgin to some shepherd or other.

Nonetheless those craven enemies quickly backed down when confronted
with the consequences of their actions. When called upon to do it, they
readily made formal retraction. The rector of the Augustinian residency on
the calle de Columela at once granted my request that a brother of that
community should from the pulpit of their Church of Saints Emmanuel and
Benedict condemn the use of calumny for political purposes. This stemmed
from my hearing a lady whom I neither knew nor wished to know speak in
their sacristy about my sister in ridiculous and indecent terms. The Augustinian brother went beyond my request and used that ugly act to point
to a papal encyclical and pastoral letter issued at the time of the republic's
proclamation that strongly recommended respect for established authority.
Further, he made rectification, not mentioning her by name by my request,
by praising the virtuous companion of the Public Man, innocent victim of
slander promulgated in a futile attack on her Husband's policies, a parishio-
ner of that very church. The brother denounced this abuse as opposed to a
spirit of Christian charity and obedience, a notorious an injustice, et cetera,
et cetera.

As I had previously announced his retraction in a comment in the columns
of *Sol,* without saying whom or what it involved, parishioners overflowed
the church at that Sunday Mass. Certainly my efforts had very limited
success. People began by taking umbrage in an unpleasant way, saying that
the crowd came from family and friends to whom I had mailed the newspaper clipping as a kind of invitation. Then, on leaving, I overheard one of
those highly Catholic ladies commenting to another, "Well, now they are

satisfied. After all, what could those poor men—meaning the friars—have done!" No doubt she went on to complain about this infringement on her freedom of speech.

In spite of everything, my Brother-in-Law had faith, and rightly, in the influence of his mere presence on people who knew him only from what they had heard or read in hostile newspapers. He even bragged jokingly about the support he would get from women once he had talked with them. This did not refer merely to four old women—or four hundred—whose interview with him provided one of the most delightful anecdotes of his life as Premier. You had to hear him tell about that success to fully appreciate it. Soon after his official installation as Premier, some Catholic ladies paid him a rather tumultuous visit by way of defending their religion, which nobody intended to attack. The first contingent had arrived at the Plaza de Colón with no object beyond making an angry demonstration before the Castellana entrance to the Premier's office. City employees stood by, ready to disperse them with a fire hose, but the Premier, aware of the situation, decided with very good grace to ask them to come up for a special interview. He wanted to know what complaints lay behind their virtuous shouts of "Long Live Christ the King!" This conference was only partly impromptu, since it seems the group's president had requested it.

I heard about that event long after it happened, but he kept on telling the story mirthfully for years. First, surprised by the persuasive gentleness of his voice, and then by his obliging words and promises, the most ingenuous of them exclaimed, "Well, he isn't so ugly after all!" Then, highly jubilant, seeing that he did not react like the fanatic whom she had probably expected, she let out a shout, "He's on our side! He's on our side! God has done it! God did it!" Despite the joke he made of that good woman, describing her as truly ridiculous in her exaggeratedly modest clothing, with glasses that emphasized the ugliness of her round, herpetic face, he could not hide his entire good will. He always acted as naturally and simply with the pure in heart, however insignificant, as he did in resolving political business of the highest importance.

Another lady of a very different order had become a subject of amused gossip in the world of embassies and legations. I think that my Brother-in-Law met Princess Elizabeth Bibesco at the Greek Legation, or anyhow at one of many more or less official dinners he attended. Her title came from her husband, a Rumanian prince who at that point represented his country in Madrid. English by birth, she was the daughter of Lord Asquith, the British prime minister of the Liberal coalition that had served during the first great European war of our time. The princess had a yearning for notoriety like her mother, whose *Memoirs* recently published in England had provided quite a lot to talk about. During that evening at the legation, the princess spoke somewhat impolitely when she met this man, then merely Minister of War in Spain's government. No doubt she wished to treat him according to her estimate of his worth, as a newcomer in those elegant circles. The Minister retained a bad impression of the lady because of her efforts to shine through glib cleverness. After all, he could hold his own, and he had decisively put her in her place, as the saying goes. If my Brother-in-Law did not feel well disposed toward the princess, she, on the other hand, came to feel drawn to him as outstanding among the "public men" whose friendship she undertook to cultivate; these included Hitler, Mussolini, and Stalin.

My old friend Justo Gómez Ocerin, then secretary of the Ministry of State, introduced me to the princess one evening at the German Embassy. She in turn introduced me to her husband, and they both gave me their theatrical writings to read, hoping to have them translated and performed at the Español. After that they asked me on several occasions to the Rumanian Legation, located in a house rented from the son of Infanta Eulalia on the calle de Quintana. A great friend of José Antonio Primo de Rivera, the princess undertook to bring my Brother-in-Law together with this young leader of Spain's first fascists. Both of them—with greater indifference on the Premier's part—avoided a useless encounter. After the first meeting, and with better grace, the princess undertook to attract the Premier's friendship through continual attentions. A great admirer of her own father, she often compared the two men's parliamentary skills, even in a letter after hearing the Premier speak in the Cortes. Following a current fashion of driving out to a café or inn near the Illustrious University in Alcalá, she often traveled that highway, and she called it "the most beautiful road in the world." She certainly exaggerated her delight in the countryside, typical of Madrid's environs. Her new, favorite friend, the Premier, had more deep-seated reasons for his special pleasure in that drive.

Meanwhile our political factions became increasingly clear. True, Casares Quiroga had strengthened the Republic Action party by joining to it his ORGA coalition (*Organización Republicana Gallega Autónoma* or Organization of Autonomous Galician Republicans). On the other hand the group headed by Martínez Barrio, who had served as minister in the Provisional Government under both Alcalá Zamora and my Brother-in-Law, refused to accept party discipline under the latter's leadership. The Radical Socialists took the same position, and among them the famous "wild boars" behaved with utmost independence in parliament. Ortega y Gasset wittily called them that because they attacked both right and left. The solid bloc of Lerroux's Radicals had, of course, also assumed an independent position. All of this meant that the Premier increasingly based his leadership on a Republican-Socialist program with continuing support from the UGT. He insisted that he intended to keep revolutionary reforms needed for the renewal of Spain's declining society within norms of a progressive democratic regime. He would keep the regime as democratic as seemed compatible with existing circumstances.

In his opinion, according to an unshakable belief clearly based on the usages of other countries, parliament represented the nation and manifested the national will. This parliament governed through authority delegated by the people; in its turn it delegated executive authority to a ministerial cabinet and to the premier who headed that cabinet. The premier stood responsible to both parliament and the president of the republic. My Brother-in-Law did not, in principle, believe in limiting the president's power to dissolve the Cortes and call for new elections before the five-year limit established by our constitution for each legal term. A situation might arise, after all, where representatives could not otherwise continue their work. He believed, however, that the president must support cabinet and premier so long as parliament showed confidence in them through its votes. He believed unconditionally that so long as he or someone else had the support of a majority in the Cortes, the president must also support him. The president ought not to take a personal stand; he acted as the delegate and discerner of general public opinion. Only if no way remained to form any cabinet with a majority in parliament could and should the republic's president call for new elections. Thus from the first magistrate down to the last voter, and especially including each and every deputy, all remained continually accountable for maintaining intact the regime's principles and for guiding it in accordance with that healthy discipline which must govern the public affairs of free peoples.

When the Premier rose to speak, either on an announced occasion or in an impromptu way, his fluent eloquence overcame the close reasoning of his speeches, and he won support from a majority of the deputies. He silenced not only parliamentary opposition but even enemy rancor. His strength lay not so much in oratorical brilliance in the style of Emilio Castelar as in the force of his logic, his choice of words, and the impeccable structure of his sentences.

Did the opposition fulfill its allotted role of helping to shape laws by discussing them? Did the republic's president maintain a position of lofty contemplation, disdaining the capriciousness of a party chieftain—one might even say of a provincial party boss? By no means. The Radicals, headed by Lerroux—that large faction which might have spoken for the republican bourgeoisie, or city people—moved increasingly from their natural position toward the reactionary Right, acting to protect their privileges, which at that point remained merely threatened rather than actually lost. Government Socialists responded to the insidious and delaying parliamentary campaign of the Lerrouxists by publicly denouncing their scandalous practices.

The Premier varied his normal duties with speaking tours in a legitimate effort to seek support for his party at rallies in Santander and Valladolid. I went along on both trips as part of his entourage of supporters and friends. The Santander speech marked the first stage in a campaign to launch a real and true republican mission. He spoke against divisive competition among republicans based on their identification with the personalities of leaders who had no real differences in their beliefs. In Valladolid he spoke more concretely about a unifying formula for pulling together one single organization of the Left to represent electoral and parliamentary forces that had no doctrinal division. The climax of his campaign for union came at a banquet held in his honor at Madrid's Central Fronton. Here he developed his plan beyond current politics to a truly comprehensive scheme indicating a larger blueprint. He did not look to the establishment of an ephemeral dictatorship; his comprehensive statesman's vision looked to past history for a real sense of our nation as a whole. He hoped for nothing less than total integration of our social republic into a united body, organized in accordance with universal principles that would guide our country in its inevitable, inescapable revolution. The huge audience of enthusiasts, many of them women, overflowed from seats on the fronton court into the stands. His speech created a sensation.

Conservative supporters of ancient privileges and procedures became increasingly alarmed by the Premier's accelerated pace in establishing his renovating policies, always without seriously disturbing the tenor of national life. They found it impossible to upset the coalition in the Cortes, which sustained him in vote after vote and which also triumphed over intrigues and schemes, delays and resistance that they attempted through the rulings of a court system openly hostile to the overwhelmingly liberal popular mandate. Therefore his most militant opponents again ventured surreptitiously into paths of subversion. Extremes approached each other, for opposing parties easily form a temporary alliance in a common effort to overthrow a fortress. Certain Lerrouxist deputies of the worst sort now got together with agitators among the Andalusian syndicalists. Others whose real interests lay in mere preservation of public order concurred with them, perhaps not realizing the consequences. All these people allowed their destructive impulses to prevail over any consideration of the most elemental prudence, and ruin and havoc resulted. It was neither the first nor the last occasion when well-to-do classes of Spanish society preferred the tremendous risks of playing with fire to a compromise that would provide them with representation in the cabinet.

Thus it happened that a story appeared in newspapers about highly lamentable events in the town of Casas Viejas near Jerez; at first these events merely caused a parliamentary inquiry. The subversive campaign worsened, and a few days later, with syndicalist anarchists upsetting the tranquility of Andalusia's countryside, the mayor of Jerez telegraphed a warning about an explosion of revolutionary violence that he expected to come from Casas Viejas against his city. All of this caused Interior Minister Casares Quiroga to proclaim the harvest as sacred, to make it clear that he would tolerate neither revolutionary excesses, however sporadic, nor the outrages committed with frightening frequency against landowners and overseers. The governor had already asked for police reinforcement, and Arturo Menéndez, still general police commissioner, sent down Civil Guard Captain Rojas, who turned out to be the brother-in-law of Major Saravia, the secretary in the Premier's Ministry of War.

The first time a deputy rose in Congress to inquire of the Premier about Casas Viejas, his minister of the interior was not present. The Premier merely turned to his under secretary, Carlos Esplá, sitting behind the blue bench, for a pertinent answer, since he himself did not know what might have happened in Casas Viejas. After his under secretary explained in a few words what information he had, the Premier turned again to answer his captious questioner with that certainty which always assured him the confidence of his many partisans. "Nothing has occurred in Casas Viejas but what had to happen."

Arturo Menéndez informed the Premier that he had not given Captain Rojas authorization to take precipitate action. The question of such authorization provided the basis for a virulent attack in the extremist press, both syndicalist and rightist, with *ABC,* of course, in the lead, and it went beyond denunciation. Those very persons who a few days before had clamored about the defenselessness of so-called orderly men living in terror in their fiefs in the Jerez region now shuddered about this crime committed by the Civil Guard against anarchists and tried to implicate the Premier in it.

As a faithful observer of the law, my Brother-in-Law broke with the standard policy of all governments up to then, monarchical, liberal, and conservative. He, his minister of the interior, and the cabinet did not, as in the past, stand firmly behind excessive police reaction—and it now became quite clear that such a reaction had occurred in Casas Viejas. He allowed the examining magistrate to act freely in open court on the basis of facts. He agreed to the resignation and indictment, with prior arrest, of the general police commissioner, who was later exonerated. Captain Rojas took full responsibility for his actions, though he might have claimed exemption on grounds of fulfilling his duty while representing the government. It all proved useless against the recalcitrant wickedness of the old enemy entrenched in sacristy, barracks, editorial offices, boudoirs, and even in the immunity of the telephone—"wasted steps"—room, more sacred then the immunity of the halls of parliament. Whether or not someone had invented it earlier, there now surfaced in Luca de Tena's newspaper that unbelievable, unverifiable phrase which did so much harm to the Premier, its source never identified through mistaken respect for press freedom. It asserted that he had ordered the general police commissioner to "shoot them in the belly."

Violence from the opposite camp did not in any obvious way diminish the Premier's parliamentary authority. He continued to control enough votes to indicate clearly the favorable opinion of the Cortes toward his government. Now, though, for the first time he had fallen into manifest error through lack of information in speaking to the Cortes. The governor of Cádiz and the minister of the interior shared blame for that glaring indiscretion with the under secretary who dismissed the importance of an event he did not really understand. As assuredly as he always affirmed his conduct in important matters, the Premier had said, "Nothing has occurred in Casas Viejas but what had to occur."

34

The Republic is Done For

From then onward the campaign against the cabinet accelerated. Monarchists, anarchists, and antirevolutionary republicans all more or less openly challenged the Premier, setting up barricades in parliament, waging social campaigns, and stirring up skirmishes in streets and countryside. Everywhere ambush and intrigue obstructed efforts toward fundamental reforms by the Republican-Socialist alliance that controlled the government under the leadership of my Brother-in-Law, former Ateneo Secretary.

The republic's enemies frustrated his efforts to gain party support for establishment of a dictatorship of the Cortes directed by the cabinet, which he had suggested in August's heady days. Yet he refused to fall back on the expedient of suspending constitutional guarantees, so much used and discredited during the regency and reign of Alfonso XIII. Instead the Premier utilized certain laws of exception to protect his programs. Thus, without interfering with our fundamental law code, he could undercut the malicious opposition of persons manifestly trying to subvert his policies.

Scandalously, the president of the republic himself led those who challenged our recently adopted constitution, though the Cortes had still not enacted the complementary laws so essential for establishing republican roots. Now Alcalá Zamora pretended to change his colors, coming out for strong socialist measures but insisting on no impingement on any right of the free citizen. Still worse, he proposed a campaign for constitutional reform.

The Premier tried to respond to these various challenges by utilizing the Law for the Defense of the Republic. Through it, without suspending individual or political rights for most citizens, the government did have extraordinary powers to take action in exceptional circumstances in dealing with particular cases of certain kinds of political delinquency. Some jurists felt that these powers transgressed the democratic principles on which the republic was founded.

The campaign for strict judicial control over acts of the government had several prominent supporters. Chief among them stood an outstanding jurist and committed republican, Don Ángel Ossorio, our good friend, who would become a still better friend. Possibly because he remained independent from any party identification, Ossorio clung to his past orientation as a Conserva-

226

tive under Don Antonio Maura's leadership, and he spoke admiringly of the resemblance between Maura and the Premier—he certainly did not mean physical resemblance. Yet Don Ángel published a notable article treating "the disturbing matter" that suggested dictatorial tendencies in the Head of Government, though he did not go so far as to accuse him of wanting to become a dictator. His article appeared in *Luz,* most of whose editorial staff, led by Ortega y Gasset, had recently defected from *Sol.*

Among the Premier's colleagues this kind of warning stirred up alarm reminiscent of the morning of August 11 after Sanjurjo's coup. Many within the parliamentary majority who admired the Minister of War's executive decisiveness felt unwilling to follow him in pathways that seemed to weaken the pillars which supported judicial control over government procedures. Many times afterward, in a far more hazardous period, my Brother-in-Law recalled that warning by our friend Don Ángel, who later became a decided proponent of his personal leadership and looked to him to galvanize the defensive resistance of Spain's people, then goaded by international fascism.

After offering me an editorial position on *El Sol* just after the republic's proclamation, Manuel Aznar tried a more direct approach to the Premier. Aznar decided to ingratiate himself with his former colleague Ortega y Gasset by bringing together this philosophical mentor of Spanish youth with the pragmatical former Reformist Secretary of the Ateneo, a more viable politician. Ortega and leading intellectuals of his group voted with the Socialists, mainly at the suggestion of Fernando de los Ríos. On the other hand, they had not joined that party or any other. Instead they constituted a separate coterie vaguely called "In the Service of the Republic," as though they wanted to indicate that they did not feel limited by fixed principles of a tactical sort and so operated above contingencies of practical politics in a realm of unblemished idealism. I have already indicated the Premier's opinion about the usefulness of that approach to politics. He believed that individualism had its place, but also that persons ought not to exercise their responsibilities within a democratic system by changing their course with each changing breeze.

It seemed altogether intolerable to my Brother-in-Law that anyone should refuse to identify with a party or organization, in the name of safeguarding his independence, in order to form a kind of Sanhedrin or to make himself an oracle. Elected agents of the government certainly ought not to have to render surreptitious homage to such a person or faction, paying slavish attention to their words. My Kinsman also questioned the usefulness of recruiting a contingent of intellectuals into his own party, except for votes their readers might cast, in order to gain their support and praises in newspapers. He just could not accept the proposition that the unquestioned literary preeminence of Unamuno, Ortega y Gasset, or Pérez de Ayala—not to mention their lesser kindred—would benefit his party enough to compensate for their individualistic capriciousness toward government policies. It did not take much perspicacity to recognize the great divide that had for some time separated the pragmatic Premier from Ortega the professional essayist-philosopher, not so much in doctrinal beliefs as in their different approaches to politics. The people as a whole are not usually deceived, though individuals occasionally can be, and they did not err in choosing as their leader the man who spoke out in a forthright manner, simply and clearly, without, like the other, protecting his reputation as a sibylline oracle by making a thousand distinctions and reservations.

Still, Ortega y Gasset had surprised us the first time he rose to speak in the Chamber with a maneuver as elegant as it was unexpected. He had, in fact, seemed to be taking the lead in Aznar's move toward rapprochement with the Premier. He had called for a round of applause for the Minister of War as author of the military reforms, affording deputies an opportunity to show their appreciation in a way they had not done so far. Ortega remarked that those reforms stood as an incontrovertible part of the republican system, a constituent of its political foundation, and an anchor for the new institutions currently under discussion. The Premier felt sincerely gratified by the ovation with which parliament had responded to the initiative of Ortega, who thus easily enhanced his own prestige by affording this opportunity to others less astute than himself. This gracious gesture, however, did not develop into any really useful support or closer association.

Occasionally Enrique Ramos suggested the usefulness of trying to attract Ortega's explicit political support for the Premier. The philosopher, after all, proclaimed himself as a convinced democrat, and on that ground he made a show of controlling a certain number of votes. They might work out some kind of compromise toward effective collaboration. If Ortega did not want to join the Premier's party, he might preserve his special eminence and still agree to follow the Premier's leadership in actual political activity. Thus, avoiding any question of competition between dominant personalities, Ortega would contribute support within the framework of an alliance committed to democracy. Given this state of affairs, then, it occurred to Aznar to arrange a meeting between the two statesmen. My Brother-in-Law agreed to it without much enthusiasm, mostly to avoid any charge that he had refused an opportunity for which both Aznar and Ortega seemed eager. The three men met for a meal one fine day at his old favorite Lhardy Restaurant. Things never progressed beyond polite after-dinner conversation, which had no importance even of a journalistic sort since discretion prevented the host from mentioning it in his newspaper.

After that Manuel Aznar spoke to me frankly about his ambition to serve as an ambassador for our republic. This bid for an important diplomatic post proved that scrupulosity was not one of his outstanding qualities. A little before 14 April 1931, as editor of *El País* in Havana and also in writing for the *Diario de la Marina,* he had seemed convinced that Alfonso XIII would continue on his ancestral throne. Later, under the republic, he supported policies that favored a shady capitalistic venture in which he had some involvement and from which he stood to make a profit.

I hardly dared to suggest his nomination to the Premier. My Brother-in-Law's good friend Martín Guzmán also considered it hopeless to ask it of him, all the more because he might expect to reap considerable political benefit through the newspaper by supporting its ambitious editor in so unlikely a nomination. Guzmán suggested, however, that I might do the Premier a service by plucking up my courage in this matter. Even against his own better judgment, I might put at his disposal virtual control of this daily paper with wide circulation, sound financial backing, and considerable influence on public opinion. Why couldn't I go straight to the minister of foreign affairs, our good friend Luis de Zulueta, and suggest Aznar's appointment, explaining the usefulness of satisfying his diplomatic ambitions. At least it would remove him from editorship of El Sol, where he would never completely support the Premier; otherwise his job seemed permanent, as his contract with El Sol was protected by a large indemnification. Zulueta, to degree supporting Aznar, saw our point, and he promised to present his nomination to the cabinet. We assured him that the Premier, while not backing it, would not oppose an initiative coming from the minister of foreign affairs. In fact our ploy had no success at all. When Zulueta suggested Aznar's nomination as ambassador to Río de Janeiro, Indalecio Prieto spoke so appositely against it that he did not pursue the matter, and no one took the trouble to rebut Prieto or to urge the appointment.

I did not tell the editor of El Sol about what had happened in the council. In fact, I heard nothing about it at the time from either my Brother-in-Law or the minister of foreign affairs, but only later after asking. Certainly someone, neither the Premier nor the minister, did tell Aznar exactly and in detail. For a long time he had shown little sympathy for Prieto; now he undertook a newspaper campaign against Socialists in the government. As a result the Premier made it quite clear to his office staff and to the cabinet that he considered this kind of procedure inappropriate, since the public took for granted the involvement of his own friends. As the only consequence of this negotiation, then, my Brother-in-Law absolutely insisted on his disinterest in El Sol, not merely as his journalistic voice but to the point of refusing to make available to it official information to clear up questions for its contributing journalists like Luis Bello.

The Premier did not need to condescend to using any journal to print up versions of the news to suit his policies—versions that might contradict what appeared elsewhere. It distressed him, though, and he complained of it to me, that editors who supported him seemed incapable of taking an independent stand, that they felt they must completely endorse the cabinet's position on every issue. El Sol and other newspapers identifying with different factions seemed unable to get beyond merely repeating what they heard. Instead of commenting on the Premier's speeches by expressing their own viewpoints and positions, explaining the clear advantages of his proposals, they just published the whole text with remarks ranging from eulogy to dithyramb. If the enthusiasm of their praises gratified him, he could not help recognizing the limitations of such comments as effective propaganda. The approach of these editors seemed even emptier and of less consequence than the poisonous diatribes of the opposition press against doctrines set forth in his speeches.

Certainly the people's passiveness annoyed him, their lack of serious involvement and their merely repeating concepts and standard phrases they had learned. Forever brooding on his own thoughts, it always surprised and irritated him that nobody, or very few people, knew how to think for themselves. It followed that when he felt justified satisfaction in the depths of his soul about some public demonstration in his favor he also reacted with weariness because of the commonplace nature of the praises.

In a multitude crowding around when he and other ministers passed by, the Premier valued a single manifest dissenter. An indifferent loner provided an incidental but highly characteristic point for one of his best speeches. Driving one afternoon in Madrid's environs, as he often did, he passed through a village in the Castilian sierra. His car stopped a few minutes, just long enough for the neighborhood to discover the traveler and crowd around him, as much from curiosity as to applaud him. There, again, he found *his man* among the fatuous enthusiasts. Answering the summons of those who called him to the doorway of, I think, his blacksmith's forge, this man briefly left his work and looked out still wearing his leather apron. With an unmistakable gesture of his own superiority, without braggadocio but with the dignified bearing of one who does not need to make a show to demonstrate his self-assurance, he regarded the Premier as if nothing special had happened, and, without disdain, he returned to his work. Neither protesting nor dissenting, this man showed himself one of those philosophers unwilling to allow the world's great people to deprive them of their place in the sun— and also of shade from the sun. On the other hand, what a chasm lay between the Leader of Spain's republic, a man without vanity, and that blacksmith whose pride he so ardently praised.

"I wish that I could wear a leather apron!" repeated our old friend Juan Uña, and his allusion was not Masonic. He referred to the Premier's most talked-about speech of the moment in which he had extolled that Castilian's attitude toward his own passage through the village, an attitude he so much admired in his countrymen. Juanito (we went on calling him that because, though older than us, he already seemed our junior) spoke with such enthusiasm to my sister about that speech that she bought him one of those little leather aprons.

I rarely got to see or talk with my Brother-in-Law alone now. He seemed to me overly concerned about talk—and not all of it critical—of my meddling in state affairs. He said nothing about it, but he wanted to make it clear that I had no influence at all. I did continue to join him and my sister for meals along with one or another guest. My Brother-in-Law did not avoid dealing with admirers, but however much he enjoyed their company, nobody ever involved him in an illicit deal. We used to go sometimes to eat at Fuentelarreyna, an elegant restaurant on the Pardo highway, or we would stop for a snack on the way back from our customary ride to Alcalá, the Escorial, or Las Rozas.

Many afternoons I went to look him up after dinner, and we drove to the "La Quinta" villa at the Pardo where he was undertaking a restoration of earlier French gracefulness from an ugly mess left by the last Bourbons, who had apparently turned it over to the unfortunate prince of Asturias for his hobby of raising poultry. The Premier wanted to assign this rehabilitation to Winthuysen, the landscape architect who had supervised similar work on the gardens at Moncloa. Finally he settled for Cándido Bolívar, son of the famous naturalist and his father's heir in that profession. My Brother-in-Law felt gratified to have an affiliate of Republican Action in the post. Going to the Pardo reminded me of entering his Alcalá orchard in the old days. Now more justifiably, if disinterestedly, his face lit up as soon as we left the highway and turned through the Iron Gate onto a road leading through woods to the villa. He laughed at José Ramón and his questions. "Yes, that is the 'Iwon Gate'; what do they call this one?" the child asked about a little wooden gateway. "Sticks Gate!" his Uncle answered, pleased and interested in pointing our landmarks we passed on our excursions.

When he took me there the first time, he pointed out an avenue of tall trees leading to the villa's unkempt pleasure-ground. A summerhouse in disrepair stood at the end of that avenue of overhanging boughs. An agricultural expert from Valencia had dug up its garden to plant pasturage for pigs, and he had built a poultry yard whose model chicken houses—not exactly the Petit Trianon—spoiled the natural rusticity of those hills and woods. Halfway up the hillside came a simple neoclassical reservoir with decorative planting of hedge-mustard and ivy, one of several surrounding the mansion. On top of that hill stood the one-story house fashioned like a French pavilion and similar to those at other royal retreats. Inside, its walls were hung with wallpaper dating from the beginning of the last century, the first used by Madrid's court. It had a charming Chinese pattern of pagodas and palanquins, little bridges and lakes, sycamores and willows under a moon; over and over it repeated scenes copied from teapots, of mandarins and little princesses, or rice fields and a lacquered sky. Walking over the villa's fine straw mats we thought of royal summers in the country a century before. As on so many other occasions, he grieved over the desolated wasteland Spaniards, with the best of intentions, made of any culture. He had various plans to tear down the polluted dovecotes and thatched farm buildings, to recreate surroundings that would set off the fine buildings and beautiful natural scenery.

He did not feel that republican administrators fully appreciated the artistic value of the various royal residences. He believed that we should follow the French example and turn over former crown properties to supervision of an official national administration to keep them out of the hands of an unenlightened populace represented by municipal councils and republican committees. He himself undertook to save from demolition some buildings, gardens, and woods like those of the Pardo which he cherished so much. The spectacle of the Casa de Campo on Mondays made him realize the unsuitability of allowing uncontrolled admission. The crowd, excusing it as the Madrid custom of picnicking from refreshment stands or celebrating Saint Eugene's Day, left the grass and thyme strewn with greasy papers torn from *El Heraldo* or *El Liberal,* or they risked burning down the evergreens and avenues of trees with their bonfires.

My Brother-in-Law also found unsuitable the use of the Riofrío Palace as a school; it housed the children badly, and they inevitably damaged the building. He wanted it converted into a national museum of hunting, as Valle Inclán had suggested, or preserved as a hunting lodge to put up distinguished foreign visitors as the French had done at Rambouillet or Compiègne. Through his initiative Valle Inclán became curator of the Aranjuez tapestry museum, but this did not mitigate that great writer's capricious, biting satire; to the end he remained an enthusiastic and perspicacious critic of everything. Though the Premier did not have time for all the tearing down and building up his imagination suggested, he did establish guidelines for good republican administration of Spain's patrimony from past centuries. Leaving by the villa's back door, then walking up a roadway planted with grapevines on both sides, one's view and one's spirit were filled by the opening up of a square in front of the barracks that the Pardo Administration leased to a hunting society.

The Citizen of Madrid made it one of his special concerns to protect the Pardo's woodland from the urban infringement that threatened it, one time with a working-class housing development, another time with a tuberculosis sanatorium. He understood the abiding value of preserving that Velázquez countryside near Spain's capital. This attitude did not come from a conscious choice or an intellectual decision; it came as the reaction of a sensitive spirit, from his joy in open countryside. I remembered that joyful relaxation from earlier years of our carefree tramping through Spain's fields, sometimes in those very environs of Madrid.

My Brother-in-Law intensified his ineffable pleasure in rustic scenery through its purest expression in music; his favorite symphonic motif was the identifying theme of Beethoven's *Pastoral* Symphony. In the spacious, easy freedom of his days of leisure very few books freed him as the *Pastoral* did from his serious concerns. In moments of rest in his present schedule, music still continued as his best relief from worries and daily chores. Long a member of the Madrid Philharmonic Society, he had not time to continue this membership after his marriage. He did attend concerts of the Pérez Casas Orchestra, which had made him its honorary president, a position in which he had succeeded La Cierva, his antagonist as minister of the interior in so many unpopular monarchical governments.

In his early days as Minister of War, fellow members of Republican Action once came to get him from his box at the Español Theater, where he sat absorbed by the music of one of "his" orchestra's weekly afternoon concerts. They wanted him to appear at the María Guerrero Theater to close the party's first convention after the republic's proclamation. He had not planned to attend, much less to speak; but in the end he could not refuse. In a very bad humor because they had interrupted the concert, he agreed to say a few words, and it remains one of my lasting regrets that I missed them. He left one theater for the other too unexpectedly, and I was too far away to share what, judging from the reaction of those who did hear him, proved a delightful surprise. Accustomed to the firmness of his decisions, the convention's organizers did not really expect him, so that when they saw him coming through the door and up to the dais they did not have a stenographer ready to record his speech or time to send out for one. Thus we lost one of the finest improvisations of his shining oratorical career, or so his captivated listeners later asserted. "Do you know why I spoke so well?" he later explained. "I had just heard Mozart's *Jupiter* Symphony."

In 1933, at the time of the Casas Viejas incident, I sat with him in a prominent box at a Philharmonic Orchestra concert held at the Price Circus. I witnessed a highly significant surreptitious protest against an enthusiastic show of support for him during intermission. His greatest support came from people sitting in the bleachers.

On his birthday Princess Bibesco asked us to luncheon. For greater intimacy on that signal occasion, she had only my sister, my Brother-in-Law, my wife, and me, with her husband the ambassador, herself, and a few others. I think that she invited the English ambassador, a secretary from that embassy, Carlos Morla the Chilean ambassador, and his attractive wife. We all felt quite relaxed, and with my sister and Brother-in-Law taking the conversational lead, our meal passed amiably. The princess always somewhat overdid her sallies, and on that day she peaked. First, when the dessert cake arrived, decorated with candles to indicate how many years the celebration marked, there came a momentous silence, happenstance or not. Very graciously, she broke that silence, "Don't bother to count them; we put on thirty-seven."

Later, however, she yielded to an unfortunate temptation and asked, in the badly accented French of our conversation, "And how is your friend the blue-eyed murderer?" My Brother-in-Law pretended not to understand, but the princess insisted, heedlessly, so that he could not possibly miss her reference to his minister of the interior, Casares Quiroga. The Premier's sharp rejoinder abruptly ended the casual ease of that meal. I had hardly arrived home afterward when a phone call came from Princess Bibesco to apologize to me for her remark. She explained that both her usually indulgent husband and the English ambassador had strongly criticized her for the impropriety that she had intended as an innocent joke. She kept insisting until I agreed to bring the Premier to her house again a few days later—this time just the three of us. He accepted her apologies but absolutely refused the princess's attempts to reestablish a close friendship. As we left, he commented to me with a weary grin that he would have felt readier to make it up with her twenty years before.

At that time, too, M. Herriot, the former French premier and long-standing mayor of Lyons, turned up in Madrid, unexpectedly and incognito, with the pretext of taking a vacation. I say unexpectedly, though we learned afterward that the French ambassador, M. Herbette, knew of the plans and had a hand in formulating them; but Spain's government learned of the trip only at the last minute. The antirepublican opposition gave this visit unjustified significance and expressed shock and alarm against any action that would subordinate our foreign policy to French interests. They scared off the game, as the saying goes. Of course the Premier regretted the journey's inefficacy, since it represented a serious, personal initiative by their ambassador. Apparently Herbette had insisted that Herriot's presence might bring pressure on Spain's government toward some kind of chimerical plan that finally did not work out.

The Spanish Premier resolved to keep to the strictly constitutional limits of his office on this occasion and not to commit himself to any course of action that the French ambassador might propose, apparently without any official sanction. He received M. Herriot in a formal audience, but the best opportunity for serious discussion came during an automobile excursion to Toledo arranged by Ambassador Herbette. Here again the Spanish Premier, as he later told me, held strictly to the rules of diplomacy and did not let the conversation stray far from El Greco. I myself went with my sister and Brother-in-Law to an evening party at France's embassy in honor of the distinguished visitor. In connection with the musical program that evening, my Kinsman showed off his wide reading in the French language and spoke opportunely and intelligently about his visitor's book on Beethoven. M. Herriot had written many books during the course of his long political career, but this remained his best.

To counteract with a show of friendliness the hostile reception our antirepublican press had given to the French politician, a large group of us went to see him off at the North Station a few days later. Nothing more happened, but my Brother-in-Law spoke to me more than once of the consequences, at the time unsuspected and unpredictable, of that impromptu, unexpected visit. M. Herriot must have felt annoyed with his old friend the ambassador, who had undoubtedly made rash promises about an eagerness for friendly understanding on the part of Spain's government. Shortly afterward France and Spain did, indeed, sign a commercial treaty. In its negotiation our government fought hard to defend the special interests of Spanish manufacturers. France's ambassador made the primary issue, the *sine qua non,* Spain's obligation to make all of her foreign arms purchases from France.

That summer my father died after days of much suffering. Even his passing provided an opportunity for cruel enemy hypocrites to hurt us, this time in the heart of our family. Though indifferent, like most Spanish men, to details of religious observance, my father had always respected the feelings of his wife and daughters in these matters. My sisters and my mother's sister, who had lived with us after her husband's death a few years earlier, had not wanted to ask my father to make his confession while he was still conscious, but they did want Holy Oil administered to him afterward. So it happened that on one of the last nights of his life the Saint Jerome parish priest gave him Unction in the women's presence. We men had retired to a back room; the Premier shared with us the distress and pain of those hours. We all wanted outsiders to respect our mourning, especialy priests of Christ. Only the priest or his sacristan, however, could have provided the information that the perverse *ABC* published prominently with this inexact heading "Father-in-Law of Premier Seeks Last Rites."

Perhaps as a trick of fate, my father had a very distinguished attendance at his funeral. He had always considered presence at a friend's burial one of the most important obligations of social life, as a public testimony of friendship. Certainly he was not motivated by the reason indicated in one of his favorite proverbs: "If the governor dies, go quickly to pay your respects, but if the governor's wife dies, go even more quickly because the governor remains alive." My father's vulnerability to disillusionment always put him on guard against it. His death represented that of the father of the governor's wife in that little adage, and many people attended, as many, in fact, from the world of government as from among his own many surviving friends. At the cemetery, just as they laid him to rest, my cousin Rafael Sanz came forward to read a response. This priest and I had played together as children in my grandfather's village. His brother, the cavalry lieutenant, had made that unpleasant remark about my budding friendship with my Brother-in-Law at the station while I waited to return to Madrid from my first visit to Alcalá. Involvement in the August 10 rising had bought the lieutenant a mild punishment of dismissal from the army.

Taking off his mourning band as we left the cemetery, Santiago Alba, the former minister harassed by Dictator Primo de Rivera, warmly expressed to me his gratitude for my father's generous behavior toward him. Alba felt no obligation, however, toward his Son-in-Law, the Premier, who in a mere three years had risen from that podium in Madrid's bullring, through a memorable election, to head the blue bench of the republic's Constituent Cortes. Now Alba, mocked horseman of the Apocalypse of that day, chomped at the bit, never letting up in his opposition toward his disdainful and triumphant rival.

The Premier and his party felt bound by no commitments beyond their public responsibilities toward their constituents; until he became Minister of War he did not even enter Masonry. He retained a hilarious recollection of a visit by some ingenuous French Masonic brethren who, believing him firmly attached to the movement, gave him a ritual welcome including a kiss on his cheek. He did allow himself to be initiated to please many friends—men of high Masonic degrees. He remained a passive member, however, and did not return to the Lodge after his initiation. He did not believe membership necessary or even very efficacious in these days. Perhaps he deprecated too much the social and political support his new brothers might have brought him in the government against the Catholic Church's reactionary strength. No one knew better than he the Masonic contribution in achieving French republicanism, but he considered Spain's situation different. Most Socialists in the ruling coalition had no connection with the Masonic Lodge, though exceptions proved that rule, and some of them even felt hostile to Masonry. This widened the rift between the Premier and the Radicals, whose historic anticlericalism had its deepest roots in Masonry.

All of that may help to explain why Martínez Barrio, then acting Grand Master, took the responsibility of belling the cat. I don't even suggest, of course, that a Masonic decision lay behind the rough tone taken by that recently deposed minister toward my Kinsman in a famous speech during the debate about Casas Viejas. From that speech came an angry phrase seized upon by his open and dissembling enemies: Martínez Barrio said that nothing would come from the cabinet's policies but "filth, blood, and tears." Though the Premier's voting majority in the Cortes remained clear, he now called upon the president for a test of parliamentary confidence in his leadership. Don Niceto had begun to disagree openly with his Premier, to the point of sending back to the Cortes a law presented for his final approval. Now he accepted my Brother-in-Law's resignation as a challenge and called upon Lerroux to form a new cabinet.

Just my Kinsman and I rode in a car that took him to present his formal resignation at Don Niceto's house on the night when this crisis came to a head. He said, "The republic is done for." Nothing more. I repeated to him his own argument, reiterated so often to his intransigent supporters: the regime could not remain exclusively identified with him. He answered that he did not talk that way because of his mere retirement. No, he said it because the president was precipitating a dissolution of parliament contrary to the constitution's republican intention. Absolutely no justification existed for holding new elections when a premier had a clear majority behind him and could, in any case, reshape his cabinet on the basis of other viable political alliances without betraying the people's will.

1933–40

35

The Tenant of 38 calle de Serrano

Lerroux formed a cabinet without Socialist support; they would not have joined him if he had asked them. He appointed as minister of foreign affairs Claudio Sánchez Albornoz, a history professor, at that point in the middle of the Atlantic Ocean on his way home from an academic assignment in Buenos Aires. Lerroux had not even consulted the former Premier about including Sánchez Albornoz, a member of Republican Action, in his cabinet, and in a subsequent parliamentary debate my Brother-in-Law referred to this professor as "the adrift minister." As a result of that speech the Cortes refused Lerroux the vote of confidence he asked for on his new minister, and he lost his premiership. Lerroux called his predecessor a serpent and himself a lion, but Don Niceto had to find someone else to resolve the crisis he had so inexpediently brought on by his obstinacy and capriciousness.

Doctor Marañón came to visit the former Premier in his third-floor apartment at 24-B calle de Hermosilla, where he and my sister had returned after their speedy departure from Buenavista Palace. The doctor did not, of course, come in a professional capacity but as the prominent politician he had remained since that moment when Don Niceto and the count of Romanones had, in his house and with his intervention, arranged the transmission of power that had brought our republic into existence. My Brother-in-Law informed him, as he had said publicly and in the president's office, that he remained ready at any time to give full support to any republican coalition—especially to a Republican-Socialist coalition—that could attract enough votes to govern the present Cortes. He believed anything preferable to a dissolution and new elections because he believed the present Cortes had not yet finished its mandate. Further, he believed that, though the Constituent Cortes had no established legal term, nothing would foster our republican regime so much as allowing this Cortes and other basic units of government to serve the full terms established by our constitution.

Putting aside all consideration of his own self-respect, my Kinsman gave full support to Martínez Barrio's attempt to form a cabinet after the parliament had rejected Lerroux. He even went so far as to make the very considerable sacrifice of visiting that fallen lion one night along with Marcelino Domingo, but Lerroux absolutely refused their request that he allow Radi-

239

cals to serve in a cabinet headed by his disloyal friend. In spite of this, Martínez Barrio did finally become premier. Once in office, however, he forgot all his promises made to the republican coalition in return for their support. Instead, he agreed to countersign a presidential decree suspending sessions of the Constitutional Assembly, dissolving it, and so making new elections inevitable.

An ill wind might still blow some good. Like it or not, hope still prevailed; dissolution of that first republican Cortes might turn out for the best in spite of its not having completed some very important tasks. We could still hope that believing republicans would have enough instinct for self-preservation to protect them from manipulation by the enemy in their midst. We could hope that in the imminent elections republicans would show the same cohesion that had brought their triumph on April 14. The former Premier's argument remained undisputable: if in forthcoming elections the Republican-Socialist coalition that had held power for two and one-half years presented voters with that same clear confrontation between Right and Left in the same militant way as before, these elections would come out the same as the others. They would expose the president's stubborn capriciousness. Public opinion would gainsay his opinions about a need for political change, and he would find himself in the position of General MacMahon facing Gambetta in France in 1877: "Submit or resign."

It did not turn out that way. Socialists disagreed among themselves about the usefulness of preserving their electoral coalition with Left Republicans—the name adopted by a new party formed through merger of Republican Action with the Radical Socialists. A majority of provincial Socialist organizations wanted to run their own candidates autonomously. This also represented the position of Largo Caballero, who delighted to hear himself called the Spanish Lenin by people who cast my Brother-in-Law in something like Kerensky's role in the Russian revolution. This secretary of the General Confederation of Labor firmly believed that Socialists would win the election without Republican collaboration. Republicans in their turn, in particular Left Republicans, refused to adopt an arrangement proposed at the last minute that might still have saved the situation. Madrid's Socialists suggested resolution of the division in the capital by presenting one single electoral list with all Socialist candidates under a single Republican leader, the former Premier. My Brother-in-Law was certainly not a man who would accept that kind of proposal, "How could I accept something like that? Impossible!"

Yet, daring as it seemed, I thought that it truly reflected political realities, however much it scandalized desperate Republicans. Beyond his limited position as party leader, the former Premier represented a broad constituency. His fellow party members realized this and tried to capitalize on it, but they themselves lacked sufficient support among voters to really utilize it. Though I believed that the Left Republicans should accept the Socialist proposal, however audacious, the interested Party would not consent to my saying so to anyone but himself. He went so far as to say that he disagreed with me. In the first place, nonetheless, I felt that the proposal rightly emphasized him as a political figure transcending party differences. More practically, once this compromise had overcome difficulties about renewing the electoral coalition in Madrid, almost certainly deals would follow in other districts to balance lack of equity in the capital. This particular imbalance did not seem so great a problem to me, anyhow, since in Madrid the Socialists would present a ticket of outstanding candidates. Except for the former Premier, no potential Republican candidate could compare to them. It also seemed to me that the Socialists were doing my Kinsman justice, recognizing his merit as most people had from the very first where his fellow party members failed to fully acknowledge it.

On the other hand, and as it turned out, when they did not reach an agreement in Madrid, provincial organizations followed the capital's bad example, each going its own way and taking its own risks. If Prieto had not enforced his own decision to maintain the Republican-Socialist coalition in Bilbao, the former Premier himself might not have retained a seat in parliament. Of course, he might have been offered a seat from Barcelona, but he would never under any circumstances have agreed to accept that. His self-respect would never have allowed him to receive something that might seem payment for past services.

At the request of fellow party members he went to speak in support of the election of Left Republican candidates in eastern Spain, and I went with him. We departed one fine morning for Alicante; a city with a notable republican tradition, it gave the former Premier a triumphant reception. Carlos Esplá and his friends who had organized the trip took due pride in that. Clouds soon dimmed that brilliant reception. Even during the first rally in Alicante's large theater we heard the cries of "How about Casas Viejas? Casas Viejas! Casas Viejas!" that would accompany us all day. A predominance of women's and children's voices showed us clearly a lack of spontaneity in those cries. We had dinner in Alicante along the seashore and went on to a rally in Elche's bullring where syndicalist hatred abetted efforts to create a scene. From the podium, the Orator challenged a youthful protester to stand up. Hardly twenty, the young man did not have enough effrontery to answer the Premier's direct question, "Well, let's see! What do you want to know about Casas Viejas? What have they told you about it?" Flustered and confused once my Brother-in-Law challenged his juvenile insolence and singled him out to speak for the wrathful devotees, he had nothing to say. The cub hurried from the stands and the arena, no doubt to give an account of his courage to those who had sent him.

A niece, married to an agricultural engineer and living in Almansa, came down to hear her Uncle and joined us in Elche. After his marriage my Brother-in-Law had renewed relations with his own family, never entirely broken off but less close after his brother's third marriage. This brother, at that point, served as presiding judge of the court at Zaragoza. A few months earlier my Kinsman had attended this niece's wedding when her father was temporarily serving as governor. The Premier's entrance into the Cathedral of the Virgin of the Pillar on that occasion afforded a perfect opportunity for Zaragoza's *señoritos* to make a demonstration. They took full advantage of it, confident that family feelings would prevent us and the acting governor from interfering with them.

In Elche our supporters took us to a famous grove of palm trees called the "Curate's Orchard." My Brother-in-Law had no liking for that tree; he called it "absurd, like giraffes in the animal kingdom." Thus he gave no more than token witness to that regional glory, just signing his name in a proffered book as so many visitors had done before him. We journeyed by car from Alicante to Valencia, and if the desolate panorama around Ifach seemed more like Africa than Greece, the coast near Denia stirred up thoughts of the Hellenic world. In one of those towns they urged him to speak from the city hall balcony, and as in the days of his apprenticeship in Novalucillos in Toledo Province, opponents interrupted him with shouts. They did not seem numerous, but local police stood by fully ready to protect them in defending their opinions, and that sufficed to intimidate our partisans from interfering.

Sigfrido Blasco, the errant son of Blasco Ibáñez, and his cohorts had prevented our supporters from organizing any political meeting in Valencia, a Lerrouxist stronghold. They launched an infamous propaganda campaign against the former Premier; arrogant notices in *El Pueblo* warned us of what to expect in Játiva, where our partisans had arranged a rally. We found a hostile crowd whistling and jeering along our entire route from the edge of town to the theater, and, according to what we heard, city hall counselors stood in the front ranks. Our people from Játiva and surrounding villages entirely filled the theater, with no opponents admitted. All during my Brother-in-Law's speech, however—and it was too fine for the occasion, town, or theater—tumult continued outside, enhanced by church bells ringing, not by way of celebration but to make as much racket as possible.

The former Premier also visited Bilbao and Barcelona during this electoral campaign. I did not accompany him to Bilbao. There somebody threw tear gas bombs during a rally in the fronton, and both Indalecio Prieto and my Brother-in-Law suffered from the effects on their eyes for a long time afterward. I did go with him and Prieto to Barcelona. President Maciá had died a short time before, and Lluís Companys had succeeded him as president of the Generalitat. My Brother-in-Law amusedly commented afterward about Prieto's juggling act with Maciá's heart, his sentimental words about the missing patriarch during a great rally in the bullring. We all went to call on the widow.

Prieto also accompanied us on a visit to Jaume Carner, now restricted to his house though not to his bed, past all hope of recovery from the cancer that killed him a few months later. "What are you telling me?" he barely murmured, obedient to his doctor's orders not to talk much, especially not to strain his voice. With gestures and looks more eloquent than anything he might have said, he sadly shook his head, grieving with us about the direction our republic had taken, heading straight for destruction. My Brother-in-Law parted from Carner that day in anguish, knowing that he would not again see him alive. He believed that when Carner died we lost our best chance of incorporating Catalonia into the Spanish nation through truly republican means. He greatly esteemed the man and said that he lacked only parliamentary eloquence to become a fine premier of Spain. An able financier, Carner had much influence with Barcelona's upper bourgeoisie, and he maintained the highest principles in his public and private life. This great Catalan did not seek popularity by lowering his political standards; in particular, he did not need to venture into the abyss of anarchical Catalanism to gain the votes of his countrymen. "If we had him as president of the Generalitat—as we should have—the story would have turned out differently."

Defeated in Madrid, the former Premier triumphed in Bilbao, and thus he saw fulfilled his predictions about Republican-Socialist electoral coalition. A few months after the election a Radical cabinet put together by Don Niceto himself and headed by the Valencian Richardo Samper replaced the Martínez Barrio cabinet. Now my Brother-in-Law stopped attending parliament. From this period of his withdrawal into domestic family life dates the very loyal friendship of Santos Martínez, one of his most devoted adherents from the Ateneo's most recent generation.

Santos and some other party members felt that, partly for personal safety, the former Premier should have a car now that he no longer had use of those connected with his official positions. Overcoming his scruples on the basis of a rather large pool of persons from whom my Brother-in-Law felt he could receive such a gift, Santos bought him a Ford. In it we continued our drives, always accompanied by a police escort that very much annoyed the interested Party. Durán and Santos regularly joined us and so enriched our outings.

Thus at the end of spring and beginning of summer we renewed our evening excursions. Almost invariably he would say to me when we got into the car, "Where shall we go?"

I would reply, "Anywhere you like."

And he returned, "What a bother that I always have to decide."

"All right, I will decide. Let's go to Alcalá."

He grimaced as though he didn't really want to go to Alcalá, and our dialogue continued.

"To the Escorial." "Again?"

"To Navacerrada." "So late?"

"To the León Heights." "Do we have to go there every day?"

Finally he would tell the driver to take the Guadalajara highway, an ingenuous euphemism to hide his intention. I knew that we would turn off at the Alcalá exit and end up taking a walk through the shadowy Chorrillo. Occasionally we just walked through deserted streets. Some afternoons we visited his sister and his perennially ill brother-in-law in his paternal home on the calle de la Imagen. One day during his ministry we called on his old friend Vicario, who received him joyfully, and they chatted together as in the past on the same courtyard bench. Another time we went to see his cousin and wedding attendant, the wife of General García Benítez, commander of Alcalá's garrison. She still displayed in her drawing room presentation photographs the king and queen had dedicated to her husband when he served as colonel of their honor guard.

Whether we took the Guadalajara highway, the connecting road to the Escorial, or the Manzanares highway, when we got out of the car and began to walk he wore out his police escort and younger companions. "I think I can smell the sea. We must be getting close to La Coruña," the former Premier joked one evening when he had led us on a long walk beyond Torrelodones, moving fast as always and leaving Casares Quiroga panting for breath. On one of those drives when he still had the official car—whose drivers always very willingly made an effort to satisfy his taste for high speed—another project occurred to him. They might convert the reservoir at the Santillana Dam, inadequate and unsafe as a source of drinking water, into a recreational lake for Madrid. Our conversations on these rides ran more to urban planning than to affairs of state. His most grandiose vision even outdid Philip II's plans to develop Madrid as the center of his government. The former Premier thought of extending our capital right up to the sierra at the León Heights and Siete Picos between Los Molinos and Cercedilla.

One afternoon when I had not gone with him, he came to tell me about an incident that had happened at an inn on Madrid's outskirts, a fashionable place where "the smart set" went for afternoon refreshment. Unexpectedly the bullfighter Ignacio Sánchez Mejía sat down at a table near his, accompanied by a then famous dancer, "La Argentinita" [Encarnación López] a great friend of mine. Without quite recognizing her, my Brother-in-Law looked at her as though he knew her. The valiant toreador finally came over, "Allow me to introduce myself, to fulfill a wish I have had for a long time and which Cipriano has promised to satisfy. I didn't want to take the liberty with you still in office. I am one of your followers, though not a member of your party." When the former Premier smiled and urged him to put his convictions to more positive use, Ignacio insisted on continuing about how wise he found my Brother-in-Law's policies. "I speak as a conservative and an Andalusian landowner." "Some of your countrymen don't feel as you do," the former Premier replied. "Then they will have their heads chopped off. I mean what I say."

That man made an excellent impression on my Kinsman, though he had not seen him perform in the ring. He had not gone to a bullfight for years and had never been what they call a true aficionado. I, too, had stopped going years before. Anyhow, we didn't usually esteem *señorito* bullfighters and still less the latest mode of "intellectual bullfighters" who figured in books and plays and had become cult figures for bookish young people who had rejected all other idols. Beyond that, Ignacio's well-known friendship with Sanjurjo would have alienated us if we had not recognized it as the principal source of his admiration for the former Minister of War. After all, my Brother-in-Law had risked the unpopularity that might follow his pardon of the insurrectionary general as courageously as he had confronted Sanjurjo's rebellion.

[Sometime in the spring or early summer of 1934 the Azañas moved from 24-B calle de Hermosilla to a larger apartment at 38 calle de Serrano. They had made the move before they went to Sant Hilari in July.]

That summer he did not go to the waters of Corconte in Santander, which from his last bachelor days had helped to combat a painful and recurrent nephritis; instead he and his wife went to the spa of Sant Hilari in Catalonia, highly recommended for that affliction. Though uncomfortably lodged, he had a good time there, gratified by the enthusiastic affection the Catalans showed him. Nevertheless, he complained, somewhat unreasonably, that they would not let him alone to enjoy his vacation.

As one of the most memorable treats of his stay at this spa, he and his wife shared an intimate dinner at the poet Eduardo Marquina's home in Cadaqués. The former Premier had accepted this invitation only because that volatile poet strongly insisted and went on at length about how enthusiastically he supported his policies. Returning from this excursion on the yacht of some friends and battered by a typical Costa Brava storm, they faced some danger before they put in at Rosas. This experience did not prevent them from sailing those waters afterward, enjoying the splendid panorama and an enthusiastic welcome from the populace—especially urban workers. At that time, too, he came to know the famous archeologist Bosch Gimpera, who showed the former Premier around his magnificent Hellenic excavations on the Gulf of Rosas.

My Brother-in-Law little suspected, coming back to Madrid from Sant Hilari's beneficial waters, that he would soon have to return to Barcelona. Nor could he guess the serious consequences of that trip which would endanger his personal safety in the midst of a general national upheaval.

36

His Rebellion in Barcelona

Prior to my Brother-in-Law's visit to Sant Hilari, I had spent the Saint John's season in Barcelona with the Español Company. Before returning to Madrid, I paid a courtesy call on the Generalitat's new president, and he took that opportunity to give me a letter for my invalid Friend urging me to take very good care of it. His letter spoke of increasingly tense relations between the republic's government and the Generalitat, which had developed from the problem of *rabassaires*. This involved litigation dealing with a special kind of lease and usufruct peculiar to Catalonian law. The problem had political repercussions as it caused conflicts between Right and Left that the Radical Samper ministry could not resolve. Extremist Catalans went on to deduce further conclusions from the conflict, but the Resident of 38 Serrano did not consider them relevant. This particular problem had nothing to do with the Statute of Catalonia.

Elsewhere, and more seriously, members of the General Confederation of Labor, particularly in Asturias, felt increasingly concerned about the bold-faced reaction encouraged by Samper's cabinet, to which the middle classes were now turning from fear of some kind of revolutionary hydra. Enemies of the republican regime now discarded secrecy and openly bragged about their provocations. All of this, of course, encouraged insurgency. Socialist leaders, in turn, declared that they could not control the aroused strength of their members, who now felt disposed to counteract once and for all the schemes of the republic's enemies and those who sought to control our republic to prevent social reform. This undercut the republic's basic reformism. The Resident of 38 Serrano despaired when he saw responsible persons simply accept as inevitable an unrestrained and virtually undirected revolution carried out by agents of the unstable, unthinking populace that seemed ready to let chips fall where they might.

At this point, in mid-September 1934, Don Jaume Carner died, and the former Premier went to Barcelona again for the painful duty of attending his burial. Indalecio Prieto and Fernando de los Ríos went with him, and the profound and dignified silence of a huge crowd when the funeral cortege passed by impressed all three visitors as a powerful sign of general mourning. Before these distinguished delegates returned to Madrid, the Catalans honored them with a private dinner at the Font del Lleó Restaurant in the Tibidabo District. There Fernando de los Ríos, with the somewhat cautious endorsement of his comrade Prieto, repeated a suggestion in favor of an uprising that he had made to the former Premier a few days earlier. Alone, and against the prevailing opinion of his Socialist colleagues and members of the Generalitat, my Brother-in-Law spoke in favor of doing anything that would calm down the masses. The extreme Right deliberately stirred up popular agitation to provide an excuse for repressive measures. The unlawful holders of power had already begun preparations for that repression. He called them unlawful because, though they had an undeniable majority in the Cortes after the recent elections, their parliamentary control depended on a monstrous coalition of Radicals with the Right. Thus it happened that my Brother-in-Law judged it useful to remain in Barcelona, where his presence might possibly avert a rupture between the republic's government and the Generalitat.

Now an anticipated parliamentary crisis in Madrid complicated everything, a crisis only temporarily averted by the formation of a new ministry. Lerroux became premier with strong backing from the CEDA (*Confederación Española de Derechas Autónomas* or Confederation of Autonomous Spanish Rightists). Gil Robles, leader of the CEDA coalition, though a deputy from Salamanca, actually represented the Jesuits; and he now sought nothing less than the portfolio of War. The former Premier naturally thought it execrable that the republic's president agreed to cabinet positions for CEDA members who had made a point in parliament of refusing to swear allegiance to our constitution. "The republic for everyone, certainly," he often repeated, "but governed by republicans."

Left Republican friends also considered it best for their Leader to stay in Barcelona for the additional reason that it would afford him protection from the personal danger he might face in Madrid during this crisis. Everyone now expected an explosion, more revolutionary than political, characteristic of our people who always spoil everything by insisting on settling affairs all at once—affairs whose real resolution would require compromises and patience. My sister and I agreed that his absence right now could prove useful, even if it merely kept him away from enemies or friends who might in a crisis push him into actions that ran counter to his usual way of thinking. None of us anticipated any danger in Barcelona, certainly nothing of the sort that did occur there on October 6. A nationwide general strike called for that day intended to prevent the admission of CEDA ministers into the cabinet. While the former Premier opposed admission of CEDA ministers, he also opposed the strike. He feared the negative impact of any act by the populace that went beyond politics and civil protest.

The government broke the strike in Madrid on its first day. I heard shooting in the calle de Toledo and also later at Left Republican headquarters on the calle Mayor. I had gone there to look for friends who could give me some news. From then on I walked in the middle of the street with my hands raised over my head almost all of the way from the Plaza del 2 de Mayo (Casares Quiroga, carefully hidden, was in one of its houses) to my own house at 38 Velázquez, lowering them only on boulevards, on Génova and on Goya after the Plaza de Colón. I found my own street deserted at nightfall in accordance with warnings from soldiers that a state of war existed and that they would shoot anyone who even slightly disobeyed orders.

Shortly after dinner my sister called. Naturally worried and listening to an official radio news broadcast, she had just heard an unconfirmed report of the arrest of the President of the Left Republicans and former Premier. The army had captured him in a Barcelona hiding place. I hurried to her. Uncertainty distressed her more than anything. The news report did not reassure her; it would relieve her to know that some responsible authority had her Husband in custody. It occurred to me to telephone directly to General Batet, captain general of Barcelona. He had seemed solicitous and very friendly when Joaquín Montaner introduced us recently, friendly enough to justify my asking a favor. He soon came to the phone, and in a few words I identified myself as a spokesman for my sister naturally anxious about her Husband's fate. We knew nothing except his detention. Batet answered coldly that I should consult the judge advocate's office; he knew nothing about it. We found out a few days later that he had lied to us. At the moment when we telephoned he had the former Premier under arrest, seated on a bench between two Civil Guards in the patio of the Captaincy General. In that position my Brother-in-Law afforded some amusement, a source of derision and curiosity for garrison officers passing by. At that point I made up my mind to avenge myself on that general, but he more than paid for it. His death vindicated his memory for me; later on, his sacrifice wiped out my rancor.

The former Premier had taken refuge in the apartment of the son of a Catalonian magistrate. Shortly before that he had intervened with Generalitat officials to facilitate the departure from Barcelona of Mr. Brauns. Brauns, a German citizen and manager of Siemen's Madrid office, was the father-in-law of one of my wife's brothers. In return, Mr. Brauns offered to deliver to my sister and me a letter in which my Brother-in-Law urged us to remove the contents of a safe-deposit box in the Bank of Río de la Plata. He told us to use this material in any way that might seem suitable if the government took action against him personally. He heard from all sides of their animosity toward him. In fact, much later the police did search his home and mine, where I had that treasure from the bank safely hidden. So far as I can remember, it consisted mainly of irrefutable photographic proof of a recent swindle involving Alejandro Lerroux and some landowner from Estremadura.

After the government had broken strikes in Madrid, Barcelona, and the rest of Spain, they directed a terrible reprisal against the Asturian miners' uprising. It proved a mild preview of the uncivil war launched against our republic two years later by the blackest reaction that ever darkened the pages of Spanish history. Then our soil and our blood would witness another chapter in the infamous struggle for control of our land and our destiny between invincible spirit and the brute force that has challenged it through the ages.

As we heard nothing about the release of prisoners or their possible transfer to Madrid, my sister and I decided to go to Barcelona. Those held included the former Premier, the whole government of the Generalitat, and many distinguished Catalans. An anonymous woman had called my sister from Barcelona, speaking as a friend, to say that she had succeeded in seeing my Brother-in-Law but that now they were holding him incommunicado. Friends whom we considered overly cautious advised us to give up our planned journey as too dangerous. At the last minute Mariano Ansó, deputy for Navarre and part of the group seeing us off, jumped onto the train to accompany us, since others closer to us or with greater obligations stood by allowing us to leave alone. When our train pulled out of the station, its lights out, porters requested that we few passengers should lie down on the floor as a precaution against shots strikers often fired at the express train leaving Madrid. Ansó and I finally agreed to spend those first few minutes in the passageway between two cars.

We arrived in Barcelona on the morning of October 12, but for several days my sister could not see her husband in spite of efforts by several people who tried to assist us. One of them, a magistrate who spoke of himself as a great friend of my Brother-in-Law, and Don Juan Moles proved especially helpful. The latter, a well-known lawyer, was also Eduardo Marquina's brother-in-law. Left Republicans, and notably the president of the local branch in whose home they had captured the former President and Luis Bello, got in our way more than they helped. We found them either pusillanimous like their Madrid cohorts or absorbed in squabbles with the Catalonian Esquerra. In the end my sister did get authorization to see her husband aboard the steamship *Uruguay,* where he lived in crowded confinement with many other prominent prisoners including Lluís Companys and Joan Casanovas. The latter had a highly publicized relationship with a good-looking Mexican star of a review, and it scandalized ladies waiting for hours at the gateway in inclement weather to see officers of the guard allowing this charming and pushy chorus girl to go right aboard without delay.

I finally got to see my Brother-in-Law along with his wife on one of the last days of his residence on that old liner converted into a prison. We met in the ship's main salon together with several of his fellow prisoners under surveillance by the Civil Guard. He could not hide his irritation. "Do you know how many telegrams I have received? Seven. A few months ago I would have received seven thousand." I explained that seeming lack of support. Certainly many friends and partisans had held back from fear for themselves or for him. Many, however, had undoubtedly sent telegrams. Allowing just seven to come through showed perverse cleverness on the part of the authorities, giving him an impression of abandonment by his followers rather than of the government's holding up his mail.

Our friends' passivity in the face of enemy aggression irritated the former Premier very much. He wrote to his lawyer, Don Ángel Ossorio, and I telephoned him. We both urged Don Ángel to emphasize at the trial his Client's unjust treatment. Don Ángel judged, instead, that the advantage of this treatment must lie in an inscrutable exaltation that Christian doctrine promises to those who suffer humiliation. Unfortunately my Brother-in-Law did not know how to accept humiliation, and he did not want to accept it. To me it seemed monstrous for our friends to tolerate without violent revulsion the attitude of Santiago Alba, president of the Cortes. Only malice could explain his failure to exercise his primary duty to defend deputies' parliamentary immunity, and beyond that to secure decent treatment for a personage like my Kinsman. Santiago Alba's personal obligation to my father's memory made it worse. As for the president of the republic, I need not say that Don Niceto found neither ways nor means of offering any opposition to Lerroux and his rabid colleagues, now so wretchedly demeaning their own positions by harassing the former Premier. When I spoke and wrote to Don Niceto's private secretary his evasive answers echoed the president's cold response. This culpable abstention disguised as incomprehensible torpidity further infuriated the Prisoner in his offended dignity. He found his role as victim highly uncomfortable in spite of all predictions that it might serve him well and prosper his cause in the future.

He also found it intolerable that people should identify him, whose respect for legal authority had constituted the essential norm of his political career, with the subversion he had tried to avoid by all possible means. In our first conversations he eased his bad humor by going over meetings with influential Catalonian politicians in the Colón Hotel where he was staying. He had urged them not to commit themselves to a course of irresponsible violence, characteristic of Catalonian extremists but unsuitable for members of the Generalitat. He also found the Socialist position highly imprudent. He talked a lot to me about his dramatic discussion with the deputy Lluhí, whom he especially admired among young Catalonian politicians. He had argued the wrongheadedness of persons with means of power in their hands resorting to insurrection; they ought, rather, to use their positions to achieve their ends. He remained inconsolable about the folly of the republic's government and the Radicals who had led that government into a criminal alliance with the Right. This had in due course triggered the popular reaction that had proved too disorganized and weak to succeed.

My sister and I saw some evidence of that popular reaction, unimportant but still significant. On one of our first days in Barcelona in the Colón dining room's vast loneliness, I heard a couple, a man and a woman at a table near ours, the hotel's only guests besides ourselves, commenting on a newspaper story. "It seems that Rivas Cherif, this Bum's brother-in-law, has withdrawn from the bank all the money he stole." My sister, somewhat hard-of-hearing, had not understood, so it amazed her when I calmly called the waiter. "Please tell that gentleman that I am Mr. Rivas Cherif, my sons are nephews of 'that Bum,' and he had better get out of my sight." That fool, dumbfounded and confused when he realized his blunder, hurriedly settled his bill and left with his companion, his departure sped by the waiters. It had all happened by a curious, inopportune chance. How could he suppose we would hear him repeat that bit of gossip from an equally false barrage? I had hardly finished speaking when the headwaiter, the manager, and even one of the cooks came up to offer their support to us; they had picked up the story of my defense from the waiters.

A few days later two obvious foreigners came to share the solitude of our lodging place, husband and wife according to the hotel register. The waiter, apparently an anarchist but very proud of serving as captain of waiters, identified M. and Mme. Strauss as Dutch citizens. She, though no longer young, attracted attention with her platinum blond hair in the extreme fashion of the moment and was always accompanied by several unusual dogs. He had become very famous in Spain as the focus of a scandal arising from his connection with a kind of crooked roulette its inventors called *straperlo*. The Radical minister of the interior and his accomplices had authorized it, and it had become a major attraction at casinos in places like San Sebastián and Majorca where big shots go to lose their pesetas. Thus *straperlo* became a kind of synonym for flagrant fraud.

One of those evenings my sister and I sat talking in the hotel lobby with Braulio Solsona, a well-known Barcelona journalist and until recently a provincial governor, who had joined us for dinner. Another friend came in, Max Aub, German but a naturalized Spaniard from childhood, whose life revolved around literature and its attendant friendships. He told us, and his alarm immediately infected us, that he had just heard in a movie theater from a friend, an army major, that the army was taking over the government. Seeing my sister's panic, her sudden paleness, I challenged the truth of this rumor with such vehemence as to cause an embarrassing silence. Braulio Solsona broke the impasse, making me laugh, by replying seriously, "Well, now that we have scotched that rumor, would you like me to phone up the newspapers to hear what they have to say about it?"

After consulting me, but without consulting my Brother-in-Law, Braulio Solsona arranged for his transfer from the *Uruguay,* where he had remained in crowded confinement to a gunboat, the *Alcalá Galiano,* anchored with other warships in the harbor. Solsona managed this by an appeal to his friend Rocha, then minister of the navy and at that point visiting Barcelona; Rocha had recently served as ambassador to Lisbon. Though the interested

Party protested against special treatment for himself, he had a better frame of mind in his new prison. If equally unjust, it did afford greater comfort as he occupied the Second Officer's quarters, and right away the captain made a special effort to show his goodwill. My sister could visit him the morning after his transfer, and, after obtaining authorization, I could accompany her every day. Other friends came to Barcelona as soon as they learned of this new arrangement: Enrique Ramos, Amós Salvador, Martín Luis Guzmán, Marcelino Domingo, and his wife.

Don José Giral came first of all, and I saw him weep when he took leave of the former Premier, as did Casares Quiroga's wife. Casares and his wife came with us several days to visit my Brother-in-Law, and they stayed with my sister and me in Margarita Xirgu's Barcelona house. We had moved in at her insistence. After learning that the manager of Valencia's Teatro Principal had removed my name as director from the company's posters, I at once offered to cancel my contract so as not to prejudice Margarita's interests. She not only declined this but went so far as to say that she would retire from the stage if I insisted on withdrawing from her company. As I refused to accompany the troop to Valencia, she urged that we use her beach house at Badalona, otherwise closed during her absence. Enrique Borrás, her colleague, impresario, and leading man behaved far differently. Previously he had embarrassed me with continual encomiums about my Brother-in-Law, and he had insisted that the former Premier stay with him in Barcelona on his way to Sant Hilari. Now Borrás did not dare even send me a postcard from Valencia, and he advised Margarita to refrain from any show of support for the Prisoner.

Margarita had a curious telepathic experience, confirming this not uncommon phenomenon. On the night of my Brother-in-Law's arrest, at a time when nobody in Zaragoza could have known what had happened in Barcelona, she woke up with a start. Nervous and distraught, she called to her husband and insisted that he find someone to go to the assistance of the former Premier, whom she *saw* at that moment in very difficult circumstances.

A few days later misfortune brought my Brother-in-Law further anguish. His brother who had suffered from a cardiac condition got worse and died in Zaragoza without his having the consolation of a final visit. The *Alcalá Galiano*'s captain offered to ask the minister's permission for the former Premier to go to the dying man, sure that he would grant it. My Kinsman refused to have the request made because he would have to go in custody of a Civil Guardsman. I accompanied a large cortege from Zaragoza to the family crypt in Alcalá. Heading the mourners, General García Benítez joined the dead man's son; this young man would be murdered two years later in Córdoba early in the military rising against our republic. General García Benítez made a bad impression on me when he silenced with an angry look and a violent gesture a simple citizen of Alcalá. Entering the cemetery this man had shouted "Long Live the Republic!" to honor the dead man and the absent man.

The former Premier regained his freedom on December 28, the Feast of the Holy Innocents [in Spain equivalent to April Fool's Day] though the coincidence seemed too farfetched to apply to him. We stayed in Badalona to give him a few days of peace and rest before returning to Madrid. Nevertheless, continuous visits interrupted that rest. Now people no longer felt restrained or fearful about showing respect for him. We wanted to remain in Barcelona through New Year's Day 1935, and he received such an avalanche of telegrams that it required volunteer overtime service to transmit and deliver them. All those bags of mail came in a special little truck; the usual bicycles did not suffice. One telegram from Bilbao had thousands of signatures on I don't know how many pages.

We decided to return to Madrid at once. Cándido Bolívar came for us in a car with Fernando, Amós Salvador's little boy. Others of his friends, now ours, accompanied us in other cars. Friends had filled the apartment at 38 Serrano with flowers for my sister, and all kinds of people came to show their enthusiastic support. So many people came, in fact, that they had to hire a young boy, Antonio Lot, just to answer the door. Bright and quick, he regularly performed this duty in my brother the occulist's office. A model of faithfulness, Antonio had the consolation of accompanying his master the Premier when I no longer could.

37

Speeches for the Multitudes

Well into January it occurred to Ramón Pérez de Ayala, who remained our ambassador in London, to forward a letter Princess Bibesco had entrusted to him in the first days of the former Premier's detention. Rumania's government had transferred her husband to Lisbon, and the princess was at that point in England. Knowing about events in Spain only from newspaper reports, she had rushed to our embassy. The ambassador made a joke of her concern when he told us about it afterward; our friend, in her anxiety had offered to ask the king of England to intercede in my Kinsman's behalf. After Pérez de Ayala had pacified her, the princess wrote to express her friendship as something transcending all circumstances, and she gave her letter to him as the surest way of transmission. Until January he had not found an opportunity to send it on. She had also sent some books bought in London to help the former Premier endure his days of imprisonment. By his delay, Pérez de Ayala had also succeeded in denying him that pleasure. The princess showed very good choice in these books. I remember one on Cisneros, an old book like the others. She used to compare my Brother-in-Law to the cardinal-statesman when, as on that occasion, she wanted to flatter him.

In transmitting that letter and those books, Pérez de Ayala asked pardon for his negligence and the delay, since there seemed little point to it with the Captive freed. He felt more comfortable handling this transmission through my mother-in-law, now widowed from her second husband, the poet Enrique de Mesa. He was an old friend of Pérez de Ayala—proof that opposites attract. The ambassador knew what I thought of his policy of representing our republic without a full commitment to it, and in his cover letter to my mother-in-law he sent me greetings and asked my indulgence toward him. I merely replied that his new friendliness toward us suggested a political shift to the Left sooner than we had anticipated.

I had failed to convince my Brother-in-Law to turn to writing as a means of alleviating his incarceration. He found imprisonment so insupportable that he could not command sufficient inner tranquility for creativity, neither in the *Uruguay*'s uncomfortable confusion nor in the peaceful quiet and respect that surrounded him on the gunboat. Later in Madrid, after the first reunions with friends and family, he undertook to give an exact accounting of what had happened. Whereas on other occasions he had turned to me for help in finding titles, this time he quickly hit on a really apt one. A few months later he published *My Rebellion in Barcelona,* a record of how he had gotten caught up in the recent crisis. It had great popular success. Malevolent persons had wanted to eliminate him at any cost, recognizing his entirely constructive spirit as the republic's best affirmation.

He refused to collaborate in a parliamentary opposition cowed by a dominant uncivil majority. A patriotic reaction surged up everywhere against a policy that differed markedly from the amnesty granted at once to the August 10 insurrectionists. Repressions in Asturias by republican reactionaries exceeded atrocities committed in the past by the king's guardians of order, acts that caused Spain's people to lose faith in monarchy. Don Niceto's failure to respond to that repression with veto and protest exaggerated everything. Now the former Premier saw fulfilled that facile prophecy his lawyer, Don Ángel Ossorio, had made when abandonment by a silenced populace had caused him to despair.

Every spring since the republic's proclamation a rally had been held in Valencia's Mestalla Stadium. Organizers of that event in 1935 might well find satisfaction in the great city's enthusiastic and spontaneous welcome to the former Premier a year and a half after that organized jeering at Játiva. It proved ample compensation. The Orator somewhat dampened popular enthusiasm by refusing to appear on a balcony of the Victoria Hotel when he arrived rather fatigued from his automobile trip. We anticipated a great speech, though, because he told us early on that rainy morning that he had a headache. Incessant traffic of cars and trucks had kept him from sleeping. A multitude came to Valencia to attend the rally.

This crowd filled Mestalla's stands long before the hour announced for his speech; its field seethed as different persons came up to the microphone to entertain a packed audience and to keep up their enthusiasm for the main event. Each speaker tried to identify himself with the former Premier and vindicator of the people's rights. His own entrance proved particularly moving as did blind Mario Blasco's welcoming embrace. Blasco Ibáñez's stalwart son wanted to appear before Valencia's people and all those others from the rest of Spain gathered to salute the recognized Leader of the Left Republicans, a man representing the true spirit of our republican revolution in his challenge to renegade republicans and recalcitrant reactionaries. That delirious and exultant assemblage deserved my Brother-in-Law's magnificent speech. In spite of similar, even bigger demonstrations that came later, to the end of his life my Kinsman kept a precious album of photographs evoking that unforgettable day, indelible in the minds of true Spanish democrats. Very rarely had the patriotic feeling of a great crowd so clearly manifested itself with all hearts beating as one.

The Orator spent most of the rest of that afternoon in *El Mercantil Valen-*

ciano's editorial office correcting proofs of a stenographic text taken during his speech, which that newspaper and principal Madrid dailies would publish the next day. He always took special care and pleasure in this task. In an extraordinary way, he remembered each word, each inflection as indicated by either a comma or a dash, so that none of the rest of us could quite satisfy him when we tried to make these corrections.

That Valencian event had tremendous repercussions. Vizcayan Leftists immediately undertook to organize something similar in Bilbao. Needless to say, Socialists identifying with Indalecio Prieto, also editor of *El Liberal,* asserted their full support for the policy of republican union that their Deputy represented in so eminent and eloquent a way. That rally took place in the early summer on a field in Baracaldo. Though beautiful and effective, the Baracaldo speech could not possibly have so great an impact as the one given at Mestalla in Valencia. At least, it confirmed for us a warranted revival of the President of the Left Republicans' political popularity. Many thousands of voters unanimously acclaimed him here in a manifest plebiscite.

These enthusiastic crowds also wiped out humiliating memories not only of jeering at Játiva but also of the La Coruña rally back when Republican Action and the Radical Socialists had first fused into Left Republicans. Our friend Casares Quiroga had wanted to demonstrate to us the strength of his regional organization in Galicia, which had joined with Republican Action earlier. My Brother-in-Law had wanted at least to test the attitude of La Coruña's syndicalists and had stood forth bravely, along with Marcelino Domingo, in the bullring. Given the authorities' passivity under the newly elected reactionary government and the turbulent opposition that interrupted him continuously, we had been lucky to escape without physical injury.

Two highly successful productions at the Español coincided with the renewal of republican spirit expressed in those 1935 popular rallies. García Lorca's *Yerma,* which we staged at the beginning of that year, had an extraordinary triumph. Then Margarita brought to culmination her dual talents as an eminent artist and a popular actress in a brilliant political statement in our production of Lope's *Fuenteovejuna.* Soon after its President was released from imprisonment on the gunboat, the Left Republican party paid tribute to this great actress, my colleague, who had kindly offered her home to him. We decided to attend the theater en masse on a given day to present Margarita with the Order of the Republic, already awarded to her. She came down from the stage to his box, to receive her decoration from the Author of *The Crown* before a public cheering with enthusiasm. The republic had honored only one other woman, also an artist, in this way. Earlier my Kinsman had presented [the Order of Isabel the Catholic] to Antonia Mercé, "La Argentina," at the Español. That award had resulted from my article in *El Sol* pointing out her importance in promoting internationally the reputation of the Spanish theater. She had become the artistic heiress of the Russian ballerina Pavlova as the greatest woman dancer of her times.

Meanwhile my Brother-in-Law promised my sister a second honeymoon in Italy's lake country after the hazardous years she had endured without respite since our republic's proclamation. The Xirgu Company was planning a theatrical tour, also in Italy, but that country's declaration of war against the Abyssinian Negus delayed our plans and finally changed them. Chatting in his home with a circle of friends about the first incidents of that one-sided war, my Kinsman countered some exaggerated declaration of support for Haile Selassie, King of Kings of the Parasol, made in some connection or other. He said that, after all, he felt himself more a Roman of Tarragona than an African of Ethiopia. Imagine my surprise when, the very next day, Italy's press attaché in Madrid called me on the phone to tell me of his pleasure in hearing about the former Premier's travel plans. He said that the ambassador, who knew of those plans and of his judgments about the Italian-Abyssinian war, wanted to speak to me confidentially.

In this year of Lope's third centenary Mr. Pedrazzi had replaced our friend Guariglia who had brought a branch of laurel from the Capitoline Hill to Mérida for the Xirgu Company's presentation there of *Medea* in 1933. We had heard that this new man's assignment to Italy's Madrid embassy came from his friendship with the Duce rather than from his having risen through the diplomatic corps, to which he did not belong. Margarita and I had met him at a Lope festival in the Retiro even before he formally presented his credentials as ambassador. Now, hearing of our planned trip to Italy, he seemed interested in talking to me about it in a friendly way.

He received me privately and spoke with unusual frankness about his admiration for Spain's people; he compared our republican revolution with Italy's fascist revolution because both represented a break with a mediocre past. In this sense he considered himself an extreme revolutionary, and he proudly cited an article he had published in one of his country's leading periodicals, I think *Il Corrière della Séra*. In it he highly praised my Brother-in-Law, comparing him to Europe's great innovating statesmen of the recent past. Now he expressed delight in hearing that the former Premier planned an Italian trip and said that he would receive the welcome he deserved. I interrupted to say that, in any case, my Kinsman planned a strictly private visit, limited to the lakes, where he intended to take a restful vacation. The ambassador insisted that he would see a demonstration of the deep admiration felt for him in Italy with no disturbance of his privacy. He would also, however, and unavoidably, have to meet with the Duce. Ambassador Pedrazzi emphasized his own support of Mussolini, possibly because he had not been a fascist from the days of the first Blackshirts but came from the Nationalist party.

As soon as I mentioned my conversation with the Italian ambassador, my Brother-in-Law changed his plans. "Don't worry," he said to his wife with a smile, always enjoying the role of tour guide. "You will have your trip. We will go to Belgium. I very much want to see it again"—he had spent a few days there during his Paris residence twenty years earlier. "You will like it, you'll see." And, turning to me, he went on, "You understand that we cannot go to Italy under these conditions. We will save that for another time when we can go together as two couples. No, I cannot even consider it. The least they would say—I can hear it now—would be that I have sold myself to Mussolini."

He did not fully realize the importance of Hitler's rise to power in Germany. I happened to be the guest of our ambassador in Berlin, Luis Araquistáin, in 1933 on the day of the elections that assured the Führer's triumph, with the Reichstag still smoking from a fire caused by Nazis but blamed on Communists. I don't believe that Araquistáin guessed the tremendous consequences of that impressive electoral victory any more than I did. After all, neither did the English or Americans.

My Brother-in-Law and sister traveled to Paris, then, and on to Belgium and Holland to enjoy a month of summer rest, and they gave our representatives abroad a chance to show their antirepublicanism. Mr. Cárdenas, ambassador in Paris, felt obliged to inquire from the minister of foreign affairs about what attitude he should adopt during the former Premier's stay. My Kinsman made things easy for him by maintaining the strict incognito he so much preferred; he did not even call at our embassy. Aguirre in Brussels, more discreet or a better judge of the future, took a different approach. He met with the visitor and offered to show him around or to lend him an official car. He said, though, that he would not undertake any formal entertainment since no other possible guests remained in Belgium's capital at that season.

Delighted by Holland, which he had never visited, my Kinsman insisted that I should go at the first opportunity, to discover Rembrandt, to visit the Haarlem Museum, and to see Antonio Moro's portrait of William the Silent in The Hague. From Paris he brought back old and new memories, among them a performance of Gluck's *Armida* at the Opera. My sister's sensibility and her manifest enthusiasm delighted him. Now he shared with her, as he had with me in the past, confirmation of his earliest feelings about that city. Let anyone say what he liked about the polished stones of Paris, for him the whole city remained the touchstone.

As soon as he returned to Madrid the former Premier began work on a speech that would climax the campaign initiated in Valencia and continued in Bilbao. I was in Barcelona making final preparations for the Xirgu Company's Mexican tour that we had substituted for the Italian tour, suspended indefinitely because of their Abyssinian war. Thus I traveled to Madrid on that memorable October day to attend the immense assembly, an unprecedented political demonstration for an orator, that took place on what they then called the Field of Comillas.

The Mestalla field had at first seemed too large, and, though that crowd had far exceeded our expectations, the choice of the vast field of Comillas seemed far more risky. True, mere announcement of the former Premier's speech had aroused interest throughout Spain, presaging the enormous mass of people who did assemble there. Even the Ateneo cat attended, always part of meetings at the Learned House, brought to Comillas in a cage to witness that apotheosis which culminated its former Secretary's popular glory. Nobody could miss the moment when the Orator approached that rostrum; an extraordinary acclamation burst into the air, and all of Spain heard his ironic confirmation of a multitude before him. Looking out over that assemblage blackening the whole vast esplanade and speaking before he realized that the microphone was on, he commented, "hardly anyone." Some opposition journalist had predicted that as the probable attendance.

Two moments in particular brought home to me the event's immensity. First, when he began to speak, his voice, projected with an obvious delay and carried over the great distance, came back like an echo from the farthest loudspeakers. The other was a waving of handkerchiefs giving an impression of doves in flight in a triumphant salute to the podium.

"What did you think of that?" he asked, turning to me down below the rostrum during a pause forced by an uproarious ovation. He had a little trick of trying to seem unperturbed to me when, in fact, his effort to control his feelings weakened his voice and gave it a different quality just because of that effort to make it seem natural.

Hundreds of thousands of people congregated there, listening and shouting, but their mere numbers did not make the greatest impression on me that day. Perhaps they could understand his words only imperfectly. Rather, an admonition by the Orator especially struck me; indeed, I understood it more fully than anyone. He said that we should not base our foreign policy on considerations about forms of government in other nations. Foreign policy should depend on geographical considerations, not on similarity of political systems. Then, hitting the nail on the head, he added that he saw nothing incompatible between a strong Italian presence in the Mediterranean and preservation of Spain's inalienable rights there. He did not mean that he felt the least inclination or sympathy toward Mussolini or fascism. (He did not even like to use that word, and he found its Castilian forms, *fascismo* and *fascista,* beyond the limits of linguistic toleration.)

He himself recognized this as the most important thing he said that afternoon—and the riskiest.

38

A Confidential Testimony

That Comillas rally proved a major signpost directing Spain's freedom forces toward the Popular Front. Republican ideals spurred them onward, their resolve strengthened by their opponents' reactionary policies. With that rebirth of the enthusiasm of April 14 in our common people, ingenuous men of faith might believe that Spaniards would now face up to their responsibility to join together in a truly national government. Unfortunately, not everyone supported the Orator of the Field of Comillas. He himself had no illusions and always rated things at their true worth. He did not overestimate the commitment or, better, the efficacy of that coalition he had brought together. He understood that the enormous mass of people at Comillas represented many constituencies, distinct in shades and values, and that they had come together to present a united front only through force of circumstances, especially the prospect of new elections.

The republic's president remained true to his wretched policy of governing through confusion and setting different forces and political factions against each other. This increased his own power, since successive minority governments turned to him when they found that they could not take control of the middle ground where liberal democracy must find its strength. New signs now appeared of Don Niceto's political identification with the politics of the last Bourbons based on king and cacique. When the monstrous liaison of Radicals and CEDA broke down, the president turned power over to Portela Valladares. Portela personified the fraud our republic had come into existence to uproot. He represented the merely corrupt liberal counterpoise that had alternated in power under Alfonso XIII with equally corrupt, ferocious conservatism. Martínez Anido had represented the conservative prototype in Barcelona, nerve center of Spanish politics for the past twenty years. Portela Valladares had an untested reputation of being an in-house democrat; no one doubted his cleverness, his unscrupulousness, or his identification with Freemasonry.

This man used his position to serve Don Niceto's interests. Faced with a now unavoidable confrontation, the president still used dilatory tactics in dealing with the approaching showdown. Perhaps he hoped through political maneuvering to establish a middle-of-the-road faction that could attract voters from Left and Right. He remained unconsoled for the failure of his first plan, the alliance of Lerroux's Radicals and Gil Robles's CEDA; thus he failed to recognize as his best remaining opportunity, his only viable alignment, identification with Republican Action and the former Premier whom he had treated so badly. Alcalá Zamora had not seen, and he did not see now, his good fortune in having so strong a collaborator, a man who made up in popular support for his lack of presidential support. Portela Valladares may have seemed highly promising, doubly cunning as a Galician and a professional politician. Certainly he readily acted in accordance with presidential policies, weakening solid alliances, breaking up legitimate relationships, unmaking coalitions, and violating agreements. A crisis had arisen, however, that required more than this. The discontented Left and the insatiable Right were both pushing for an inevitable resolution of long-standing problems in the life of Spain's people—though perhaps not for definitive solutions; that lies beyond humanity's reach.

Both Right and Left had united in solid blocs, reversing the reactionary concubinage of Radicals and CEDA through which Don Niceto and others had made such poor use of delegated authority. That impressive demonstration on the Field of Comillas indicated effective cohesion on the Left. Both sides blamed Don Niceto. His first, leftist collaborators felt betrayed by him and paid him back for October 1934 by charging to his account responsibility for the terrible repression in Asturias. Catholics of the CEDA proved far more indignant, having counted on passivity, if not open collaboration, in achieving a transformation of the Spanish state from democracy to totalitarianism in the pattern of so-called "national revolutions" in Italy and Germany. Young Primo de Rivera had not made his journey to Rome in vain, though the Duce, who had seen through Primo's father in one disillusioning interview, now rather distrusted the son's political effectiveness. Similarly General Sanjurjo and Gil Robles had traveled, each in his turn, to Berlin to test the waters there concerning a possible commitment for which circumstances would provide an opportunity very soon.

With the Español Company's Italian tour suspended indefinitely, our American excursion became imminent. We had gone on postponing the trip, but, in spite of my desire to stay in Spain, we could no longer delay our departure after we made specific arrangements with Mexico's government to perform in their Theater of Fine Arts. I like travel and looked forward to going again to the New World and to visiting the United States, but it seemed a bad time to be away from Madrid. It also saddened me that my Brother-in-Law raised no objections to my travel plans, that he felt he could spare me for the present. More signs of regret would have made my impending departure easier.

Early in January, on the eve of our journey, the former Premier took me for a farewell drive one afternoon on the La Coruña highway. For years we had not had so long a period of time alone together. He began by excusing himself for not having made an effort to keep me from going. He had not believed that he should ask me to forgo the material opportunities the American tour offered without some sure compensation. I told him that my own reluctance came from a feeling that my absence would come at a time when success would crown all our political hopes. Margarita and her husband, our company's business manager who understood this side of the theater, felt that absence from Spain for a season or two would prove very useful, and she wanted to follow through on our plans. My Kinsman countered my optimistic prediction. Everyone on the Left did not support him, far from it, and it certainly made no sense to make a sacrifice in order to share something that would not happen so easily as some enthusiastic proponents of the Popular Front hoped.

He felt greatly concerned that preparatory efforts had not developed a homogeneous, solid bloc of aligned forces with a defined program that the acclamations on the Field of Comillas had promised. For success, the Front needed more than victory in forthcoming elections. They needed to follow through in a positive way in the government after those elections. The unmistakable commitment of the multitude, indicated by unanimous applause and stentorian cheers, supported a "common platform," a term in use at that time coming from a literal translation the Orator did not much like. Unfortunately delegates from various parties and groups had not followed up on this clear mandate with negotiations; instead they had turned to niggardliness, deceit, tricks, and egoism.

That very day, or the day before, he had talked with our friend Amós Salvador, who had shifted with the republic's proclamation from his earlier identification as a Constitutionalist and become a faithful supporter of the President of Republican Action, now of the Left Republican party. Amós, a liberal conservative, had spoken of the recent democratic triumphs identified with my Brother-in-Law and of his own bitterness in connection with negotiating electoral agreements toward a Popular Front victory. Disputes among its constituent parties threatened to frustrate the people's unquestionable insistence and decision for unified leadership—as indicated by that eloquent plebiscite on the Field of Comillas with four hundred thousand people in fine feather.

Amós had complained about his colleagues. With all signs indicating early elections, they had turned to ridiculous scrupulosity and nitpicking about each party's representation in relation to its actual strength in various districts. A tendency to schism at the heart of the Socialist party complicated things. Furthermore, the Communists justifiably claimed a leadership role because in Moscow the famous Dimitrov had devised the Popular Front alliance formula as a common point of departure for all democratic countries in their struggle against fascism. Other divisions appeared within Martínez Barrio's Democratic Union. Even the Left Republicans had split between those who had come from Radical Socialism and those who had come from Republican Action. Finally, other clearly dissident small groups had never joined the new union, and federalists, though never numerous, always seemed ready, in the name of local autonomy, to obstruct effective cooperation. Altogether, prospects for the immediate future caused my worried Brother-in-Law to wonder, "Who knows? Perhaps it would serve us better to lose this election!"

When I cheerfully refuted that, simply saying that he could talk in such an absurd way because he knew that they would certainly win, he insisted. "Don't be so sure; don't be so sure. If we win, we will have so narrow a margin of votes and such strong opposition that we will find parliament uncontrollable. You can see disorder already in the Popular Front Committee; they can't agree on anything. Communists don't care about anything but beating the Socialists, but all this contention will hurt them more than the rest of us and outweigh any possible advantage they might achieve by it. To me it seems not merely right but necessary for the Communists to have representation in the Cortes. Altogether, nobody wants to face up to the real situation; they care only about maneuvering for position on electoral lists on the basis of votes they claim to control but don't really control." The syndicalists represented an altogether different problem. He blamed their mistaken apolitical attitude for their entering into abominable alliances, and he felt that it ruled out any possibility of the CNT entering into a sincere collaboration with anyone. In this their tactics differed entirely from the French CGT (*Confédération Générale du Travail* or General Confederation of Labor), which collaborated as honestly with the Left Republican cabinet as the UGT did in Spain.

I insisted that we would have a decisive victory, basing my opinion on gossip in café *tertulias*. My Brother-in-Law tried to dismiss this, but, in fact, it impressed him as a sign of the general feeling, all the more as it did not reflect any special party bias. Decades earlier, Don Antonio Maura, that oracle in a frock coat, had pronounced that one must pay attention to the neutral masses. Yes, not only would we have a sufficient victory to make government possible, but the former Premier himself would govern as President of the republic. I made my prediction too boldly for him to ignore it.

He responded, "In the first place, I neither should nor want to head this first cabinet. People have to stop thinking of me as indispensable, and they also have to see the desirability of each person in turn assuming these responsibilities. No, no! Let Don Diego (Martínez Barrio) become premier." He spoke even more explicitly and decisively about his conjectural presidency. "What a crazy idea! Nobody could accuse me of loving Don Niceto, but I have said, and I repeat it, that people have got to get used to the idea of republican continuity. As a beginning, the first president should serve out the full legal term to which they elected him. We must work with our republican formulas; we must direct the regime according to its own rules."

I had no trouble answering this, using his own arguments. They might well use the constitutional provision for presidential resignation after a vote of censure by the Cortes. This might very well result from discussion of dissolution of the Cortes in 1933 as a protest against the president's policy of too-frequent elections. Both Right and Left had become disillusioned with Don Niceto, and no recourse remained but to dispose of him. No other substitute as president appeared likely but my Brother-in-Law.

This all seemed crazy to the interested Party. As before, when Maura had predicted in my presence that he would soon head the Provisional Government, he now argued that he had enough to do in heading a ministry and a party, and that in limiting himself to these he would best serve in conditions that would follow the coming elections. I answered him by again repeating his own arguments. Hadn't he once said that our republic needed guidance and that he disagreed with the usual interpretation that our constitution intended a merely passive role for the president? Instead, he believed that the whole direction of public policy devolved on this office. It showed in the president's suspensive veto over legislation. Most important, it appeared in the requirement for presidential authorization of each succeeding cabinet. In fact, the president held a key position, and though we did not have what they call a presidential republic, this remained our government's paramount job. Who else but the former Premier could, as president, engineer the statutes for regional autonomy?

"No," he said again, "you will not convince me. And, besides, who even thinks that way?"

"Well, you will write to me about it when it happens. Because I don't believe that our *tertulia* has just dreamed up the impossibility of Don Niceto's remaining in office, and this is in Madrid. If you had come from Barcelona as I have, you would know that everyone there takes it for granted that he cannot continue as president. And after he goes, well you will write to me all about it!"

"Bosh!" and he remained quiet for a moment. Then, smiling as at a rather simplistic idea, he went on. "If things did turn out that way, and, in fact, Don Niceto really could not remain in office, maybe they should choose as the next president a man like . . . Giral." Anticipating my reply from my gesture, he went on citing his friend's undoubted, if unrecognized, merits. Giral combined caution with modesty, the consequences of his lack of eloquence. His republicanism was unblemished and his background irreproachable. No one surpassed his discretion, and very few had a better understanding of national politics; he gave constant proof of that to those who knew him well.

I answered, "You have pointed out the problem exactly. Not many people know Giral well. Most of our people have never heard of him. Very possibly Don José's virtues would suit a president of France, where a republic has existed for more than half a century. I am trying to show you how the man in the street thinks, and I know more about him than you do at this point because, like it or not, you have not gone around in our streets for a long time." (How often he had said to me that he would like to get out of his

official car, walk for a while, and jump onto a streetcar at the Goya station!)
"We will have elections a month from now. No? Apparently your triumph
will come as a surprise to you and to the few people who think as you do.
You will have no choice but to take charge of the government at once, as
Premier, and, say what you like, get ready to become President of the repub-
lic. If you don't believe me, time will tell."

He answered, "Of course, it could eventually occur. . . . Stranger things
have happened. . . . But, after all, who knows? Perhaps we need a governor-
general of the republic instead of a president." Now, I think, for the first
time he said to me that his first period of government had failed from lack
of fifty civil governors. (He considered a failure what seemed to everyone
else the revelation of an exceptional republican leader.) I asked him, smiling,
"A governor-general? A Cromwell?" He replied, "No, not a Protector. I
don't like the idea of a Protector. A governor! Governor!" We agreed that
Spain's people had to have liberty imposed upon them. Hadn't he said that
when we spoke of "the republic for everyone but governed by republicans,"
and "there are no liberties against liberty"?

We fell silent as we so often had in past years coming back from rambles
along that same Pardo highway. Now traveling by car we went too fast for
me to take leave of those trees; they and others on the parallel, higher
Florida boulevard had witnessed my walks with friends and my youthful
love affairs. After so long an interruption in our confidential, private talks,
after so much chattering in larger company, he had again confided in me his
doubts—uncertainty more than discouragement. That conversation could
have left me disconsolate, and I did embark on my journey with mixed
feelings. He had showed me contingencies clouding his plans, but they left
him unfazed. I left consoled that he had turned to me and certain of his
triumph and apotheosis in the near future, though I would share it only
indirectly.

A few days later my Brother-in-Law and a considerable party of friends
came to see my wife and me off at the train that would take us to the port
where we planned to embark for New York. Margarita had preceded us; the
rest of our company would come later. As we leaned out of the train window,
saying our last goodbyes in those trite phrases that help to get through the
last difficult moments of this kind of leave-taking, someone pushed through
the crowd and took my Kinsman aside. We almost missed our last hand-
shake. "Do you know," he asked me, with the train already moving, "whom
the Right intends to make president if it wins this election? General
Sanjurjo!"

A lady, a widow in deep mourning, still rather young, and looking out at
a window on the same corridor, stared at us hard, with clear hostility. I can
still see that little group as we pulled out, crowded together, surrounded by
curious people who made room for them.

39

President of the Republic

We stayed three or four days in La Coruña, very well entertained by friends of Casares, and I took advantage of that required sojourn to make a quick trip to Santiago, where my dear friend, the great writer Valle Inclán, had died a few days earlier. It turned out that the *Marqués de Comillas,* supposed to take us to Havana, ran aground at Vigo, and it seemed that the Transatlántico Español would not provide us with transportation soon enough, so we went to France. We got to Le Havre just in time to embark for New York.

When we arrived in Havana, before I even had time to leave my card at the Spanish embassy, Ambassador Luciano López Ferrer sent his First Secretary, a member of a Cuban family known in the capital for its conservatism, to greet me. As soon as I did visit our embassy, the ambassador returned my call with a promptness that my own position did not justify. His daughter accompanied him to welcome my wife; his own wife, member of a wealthy Madrid family, did not accompany them. According to gossip, a rather attractive and very willing secretary had replaced her in his affections. This secretary openly flaunted her authority over the embassy's career personnel. When I presented to Don Luciano my Brother-in-Law's letter of introduction, he outdid himself in praising the former Premier. He had good reason for gratitude. My Kinsman had promoted him from civilian technician to high commissioner in Tetuán in order to replace a military man at that post. Enrique Ramos had highly praised the ambassador's tact and intelligence to me. I had enough experience to make up my own mind about our diplomats and to make allowance for what a blind man could have seen. Still, the clumsiness of his pretense at sincerity surprised me.

He began by flattering me, saying that my reputation as a writer and man of the theater required no other introduction and that he was pleased to meet me quite apart from his esteem for the letter's Author. "As an ardent admirer of your Brother-in-Law," he went on, "I regret all the more that he has again allied with Socialists in the coming elections. I feel absolutely certain that even now (just eight days before the February 16 elections), if he would publish a statement separating himself from them, all of the Right would vote for him." I answered that even if that happened I could not imagine what my Brother-in-Law would do with those votes or what the ambassador could admire about his politics. The former Premier, I continued, precisely because of his moderation, could have no dealings with his born antagonists except as opponents in the Cortes.

On the night of February 18 Ambassador López Ferrer came to greet me at the theater, quite solicitous, though it did not occur to him to congratulate me on the Popular Front victory and the formation of a new government. He did say that Cuban opinion had reacted very favorably to Augusto Barcia's appointment as minister of foreign affairs. Barcia's father-in-law, Don Rafael María de Labra, a former president of the Ateneo and now dead, was Cuban-born. Of course, Don Luciano asked me to put in a good word with the new minister about his own performance as our representative in Havana.

Still, López Ferrer may honestly have admired the President of the Left Republicans. I realized that when we paid a call together on Colonel Batista. Though Batista no longer headed Cuba's army, I recognized his great influence on all aspects of his country's public life from our having to seek his approval to stage an outdoor show. Normally this would have fallen within the province of the Department of Fine Arts or even Havana's city hall. Anyhow, López Ferrer introduced me as the new Premier's brother-in-law, not quite my role in coming there, and he compared my Kinsman's statesmanship with Batista's.

At this time I got acquainted with a young journalist, Manuel Millares Vázquez. He and other Spanish residents had founded the Left Republicans of Cuba. He took me to the opening of a picturesque nightclub in Pinar del Río where my Brother-in-Law had an enthusiastic following, as he did in a similar nightclub in Havana.

Only after three years, whose length in the souls of Spaniards far exceeded their sum in months and days, did I hear a full account from my Kinsman of the monumental events that followed the 16 February 1936 elections. Someday that signal date will again assume its rightful importance in the record of contemporary Spanish history, though it now pales before more ephemeral events of the tremendous war that took place on our soil. As I had predicted easily enough, no sooner had general elections brought an irrefutable triumph of leftist candidates than the former Premier had no choice but to resume the leading role in the tragicomedy of Spanish politics. Premier Portela Valladares called him with anguished urgency. Before the elections Portela had been full of subtle predictions about how, backed by the president, he would occupy the fulcrum of our uncertain national political picture, and, somehow, his mediocrity would balance the extreme virulence demonstrated by Left and Right. Now, like Morón's cock, his tail feathers gone, he crowed with fright.

The governmental Left's unquestionable Leader tried, as always, to direct an incipient crisis in a way suitable not just to the moment but to the future. He tried in vain. "I had never spoken to Portela," he said to me much later, "but I encountered a very different man from what I had imagined. Distraught, he wanted to leave office that very night. 'I can do nothing,' he said to me. 'All the governors are resigning, and nobody pays any attention to what I say. You must take over at once.'"

My Brother-in-Law told him not to do it, that people had to get used to things happening on schedule. The two premiers, old and new, ought to act in a prudent, normal way, convening the Cortes at its scheduled time and letting it deal with this crisis through its votes. Until then Don Niceto, as president, could handle routine government affairs without having to resolve major problems under pressures of the moment. Unfortunately it became a question of public confidence in the government as Portela Valladares insisted strongly on turning over control that very night, not even waiting until morning. The former Premier faced up to the responsibilities of power, now in circumstances far more ominous than the first time, though he did not see it that way then.

Nothing more happened at that interview, and nothing less. The departing premier did not even suggest that any general, much less Franco, had indicated a possibility of military rejection of the manifest electoral verdict. Portela carefully avoided any reference to anything like that. So much so that my Brother-in-Law could hardly believe a rumor—later verified by Portela himself and corroborated by the adventitious victor in our struggle—of an official warning and an offering to overturn the people's decision made to a man then still premier but on the verge of precipitate resignation. At that later date my Kinsman headed a republic ferociously attacked by all kinds of people, and he could not correlate this account with his predecessor's simple wish to flee from office. He found it impossible to believe that Portela Valladares, still premier, would have hidden from him a matter of such extraordinary seriousness, thus contributing by culpable silence to an impunity that the conspirators enjoyed from the start in their extensive planning for insurrection. Nonetheless it seems to have been so.

Nor did the popular acclamation that again swept my Brother-in-Law into the position of Premier cause him to forget his pessimistic comments of forty days earlier about the unlikelihood of relatively peaceful government if the Left had a narrow victory. He did not believe that his mere presence would somehow magically dissipate insuperable political difficulties. Recognizing the moment's tremendous seriousness, he separated himself from a great majority in both of the hostile bands contesting control. While he spoke "words of peace" to Spain's people, extremists on both sides made preparations for the most atrocious and ruthless of wars, and other more responsible persons on both sides did not realize how far things had gone.

It meant little that a very important sector of the country did accept the electoral results and receive with hope their Premier's nation-wide broadcast. It deeply pleased and flattered him, in spite of his previous discouraging experience, to hear that some elegant ladies drinking tea in a Castellana pastry shop, agreeably surprised, had praised that first declaration by the government's new Head. Other reports meant more. His pacifistic approach disenchanted more than Socialists, Communists, and revolutionary anarchists. Some at Left Republican headquarters on the calle Mayor tore up membership cards in angry protest against their Leader's moderation. Had they won the election for this? I need not say that his speech did not cause the Rightists to disarm, far from it.

Parliament assembled facing a very difficult discussion about the constitutional crisis caused by Alcalá Zamora's 1933 dissolution of the Constituent Cortes. My Brother-in-Law learned from reliable sources that the president intended to openly repudiate his identification with the Left cabinet and the republican tradition. "Everyone talked about it then as openly as they do now," he said to me some time later. Calvo Sotelo went so far as to say in Congress that Don Niceto had committed himself and stood ready to remedy the current crisis by a new dissolution of the Cortes.

In this situation, no question could remain about the next step. The president of the republic had become increasingly and obviously reticent in meetings of the Council of Ministers, and he lost no opportunity to weaken its authority by exaggerating the growing public concern about frequent disorders. Certainly anarchist elements did commit scattered acts of armed violence, though this represented their response to similar actions by persons of the so-called Right, and they often put up with everything. Later Luis Araquistáin told me that Rightists identified with *El Debate,* then the recognized voice of the CEDA but always of the Jesuits, had tried to get the Premier to follow Don Niceto in more or less explicitly withdrawing from the Popular Front. When I questioned my Brother-in-Law about it, he did not deny that they had made an approach, but certainly nothing open. In any case, this would have occurred in the days just before the election, about when the ambassador in Havana spoke to me of that possibility as his strong hope.

The cabinet heard that Socialists intended to propose a vote of censure against President Alcalá Zamora during the debate on his dissolution of the previous parliament. When my Brother-in-Law undertook to advise Don Niceto to resign in order to avoid the awkwardness of being deposed, he took it amiss and obstinately refused any effort to hide his complete break from supporters who had established his presidency five years before. Some of them had supported it with enthusiasm; others, like myself, distrusted him and had done it less enthusiastically. Alcalá Zamora's presidency ended immediately and according to the constitution, when a requisite vote of censure passed by an absolute majority. In the unavoidable interim before the new presidential election, about a month away, Don Diego Martínez Barrio, president of the Cortes, assumed the duties of highest magistrate. He took possession of the National Palace at once. The departing president, in his perturbation, did not even bother to greet his interim successor.

Dense clouds and lightning warned of a coming storm; thunder soon exploded. The clash of extremists took the form of attacks on individuals, and several innocent bystanders got killed. Italian Fascism and German Nazism had found their earliest inspirations in anarcho-syndicalism, which, in a regression to medieval justice, turned to direct action by its militia for defense of its members. This chaotic system of judicial vengeance had earlier brought the death of Manuel Andrés, the best police commissioner our republic had. His assassins had killed him treacherously in San Sebastián, where he lived, in retaliation for the immediately previous murder of a well-known representative of the Right. As with so many other irreplaceable young men (especially the devastating death of his nephew Gregorio), my Brother-in-Law could never accept the loss of Andrés. He always remembered, too, and with great indignation, that some concerned friends had tried to get him to withdraw from the sight of that commissioner's dead body, fearing that he would collapse. He had come from Madrid to attend the burial, and he had lingered a moment at the coffin with his hand over his eyes in an attitude of sorrowful recollection. ("They thought I would faint; that's what bothered me!")

The first public manifestation of violence came on April 14 during a military parade on the Castellana when some agitators sowed confusion by throwing firecrackers near a stand where Martínez Barrio presided. This would have meant disaster if panic had spread to the crowded avenue. Instead most people remained calm, following the example of their Premier sitting in the front row. Nothing happened that day beyond a few firecrackers exploding, but some foreign representatives threw themselves to the ground, the first indication of a cowardice that would cause them to desert their posts a few months later. They gave no thought to ministerial wives, with my sister also in the front row. She followed her husband's example, advising calmness, and from then onward she never deserted her post beside the man whose fate she had made her own.

So far I had received only two or three letters in Havana from my Brother-in-Law, precious to me since he was always his own best witness. In the first he told me briefly, with no details, of his February 16 interview with Portela Valladares. In another, after Alcalá Zamora's deposition, he told me that he had accepted, mainly at Prieto's behest, candidacy for the republic's presidency. Without referring to our conversations of two and one-half months earlier or to my predictions, now so soon confirmed, he repeated as his justification for taking that post the very reasons I had given to him then. Before that and afterward he played devil's advocate in his own case, arguing with me against a position I very well knew corresponded to his deepest wishes. Denying it to me, he wanted to have me confirm him. I had not even ventured to seek permission to ask the editor of *La Libertad* in Madrid, a good friend of mine, to reverse his stand and urge it as necessary that our Premier become our president. Many opposed it, including Left

Republicans who believed, as followers of Lerroux had in the past, that exaltation of their leader would decapitate their party.

My Brother-in-Law finally decided that he had to accept nomination for the presidency when our old friend Araquistáin openly proposed Álvaro de Albornoz for the position, more to spite Prieto than for any other reason. My Kinsman judged that this choice had all the disadvantages I had pointed out in Giral; Álvaro de Albornoz did not have unquestionable prestige with the mass of voters. Besides that, it might mean that Araquistáin, who inclined to play the role of Ninfa Egeria, would come to have a commanding role in Socialist party councils through Albornoz. Later, using Largo Caballero, he did assume this kind of position with no less harm. Anyhow, Prieto's nomination of my Brother-in-Law triumphed when our people and others clearly understood that the Candidate not only agreed but felt convinced of the necessity of his election as President. After the Socialists decided to support the Premier as their candidate, no real dissent remained or, for that matter, any other candidate to challenge him.

Of course Socialist obedience to party discipline assured that party's unanimous vote. Nevertheless, an incident among the delegates assembled in the Retiro's Crystal Palace clearly indicated underlying division about the choice. Julián Zugazagoitia, fellow Socialist and friend of Prieto, slapped the face of Luis Araquistáin, also a Socialist but resolutely opposed to my Brother-in-Law's presidency. Araquistáin interpreted this choice as a personal defeat, though he had not otherwise shown himself an enemy and had sometimes seemed the Premier's advocate. Zugazagoitia had heard from sources he considered reliable that Araquistáin had consoled himself about the outcome by saying, "All the better. Now he will fall from a higher place." The President told me about it months later, with a certain melancholy irony, when I questioned whether or not he had the full support of Araquistáin, then our ambassador in Paris.

In the meantime Margarita's husband [Don José Arnall] had died in Havana, and López Ferrer attended his burial as official representative of my Brother-in-Law, then still premier though Don Niceto's return to private life had become imminent. Margarita's innate discretion led her to turn down the ambassador's offer to use the embassy chapel for the funeral. This gesture of ambassadorial obsequiousness did not, however, counteract the effect of his almost explosive disagreement with me about celebrating April 14. López Ferrer wanted to avoid the celebration, whereas I insisted on it and put off our Company's departure for Mexico to publicly expose his equivocal attitude. A little later he lost his post, about when we awarded the Order of the Republic to that young journalist, Millares Vázquez, who, as I have said, founded Republican Action in Cuba's Spanish colony. Up to then the ambassador had not paid much attention to him. The Premier chose the opportune occasion of López Ferrer's obligatory farewell banquet for presentation of that award. I need not say that the insurrection against our republic in Spain had hardly begun when our former ambassador to Cuba confirmed my first impression by offering his services to the Junta of Burgos, the insurrectionists' governing body. Still, his support of that treason did not gain this traitor any significant diplomatic post after foreign powers recognized the new Spanish government at the end of our civil war.

I first read about the new President's apotheosis and inauguration in a Mexican newspaper. Later a family report came by mail. These letters from my sister and especially from him helped to alleviate my distress about missing a spectacle I had imagined so many times. Leaving Madrid at that point meant missing this and other personal joys.

Right after taking his oath of office the new President offered the premiership to Indalecio Prieto. The Socialists, however, increasingly divided about how far they ought to support Republican cabinets, now adopted a policy of voting with the Premier in parliament but not serving as ministers. Thus Prieto foresaw his party's unwillingness to let him serve as premier, and he felt unwilling to risk a schism by refusing the discipline of a party to which he had always belonged. This undercut the incoming President's expectation of maintaining a Republican-Socialist coalition with a liberal Marxist premier, that is to say, someone who would not link the social revolution so indelibly cemented in the republic's fabric with the political forms of Soviet communism.

Consultation with the Chamber's president and other important political leaders brought unanimous agreement in favor of authorizing Santiago Casares Quiroga to form a cabinet. This completely fulfilled a prediction I had made to my Brother-in-Law a few months earlier. Contrary to his own opinion—that needs emphasizing—I had ventured to foretell his presidency, in which he would have as his premier an invaluable collaborator in this close friend and former minister of the interior. I saw this as a great advantage because my Brother-in-Law as Head of State and Casares heading the cabinet would function as one person. That idea seemed absurd to my Kinsman. From a strictly republican viewpoint, he insisted on separation of powers and variety of responsibilities as inviolable principles. He also believed that I erred in believing that Casares as prime minister would prove absolutely submissive to presidential directives, their close friendship notwithstanding—indeed precisely because of it. On the contrary, he felt sure that once Casares became premier he would make a point of asserting his independence and individualism, as much from fear of criticism as from his own inclination.

Yet in hearing of the nomination I recalled only my own strong arguments. At first and in letters, the President could not indicate my clear and fatal mistake; he could later. Though, like myself, he valued Casares's talents, he recognized other less helpful qualities. Characteristically, Casares and I had founded our own private party; I invested him with its mock leadership and thus became myself the whole party membership. We called ourselves "The Immoderates" from a nickname he had given me.

When our family in Madrid became alarmed about my eldest son's illness, I decided to send him, and later his brother as a precautionary measure, to a sanitarium in the Guadarramas run by Dr. Gómez Pallete. The doctor was a childhood companion of my sister Lola and brother Ramón, for whom we had named the elder boy. The President and his wife took our third, youngest son with them to the Pardo where they established their principal residence in the La Quinta villa. They settled down happily there to get some rest from the strenuous efforts of those months up to February. Meanwhile the President was having rooms formerly occupied by Queen Cristina in the Royal Palace prepared as his Madrid residence.

Against Margarita's wishes, but driven by some pressing, undefined uneasiness, I decided to advance the date of my wife's and my return to Madrid. I accepted an offer from a movie studio to try out cinematographic direction. I also anticipated a new contract from the Español, though my impresario and collaborator predicted that we would not find Spain's political situation propitious for our theatrical enterprise.

Leaving the embassy one day in July, after having dinner with Ambassador Gordón Ordaz, we heard newsboys shouting about the assassination of Calvo Sotelo in Madrid. On July 18 my wife and I embarked on the *Cristóbal Colón* at the port of Vera Cruz. That morning during a visit our friend the consul had received a telephone call. When he hung up, trying to discount its importance, he spoke of unconfirmed rumors of an army rising in Spain. Just as we embarked at midnight the consul communicated to us that an African garrison had, indeed, revolted, though it had no other consequences than to temporarily alter the course of ships sailing for southern ports of the peninsula. He promised to keep me informed as well as he could.

40

Temporary Quarters in the Palace

Two days later, at sea, in response to my own urgent message, a telegram came from Domingo Barnés, our new ambassador in Havana: "Reports unclear. Please accept lodging in embassy." My wife felt somewhat unwell, and I did not want to tell her my impression of that message. I feared total disaster, since my friend the ambassador clearly meant that we could not continue our voyage. What had happened? What about our family? A few hours later another, somewhat reassuring, message arrived, this one from Cándido Bolívar, the President's executive secretary: "Madrid and Barcelona in our control. Alcalá, Guadalajara retaken. . . . " I read no further. How far had the rising spread? Soon Barnés sent another telegram: "Rising over. Will meet you at port." Only then did my traveling companion, Comenge, our commercial attaché in Mexico, tell me what the consul in Vera Cruz had told him on the day of our embarkation. In that telephone call during our courtesy visit he had heard from New York of my Brother-in-Law's assassination. He had held back and had not said anything about it since he had no confirmation. We had, however, noticed a contrast between his great show of concern to be of service to us when we passed through earlier and his later evasiveness and uncommunicativeness.

The ambassador did meet us at the port in Havana with a sizable party of friends. As our ship moved into its mooring, he ostentatiously waved a newspaper to show me headlines that took up much of the front page: General Sanjurjo had died, victim of an airplane accident as he took off from Lisbon's airport. Everything, then, had turned out as well as possible for our side. Answering my gesture of doubt, my reaction against his exaggerated optimism, as earlier doubt had protected me against despair, Barnés insisted.

"It's all over. Finished. According to what my brother says—the minister of education—they are finishing it off now."

"I don't know. It seems to me that we have a civil war on our hands like the other time," I replied.

He asserted, "For better or for worse, Spain today cannot stand seven years of war."

I answered, "I don't know about seven years, but something like seven months. . . . That's what we will have. You'll see."

Millares Vásquez joined us in Havana and traveled with us to Madrid. I will not relate here the events of that hazardous voyage. With the *Cristóbal Colón* scheduled to land first at Vigo, we had planned when we left Mexico to go on to Santander to meet the President, my sister, and our children. They had rented a very comfortable house in Piquío, and they had written to us about its splendid site overlooking El Sardinero. Circumstances changed our plans. Instead, we docked first at Southampton and got off the ship at Le Havre where we took a train to Paris. Until then I had not known that the insurrectionist attack on Irún had obliged Spain to close its Hendaye frontier. We were obliged to enter our country by way of Port-Bou, and after a few hours stopover in Barcelona we traveled on to Madrid by way of Valencia as the rebels had occupied Zaragoza from the first.

We found our children waiting for us on the platform at the South Station with their aunts—my sisters and my wife's sisters. We later learned that most of the crowd on the platform had not come to meet incoming passengers but to wait for hours, even for days, to get on a departing train. Our boys, especially the youngest, made a great show of raising clenched fists and shouting joyfully, "U! H! P!" [*Unidad Hermanos Proletarios* or Proletarian Brothers Unite, the slogan of the 1934 Asturian rising].

I lost no time in hurrying to the National Palace. My taxi dropped me off at its Prince's Gate entrance at the foot of a flight of stairs leading up to the Horses' Esplanade and a doorway into the palace's ground floor. Rapidly greeting friends in passing, I went through two narrow rooms with high ceilings used as waiting rooms and offices for assistants. In the third, the republic's President got up from his armchair when he saw me enter. Extremely pale—even more than usual, he gave me a hearty embrace. "See what we have come to!" He found nothing more to say, and I didn't know how to answer him. We quickly got over our mutual emotion, and I turned to shake hands with some other friend. Cándido Bolívar, the President's executive secretary, stood tall and erect with fitting circumspection. I think that Sindulfo was also there. My sister could not hide her tears.

Inevitably our conversation turned to the events of my ocean voyage. I didn't realize what risks it had involved and what suffering they had caused my Brother-in-Law. He had followed the vicissitudes of the *Colón's* passage with his heart in his throat. They knew in Madrid that the insurgents had sought out our ship and then followed it, intending to capture it and its cargo. I myself had represented a significant part of that cargo because of my close family relationship with the President. He emphasized this to me with some reproach in connection with a story printed in the newly founded *Frente Rojo* about a telegram I had sent from mid-Atlantic to the *Pasionaria* [Dolores Ibarruri] after hearing her emotion-filled voice in a radio address to Spanish America.

I stayed for dinner. New faces among the aides. General Masquelet, chief of the President's Military Cabinet; an admiral whom I soon learned they suspected of leanings toward his rebel colleagues; Riaño, an old acquaintance of mine. An awkward pause followed when, among my first random questions, I asked about Casares. Casares, I later learned, no longer came to the Palace. I went on talking about our voyage. Various passengers on the *Colón* had great hopes for Martínez Barrio's ministry as a barrier against revolutionary excesses that might follow the military rising. That ministry had not lasted long enough to take the oath of office. In this dire emergency Don José Giral had taken over as premier. Saravia, presidential private secretary when I left, had become minister of war. Impelled by an optimism that nobody contradicted and that was not dissipated even by my Brother-in-Law's brooding, melancholy seriousness, I suggested that everything seemed to be going well. From the frontier to Madrid, but especially from Valencia and increasingly as we approached the capital, spontaneous manifestations of public enthusiasm indicated a high level of popular morale, an irrefutable confidence in certain victory. I could not believe that the insurrection would last long. The prospective war appeared to have dwindled into a failed coup in spite of the insurrectionists' elaborate preparations.

The President, always concerned about details of the lives of my little children, said to me that he did not like to hear of their playing in the calle de Velázquez. Agreeing with him, I answered something about the greater opportunities they would now have for walks in the Casa de Campo and Campo del Moro. "In the Casa de Campo?" I especially remember the look on Sindulfo de la Fuente's face and my Brother-in-Law's pained smile as the others turned to him. Mixed feeling converged there to create a kind of sad sarcasm that ended in an inexpressible grimace. Thus I learned that we could not go into the Casa de Campo because it had become a dumping ground for the first *paseos,* a terrible term describing a new custom of clandestine murdering of enemies, or even suspected enemies. That alone would explain a terrible grief in the President's soul. Legal authority could not halt these criminal excesses committed in the name of purgation, like that supreme crime of the civil war which rebel soldiers had declared.

Our eagerness to talk prevented any order in our conversation that first night, so I learned by fits and starts what had happened in the first hours of the rising. Still at the Pardo's La Quinta villa, the President had received an urgent message on the afternoon of July 16 to leave for Madrid in view of reports of a rising of African garrisons. If conspirators in the communications regiment stationed at the Pardo had been more alert they could easily have taken him prisoner. Only a few days before, one of their officers had made some kind of radio installation in the presidential residence. On July 16 my sister had gone to visit our two elder boys at the Guadarrama sanatorium, and Secretary Bolívar went to find her to urge that she join her husband at once. As the President had already left the villa when she got back there, she hurried to the palace in Madrid. A knotty strike of construction workers sponsored by the CNT had delayed work on Queen Cristina's apartments for more than a month, so the President and his wife settled in rooms on the lower floor, where we had eaten our dinner. My unmarried sister had recently joined them at La Quinta and now lived with them in the palace.

My Brother-in-Law cut the evening short in spite of my wish to soak up, to relive through that disjointed narrative, events I had tried and failed to imagine during my ocean voyage. He strongly insisted that I get home early. He said that streets became unsafe after midnight, though the official car of a presidential secretary seemed sufficient protection to me.

At home I tried hard to convey to my wife my impressions of the President, but could not get beyond the undoubted grief that showed clearly in his ravaged face. My mother-in-law seconded me about the impact of the insurrection's very first days. Only twenty had passed; the calendar showed August 7. "Especially his hands," she said. "You cannot imagine the effect those hands had on me when I saw him after the first two days when, among other things, he had hardly slept. So white, so helpless, resting on his knees or just hanging free of his body! He was sitting down, terribly pale, looking defeated . . . and those hands!" Of course, now, I did not get the same impression of anguish about him. No. He did seem to have grown much older in a short period of time, but he had never looked really young in the years of our acquaintance. Still, as soon as he began to talk, however great his agony, his spirit revived, dignified and serious unless circumstances called for a joke. He never surrendered to adversity.

The next morning I lost no time in getting back to the palace. He continued to occupy Don Niceto's office, as we called it, a little room they had fitted up for Alcalá Zamora in apartments identified with the duke of Genoa. He looked better and seemed happier. Quite a lot of that came from seeing him in daylight, fresh from a good night's sleep. I had arrived at day's end and after many weary days, aggravated by worrying about me. Besides, those gloomy rooms made everything worse, entirely lacking the comfort and graciousness a suitable and pleasant retreat should afford, hung with dark red tapestries, and one sad lighting fixture high up near the ceiling. (Ossorio told me months later in the Paris embassy, where he had replaced Albornoz, that he believed much of what he regarded as the President's exaggerated pessimism came from the shadowy sadness cast by that depressing fixture.) My Brother-in-Law took me to a balcony overlooking the Campo del Moro. "Do you see that smoke?" he said, pointing to the blue line of the León Heights. That's where they are now. Someday we will see them in the Plaza de Oriente.

He countered my naive optimism, until then unchallenged, in telling me what had happened. Certainly the government had put down the rising in Madrid, but not through foresight. Almost daily knowledgeable persons had told Casares about preparations for a coup. Instead of heeding them, and without taking into account how things had changed since the crisis of 10 August 1932, he depended to a great extent on information from his son-in-law, a military man but obviously not very conversant with plans of other officers. Casares had taken this young man with him into the Ministry of War; he had assumed that office himself following the fashion set by my Brother-in-Law in his first premiership and copied in turn by Lerroux and Gil Robles when they served as premier. Casares had responded to warnings with jokes and sarcasm. "Alarmism!" As my Kinsman had predicted to me in deprecating Casares's aptitude for the premiership, he had not continued daily contact with the President but had allowed days to pass and once even a week without appearing at La Quinta. It got to a point where my Kinsman had to call his attention to it in a friendly way.

My Brother-in-Law accepted much blame himself for having yielded to fatigue left over from his efforts earlier that year and the tempting delights of his short country vacation. To some degree he had neglected that part of state business for which he had no direct responsibility. He had trusted in the Chamber's obvious confidence in the premier.

After those first reports of a rising in Africa, when he began to receive messages of governmental authorities in one province after another more or less willingly yielding to insurrectionist intimidation or force, the President consented to distribution of arms to the people. He went still further. He tried to counteract this revolt of the majority of army officers by excusing troops from obedience to any superior officer who proved false to his oath to the republic. This measure had proved largely ineffective. My Brother-in-Law knew well enough, and he continually repeated it to his Socialist colleagues, most of whom believed otherwise, that the common soldier obeys his sergeant, the sergeant obeys his lieutenant, the lieutenant obeys his captain. The captain obeys the major, and the major obeys the colonel. Thus the colonel exercises effective command of our troops. Colonels bring troops into the streets or keep them in their barracks.

As to the generals, and nobody ever got him to yield on this point, he insisted that no Spanish general had sufficient political or military prestige to resist forced retirement into the reserves or a change of assignment. Certainly, as Minister of War, he had applied prudently the laws he had created, though without lessening their force. He had tried to attract support by accommodating any officer who, whatever his politics, had a feeling for the strictly military dignity of his position. As a fundamental part of his own political strategy, however, he had retired any general with pretensions to head a political faction and any who believed in strong-arm techniques that subverted orderly public administration. He found it intolerable that those who had succeeded him in the Ministry of War in the past two years had restored to military command persons involved in the August 10 barracks revolt, persons who had more or less openly kept its spirit alive.

The President had little sympathy with the frivolous attitude of many Madrid citizens toward the war, their treating it as a festival. What had seemed to me nonchalant, joyous heroism seemed to him foolish, inconsequential showing-off. He told me that people visited the sierra front as a Sunday excursion. One might expect this kind of thing from newly recruited peasants and café warriors, but even some professional soldiers approached the war in a highly casual way—not to call it something else. All of it prevented him from foreseeing the easy and early victory that I, caught up in the enthusiasm of the streets, insisted on.

"I cannot make you realize," he kept repeating to me, "how crazy people became. On the day when we took Montaña Barracks a stranger came into the palace, into my office, and, beside himself, boasted, 'I killed Fanjul!'"—and he thumped himself on his chest with both hands, imitating that man's maniacal gesture. In fact General Fanjul, taken prisoner when the barracks fell, was tried by a summary court-martial and shot a few days later. Openly opposed to the reforms of the republic's first Minister of War, Fanjul had served as deputy in the Constituent Cortes but had failed to galvanize parliamentary opposition in that first period of republican success. Relegated to the reserves by the law on retirement, he had never let up on his lawful but ineffective campaign. Finally he had joined the conspirators who intended to finish off in Madrid the coup d'état begun by army revolt in Africa.

After Colonel Asensio had replaced General Riquelme in command of the forces guarding the Guadarrama pass, the President wanted to visit that front, and we went one August evening without giving prior notice so as not to provide our enemy with useful information. My friend Millares Vázquez joined the retinue; I had introduced him to my Brother-in-Law as founder and stalwart proponent of the Left Republican Party in Cuba. At nightfall we got to a settlement mainly comprised of sanatoriums. Soon after that we parked and followed the President out of his car. Informed of this visit a little before, Colonel Asensio and his staff welcomed us. As we climbed some distance toward the mountain, silence seemed to increase with the darkness. We went into a small hut where my Brother-in-Law looked at a map of operations in that sector and then through a window at the nearest enemy outpost in some nearby boulders—so close that those who accompanied us kept urging us to speak very softly or preferably not at all. A blue-colored light bulb and its green shade seemed to obscure the room more than to illuminate it. We also looked out through cracks in venetian blinds that covered the windows.

Returning on the Escorial highway, my Brother-in-Law highly praised Asensio, calling him a good soldier. He also pointed out unmistakable evidence of aerial bombardment of that very sanatorium where Bolívar had surprised my sister, on a visit to my two children, urging her to return at once to the Pardo at the war's outbreak. We had often traveled this road on drives as a break from his ministerial labors, and more than once we had gotten out of the car to look at some herd of bulls peacefully grazing.

Even the President's supporters sometimes criticized him as too pessimistic. I, too, got caught up in the prevalent optimism, heedless of the counsels of reason and the voice of experience. My Brother-in-Law also felt in better spirits that evening when he could momentarily share hazards with our fighting men and get away from that depressing palace apartment where the prince of Asturias had languished. He found it insupportable that the men responsible for his personal safety preferred his staying shut in, to the point of not even allowing him a walk through the Campo del Moro. One typical, suffocating Madrid August afternoon he insisted, so his assistants, another friend, and I trooped after him down the Horses Esplanade ramp. I think that General Masquelet accompanied us, but clearly remember Major Casado, commander of the Presidential Guard, commenting on the imprudence of our walk—dull and boring as it turned out. Gates leading to Saint Vincent's Hill and the Plain stood wide open for any malcontent who wanted to do mischief. Somewhat annoyed, I commented that it had not occurred to them to lock those gates and give the President an opportunity for a little outing.

It shocked and concerned me to learn from Casado that many families continued to live in upstairs palace rooms from the days of the *Señores,* as service personnel continued to call the royal family. That situation had continued through Don Niceto's grace or neglect. It also shocked Casado, but he felt that not he but the Administration of the Patrimony had jurisdiction over this problem. Certainly two unmarried sisters who had charge of household linen and bedding or a few porters posed no threat, but other more recent guests did. Among them my Kinsman discovered and finally evicted the brother of Lahoz, that armed man arrested opposite the Español Theater's private entrance on the calle de la Visitación during *The Crown*'s dress rehearsal in 1932.

At this point Rosenberg, the first ambassador of the USSR, arrived in Madrid; up to then they didn't even have consular representation in republican Spain. This arrival helped to balance the flight of other accredited representatives, but it also worsened our international position by feeding insurrectionist propaganda, which claimed that their military intended no more than to restore a social order threatened by some kind of communist revolution. On the afternoon preceding the official reception Major Casado himself told me that, because of prior announcement of this ceremony, he feared fascists might spoil the ambassador's presentation of credentials by dropping bombs on the palace. When the minister of war visited the President that night I took the opportunity to pass that along to him. The actual possibility of an incident bothered me less than the lack of confidence indicated by Casado's comment.

Having no official post, I witnessed Ambassador Rosenberg's entry into the Plaza de la Armería from the foot of the palace's main stairway. As his official party drove through the plaza's gateway, a band began to play the solemn "Internationale," and under those circumstances it seemed both ironic and melancholy. A sizable group of young Communists surrounding the car cheered and applauded the Soviets. Just as the ambassador got out of his car, Major Casado's horse took fright and reared, threatening to throw him to the ground or trample us bystanders.

The President did not find this Russian ambassador a very agreeable person. Cold and circumspect, Rosenberg limited himself to a set speech and necessary conventional words of greeting and conversation following the ceremony. A Soviet presence, and this man in particular, did not compensate for the unexpected desertion of French and English ambassadors who, in their imprudent withdrawal to Hendaye, had carried in their wake nearly all of their colleagues from other nations. Those who did stay on, some representing major South American republics, organized in their legations and embassies asylums for supposed refugees from revolutionary excesses. These refugees proved willing agents for sedition, and embassy annexes kept growing to hold more and more people.

The insurrectionists were using against our republic Moorish troops of the Sultanate of Morocco regularly assigned to the Spanish Protectorate. Now the President and his cabinet demanded that France's government order the sultan to withdraw these troops in accordance with provisions of 1912 Franco-Spanish treaty. The French culpably avoided taking any action, thus acting contrary to the treaty's spirit and its specific provisions. This left Spain's government with nothing to do but protest to His Cherifian Majesty, the sultan; that gave minimal satisfaction and achieved nothing. To complicate our position further, the caliph of Tetuán sympathized with the military insurrectionists, whose movement had first broken out in his zone. Later the French government also refused to allow us to buy armaments in their country though they had this obligation both by international custom and by the recent commercial treaty that required us, to our disadvantage, to buy all our arms in France.

I could not accept Casares's absence from the palace, whatever his reasons, nor could I simply accept the opinions of persons inside and outside the palace who blamed him for lack of foresight about the rising and so blamed the war on him. My friendships, then an now, go beyond accidents of fortune. I went to his house, then, where he greeted me much hurt because the President had summarily replaced him on July 19.

When I spoke to my Brother-in-Law about that visit to our old friend, undertaken on my own account, he added one more detail about Casares's state of mind when the rising surprised him. He had telephoned the President that evening with an urgent message about an attack on Madrid by the Carabanchel artillery garrison. No other evidence confirmed this warning, but my Brother-in-Law had to take seriously a threat of insurgents arriving at the palace at any moment—you could see the road leading straight to Carabanchel from its western balconies. Thus he felt that he had to follow the premier's urging to abandon his official residence and go into hiding. Saravia, still only his private secretary, quickly arranged a suitable refuge. My Brother-in-Law imagined for us a scene tinged with his special irony, his indignation tempered by commiseration for himself and others. With two cars waiting at the Prince's Gate for him, his wife, and their indispensable retinue, he took leave of his staff. "Gentlemen, farewell until we meet again in the Third Republic!" Before that happened, his telephone rang again, and Casares told him that it had all been a false alarm based on a mistaken report. "What do you think of that!"

Anguish about family members added to inevitable unhappiness entailed in his presidential responsibilities in these awful times. In the rebellion's first days his sister and chronically ill brother-in-law had nearly fallen into the insurgents' hands during their ephemeral control of Alcalá. Seeking refuge on the husband's farm in his native Murcian village, they had found neither security nor relief. Local revolutionaries seized their property, persons who refused obedience to any government that would not immediately sanction their own false claims for social justice. These revolutionaries might have better achieved their vision of justice by joining the fascist revolutionaries, our common enemy. On top of that, one night the daughters of General García Benítez, the President's cousins, appeared at the palace. Their mother had served as matron of honor at his wedding. These young women had come to ask him to arrange a pardon for two of their four brothers, soldiers and artillerymen for whom their cousin, the President, had shown unmerited affection. Just hearing that they wanted to see him brought such anguish to her husband's face that my sister wanted to avoid the interview. He answered, "How can I turn them away?"

He explained it all to me. On the evening after rebellion broke out his phone rang, and an assistant answered, "The President has no rebel cousins." Hearing this, my Brother-in-Law asked, both curious and alarmed, "Let's see. Let's see what it's all about." "It's nothing," the assistant answered. "Some rebel officers captured near Carabanchel. The police say that they claim to be your cousins." It turned out so. Saravia had to intervene that night, and he at least saved them from a summary court-martial. Now the daughters of General García Benítez had come to try to prevent their brothers' scheduled trial a few days later. The President promised to intervene again with the minister, but he warned them that he could accomplish only so much. Their brothers had gotten actively involved in rebellion, and that went beyond family concerns. Then, returning to the present, he said to me, "I asked them whether they knew anything about their cousin Gregorio."

In this way he reproached these young women whose father had participated in the military rebellion from its inception but had made no effort to help the President's nephew. Up to then I had heard nothing of Gregorio's presumably unfortunate fate. During my absence in America he had received his first assignment, as public prosecutor for the court in Córdoba, and he had gone there a few days before the army rebellion broke out. Though nobody really knew what had happened to him, everyone fell silent when the President projected his probable death. We knew only that in the revolt's first hours Gregorio had dutifully offered his services to Córdoba's civilian authorities. My sister decided not to burden her husband with an unconfirmed report about Gregorio. Somewhat later, serving as a hospital nurse, she heard from a Córdoban whose father had suffered the same fate that they had perfidiously shot Gregorio without trial or even sentencing. Her husband had wanted to spare her the depressing sight of wounded persons and the unpleasantness involved in ministering to them, but she had volunteered to do nursing and gave assiduous service.

During that same period General García Benítez had presided over the summary court-martial in Burgos that had condemned General Batet to death by firing squad. Thus fate decreed that Batet pay a debt contracted in October 1934 more quickly and inexorably than he could have imagined. After Batet had incarcerated my Brother-in-Law in Barcelona, Don Niceto had named him head of the Military Cabinet of the President, and Martínez Barrio had kept him on during his interim presidency. My Kinsman had confirmed him in that post despite the general's insistence on resigning. It made no sense to the new President to leave Barcelona's former military commander without assignment merely because of his own suffering a year and a half earlier. That gracious, elegant action, characteristic of a man who judged each case by its merits, so impressed Batet that he wanted to match it with the appreciation it deserved. The unfortunate military rising against the republic provided him with his opportunity. Batet judged erroneously that through his personal intervention in Burgos he might convince his comrades in arms to agree to a compromise settlement. The President did not believe his plan likely to succeed, but the general insisted so urgently that he could not refuse to let him try. On the other hand, it would have seemed preposterous to suppose that Batet was risking his life by going to Burgos. It greatly distressed my Brother-in-Law that García Benítez presided over this trial, so inexorably revolutionary in terms of traditional military conduct.

Anxiety about assassination behind the lines on both sides, which was the culmination of our fratricidal war's horror, greatly burdened the President. Many newspaper stories treated the *paseos* that existed on the fringes of Madrid's police department, but one journalist really went too far. He spoke admiringly of services rendered by the "Sunrise Brigade." The President felt that our people had some justification for taking justice into their own hands in those first moments of military treason, notoriously supported by a barbarous clergy and a suicidal bourgeoisie. He could not, however, excuse any representative of our government who degraded its legal authority, already weakened by bands of delinquents who used the rising against our republic as an excuse for killing and robbery. It did not matter that the other side supported military insurrectionists by acquiescing in equally ferocious actions and even methodically organizing them. The Church's blessing crowned the outrageousness of those antirepublican atrocities. At least the republic did not officially condone terrorism.

One August morning I sensed some crisis from the way officials on duty at the palace greeted me. Santos Martínez briefly told me about a massacre at the Model Prison. The previous afternoon some inmates had started a fire to create a distraction so they could escape. After the fire's extinction Madrid's populace had responded to this trick by attacking the prison and killing many persons held there. Ironically, the government had incarcerated some persons in this prison for their own protection. (I heard that Álvarez Valdés's son had even asked for his father's detention to protect him from the dangers of persecution by extremists on the outside.) Tumult and killing had lasted all night.

I found the President in his "audience chamber," one of the duke of Genoa's rooms hung with yellow tapestries and decorated with precious small paintings by Tiepolo; Don Niceto had received me there once. I found my Brother-in-Law sitting at a marbled table in the middle of the room, his head pressed between his hands. He looked up at me, his face contorted as I had never seen it.

"How should I feel!" he responded to my usual greeting in a tone, not of sadness or irritation, but of desperate, bitter indignation. "They have murdered Melquíades!" And he returned to his self-absorption, paying no attention to me. I didn't know much about it and wanted him to talk, but my questions seemed cruel to him, making him repeat things that caused him deep sorrow. Victims included not only Melquíades Álvarez but Martínez de Velasco and some thoroughgoing fascists like Ruíz de Alda who had instigated the whole business. Not knowing what to say, I began leafing through *El Liberal,* which lay among other unopened newspapers on the table. I finally commented, "Why don't they tell what happened at the prison?" Again he looked at me with astonishment and indignation. "What more do you want them to say? What should they say?" "The truth," I ventured to answer. "Why can't they tell that some prisoners revolted and that an indignant populace went into the prison to attack insurrectionists who had earlier attacked them?"

He fell silent and said nothing more. I went back to his assistants' office, and Santos finished telling me what had happened the previous night. The government had decided to establish a special court now already functioning right in the prison. Listening to his words, the event he described just did not make that tremendous impression on me it had on the President. "Not this, not this!" he had repeated in anguish. Raising his hands violently to his throat, "I'm sick of the blood; I have had it up to here. We will all drown in it." I pointed out that he had absolutely no responsibility for these outrages—on both sides, the terrible by-product of our fratricidal conflict. I mentioned, too, that insurrectionists perpetrated atrocities even worse in their zone. None of it helped. All those cowardly and insolent crimes had brought him to despair about the justice of our cause.

"What can we do," I wondered aloud to Santos. We had no time to lose. My Kinsman hadn't actually said it, but I feared that discouragement would cause him to resign the presidency. Whom could we call? I could think of no way to relieve his overwhelming distress. All at once the only possible remedy occurred to me. Don Ángel! In spite of strong reservations in the President's estimation of Ossorio, I could think of nobody who could have a better influence on him in this state of deep depression. It didn't take Don Ángel Ossorio a half hour to get to the palace in a car I sent. I hadn't returned to the office except to tell the President my decision. He seemed indifferent, "What did you call him for?" "So that you would hear from him what you will not listen to from me." I was explaining to Don Ángel the President's state of mind and why I had ventured to call him as best qualified among our close friends to help when the office door opened suddenly and my Brother-in-Law appeared. I had no time to finish briefing the newcomer, who also did not know much about what had happened at the prison.

They came out again about half-past one; Don Ángel refused the President's affable invitation to stay and eat with us. Now my Brother-in-Law's face had begun to assume its usual look of a dominant irony tempered by that melancholy which softened his customary critical attitude toward the world around him. At the street door Ossorio gave me his impressions in answer to my questions.

"What did you say to bring that change?"

"What I had to say to him. I have said it to him before, but believe it more now than ever. I said that he had been deceiving us all this time with his mask of cold indifference. Now we see the Ogre unmasked, grieving in his heart because they have killed Melquíades! I said that Melquíades, if he had the chance, would have let your Brother-in-Law die to save himself. He does finally seem calmer now. He even talked of resigning. I said to him what I had to say."

As we parted Don Ángel indicated how moved he felt that I and the Ogre had turned to him before anyone else. And that he had been able to give us some help.

"Ossorio never changes!" the President commented to me. I did not hurry back and sulked a bit when I did join him because he had listened to my arguments only when they came from someone else. He went on talking, paying no attention to my attitude. "Still, I told Don Ángel that he could say what he liked, but he would feel the same way in my shoes."

Negotiations continued through August about the motion picture director's position that had prompted my opportune return from Mexico, but it became clear that they would amount to nothing. Anyhow, I wanted to contribute to the great effort for our republic's defense in a way best suited to my talents, and it occurred to me to help with organization of official propaganda, then just getting started. I spoke about this to Giral and Esplá the President's under secretary. The premier replied only that it seemed a good idea. Then, after a few days and a heated conversation with our friend Barcia, minister of foreign affairs, who I felt did not fully understand the attitude of our career diplomats, his under secretary surprised me with the offer of our Brussels embassy. I turned it down, believing that we needed an ambassador there of some political stature, someone like Ossorio. He also suited the post because his Catholic identification would counteract the tremendous propaganda efforts against the republic along those lines, especially from clergy. When I spoke to the President about it, he agreed about the unsuitability of my nomination to so high a position, but ultimately he did not agree with my wish to remain in Madrid to support him.

It saddened me to find myself once again facing separation from my Brother-in-Law and at so difficult a time. Nevertheless, finding it all decided and that he felt more comfortable having me away from Madrid, I accepted nomination as consul general in Geneva the day after turning down our Brussels embassy. This consulship had no great political importance, but a position close to the permanent secretary of Spain's League of Nations delegation gave me a very favorable listening post to learn about attitudes abroad. It seemed a good arrangement to the President; it seemed preferable to me to one of the foreign assignments my Brother-in-Law afterwards arranged with less justification to enable many persons to avoid more peremptory responsibilities in Spain.

Giral's cabinet fell because of the failure of military operations to impede the advance toward New Castile of insurrectionary troops from Africa that had landed at Algeciras and had been reinforced by Andalusian rebels. After General Miaja's unsuccessful attempt to take Córdoba in the war's first days, circumstances relegated him to secondary objectives until he took charge of Madrid's defense, evermore identified with his name. Now the President urged Saravia, minister of war, to stop the approaching rebels, whatever it cost, at Mérida. As Minister of War himself he had given the same orders to Saravia another August four years earlier in connection with General Sanjurjo's capture. Later failure to destroy a bridge over the Guadiana in spite of those orders seemed to him an irremediable loss of an opportunity for resistance. His indignation peaked when he learned that our forces had evacuated Puerto de San Vicente and the Ávila sierra, invulnerable if we had strengthened our position there in time. Its possession by our enemy assured communication between the northern insurrectionary army and that of the south. Then came the disastrous Battle of Talavera.

Above all else the militiamen's indiscipline, with each region and even each party dedicated to its own particular vision of revolution, made the President give up hope for the unity he had anticipated when he took over. When war broke out he had charged Martínez Barrio with forming a cabinet in hopes that the emergency would pull together all parties that had sworn loyalty to our constitution, from the extreme Right to the extreme Left—as in our republic's first period. By telephone he had broached the subject to Miguel Maura, then summering, I think, in La Granja. Maura considered it too late for any effort toward republican reconciliation; immediately after that he went abroad and had no further dealings with the President for a long time. Our defeats at Talavera and Maqueda came in spite of defenses set up by General Masquelet. According to what my Brother-in-Law told me, Masquelet answered very appositely to persons who blamed him more or less openly for those defeats. "Trenches become useful with soldiers in them; they do not defend themselves." Soldiers fleeing from their defeats at Talavera and Maqueda came hurrying in their trucks to the very gates of Madrid. According to my Kinsman, who had it from the protagonist, Indalecio Prieto himself went out to meet them and turn them back to the front as best he could.

It exasperated the President—I emphasize that—to know that meanwhile Catalans had undertaken a haphazard landing on Majorca, from which the enemy immediately and definitively dislodged them. Similarly the few battalions of Catalonian volunteers who came to the central front in Castile demonstrated lack of combativeness. He believed, too, that the revolt might have broken down early if officers who had joined it casually had felt able to surrender without fear of immediate execution. Many of these men, after all, may not have favored an extended war; they had counted on quick success after the coup. Another problem of command was that a natural popular distrust of officers sometimes expressed itself by soldiers shooting in the back officers whom they suspected as potential renegades.

One afternoon I took advantage of an opportunity to visit Toledo. After my quick trip I gave the President my impressions, and he talked about the situation there to several of us. It seemed to me that firing from the Alcázar had turned its besiegers into the besieged. Even our driver entered the city roundabout so as to avoid gunfire on the highway from those insurrectionists in the fortress, and our troops in the Plaza de Zocodover had adopted a similar defensive attitude. I noted the militiamen's attitude of just waiting out the siege, even joking that insurrectionist troops marching up from Mérida and Talavera would put an end to it—in fact things happened just that way. The President commented, "We can only take the Alcázar by assault, but we don't seem to be doing that. Our men got as far as the very entry to the castle's central patio and then retreated. That's not the way to do it."

At this time they tried to achieve the Alcázar's surrender by sending (then) Colonel Rojo to talk with the besieged, and later they sent a very prestigious and eloquent preacher, Don Santiago Camarasa. The President never expected success from this kind of negotiation. One night I heard him repeat to (now) General Saravia that we needed serious bombardment of that important insurrectionist fortress. He did not think that mining it with dynamite would be necessary; besides, that might also destroy the cathedral.

Instead of strengthening confidence in the republic, Giral's government lost public support. This came largely from the bellicose attitude toward him adopted by intransigent Socialists, determined to give the war a clearly popular, revolutionary character. When I dared to disparage Don José Giral as a statesman, my Brother-in-Law cut me short, saying that he rated this man's service in assuming power on July 19 beyond praise. He described for me the scene in which Giral offered himself as an authentic sacrifice, with the same sincere, self-effacing patriotism as when he became a minister in the second Provisional Government.

In one of our last conversations before my departure for Geneva, I suggested to my Brother-in-Law, again acting as spokesman for the cafés and the talk that filtered into them from the streets, that he should listen to public opinion and make Largo Caballero premier. In answer to his various objections, I argued that this would prove useful, however it turned out. If Largo did prove to be the Spanish Lenin, then he would win the war, and we needed that. If he did not, then he would founder and take down with him the scarecrow of his prestige.

The President responded with irrefutable certainty. "He is not the Spanish Lenin, and he will founder, taking our republic down with him."

41

Guest of the Generalitat

The day before my departure for Geneva, my Brother-in-Law led me into a room next to his office and removed a carefully wrapped package from an Isabelline commode. It contained a manuscript in several notebooks of memoirs covering the period since 1931, and he asked me to take it with me. He had not read me any of his writing for a long time. He laughed delightedly when my sister praised to me the contents of these pages he had kept secret. One day he had come home unexpectedly and caught her reading them, seated at a table in his study.

My wife and I and our three boys left early in September. Our friend Sindulfo's wife accompanied us to Geneva; her husband planned to join her there to go on to her native Poland to clear up some kind of inheritance. At the station and later on the train I ran into José Ortega y Gasset convalescing from a serious illness, so much aged that at first I recognized him only by his brother who had come to see him off. He was headed for Alicante like myself, and also accompanied by a wife and three sons all older than mine. I later learned that at least one grown-up son had received dispensation from his military obligations by special government permission so that he could accompany his father.

At the hotel where we stayed in Alicante I spoke with Sánchez Román and other acquaintances. This fugitive's hopelessness impressed me. I had hardly known him, indeed had not even spoken to him before the republic's proclamation and in its early days. Rather taciturn and not one of my Brother-in-Law's best friends, his attitude during the Constituent Assembly did not encourage me. He had headed a small group on the fringes of the great governing parties, contributing to a division of our republican forces, which so badly needed cohesion. He had used his unquestionable prestige in trying to exercise influence while keeping aloof from the responsibilities of power. His negative impact showed in the respectful attention paid him by such disparate personalities as Indalecio Prieto and Miguel Maura. His relationship with the latter seemed more natural than that with the Socialist leader, and I asked my Brother-in-Law about Sánchez Román's generally recognized influence with Prieto. He explained it as the dazzling effect that self-confident professors exert on uneducated persons. While the man of action despises intellectuals, he still recognizes his own inferior training.

All my reservations about Sánchez Román dissipated, however, when he called me to his office on my return from Barcelona in 1934 after my sister and I had visited her captive husband. He expressed himself so strongly in favor of the persecuted man and supported his cause with such solid republican arguments that from then on Sánchez Román's position became a kind of touchstone by which I judged the policies adopted by other men toward my Kinsman. From then on I esteemed Sánchez Román as one of our republic's indispensable men. Thus his aloofness from the Popular Front in the February 1936 elections had seemed deplorable to me. His discouragement, now causing him to leave Spain, bothered me still more, perhaps because of my own reluctant departure, my desire to stay and support the President. Sánchez Román had, in fact, come to the port of Alicante to emigrate. He inquired with real interest about the President. When I spoke to my Brother-in-Law about him a few days later, he merely reacted with regret at these departing republicans now abandoning him and the republic. Their leaving Spain much strengthened the insurgent army's challenge to the government's legitimate authority: our republic had brought about demagogic, anarchistic revolution it could not control.

In Geneva I replaced an émigré consul and found myself surrounded by subversive diplomats. My petulant, young vice-consul later proved very untrustworthy; my chancellor was very old, very circumspect, and very long established in Switzerland. Soon after my arrival Pablo Azcárate, a high-level official in the League of Nations Secretariat for some time past, became our ambassador to London. López Oliván, his predecessor in London, had resigned when Largo Caballero's cabinet dissolved the professional diplomatic corps. In fact, very soon after my departure from Madrid, the President had found himself obliged to accept the UGT secretary as premier. My prediction had not turned out so preposterous, but subsequent events proved my Kinsman also correct in his predictions and unfortunately so.

A few days afterward, on September 12, I think, the regular session of the League of Nations Assembly began, attended by Álvarez del Vayo, our new minister of foreign affairs and Spain's representative to the Assembly. A distinguished delegation assisted him; besides Azcárate, well-experienced in League procedures, it included Don Ángel Ossorio, Fernando de los Rios, Jiménez Asúa, Carlos Esplá, and Isabel Oyarzábal de Palencia. At that time Premier Largo named Fabra Ribas, formerly our delegate to the International Labor Organization, as Spanish minister in Bern. Because of some irregularity about our delegation's credentials, Vayo needed an entirely trustworthy person to go to Madrid with a letter for the premier and to bring back his response and a souvenir from the Talavera battlefield, the first shell fragment we had reclaimed from a German incendiary bomb. I offered to go, taking this opportunity to communicate my first impressions of Geneva to the President.

I also gave him a fuller account of our journey than short telephone calls had allowed, especially concerning ominous discourtesies we suffered at the hands of our "foreign friends" in Catalonia.

Believing that we would do better traveling by sea from Alicante to Marseilles instead of crossing the provinces of Valencia and Catalonia by land, I had arranged to take a French steamer, purportedly the official mailboat from Algiers. We found ourselves on a filthy little boat, though French, where we had to give up the only decent cabin to Ortega y Gasset because of his poor health. It surprised me to find him on board because he had told me only the day before that he had no plans to leave Alicante's environs. I could see an English cruiser in the port taking on fascist refugees with more or less obviously forged Cuban passports, since they could not leave Spain under their own identities. The incident of Cossío's granddaughter, a very little, frightened girl crying among those refugees in Alicante, surprised the President less than it did me. Her parents had put her on a train at Madrid's South Station. I tried to help by turning her over to the governor, but he, righteously indignant at seeing a passport and safe-conduct in enemy hands, refused to allow the child to leave with an English family who had planned to take her with them.

My Brother-in-Law found it natural that parents should want to spare their children or even themselves the horrors of civil war. He did not, however, like my having to take verbal abuse on my return trip to Spain in spite of my diplomatic status—clearly marked on my passport—or because of it. This trouble came from two FAI members established as adventitious customs officials in Barcelona's railroad station with the knowledge and tolerance of the Generalitat. [The FAI, *Federación Anarquista Ibérica* or Iberian Anarchist Federation, was the political action group of the CNT.] Not only did those irresponsible persons occupy positions they should never have held, but Director of Customs Ventura Gassol felt that he had excused them sufficiently by saying that they came from the "Uncontrollables." It dumbfounded me to see public officials indifferent to serious disrespect for government authority. Largo Caballero never turned a hair when he received Vayo's letter, which I had tried so carefully to protect. Those same anarchists at Barcelona's station had torn open its envelope.

I did not want to fuss too much about discomfort suffered by my wife, myself, and our boys during two days at sea from Alicante to Marseilles, surrounded by unfriendly passengers, crowded into the few cabins, and literally jammed into dining facilities. Predictably, the captain charged an exorbitant price to transport us. We did not enter Barcelona's harbor, but before we sailed on to Port-Vendres a party of nuns, badly disguised in up-to-date clothing, transferred to our ship from a foreign warship also anchored at sea. They crossed themselves in an obvious way whenever they passed us.

Their comments about me brought Sindulfo de la Fuente's wife to tears; for then I personified the revolutionary hydra.

At least I got the President to smile at my description of Ortega, the philosopher, about to depart from Alicante. As we weighed anchor he dramatically gestured toward the coastline—which is, indeed, calcined like the neighboring African coast, "Do you think it possible that a civilization will again arise here?" I didn't answer, but did not see why civilization should not continue there. Afterward and after some questions to indicate his pious interest in the President's health, Ortega began to speak ill of Araquistáin, whom he called a noxious man deserving exile on a desert island. Our conversation drifted to his opinion that Vienna represented the most interesting diplomatic post both now and for the foreseeable future. Thinking he intended me to pass this on, I ventured to ask Ortega's eldest son whether he believed his father would accept the post of Spanish minister to Vienna. The young man authorized me to inquire directly of the elder, and I did it next day. Though Ortega dismissed my suggestion on the basis of his physical infirmity, he never actually refused it. I wrote to Barcia about the matter as soon as we arrived in Marseilles, and neither he nor the President took my proposal amiss. On the other hand, Álvarez del Vayo, Largo's new minister of foreign affairs, did not support the appointment of this famous essayist as our republic's representative in Vienna. I believe that the indifferent attitude of Largo and Álvarez del Vayo explains much of Ortega's disdain toward the republic at war.

I returned to Geneva after two days in Madrid, having quickly fulfilled the assignment of my chief, the minister of foreign affairs. Unexpectedly at Madrid's Barajas Airport I ran into my sisters and Prieto's daughters heading for Alicante to inspect some kind of children's refuge. With my plane about to depart, Prieto, who had come to see them off, realized that I was going back to my official post, and he offered me a ride in another plane that took off moments later for Toulouse. My only fellow passenger told me of his mission to oversee a shipment of gold to France guaranteeing payment for war materiel.

The situation in Madrid deteriorated rapidly as insurrectionist troops advanced on our capital. The President realized that he had to make a decision. He might remain in Madrid with the whole government, a target for the main force of enemy attack. In this case, given the possibility that rebels might take the city, he would have to arrange for some emergency substitute government. Alternatively he might turn Madrid over to persons organizing its defense and move the presidential household and agencies of government to Barcelona. Insurrectionist entry into the imperial city of Toledo meant liberation for the Alcázar's defenders. This diversion, delaying their approach to Madrid, may explain the success of the first resistance there. Afterward the International Brigades took shape in Madrid's trenches against the manifestly German forces that constituted the attack's vanguard and leadership. In an interview General Mola, commander-in-chief of the Army of the North against our republic, gave an apposite response to a correspondent's question about which of the four columns of his army would take our capital, "The Fifth Column will take Madrid." We did not then comprehend the full truth of his assertion.

The meeting of the League of Nations Assembly adjourned without confronting Spain's conflict. Our delegation had settled for breaking with Italy over admission of Abyssinian delegates to the Assembly. I now found myself alone in Geneva. Azcárate had left to take up his post in London; our minister of foreign affairs had returned to Madrid, and his brother-in-law, Araquistáin, took Albornoz's place as ambassador in Paris. The Belgian government finally accepted Don Ángel Ossorio's nomination to our embassy in Brussels. More exactly, I should have preferred loneliness to the company of my young vice-consul, Antonio Espinosa, whom Barcia had erroneously described as very amiable because of his earlier polite and subservient attitude. Espinosa belonged to a generation of republican diplomats selected through competitive examinations administered by the Ministry of Foreign Affairs. The examining board concentrated on a candidate's brilliance in foreign languages, not considering the social background of those chosen to represent our new Spanish state abroad. The regime found itself confronting aristocratic attitudes traditionally represented by the diplomatic profession—a decadent situation made worse by our upper bourgeoisie's pretentiousness. I felt suspicious of this Espinosa from the start and became more suspicious because of his close friendship with a certain secretary in Álvarez del Vayo's retinue. That secretary had gotten his minister's permission to remain in Geneva instead of returning to Spain and had fallen in with a group of fascists from the Italian consulate.

In late October and early November I became very uneasy, having had hardly any communication from my Brother-in-Law and finding the Ministry of Foreign Affairs stingy with official news. Then, returning home one afternoon, I learned that my sisters had telephoned from Marseilles that they would arrive the next morning. My brother [Dr. Manuel de Rivas Cherif], in Marseilles for a few days with a Sanitary Corps commission, had to finish off his assignment in Geneva before returning to Barcelona, and he would accompany them. By the time I went to pick up these travelers, French newspapers had already printed a deceptive story that the wife of the President of the Spanish republic had crossed their frontier. Two days earlier, involved with the children's refuge near Alicante, Indalecio Prieto's daughters had received a message from their father instructing them to take a plane for France. My sisters, alarmed at not having had any news from Madrid except that the President had left the city, decided to accompany Prieto's daughters. They had agreed that my unmarried sister would remain with us and that the President's wife would join him wherever he was. When we got through to him we could report the travelers' safe arrival and my departure with his wife the next morning.

Very early, she and I took off by plane. We caught sight of Mount Blanc's snowy pink summit above the clouds, flew over Grenoble, and landed first in Marseilles as no direct flight existed between Switzerland and Spain. It surprised me to find a *Luftwaffe* plane waiting for us, where I had expected *Air France*. Still, this seemed all right after they explained it as routine, in spite of the anomaly of German civil aviation playing so important a role in our communications while their military aviation fought for the rebels against our republic.

Soon after taking off we landed again. It was a minor breakdown, they assured us, repairable in an hour or two. I tried to telephone Barcelona to save the President worry about our delay. He had already left for the Prat Airport, so I left a message that we would arrive soon. Only after we had taken off a second time did I realize the full extent of our imprudence. We had only a few fellow passengers, among them an obviously German woman, who, we later heard, made that trip frequently without anyone knowing why. The full extent of our danger became clear, however, only after we had arrived at our destination and I saw the violent reaction of Perico Fuentes, an old friend of my wife's family who happened to have charge of the field at that point. He reproached our pilot for disregarding previous orders by coming in for his landing over the harbor in a horizontal flight as if to attack. To avoid repetition of this maneuver, Perico gave orders that antiaircraft guns should fire even at German mail planes if they insisted on this transgression. Our pilot made no more flights to Spain, as the *Luftwaffe* suspended their service from that day.

The Generalitat had provided quarters for my Brother-in-Law in the Palace of the Catalonian Cortes located in Ciudalela Park. Regent María Cristina had stayed there when she came to inaugurate the 1888 Barcelona Exposition. At the end of a very large reception room Dalmau Costa, head of the Household of the President of the Generalitat, had built some pleasant and comfortable rooms like a ship's cabin. Here my Kinsman could withdraw from his formal duties and enjoy a sense of seclusion. I rejoiced to see his happiness in our disobedience of his injunction against his wife's sharing the difficulties of his position.

Later he told us all about it. Indalecio Prieto had become alarmed by a report that confirmed some of General Queipo's foul bombast on the radio from Seville and indicated a very real possibility of Moorish troops landing at San Juan near Alicante. Thus he had decided on his daughters' departure for France. At the same time he had communicated to my Kinsman the cabinet's willingness for him to transfer his presidential residence from Madrid, where insurrectionist troops now posed an immediate threat. The President had not yet confirmed this move with Largo Caballero when one morning he found himself part of a celebration in honor and gratitude to the

USSR. He did not much like this, not only because he disliked a festival approach to war but also because of uses enemy propaganda might make of what seemed to him excessive pro-Russian demonstrations. After that he informed Prieto that he intended to leave the capital at once. Other government agencies prepared in their turn to take the same step. My Brother-in-Law thought that he had convinced Largo Caballero to transfer the government to Barcelona, and he went there as he had planned.

Once settled in Barcelona, he got an impression that Companys, president of the Generalitat, regarded him merely as head of a foreign nation, an ally in the common defense against a common enemy. Catalans seemed overly concerned to point out the "differential nature" of their own war, though the insurrectionists had used Catalonian separatism as a pretext for their revolt against our republic. The President had moved to Barcelona, hoping to establish the national government there, in order to counteract this Catalonian attitude. His own unquestionable identification as a Spaniard, of course, came before his commitment to Catalonian autonomy. He stood firmly against any trumped-up interpretation of the Statute of Catalonia through which anyone would take advantage of our national crisis to subvert the fundamental principles of our republic. Because of this, it particularly amazed him when, against his advice, the rest of the government later settled, apparently permanently, in Valencia rather than Barcelona. This also disrupted indispensable daily contact between premier and President.

To demonstrate how little direct dealings the President had with the premier and minister of foreign affairs, he first learned from news media of so serious an event as our break in diplomatic relations with Portugal. There followed, inevitably, a break with the Reich and Italy, though their intervention against Spain's republic remained surreptitious through the monstrous, equivocal position adopted by other nations. Entering the anteroom to the President's audience room, the day after our arrival, I met Gabriel Alomar, formerly our ambassador to Rome and now minister in Cairo. He agreed with what the President kept saying about the necessity of somehow procuring English and French mediation to achieve peace. The very word mediation, however, antagonized some persons who could not yet accept a possibility of defeat or the least compromise, because justice certainly lay entirely on our side.

The conduct toward us of governments with which our republic continued to maintain normal relations seemed atrocious, and the adherence of our constitution to principles of Genevan pacifism made it worse. Under traditions of international law the Spanish republican government ought to have had freedom to purchase arms from other nations; they denied this to us with the excuse of preserving their neutrality. Normally, neutrality pertained to a declared war between two nations; now, through the neologism of "nonintervention," France, England, and others applied it to the internal struggle of our state. Our recent onerous treaty with France obliging us to acquire arms exclusively from her made this iniquity unparalleled, as the President repeated many times. Justification for this policy based on fears in England and France that any other approach would unleash a general European war made no sense to him. These nations would suffer defeat in our defeat, if it occurred; our present danger threatened them as much as it did us.

In our given position, the President believed that we had no choice but to accept the English and French doctrine of nonintervention, however much we maintained our right to assistance they denied us. We might even try to utilize the new order of things; if we could not get our friends' assistance, we might use nonintervention to achieve withdrawal of our foreign enemies. If an armistice achieved this withdrawal, and afterward hostilities broke out again among Spaniards, improbable enough, then the government's triumph seemed sure, once our military rebels were left dependent on their own resources. Unfortunately, public opinion, stirred up by prowar propaganda, rejected any suggestion of a peace settlement not based on our overwhelming victory. The Largo cabinet took any spirit of compromise or talk of concession as a sign of weakness, especially at this moment of government withdrawal from Madrid. To give any indication of yielding now might seem like admitting defeat. Only Prieto supported the President's position; homefront warriors called him a pessimist.

One afternoon, coming back to Barcelona from the President's habitual drive, a sentry detained us as we entered the city, insisting that he did not recognize the principal Occupant of our three cars. That soldier would not listen to arguments of the police or military adjutants who accompanied us; he insisted on examining each of our passports and safe-conducts. The President looked out of his car window and asked that man, with a kind of wryness, "Don't you really recognize me? Haven't you seen me somewhere? Well, then, you do right in following your orders." He could not comprehend how the Generalitat—or Spain's republic—could accept so intolerable a situation, this kind of abuse of common sense under the pretext of strict fulfillment of necessary vigilance.

Another afternoon we drove out further, to Montserrat which I had never seen. Though we found the monastery evacuated with only a lay brother left behind as caretaker, the building's structure had suffered no damage. Indeed, we found its library in perfect order; the Generalitat's agent maintained it far better than the monks had. Leaning on a parapet of the monastery garden looking at the sunset, my Brother-in-Law commented that he would like to withdraw to that retreat. I urged him to do it; nobody would stand in his way. Later, however, we realized the inconvenience of living so far from Barcelona and having to drive in every day on a crowded highway. It would also leave him exposed, especially at night, to dangers that always threaten a head of state, exaggerated by the unfortunate circumstances of our civil conflict.

Nevertheless, the President decided to establish his private residence at

Montserrat, and he moved in with my sister and their small personal staff. He kept his presidential office in Ciudadela Park in Barcelona. His decision turned out to be a mistake in every way. The President's withdrawal fed a rumor that he had become little more than a prisoner of the cabinet—which, in fact, had little dealings with him. Our friends in official positions did not like what seemed a restriction of his power. Don Ángel Ossorio in Brussels told me so in no uncertain terms, no doubt so that I would pass it on to the interested Party. My Brother-in-Law himself soon tired of the solitude, and he could only really enjoy the mountain scenery en route, while commuting to his office. He moved back to Barcelona then, in time to experience its first bombardment by a ship of the insurrectionist fleet, and he remained there into the spring of 1937. I did not see him during those months because my official responsibilities kept me in Geneva, but he telephoned me more frequently now, sometimes almost daily, for an exchange of opinions and to relieve the loneliness that he felt surrounded by so many people.

Soon after my establishment in Geneva an amiable and intelligent Italian, descended from a noble family of Trieste, had introduced himself to me. His best friends called him "Baron" because of his family title, though he never used it. At the beginning of the 1914 War Carlo A. Prato had served in Austria's army, but he had taken his airplane and joined the side of Italy, his true native country. He distinguished himself in that war as an "ace"—a combat pilot. Count Sforza later brought him into the Italian Ministry of Foreign Affairs. With the advent of fascism to power in Italy, Prato took refuge in Switzerland and founded in Geneva the *Journal des Nations*. This became the League's true voice, since national delegations contributed to it with their subscriptions and official subventions, not only for propaganda purposes but because it contained excellent reporting of matters interesting to diplomats.

Knowing that Álvarez del Vayo would like to recognize the *Journal des Nations* for its support of Spain's republic even before our civil war broke out, I proposed to him that we make a onetime subvention of ten thousand Swiss francs. About a month later a profascist scandal sheet published a photograph of the receipt for this gift signed by Prato, stolen from my desk drawer. I soon realized that my vice-consul had taken it because he kept harping on this minor newspaper scandal and attributing the theft to our consulate's faithful typist. When I told Álvarez del Vayo about it, he insisted on Espinosa's immediate return to Valencia. That alerted the culprit, and he absconded without making any more trouble, but he carried away plenty of ammunition in his baggage. He left with the knowledge and assistance of Swiss police and went directly to Salamanca and then to Biarritz to work in espionage as assistant to his former boss, my predecessor in Geneva.

Soon after that, it occurred to me to look through the memoirs the President had turned over to me in Madrid. I noticed that page numbers at the end of one notebook did not correspond with those at the beginning of the next, and also an interruption in chronology. I hastened to telephone my Brother-in-Law about it, using circumlocutions and code words, through which we partially confused the censor whose fanatical vigilance about our conversations we had detected. I hoped that my Kinsman might purposely have kept that missing notebook with him, but found him much annoyed at its loss. He attributed the theft to a maid from calle de Serrano days, when my sister had noticed other less important thefts. My wife and I felt sure that Vice-Consul Epinosa deserved the blame, and it turned out so.

Meanwhile the League of Nations Assembly met in a special session in December and ratified the monstrous nonintervention policy by establishing the London Committee made up of representatives of England, France, Italy, Germany, and the USSR but without a Spanish delegate. Through this committee Europe's eminent democracies barbarously, arbitrarily, and hand in hand with the authoritarian states that were attacking us, condemned Spain's republican government to death. At that point Víctor Hurtado, son of Don Amadeo, a stalwart Catalonian republican, became my vice-consul. Before his nomination, not afterward, Víctor Hurtado eagerly offered the services of his father, then in Paris and, he said, in complete accord with the President's position. Don Amadeo felt that his familiarity with the Paris political scene would enable him better than anyone else to put this policy into effect through unofficial relations between our government and the French republic.

Though sure of the President's refusal, I transmitted the message to him. He expressed gratitude for "the Savoyard's" support. We had earlier agreed to use this name alluding to the dynasty of Savoy, whose only Spanish king was Amadeo I. My Kinsman also very much appreciated the intentions his offer seemed to represent. Still, he wanted something understood once and for all, and more certainly as friends became involved. He would not agree to epistolary discussions or to discussions through third persons—least of all through me—with people to whom the doors of his office in Barcelona stood open. Furthermore he would not get involved in the political activities of people who had shamefully fled from active, open involvement in our politics. Even less would he consider deals with anyone who tried to serve the presidential position from abroad, surreptitiously, behind the backs of Spain's cabinet ministers and their accredited plenipotentiaries and ambassadors. After all, those hoodwinked officials would finally have to confirm any policy decision.

Apart from incorrect procedure, however, the President agreed with Hurtado about our need to establish connections inside the English and French governments, which might help to gain their mediation when the right time came. Now one could not even talk about this without scandalizing legal purists. Accordingly, in Geneva I approached M. Fouques-Duparc, an upper-level bureaucrat in France's Ministry of Commerce, a career diplomat and, apparently, a friend of "the Savoyard." I tried to present the President's viewpoint to him, explaining it to make it clearer, and thought that I had him convinced. When he asked about the USSR's controlling role in Spanish republican foreign policy since the military insurrection, I merely repeated what the President kept saying about the defection of French and English ambassadors, now ignominiously established in Hendaye.

During my stay in Barcelona, my Brother-in-Law had told me that when he first arrived there Ovsëenko, consul of the USSR, had paid him a proto-colary call, perhaps somewhat imprudently. The Russian had seemed unembarrassedly sympathetic. Ovsëenko's identification, accurate or not, with the killing of twelve thousand anarchists early in Russia's revolution gave him a somewhat counterproductive fame among the predominantly anarchist workers of Catalonia's capital. This kept his relationship with the Generalitat mostly formal, and not very efficacious. Also, Ovsëenko, like the President, did not think it useful to make a show of going to noisy rallies with Companys, nor did he have other frank encounters with my Brother-in-Law after that first one. Other than Ovsëenko, only the United States consul felt obliged to call to pay his respects after the President's arrival in Barcelona. My Brother-in-Law had to decline his very premature offer of an American warship should circumstances oblige him to leave the presidency and Spain. No doubt this American believed the most unfortunate developments imminent, but, in fact, his offer never did prove effectual.

In January 1937, while the League of Nations Council was meeting in its regular session in Geneva, the President gave his first wartime speech in Valencia. A photographic record of this event shows him walking in a university cloister toward the hall where he would speak. He appears erect, robust as ever, with a jovial and open expression; his step seems firm. Two things about that speech give it exceptional interest for posterity, both for the short run and the long run.

First, he fully explained Spain's problems in the context of European politics. Our republic's pacifism, declared in our constitution, corroborated international understandings between Spain, England, and France that dated from our monarchy's last period. A disarmed Spain occupied a pivotal geographic position and made an essential contribution to the Mediterranean status quo and equilibrium. Both English hegemony over the route to the Orient and the security of French domination of North Africa depended on it. A rearmed Spain, whatever the outcome of our war, would no longer necessarily identify with English and French policies. For this reason, His Majesty's government had already signed the Gentleman's Agreement with Italy. This safeguarded special British Mediterranean concerns and gave Mussolini virtual freedom to aid the notoriously fascist-minded Spanish reaction. England's government did not believe that this agreement injured her vital interests or the pure, liberal feeling of her people. The President also asserted in that speech the righteousness of our cause in connection with the Franco-Spanish accord on the Protectorate of Morocco. Use of the sultan's troops in the Spanish military insurrection had seriously subverted that treaty.

After that, the President predicted his own fate after the war. "My heart will break, and nobody will ever know how much I have suffered for Spanish freedom"—a certain prophecy by a serenely disconsolate mind.

Difficulties about printing the speech, which seemed malicious to me in my impatience for it to arrive, delayed its distribution in Geneva. Delegates to the League's Council received its French translation only as the session came to an end. When the President telephoned to me to inquire about the effect of his speech, I could only tell him that members of Spain's delegation, especially our minister of foreign affairs and our ambassador to London, had praised it with effusive enthusiasm. It had, however, arrived extremely late to have any impact on the Council, and so it did not have the broader influence I had hoped for through delegates of other nations gathered in Geneva.

"That's all right," the President said, "but you tell Vayo and Azcárate for me that I have not just thought up this speech in my head, on my own. Before giving it, I checked it point by point with our cabinet, and the ministers approved it, applauded it, even wept over it. Also they did not merely applaud me; they will support my conclusions and will follow through on them. This speech provides nothing less than a plan for political action, and the government supports it. Write them a note emphasizing what needs emphasis, the part about the status quo in the Mediterranean and Morocco, and tell them that I have authorized you to make these emphases. Because of my telephone contact with you, I can handle the matter more easily this way. Tell them I think they should meet there or in Paris with Araquistáin, Ossorio, Pascua, and Jiménez Asúa, (our ambassadors to Paris, Brussels, Moscow, and Prague respectively). They should work out an agreement about the policy indicated in my speech."

I interjected that they might not find apposite the actions he recommended. I knew that Vayo and Azcárate felt distrustful because of the President's reserve about our minister of foreign affairs's reports of his resounding triumphs in Geneva. My own comments had played them down, contradicting the official propaganda Vayo sent out. My Brother insisted, with Jovian anger, "Then I will put on a false beard and come to Geneva myself to tell them what to do."

Things turned out exactly as I anticipated. I carefully wrote out the note and sent copies to Vayo and Azcárate, but neither of them so much as asked me for a fuller explanation of what the President had said on the telephone. Needless to say, they did not meet in Paris or any other place, nor did they establish clear norms for an international initiative that the President, with cabinet backing, had sketched for them. This confirmed, then, my impression of their annoyance at my official intervention; but only some months later in Valencia did I learn of further developments from my futile effort.

A little before that Azcárate had gone to Barcelona and on to the Madrid front. During his obligatory courtesy visit, the President pointed out to him that he had used me as a messenger in connection with a proposal that went beyond a private communication, not because of our relationship but because, in effect, as consul I served as a permanent secretary for Spain's delegation to the League. Azcárate murmured vague excuses, as my Brother-in-Law later told me, but neither he nor Álvarez del Vayo ever altered their pursuit of their own ineffective foreign policy, which ignored the prudent considerations on which the President had based his plan. After his return from Madrid Azcárate gave statements to newspapers emphasizing the admirable fighting spirit of our capital's defenders. This seemed out-of-bounds to the President and especially inappropriate from our ambassador to London, whom he had sent to the front as a man of judgment, a former League functionary personifying the spirit of Geneva.

On my first trip to Paris from Geneva, I think, Don Amadeo Hurtado asked me to meet with Luis de Zulueta our ambassador to the Vatican when the insurrectionary movement against our republic broke out. Zulueta had yielded to enemy pressure and asked official permission to retire, though the republic never did break relations with the Holy See. After retiring he had remained in France without going to Barcelona to pay his respects to the President in a formal way. Our former ambassador in Lisbon, Sánchez Albornoz, had behaved similarly. Luis de Zulueta agreed with "the Savoyard" about the need to create an atmosphere in foreign chancelleries favorable to the pacification of Spain, especially in London and Paris. He did not, however, feel that he could himself do anything about it, officially or unofficially. The President could not accept this kind of equivocation, and he found intolerable the attitude of people like Salvador de Madariaga who pretended to represent a "Third Spain" standing between the contending parties, speaking from the comfortable tribune of "Letters to the Editor" in the London *Times*.

Above all, the President felt that these émigrés had no moral excuse for their withdrawal from the scene of war. In spite of popular excesses and criminal follies by persons on our side who adventitiously usurped authority, justice lay entirely with us, though others denied justice to us. He found it monstrously insane that a military rising against our republic, with the excuse of saving the nation from the dangers of communism, should have plunged that nation into a tremendous, unparalleled hecatomb. Governing republicans had absolutely no responsibility for that. The Communist party had won only a few seats in the 1936 elections, and those few had depended on their collaboration with other parties making up the Popular Front. Certainly that did not represent a threat of revolutionary subversion justifying so horrible a war. All blame fell on the insurrectionists, and the President could never consent that anyone should not accept that, still less that anyone should hold the two sides equally responsible for wartime atrocities. His serene vindicatory exposition of our cause, the essence of his Valencia speech, distilled much passionate violence that he had expressed earlier in conversations with friends or in the intimacy of our family. He knew himself master of the truth.

In the meantime a serious constitutional crisis had arisen in England. Under the cloak of scandalized disapproval of Edward VIII's morganatic marriage to a divorced North American woman, Mr. Baldwin, prime minister and Conservative party head, obtained the king's abdication. Thus he undercut audacious Nazi influence through the young monarch's wife. Beyond that, the king's personalist flair had threatened to upset the Hanoverian dynasty's liberal tradition of monarchical passivity. When George VI ascended the throne, preparations began for his coronation a few months later, and our ambassador Araquistáin summoned me to Paris. Saying that he had backing from our friend Don Ángel Ossorio in Brussels, he urged that the president attend the London coronation himself instead of sending some delegate. Araquistáin felt that this would afford an opportunity to explore the Spanish question with England's government, perhaps with the king himself.

My Brother-in-Law decided that he ought not to attend; certainly he would not go without a thorough preparatory discussion of the question, or even its prior resolution. A presidential visit could even prove counterproductive, hurting national prestige, if it had no results. The suggested ploy seemed uncertain, with no real reason to expect positive consequences. He knew beforehand, through useful inquiries, that no reigning monarch would attend, nor would the president of France's republic. Always careful about presidential dignity, even more in our republic's present difficult times, he did not want even the possibility of his going to London suggested to the cabinet. In our present circumstances such a trip might seem not so much an appeal for the English king's arbitration as homage to his sovereignty, with our President appearing at court along with heads of British dominions and colonial representatives of their empire. Don Ángel answered with gracious irony when I gave him the negative reply to his unofficial suggestion, "All right, we will send José Ramón to represent him as crown prince." He referred to the President's manifest fondness for my eldest son.

The President and my sisters recalled their last afternoon with Don Ángel in La Quinta's intimacy at the Pardo a very short time before the military insurrection. After their meal they had the youngest of my three children with them; and Don Ángel, though he adopted a child's tone in talking to the boy, felt sympathy for a little lamb that a kind shepherd from those fields had given him to play with. Carlitos played so hard that the animal, visibly weakened, could hardly keep on its feet after much running, pulled by a rope. Indeed, the following day my Brother-in-Law restored the lamb to life by returning it to the fields. That afternoon Don Ángel's gracious lamentations for the lamb alternated with thoughts of his own frustrated presidential ambitions. As old friends, they could relax with each other, though political differences prevented perfect mutual understanding. They respected each other enough for some familiarity, tempered, according to each man's special genius, by irony even toward his own feelings.

"Just look," Don Ángel ruminated, "at how old I have become," and he gave his age. "I have spent *so many* years practicing the law," and again he gave the figure. "I have served as deputy *so many* times, governor when I was *such and such* an age," and he cited his service as governor of Barcelona in his youth in 1909, "minister, and in the end I have become nothing."

"While I," my Kinsman answered him with some wryness, "have never been anything, and now at fifty-five I have become President of the republic."

In January 1937 Ambassador Ossorio arranged that I give a lecture on the Spanish theater in Brussels for propaganda purposes. On that occasion he mused sadly about how useful to the republic his own presidency might have proved in place of my Kinsman's. The latter would unquestionably have served as his premier, and in that position he would always have had the presidential support he lacked under Don Niceto. When I passed on to the President this entirely amiable lamentation of his friend and lawyer, he could not help recalling Don Ángel's earlier article in *Luz* warning of his dangerous authoritarianism.

Our Guadalajara victory over the Italians might have opened the way for presidential efforts to achieve a negotiated settlement of our conflict. The premier and Council of Ministers had never openly rejected that approach; indeed, Largo Caballero and Vayo had never given any reason not to try for a settlement except our need to do it with honor, after we had inflicted some clear defeat on the rebels. All the ministers, including Prieto, had yielded to that argument. Our defeat of the Italians might even conceivably have brought the two contending bands of Spaniards together, given the very small military prestige that nation, now under Mussolini, has always had among us. The President soon realized, however, that this victory actually impeded his plans. All of Europe, and especially friendly English newspapers, reacted with such a clamor of sarcasm that Guadalajara became a kind of updated counterpart of Caporetto, Italy's military disaster twenty years before in her war against Austria. This reaction made it impossible for the Duce to accept any suggestion of withdrawal from Spain through compromise. Guadalajara became our ruin because it created an indispensable need for Fascist Italy to regain preponderance by sending more troops to aid Spanish insurrectionists. The rebel cause now became linked with the name of Francisco Franco, heir to Sanjurjo's caudillist mantle after many serious disputes among insurgent leaders. Anyhow, after that victory it would have been useless to try to talk the Spanish people into settling their just cause by other means than force of arms.

The empty promise of our ephemeral triumph at Guadalajara did not, in

any case, deceive the President. He knew that French and English unwillingness to take one more step in our favor implied the impunity of Germany
and Italy—to our disadvantage. The principal argument of his Valencia
speech had not convinced these democratic nations. He had explained the
aid of Axis nations—Germany and Italy now called their alliance that—to
the rising against Spain's republic as preparation for Europe's next general
war. The President had insisted at Valencia that Hitler and Mussolini—
whom he never actually named—did not care much about the political nature of any regime in Spain. They cared about the peninsula's strategic
position and not about establishing a government sympathetic to principles
of National Socialism and fascism. He had quite sufficient recent information to know that, if Spain's republic had shown itself sympathetic toward
Germany and Italy in the advent of the new European war already shaping
up, these nations would not have supported the antirepublican whims of the
military, Spanish priests, and that suicidal segment of our bourgeoisie which
followed them.

At the time of our triumph over the Italians at Guadalajara my wife gave
birth to our fourth child, a girl. Once again my Brother-in-Law's happiness
contradicted those who judged him, if not totally lacking in feeling, at least
beyond the snares of family tenderness and affection.

About the beginning of May, I gave another cultural-propaganda speech,
this time in Holland and arranged by our chargé d'affaires in The Hague,
José María Semprún. I returned to Geneva by way of Brussels and Paris.
In Brussels, Don Ángel, always harping on the President's pessimism, said
to me that "for the present and fortunately," he had proved mistaken in his
hopeless predictions of a few months earlier. My Brother-in-Law commented about this, "Tell him that I was mistaken only about dates." In Paris,
on the other hand, Araquistáin seemed to have come around to accepting
the President's viewpoint. Of course, suggestions coming from the French
may have impressed him more; now they had become convinced of the need
to settle the Spanish civil war. Indeed, this had become part of their own
policy, looking toward possible rapprochement with Germany and Italy. Not
much time remained to effect a compromise settlement.

I also learned in Paris, and to my surprise, that Álvarez del Vayo, staying
at the embassy with his brother-in-law, Araquistáin, proposed to appoint me
as ambassador to Copenhagen. He intended this promotion in diplomatic
rank to justify my withdrawal from Geneva. I asked him very insistently not
to move me. It seemed detrimental, first because of the greater distance
from Spain, but principally because my separation from the League of Nations would deprive the President of information I could give him privately
that often considerably differed from our minister's official propaganda.

Even at the Quai d'Orsay Station, where I accompanied the ambassador
to see Vayo off for Spain, he said to me from the coach window, with his
train about to pull out, that he would sign my transfer as soon as he got

back to the Ministry. I replied in his own bantering tone, "Oho! When you get back. So you trust me that long!" I could not suspect how few hours the minister would have after he got back to Spain. Hearing of his resignation soon afterward, though, I recognized my own small part in the early stages of the President's design to use a government crisis to try to change Largo Caballero's bad war policy and the perniciously ineffectual diplomacy of Vayo, his minister of foreign affairs.

News came before I left Paris of the anarchist rising in Barcelona—some have claimed that the fascist Right participated actively in it or even planned it. It seriously endangered our cause and the President's own safety in the Ciudadela Palace. After a month and a half I learned this event's consequences and of the President's hazardous journey to Valencia to establish himself there with the rest of our government. Before that Don Julián Besteiro had passed through Paris twice in connection with his attendance at George VI's coronation at the President's behest. Up to then aloof in Madrid from any contact with Largo Caballero and not much esteemed by Prieto, he returned again to Madrid after giving an account of his journey and mission. He withdrew into his relative isolation among city government counselors, not wishing to participate actively in politics and not being called to it by his Socialist colleagues.

42

The La Pobleta Notebook and *Vigil in Benicarló*

Soon after Negrín took over as premier, I requested and received a few days' leave to go to Valencia, where the President had moved right after the May crisis in Barcelona even before full pacification of Catalonia's capital. I found my Brother-in-Law quite satisfied with the political change and so hopeful about the new premier's disposition toward him that he began our first conversation about this old Regina *contertuliano* with, "Maybe we have found our man!" The new premier had shown such solicitude, he said, that some days he appeared at the presidential residence almost at dawn to consult about some minor problem. He had even suggested casually that the President should make his inaugural address to the Cortes, as he himself was no orator. Of course, my Kinsman made no transgression, even in jest, on the norms of our republican parliamentary regime, on whose regular functioning the health of our state depended.

More from friendship than because of protocol, I went to visit Negrín and Prieto who continued as minister of defense. Like the President, each of them asked me about the effect our change of government had in Geneva. To each in turn I answered, "It has had a very good effect. From official press releases people believe we have a Prieto cabinet presided over by Negrín." Prieto hastened to correct me, stretched out on a divan in his house, his bleary eyes crinkling, looking at me guardedly, "They will soon realize that is not true." The President, my Brother-in-Law, did not believe it either. Negrín, chief protagonist of that casual international speculation, limited himself to a smile.

I explained briefly to Negrín and later repeated it at home that people regarded the change as a positive one for short-range international politics. They believed that Prieto had triumphed in his manifest struggle with Largo Caballero, a struggle kept within the cabinet, so far, and not visibly upsetting governmental cohesion. Prieto and Negrín would support continuation of the war; indeed, they intended to subordinate to its immediate requirements all the vague, wasteful, and disruptive revolutionary schemes. On the other hand, they seemed ready to abandon unreasonable hopes about the war's outcome in favor of a compromise settlement with our enemy. Our friend

Don Ángel called this a betrayal; he had no confidence in any new Pact of Vergara. He now moved from Brussels to Paris, replacing Araquistáin, whose tenure there ended with the fall of Largo, to whom he had played the role of Ninfa Egeria.

I told Negrín that it pleased me to see my Brother-in-Law happy, that Largo's neglect had depressed him. Negrín replied with a kind of casual deceit. He excused Largo's conduct, assuring me that neither ill will nor discordant policy lay behind his relations with the President. My Kinsman felt that Largo, whose discretion as minister of labor he had admired five years before, had become obsessed with his own omnipotence when he became premier. Premier Largo Caballero had consulted neither President nor ministers in making decisions, excepting only Vayo in matters of foreign policy in the early part of his tenure. Now my Brother-in-Law could only laugh sadly about the air of mastery adopted by "Don Paco the Plasterer" in connection with all things, great or small, about our war. In telling me about it, he mimicked the former premier's accent, stretching his mouth in the characteristic way of Madrid's people, especially of Largo's class. "The General Staff . . . gave it out . . . just to me." Largo Caballero attributed his fall to Communist pressure. According to him it angered Communists that he had refused to listen to the first ambassador of the USSR and had forced his recall because Rosenberg interfered in our war policy.

Negrín spoke quite openly about Largo's inattentiveness to presidential suggestions for direction of our foreign policy, so vital to our nation's destiny. "The President of the republic should not merely be kept informed up to the minute; he should carry out foreign policy because he represents continuity in general policies. He stands as the state's preeminent representative. I made Giral minister of state because of his merits, of course, but also because he and the President think exactly the same." Giral did not take this apparently quite frank comment by the premier as a good sign. "No, look," the new minister responded, "this doesn't sound good to me. It sounds as though he will blame the President for any error I may commit as minister." The President also made a wry face on hearing about Negrín's effusiveness. In any case, my Brother-in-Law did not intend to suspend all judgment about the new premier because of that kind of talk. He would make up his mind about Negrín's actions on the basis of their constancy of purpose.

People in Paris and Geneva had not realized the significance of the Barcelona rising. My Brother-in-Law told me about it with complete objectivity, basing his irrefutable commentary on solid evidence. He neither traced the insurrection back to its earliest origins nor speculated about its political impact. He simply gave me details of his own experiences, besieged in the Ciudadela Palace.

As President of the republic, more aware, better informed than others, he saw the uprising as the culmination of a total breakdown of public order, and he suffered from this more than anyone else. He had seen syndicalist ministers refusing to be called anything but "advisers." They cared more about holding strictly to anarchist principles than about a necessary spirit of cooperation that their entry into the cabinet ought to have signified—unless they regarded ministerial office mainly as an opportunity to undermine public authority. He told me, not protesting but just for my information, that Largo as premier had not even bothered to introduce these new ministers to him, nor had they had enough courtesy to pay the customary calls on him as President. Among the anarchists, only Federica—people usually called Montsény by her first name—had attended the President's Valencia speech with other members of the government.

I told him that Federica Montsény had made a very good impression on me in Geneva and also on members of the Health Section of the League to whom, speaking as our minister of health, she had made a brilliant report. He, in turn, recalled youthful Ateneo days when Federica's parents used to get up in academic discussions and read each other's papers. After reading her husband's pages, the wife would say, "Federico Urales has spoken," and in the same way, after reading her pages, he would say, "Soledad Gustavo has spoken." We went on to speculate about what innocent enthusiasm had made that ingenuous anarchist of the *Revista Blanca* change his surname from Montsény to that of the mountain chain between European and Asiatic Russia. Perhaps he thought of the Urals as summits toward which his ideals reached. In that same era, among those same Ateneo benches, Azorín would struggle to his feet, assisted by his red umbrella, and would shout out, "I am an anarchist!"

Coming back to the present, it seemed bad enough that anarchists should show such strong opposition against constituted authority when their subversive activities had provided a principal excuse for the "Nationalists" to revolt against our republic. It bothered the President even more, though, that these same anarchist factions, though "confederated" in an organization that appeared very powerful, weakened their own organization by adhering within it to characteristic extreme individualism. Of course, their representatives brought this same clearly antisocial, self-destructive attitude to cabinet meetings. He pointed out to me the small authority these ministers had asserted over CNT brethren in calling for fellow party members, the Civil Guard, and other republican armed forces to lay down their arms—which they were using against each other in the Barcelona rising. "They treated it as something no more serious than a strike, and they never went beyond appealing for individual, voluntary action." Altogether, he strongly opposed participation in government by persons who hold as an unchallengeable principle their opposition to any spirit of government.

Soon after the President's arrival, his niece's husband, an agricultural engineer, suffered a terrible death in Valencia's first air raid. I hardly knew this niece and her sisters, as they did not come to Madrid during the years of my early acquaintance with their uncle. Her marriage three years before had brought that unpleasant incident at Zaragoza's Church of the Virgin of the Pillar. I had met her and her husband, Antonio Martínez Díaz, when Margarita Xirgu's company performed in Valencia a few months before we left for America.

I had spoken at that time to my Brother-in-Law of their friendliness toward me and the satisfaction he might take as great-uncle in the extraordinary resemblance to him of their first offspring. He had replied with that customary affectionate disdain which hid so much tenderness and protected him from the snares of family affection, "Well, I assure you, that boy means nothing special to me." He didn't want him to mean anything special. He tried to detach himself from the call of blood, that instinctive tribute to race which so insistently claimed him, first in his long-term bachelorhood and then in his childless marriage. Besides, little Manolito, just a few months old, really did show a surprising family resemblance to his mother's uncle. The President did not fool me with his effort to hide the impression made on him then and two years later by that child's physical resemblance and precocious intelligence. Furthermore, the boy's serious deportment seemed to justify the honor of bearing his uncle's name.

This child's father, a good and very discreet man, suffered from tuberculosis and had gone for a cure to an asylum at Torrelodones near Madrid shortly before the war's outbreak. He had to leave when they evacuated the asylum for military reasons, and he returned to Valencia and his work in official service despite his delicate health. The President did not like to seek favors, especially for family members, but he did ask a prominent Left Republican to give his nephew an assignment in Mexico. This man, also an agricultural engineer, did not grant the request, though he had given many less justified overseas assignments to his more aggressive protégés to save them from war's terrible havoc. Soon after the President arrived in Valencia, as I said, an airplane bomb happened to hit a bus in which his niece and her husband were passengers and caused his death.

In Valencia the President lived at first in the Captaincy General, where he and I had already stayed on the occasion of Alcalá Zamora's return from a presidential visit to Majorca. Back then General Riquelme served as the city's military commander. The decoration and furnishings of that large house, redolent of Regency stodginess, had amused us. By the time I came to visit him he had already moved from that uncomfortable mansion into "La Pobleta," a confiscated estate near Porta-Coeli a few kilometers from the capital. The government had provided him with a comfortable residence. Furthermore, its decoration and furnishings pleased him as they mostly avoided the Valencian style's levantine excesses and fake peasantry.

Set back from the highway by a good stretch of road, La Pobleta stood on the outskirts of a wooded mountain, backed up by still higher mountains, and it had a delightful walled-in garden. Considerable alteration had modified this building to suit the needs of the President and his retinue, and finally it very well suited the Master of the house. The temporary residents spent most of their days in a main-floor, glassed-in gallery that overlooked the garden. I thought it the house's best feature. In the living room connecting with that gallery hung a recent portrait of my sister by López Mezquita who had painted a matching portrait of the President shortly before he left Madrid. I had taken that excellent painting to our Geneva consulate and thus spared it the vicissitudes of moving around that its Model endured.

At that point my brother, the doctor, also lived in La Pobleta with his wife who had just delivered their first child. Besides them, the President's recently widowed niece had spent a short time there before my arrival. My Brother-in-Law seemed delighted by the charm and natural grace of Manolito, his great-nephew. After I saw the boy as a newborn two years earlier, the President had assured me that he had no special interest in him. Now the child had captivated him, and it sorrowed him to tell how Manolito ran to him for protection whenever he heard an airplane. They did not even try to hide the cause of his father's death from so clever a child. After their stay at La Pobleta, the boy and his mother, about to give birth a second time, had gone to live with her sisters in a little French village near Perpignan where the President's sister and her husband—his chronic illness worse— had now settled.

Nobody mentioned Gregorio to my Brother-in-Law, respecting the silence in which he nursed vain hopes that his nephew might have survived. Then, inopportunely and inadvertently, Leopoldo Menéndez, still a colonel, had expressed condolences, believing that the President must already know of the young man's death in Córdoba. My sister told me how, now accepting a loss he had feared in silent torment, her Husband spent an entire night sitting up in an armchair in his bedroom. He gave way to tears for the sad affliction, his family name ended in so terrible, so unjust a manner with the death of his brother's only son. "How unlucky I am! What a misfortune!" That eloquent man could finally express his sorrow only in those common words from the reservoir of universal human feeling.

I mentioned again Ossorio's comment that fortunately the President's pessimistic forecast had proved wrong, his hopelessness in contrast to popular optimism. My Brother-in-Law repeated what he had said on the telephone when I called to tell him about my trip to Holland and my conversation in Brussels with Don Ángel. "I was mistaken only about dates."

"Still," I ventured to suggest, "a mistake about dates means quite a lot in a war like ours. In these circumstances, gaining time could prove important."

"True," he replied, "if we really have gained time. But so far we haven't used our reprieve for anything, while they—the insurgents—keep correcting their mistakes. See how they have given up trying to take Madrid by assault. When they could have taken it, and in fact had already entered the city, they hesitated from fear of resistance we could not then have mounted against them. We only organized that afterward. Now they don't need to take Madrid. All things will happen in due course." He went on talking to me with gloomy foresight about the coming stages of the war, and he very nearly predicted the actual dates of our defeat.

With all of the President's pessimism, however, he did not entirely accept defeat as inevitable. Without pretending to assume a commanding general's crushing responsibility, he did speak in the cabinet and especially to the premier and minister of defense about our need to confront the advancing rebels with a vigorous counteroffensive. He believed that we should muster the greatest force we could in an all-out attack, and he favored Estremadura rather than Zaragoza as the place. He saw La Mancha as key to the war; an army there could act at a propitious moment against either Mérida or Seville—the key to victory, and certainly it would provide the best means of breaking communications between insurgent forces in the north and those in the south.

We had not spoken again about the two stolen notebooks of his memoirs when one afternoon he settled down to read to me from their sequel, which he called *The La Pobleta Notebook*. At the same time he showed me clippings from a Seville newspaper including apocryphal excerpts from the stolen volumes. I noted with relief that this publicity about his writings, even as converted into enemy propaganda, did not much bother him. When those news stories had come out, our government, through the Author himself, had denied the existence of memoirs and thus denied the excerpts. This, of course, did not convince persons mentioned in those pages. One of them, Indalecio Prieto, about whom he had made some slighting allusion in one of the stolen diaries, did not seem annoyed. In fact he had seemed not to know about it until one day he came into the President's office and found him writing, smiled, and said with pretended alarm, "Not more memoirs?" My Brother-in-Law laughed in telling me about another friend, a Left Republican, who had said that he did not want even to read those transcribed pages in insurrectionist newspapers. If the President had called him stupid, he did not want to know it. Still, my Kinsman felt some slight regret that Fernando de los Ríos would read certain comments about himself. Ríos had made a slip during a cabinet meeting about some Tiepolo paintings decorating walls in the Madrid palace. He inadvertently took them as chromos chosen by Bourbon bad taste. Ríos, now ambassador in Washington, proved exaggeratedly sensitive and unforgiving about the President's amused comment on his lack of artistic sophistication, as we learned afterwards.

Carlos Esplá, who became Giral's under secretary of foreign affairs in Negrín's first ministry, spoke to me privately and enthusiastically about another work the President had recently read to him. The first time my Brother-in-Law spoke to me of *Vigil in Benicarló* I thought it dealt with a meeting held recently with Largo Caballero and Companys at an inn maintained there by the Institute for Tourism. At the time he had spoken of this interview as a hopeful political event. For just a moment enmity between the premier and the Generalitat's president had seem resolved, though their agreement did not finally amount to much. The title in question, however, had nothing to do with petty politics. In *Vigil in Benicarló* the President undertook a Socratic dialogue in the Platonic mode, using masterful artistic creativity to express concepts of his political thought. Unlike the notebooks, he did not use details from his daily life, his virtual retirement in the midst of war through the more or less open designs of various premiers. Instead, here he expressed his thoughts about the war in a drama. Now he spoke far more directly than he had in *The Crown* through different characters who conversed about our tragic civil controversy. He liked *Vigil in Benicarló* very much, and it compensated for the withdrawal from politics to which his premiers had consciously if not openly relegated him.

When I left Valencia to return to my consulate, Negrín had already begun to think about moving the seat of government to Barcelona. Giral and Amós Salvador, in his capacity as architect and presidential friend, had undertaken to look for a suitable place for the President to live. My Kinsman wanted independence from both Generalitat and the city government of Catalonia's capital, and he judged the Royal Palace of Pedralbes, official location of our republic's presidency, unsuitable as a private residence. The President did not really agree with Negrín's decision that moving to Barcelona represented the best way of dealing with an urgent crisis that might occur any day if insurgents succeeded in their clear intention of pushing to the Mediterranean and cutting communications between Catalonia and Valencia. Coincidentally, though, Negrín's plan did agree with his own earlier opinion at the time when our government left Madrid.

I had not yet left La Pobleta when news came of General Mola's death. Disagreeing with the rest of us, my Brother-in-Law believed that this event would hurt the enemy cause, primarily because he rated Mola much higher as a general than he did Franco. None of us considered the advantages for Franco in the disappearance of the only rival to really challenge him as supreme commander after Sanjurjo's death.

43

Don Quixote on the Island of Barataria

News of M. Herbette's replacement as France's ambassador to Spain filled me with joy. He had proved a traitor to our friendship, even on a personal level. It was bad enough that he deserted his post in Madrid, following the example of his English colleague, which contributed greatly to the demoralization of the diplomatic corps. On top of that, based in Hendaye, he arranged for the Spanish conspirators to have license to operate against our republican government all along that coast. Furthermore, my sister and Brother-in-Law learned from reliable sources that the ambassador and his wife had rented out facilities in the French embassy at a good price to many well-known persons, not only for their own refuge but to protect money and valuables. Herbette's replacement, M. Labonne, was expected in Valencia in July 1937 during my visit, but the government soon moved to Barcelona, and he reported there.

Early in September I went to Moscow heading a delegation invited to attend an annual theater festival held in the capital of the USSR during those years. Our good friend Ceferino Palencia, Spain's chargé d'affaires in Latvia's capital, came out to meet me at the Riga airport, very much excited—and with good cause. The day before, Munters, Latvia's premier and minister of foreign affairs, had called him up for an interview—something unusual. Munters had recently returned from a trip to Germany, where he had close friends in middle ranks of the Reich's bureaucracy. He told our representative confidentially that he had the impression that, if leaders of Spain's republican government would agree to sit down in conference with representatives of Germany's government, we might possibly obtain withdrawal of all military aid to Franco. We could easily and quickly check this out at the coming annual meeting of the League of Nations Assembly, as Munters was scheduled to preside.

Our ambassador in Moscow, Marcelino Pascua, to whom I spoke about this upon arriving and again before leaving a few days later, considered it inopportune to indicate to Munters that we even knew of his consultation with our chargé d'affaires. When I got back to Geneva our delegation to the Assembly, brilliantly led by Negrín, with Giral, Vayo, Azcárate, Jiménez Asúa, and Carlos Esplá as under secretary of foreign affairs, agreed with

Pascua, also a member of that delegation. To my great surprise, even my Brother-in-Law did not seem to attach much importance to this lost opportunity to try again the road of negotiation with those directly responsible for the success of the Spanish insurrection against our republic. Maybe it came from his concern not to see me compromised even a little. On other occasions, he had not wanted to see me venturesome, not even indirectly.

According to Vayo, Litvinov, Soviet delegate in Geneva and people's commissar for foreign affairs, regarded Munters as a crafty Germanophile, servitor of the Nazis. Later, in a Spanish prison, I learned from newspapers that, after Soviet troops entered Riga in the 1939 war, Munters had gone to Moscow, specially chosen by Molotov as an expert on Latvia, then reincorporated into the USSR.

That December we took Teruel. This triumph of General Saravia and Colonel Leopoldo Menéndez, whom he so much esteemed, greatly pleased the President. Insurrectionists soon retook the city, ending for us any possibility of an offensive toward Zaragoza, the only significant action that might have compensated my Brother-in-Law for our lost opportunity to reconquer Seville. I did not then know how closely his opinion about our strategy coincided with that of General Rojo, chief of staff of the central zone. My Kinsman had gone to Madrid early in November to celebrate the anniversary of its heroic defense by militia troops heading that city's indomitable population.

President and government moved to Barcelona in February 1938. They had found him decent accommodations in another private house, confiscated by Tarrasa's city government, ten kilometers from the capital, set on a mountainside and overlooking the highway. On the other hand, it did not seem very safe. An enemy airplane wanting to attack the presidential residence would have no trouble finding it.

My wife and I went there to see him in March. We got a great sense of security just from the change we found in the functioning of frontier customs and the attention shown us by police chiefs. Now they obviously had charge of their jurisdiction, controlled before the May 1937 insurrection by the Civil Guard and even to a considerable degree by regular military personnel. The people called these new police "the Hundred Thousand Sons of Negrín." They rightly gave our premier credit for restoration of discipline in the armed forces and for establishing government control over the military, formerly dispersed anarchistically among the two great syndicalist organizations and other political parties.

The estate where the President now lived had the name "La Barata," a Spanish version of the Italian surname of a friend of a former owner. Two or three old buildings, low in the style of Catalonian farmhouses, stood down near the highway. The main house, built by the last, unfortunate owner, stood higher up and had a more distinguished appearance, like a good private house on Madrid's Castellana. The President had lived there for some time before he learned that this former owner, a well-known Tarrasa manufacturer, had been murdered. That considerably upset the comfortable, restful spirit of the presidential household. Unable to find better accommodation for my Brother-in-Law, and knowing his extreme sensitivity about that kind of violence, his scouts had carefully kept this information from him, and he complained about it. Some weeks he drove in to the Pedralbes Palace every day, but he always went in at least three times a week for appointments and to preside at cabinet meetings. In La Barata there lived as part of the presidential household: Cándido Bolívar, the President's executive secretary; Santos Martínez, the President's private secretary; and Sindulfo de la Fuente, in charge of the finances of the Presidential Household. Renso, Sindulfo's predecessor under Don Niceto, had gone over to the enemy, taking advantage of personal leave to visit his family in southern France.

My Brother-in-Law continued to lead a retired life. Not an early riser, he read and wrote a lot; sometimes he took a walk, though not with the frequency of earlier years. Without fail he appeared at the weekly concerts of the Pérez Casas Orchestra at the Liceo. He did not like the radio and spent more time listening to a phonograph his aides had given him on his saint's day with a good supply of classical records. He enjoyed Beethoven's symphonies more than anything else.

We talked of Father Isidoro, his former teacher at the Escorial, whose strange adventures the President had told me about in Valencia and who had written to me from Bayonne since then. One fine day my Kinsman had received a letter signed simply Isidoro Martín, asking to see him. Not sure who it was, though he did not remember anyone else with that name but the friar, he arranged an appointment and, in fact, found himself face to face with his former teacher looking very old and shabby in secular clothes. Father Isidoro said that a letter from the President had saved his life. He had kept in his wallet an acknowledgment of congratulations he had sent five years before at the time of my Brother-in-Law's appointment as Minister of War. Other monks from the Escorial, held with him in a makeshift prison cell in Saint Anthony's Church in Madrid, had perished at the hands of armed bands who had more or less surreptitiously replaced the police or had taken over their functions.

The President had asked him about his García Benítez cousins, soldiers taken in a state of revolt; he had not heard their fate after he had saved them from immediate execution. Nothing the priest could say appeased the vehement protest of his former Pupil, now Chief of State, against a destiny that had undoubtedly overtaken those unfortunate young men. Father Isidoro said that they had seemed crazy and had continued to defy fate by ranting terribly, including denunciation of their cousin, the President. Certainly the friar's exculpation did not reconcile my Brother-in-Law to such arbitrary justice. That kind of action grieved him the more because he had never yielded to thoughts of vengeance in his own great sorrow over the more atrocious death of his brother's only son in Córdoba in the war's first days. The friar, unexpectedly freed through the endorsement of that old letter, had hidden himself in Madrid for a while using a CNT membership card, and then he had come to Valencia. He asked only to leave Spain. The President helped him without hesitation, gave him some money, and dispensed him from any promise to remain in France and not to return to the zone of our country occupied by rebels.

I had written to Father Isidoro from Geneva to see whether he could help us in some way. It soon became clear that he felt much more hopeless than I did about the possibilities of rapprochement between warring Spaniards. Nevertheless, I made some fruitless efforts to achieve prisoner exchanges through him. Somewhat later, I intervened for him to help another of his old pupils, the writer Sánchez Mazas, a prisoner in Barcelona for his very prominent part in the anarchist-fascist revolt of the previous year. It also occurred to me to investigate whether through Father Ignacio's influence we might get back those two notebooks of my Brother-in-Law's memoirs that my former vice-consul had stolen. This shocked the President when he found out about it, probably through Giral, whom I necessarily had to tell my plan. He would never have considered allowing an exchange of prisoners for his diaries.

The day when my wife and I left Catalonia on our return to Geneva, we heard news at the frontier that gladdened us. Ships from our navy had sunk the *Baleares* in the Mediterranean.

Our next ministerial crisis occurred some months later, and it did not surprise me when Indalecio Prieto left the cabinet. Prieto himself had prophesied it when he assured me, fully understanding the situation, that those persons erred who believed that a Negrín premiership meant affirmation of a Prietist tendency in the cabinet. As on many other occasions, I learned months later details of the very difficult position in which the President found himself, caught between conflicting political interests. Summarizing his account in a few words, he told me that the politicians involved had not so unconditionally supported Negrín as the press reported. My Kinsman believed that censorship had become stricter than wartime needs required, to serve the various parties into which the Popular Front had now clearly split.

"One after another they came to me, from president of the Cortes to the least of our Left Republicans, among them your friend Federica. Of course Companys came, and he demanded simply, 'When will you get rid of this Don Juan for us?'" Grinning, my Brother-in-Law mimicked the strong Catalan accent of the Generalitat's president. "Each of them had his own complaint, that Negrín had become a dictator, that he had sold out to the Communists, deterioration of the war situation, our people's unhappiness. . . . Ah! but one day I called together all those grumblers so that they could assume responsibility for themselves. It took no more than Negrín's getting up to speak, and everyone shut up, including Prieto's personal friends and those politically indebted to him. They all deserted him. Prieto himself accepted defeat without protest. Again he has left me in the lurch as he did two years ago when I offered him the premiership and he refused it. My own position today has not become impossible because I have remained careful and have never gone further than I ought."

When I said to him that, in any case, Negrín seemed to me as supportive of him as when he assumed control months earlier, the President answered, "I don't know. I don't know."

I almost washed my hands of everything two months after my trip to La Barata. One fine day—which turned out that way after seeming ill-starred—a telegram came for me from the premier, acting for the minister of foreign affairs, now again Álvarez del Vayo. It ordered me to give up my position as consul in Geneva immediately and to report to Barcelona. Álvarez del Vayo himself repeated this message to me; he had come to Geneva those first days of May to attend the regular session of the League of Nations Council. I called my Brother-in-Law to explain to him what had happened. Three or four days earlier a North American correspondent of the United Press had come to ask about an item published that morning in a second-rate or third-rate London newspaper. According to it, I had made official overtures to the representative in Geneva of a Spanish-American republic with a view to pursuing a negotiated peace for Spain's civil war. I absolutely denied the rumor, though it may have had some basis in my conversation with the secretary of Argentina's delegation. Like all other conversations with other representatives in those days, I had transmitted its content to the ministry in accordance with my instructions from the cabinet.

Termination of my consulship, based on abuse of my close relationship with the President to negotiate for peace, completely surprised me, and, if possible, it surprised my Brother-in-Law still more. He particularly wondered at its occurring without anyone having the minimal courtesy to mention it to him, but he restrained his indignation so as to temper mine. He advised me to do nothing until he had talked with Negrín, whom he expected back that day from an excursion to the front. He told me later about the uproar he made in talking to the premier, and my sister and the rest of that household confirmed it. Negrín passed it all off as a matter of small importance, saying that Azcárate and Vayo had requested my dismissal because of some supposed indiscretion.

I felt inclined to resign forthwith, but not to go back to Barcelona. My age exempted me from military service; besides, twenty-four years earlier the army had rated me militarily useless because of near-sightedness. I had no obligation to return to Spain. I did feel an obligation to speak out publicly about what had happened, emphasizing the glaring discrepancies between President and premier in regard to matters as basic as direction of the war and judgments about possibilities of a necessary peace. I found it intolerable that a North American journalist with a fat salary from our propaganda department had published a news item I had recently seen featured in a French periodical. Fischer wrote there of connivance between the President and Prieto in a defeatist spirit; only the Communists, faithful to Negrín's policy, could successfully confront them.

"You are the only one," my Brother-in-Law said to me in a decisive telephone call, "who cannot speak out. The day will come when you can, and then I will ask you to do it. But if you say now what you want, you will oblige me to present my resignation. Just like that." When I answered that this seemed a good occasion to protect him from blame for the bad ending that our war might well have, he insisted absolutely. "No. You must hold off until men are no longer dying on battlefields and getting shot by firing squads crying out not merely 'Long live the republic!' but also 'Long live Azaña!'"

Negrín had told my Brother-in-Law that my departure from Geneva merely meant appointment to another position. I made it a condition of my return to Spain that the promised nomination must in itself make amends for the charge of abuse of presidential confidence. "Good," the President said. "Wait and do nothing until I tell you. *Be careful. These people are dangerous.*" The next day another message communicated to me my nomination as Introducer of Ambassadors, head of the Diplomatic Household of the Presidency of the Republic. Our old friend Amós Salvador had held this post. He vacated it to accommodate me and the President.

My Brother-in-Law feared that I might say something impertinent to the premier, and he tried to avoid my seeing him in those first days after my return to Barcelona, the period of my personal installation at La Barata and my official installation in the Pedralbes Palace. When I ran into Negrín by accident, however, he came up, apparently pleased to see me, and chattered away with the old camaraderie as though nothing had happened. Vayo told me that he thought we had resolved the matter very well, and he advised me to restrict myself to protocolary affairs in the future and have no official dealings with foreign representatives apart from my duties. Anyhow, only the Mexican and French ambassadors remained in Barcelona, and the temporary absence of the latter further limited my opportunities. The President made an effort to keep me always with him, strictly attending to the nonexistent duties of my new position. At first he did not want my wife and children to come to Tarrasa; on the contrary, he had urged that they should move into "La Prasle," a country house in the village of Collonges-sous-Salève, six kilometers from Geneva. We had leased this property, foreseeing that he might need it before long; our own need for a summer retreat gave some cover for the arrangement.

In the absence of M. Labonne, the French ambassador, I called on M. Fouques-Duparc, my acquaintance of two years before in Geneva. Undoubtedly, his familiarity with the Spanish question, gained through me, explained his assignment as counselor of France's embassy in Barcelona, and I looked forward to seeing him again. It soon became clear, however, that things would not go as anticipated. My adventitious friend did not seem very friendly, or maybe he had orders not to risk compromising himself. He did not even feel that he could follow through on a dinner invitation I had extended to him in my house in Geneva.

One afternoon the President took me with him to Vich where the distinguished archeologist Bosch Gimpera, counselor of the Generalitat, had arranged a meeting with Mr. Leche, English chargé d'affaires. We had heard from reliable sources that Leche supported us. At this time England's government had sent Mr. Runciman to Czechoslovakia to resolve through arbitration the Sudeten question that threatened to upset European peace because of German pressure. The Beneš government yielded to the British government's forceful threats and made concessions that obviously damaged its national interests.

I felt sure that a general European conflict would not break out. Nevertheless, my Brother-in-Law now wanted my wife and children, whom I had just left in Collonges after a brief vacation there, to join us at La Barata as soon as possible. He wanted to protect them from the terrible possibility of war in France, which had just declared mobilization. Vayo wrote back from the Assembly meeting in Geneva, which he attended with Negrín, assuring Giral of the imminent outbreak of a European war. (Giral, now minister without portfolio, acted as minister of foreign affairs in his colleague's absence.) Though we hoped that a European war would have a decisive and favorable influence on our conflict, on the basis of what I had just read and heard in Geneva and France, it seemed unlikely that a Russian army would at that point cross Rumania to aid the Czechs. Yet Vayo reported this as probable; he spent more time on his duties as correspondent for *La Nación* of Buenos Aires than on his ministry. He was wrong, and things turned out in accordance with what I had heard. Mr. Chamberlain, British prime minister, agreed with his French colleague, M. Daladier, to attend a conference proposed by Mussolini and summoned by Hitler to Munich to bring peace by resolving their vital interests, now manifestly threatened by war. (Chamberlain promised a peace settlement that would last for twenty-five years.)

Taking advantage of Besteiro's trip to Barcelona in connection with a Commission for the Reconstruction of Madrid that he chaired, my Brother-in-Law asked to see him. He and Besteiro talked alone for four hours on an October afternoon at La Barata. "It's all over," the President said when our visitor had left. "He completely agreed with me that we will lose the war and must make peace. Besteiro called Negrín a Karamazov (alluding to Dostoyevski's novel, much in vogue among intellectuals at that time; its protagonists are four raving brothers in a state of degeneracy). He called Negrín's leadership unacceptable. Then I asked him whether he knew someone I could call on in an emergency, and he answered that he knew no one.

He stood alone. He said that he would return to his post dealing with 'the reconstruction of Madrid' to cover his political inactivity.''

Three years later, in a penitentiary, I learned from Rafael Sánchez Guerra that Besteiro had returned to Madrid with the impression that he could achieve nothing through the President. He felt that my Brother-in-Law had become little more than Negrín's prisoner.

Epilogue

44

The Exodus

Negrín surprised both his own delegation and foreigners by announcing to the League of Nations Assembly the withdrawal of foreign volunteers fighting in Spain for the republic. Returning from Geneva he visited the President and assumed a very different attitude from that of a year and a half earlier when he first became premier. Negrín knew that rival politicians opposed him but that they did not dare to challenge him. His comments to my Brother-in-Law went approximately as follows: I know what they are trying to do to me. I would not mind giving up power if the Cortes met and refused me a majority vote of confidence. I don't know, however, what effect that would have at the front; our soldiers unanimously support continued resistance and oppose a negotiated settlement of this war. I don't know what they would say or do in that situation or what I myself would feel obliged to do if the soldiers called upon me.

This matter seemed so serious that the President felt he had to warn party leaders about Negrín's attitude, especially those who had spoken to him confidentially of their opposition to our premier's authoritarian caprices. Parliament met soon afterward, and when Negrín had spoken, the Chamber's president called for a vote of confidence. All of the surreptitious opposition delegates voted along with the premier's actual supporters to endorse his policies.

On July 18 the President gave his last speech in the great hall of the Generalitat building in Barcelona. As we drove along in the car he could not contain his protest at all the banners and decorations celebrating an anniversary that the insurrectionists had imposed on us. "It seems crazy to me to make a national celebration of the dismal anniversary of a rising against the republic, and people's eagerness to treat the occasion of a civil war as a triumph shows how little sense they have. Of course they assume that we will win, but that remains uncertain at best."

Reviewing the honor guard in the Plaza de San Jaime, he moved with his usual sure and rapid step to the applause of a multitude packed together in street entrances and on balconies. When he gave his speech, though, unlike on other occasions, everyone noticed his obvious fatigue, his extreme paleness, even his lack of breath. We insisted on attributing all of it to the extreme heat, trying to relieve our own concern and that of our friends. Those clear signs gave us a sudden warning of a weakness we had not seen up to then. We had just taken for granted his apparently tireless endurance.

In the speech itself, without admitting defeat and with his usual dignity, he warned the dullest-witted hearer about his own increasing spiritual detachment from illusions of power. Yet he surveyed our darkening horizon with his indestructible serenity, which could rise above all contingencies, favorable or unfavorable. He finished with a terrible prophecy about the Spanish panorama, a peace that brought no happiness. At the end came a compassionate, agonizing dirge that anticipated justice in a victorious vindication for any defeat we might suffer:

> I will not predict the political or moral nature of Spanish society after the war; with major wars these changes remain uncertain. Ours is a nation of surprises and unexpected reactions, and nobody knows how Spaniards in peacetime will look back on what they did in wartime. I believe, however, that the greatest possible benefit we can derive from all our troubles will be the emergence of a certain attitude and that only a contemptible person would fail to feel this way. I do not share the optimism of Pangloss, nor will I reduce the message of this drama to the simplistic adage, 'there is nothing so bad that no good comes from it.' That is not true, not true. But those who have suffered from war do have a moral obligation when it has ended—and we do wish it to end—to draw from that experience whatever lessons they can as a warning for future generations. Later, after we pass the torch to other hands, to other men, they must agree that when they feel their blood boiling in anger, when the Spanish spirit again becomes inflamed by intolerance, hatred, and lust for destruction, they must remember the dead and listen to their message, the message of those who have fallen in fury while fighting for a grandiose ideal. The dead now lie wrapped in the soil of our motherland, and they no longer feel hatred, they no longer feel rancor. They send us a message of tranquility, twinkling from afar like starlight. They send us the message of our eternal fatherland saying to all its sons: Peace, Pity and Pardon.

The die was cast; he prepared to accept the consequences, adjusting to the devastation of exile.

"Well, let's see," he said to me one morning, suddenly coming into my room at La Barata during those days when I kept insisting on the impossibility of a European war to calm our nervousness about its imminence. "Let's see. What do you think I should do if Catalonia falls to the insurgents and our cabinet decides to move to—Cartagena, for instance?"

I answered without beating about the bush. "Not long ago you refused to resign; then it would have indicated your disagreement with members of the cabinet who cannot reach a consensus and are governed by the premier's whims. Now I believe that you should share their lot to the end."

"I don't know. . . . I don't know. . . . I have told Negrín, so that he can keep it in mind from now on, that if the enemy obliged me to cross our frontier, that moment would end my presidency. I cannot relate to a republic apart from our national territory."

In late September or early October M. Labonne was transferred from France's embassy in Barcelona to its residency in Tunis, and he came to say goodbye to the President. Though he seemed eccentric at first, M. Labonne had a Huguenot acuity characteristic of French Protestants that my Brother-in-Law had come to respect. Of course, he unreservedly admired everything French—and rightly so except when he sometimes got carried away by his enthusiasm about the French countryside, French gardens, French writers, French politicians, French women, and French soldiers.

The President asked the ambassador, "Can't the French see what the defeat of Spain's republic would mean for them?"

Then the ambassador told him that, when he had taken leave of France's president to begin his embassy, M. Lebrun had asked him quite frankly, "Why are you going to Spain at this point?" "France," M. Labonne said to my Brother-in-Law, "needs a Jacobin dictatorship."

"With whom in charge?"

"I don't know, maybe even Daladier."

The Spanish President always distrusted talk about the need for salutary authoritarianism. Even at that late date, many times, I heard people say to him that he ought to establish a dictatorship. Invariably he replied, "First of all you need a dictator, and I have no vocation for it. Besides, if Spain must travel that route, they have Franco on the other side."

Apart from audiences at Pedralbes, our life became increasingly limited to the La Barata family circle. He continued to get up late, read the newspapers without much interest, write for a while. Sometimes he looked out-of-doors before dinner to check on the boys' activities. It pleased him to see them dressed as soldiers of the Presidential Guard in uniforms his aides had ordered from a military tailor to surprise their Uncle. It amused him to see them at their lessons and even to climb up the mountain with them to see them skillfully manipulate an antiaircraft gun, which they treated as their own property. They had learned to operate its simple mechanism, and they looked comical playing at being DECA [*Defensa Especial Contra Aeronaves* or Special Antiaircraft Defense] recruits, standing on tiptoe, with a soldier lifting up the youngest.

Sometimes we took a drive, usually to a house overlooking the beach at Caldetas, a zone, still respected by enemy aircraft, where most foreign diplomats had taken refuge. Our government was having this house renovated as a residence for its pilgrim President; the building itself seemed undistinguished, but its garden had splendid prospects of sea and mountains. The President would amuse himself afternoons, up on a stepladder trimming a box hedge with gardener's clippers. Bricklayers paid little attention to him; through these months their lackadaisical approach to their work made it seem like putting together a jigsaw puzzle. Negrín had insisted, especially after Lérida's fall, on the need for us to move to a place farther from the battlefront. Still the new house did not seem to offer much security against attack, standing on the Llavaneras heights with no protection against an attack coming from the coast. My Brother-in-Law and I took this as a good omen for an armistice.

We would return from these afternoon excursions in time for supper. After eating we listened to the radio, and we played Russian Bank, a double solitaire; my Kinsman especially enjoyed playing it with me because he always won without the effort involved in chess. He wanted to teach us to play ombre, a game at which he was a master, but soon abandoned his efforts in the face of our stupidity and lack of interest. My wife suggested bridge to vary the evenings, but he never took to it; to him it seemed "a silly game for old English women."

He stopped attending official entertainments because they emphasized the absence of foreign ambassadors, and banquets contrasted too much with food shortages suffered by our people. He did come to the point of accepting a dinner in his honor from the French ambassador. Then he turned it down when he learned that the Generalitat's president would attend with a rank equal to his own. "We are not two presidents of two republics. Spain has only one republic, which has its government, and the president of that government precedes those of the other two governments, Catalonian and Basque. Let them ask me by myself if they like, and the other heads of government another day; but the president of the republic must rank first."

At a Liceo concert he attended with Companys, the orchestra had already played "Els Segadors" and the "Riego Hymn." Then the public, encouraged in those days by politicians making cheap bids for popularity, called for the "Internationale" and the anarchist songs now played at most public assemblies. As soon as our national anthem ended, the President departed conspicuously, making no excuses to Companys and other Catalans who remained behind. A concert by the great Pablo Casals proved solemn and moving; this famous cellist wanted to show his support for our republican cause, which he had championed abroad. My Brother-in-Law attended, very pleased to hear so magnificent an artist on so worthy an occasion. The audience that packed the Liceo auditorium gave my Kinsman an unprecedented ovation. It began when he stepped out of his car at the theater entrance; after the performance it continued until he left the building. He recognized it as his final farewell to that company carried away by enthusiasm and unaware of the rending leave-taking.

My Brother-in-Law had broken the ice of his estrangement with Casares while still in Valencia, and our old friend sometimes came to La Barata. Very few outsiders excepting Casares and Amós Salvador did share our table. One day the President wanted Paco García Lorca to have dinner with us. Federico's brother had been transferred from Brussels, where he had served as embassy secretary, to the Ministry of Foreign Affairs in Barcelona. He brought to dinner a mutual friend, another young diplomat who had served in London at the time when our war broke out. Ambassador

López Oliván had sent him down to Southampton to greet me on my return trip from America. It upset the President to remember Federico who had suffered so unjust a fate through the enormity of our enemies. Like me, my Kinsman felt convinced that this amiable genius had come to his untimely and horrible end more through some grudge than because of politics.

Something delayed the inevitable, fatal enemy offensive we expected in early December. For us these proved days of nervous tension, which the President hid under his customary self-control. His thinking and decisions always reflected this serenity, free from panic.

One night General Saravia came to have dinner with us at La Barata. Not long before, in early autumn, I had gone for the first time to his headquarters and had joined him in his inspection of a camp for retraining deserters. I had come home with a strong impression of their neediness, most notably from seeing barefoot soldiers. The general usually put a bold face on the war situation; he did not do it that night. After removal of the tablecloth and a brief after-dinner conversation the President asked Saravia to come into his office, and, unaccustomedly, he asked me to come along. There he questioned Saravia about our military prospects and probable future developments. The general believed that even after the enemy had broken through our lines, and our lines then remained unbroken, resistance could continue for two or three months in Barcelona. The President asked, further, what he believed about the efficacy of a gradual withdrawal of our troops toward the Pyrenees. How long might that resistance last? Saravia calculated it as up to six months, taking into consideration that during this period war might break out in Europe; then we could expect France and England to come to our assistance. Even with their help we had nine months in all once the enemy broke through our lines.

Certainly, the withdrawal of foreign volunteers fighting on our side caused demoralization behind the lines. Negrín had agreed to this in Geneva without any corresponding commitment from the London Committee in regard to the much more numerous German and Italian contingents now devastating our land while they aided Franco. During the solemn, final military review of the Internationals in Barcelona two incidents occurred: one of them was to a degree private, the other spoiled that procession by unexpectedly disrupting it. When the President and his retinue arrived at the platform to witness that parade on the avenida de Pedralbes a sharp dispute ensued. It echoed a dispute that had broken out during preparations for the review, between Cándido Bolívar, the President's executive secretary, and the under secretary for defense, a recently promoted Communist, though a career soldier. At first their discussion about place and precedence had gone fairly smoothly, but the Communist had then expressed contempt for the President and his party, and it took some effort to avoid violent words about my Brother-in-Law even appearing at that ceremony.

Things began with a show of the sadness that farewells always entail, especially on an occasion like this, when a shout of victory could not accompany people's applause for those departing. Now in this final hour, without the presidential party or leaders of the Internationals ever having known each other, they shook hands. Of these leaders who had brought such a lot of attention for and against our cause, I remember best the Italian Gallo and the Frenchman Marty. The President did not much regret those foreign soldiers' departure. He had never felt enthusiastic about the assistance of combatants drawn from afar by revolutionary enthusiasm or by a spirit of adventure. Thus he had two objects in his efforts to obtain from the Nonintervention Committee withdrawal of all so-called volunteers fighting on our soil. On the one hand, he felt certain that our republic would triumph if Franco did not have foreign assistance, but he also wanted to see us freed from a collaboration that had proved burdensome in every way after its first clearly positive contribution in establishing the defense of Madrid.

Defection of so many career officers had left us permanently weak in terms of command, though not at the general staff level. At the top foreign experts usually proved inferior to our own personnel. The President told us, laughing, of a delightful incident Saravia had recounted to him with his special, sly charm about a Russian instructor who, of course, had come to help us out. When he came to the command post with his *periboschi,* the interpreter, the Spanish general announced to them that before going over plans of current operations they would have a light snack of ham and wine. After they had eaten, the general went over campaign plans, illustrating them with maps, and the interpreter translated these explanations. Then the Russian responded seriously and amiably to our general, and his *periboschi,* in turn, translated his words into clear Castilian, "Everything looks very good, so let them bring on the ham!"

At that point, however, the President could not understand the dismissal of foreign volunteers. Why did Negrín with sudden docility decide to commit himself to this unilateral withdrawal after he had failed to gain an agreement through the London Committee that would really free Spain from all foreign military involvement? Somewhat later he told me that Negrín had made this decision when the USSR informed him that it intended to withdraw its few contingents from Spain because of the inevitability of total fascist occupation of Spanish territory. The Russians believed the presence of their troops might provoke Germany and Italy and lead to a European war. Of course, the aggression by those two powers against our republic had not proved such a provocation for France, England, and other powers associated in Geneva. All of this gave my Brother-in-Law the idea, since confirmed, that Italy and the USSR had offered the greatest resistance to any compromise settlement of Spain's civil war. He felt that it came from their belief that continuation of our war delayed the outbreak of a general war in Europe, something both powers feared. Though enemies, both the USSR and Italy felt that their national interests would suffer more than they could hope to gain from a general conflagration.

Enemy aircraft provided the public incident that spoiled the foreigners' farewell review. Hidalgo de Cisneros, an airman who held a high position in the Aviation Office of our Ministry of Defense, brought notice to the presidential box that planes had taken off from an insurrectionist base on Majorca heading toward Barcelona. Newspapers had announced the review, and a radio broadcast was describing it. Though encouraged by Negrín to leave, the President refused to do it until after the parade's suspension. He wanted to save city inhabitants another unnecessary tragedy from enemy aerial incursions.

We heard of the insurgent entrance into Tarragona in a movie theater in Tarrasa where we went that one time to celebrate some special occasion. A few days earlier we had our family celebration of the President's saint's day and on January 6 a more public celebration of the Day of the Three Magi at a children's refuge near the presidential residence.

The next day, or two days later, the first air raid alarm heard at La Barata awakened us. Our boys, already up, ran downstairs to a shelter we had not yet used. My wife picked up our little girl, aroused by the alarm, and wrapped her in a blanket to carry her to safety. Enrique, our second son, stopped in the main floor hallway, asking with a child's insistance for his uncle and godfather to come down "because he is the most important." His uncle, however, refused to get upset or to get out of bed before his usual time, much later; he had agreed just once to go into a shelter in Valencia, but he never used the one at Pedralbes. Before we got downstairs we saw that this plane would not fire on our house—the boys called it a "turkey," a term they had heard. Perhaps its crew, if they spotted the presidential residence, could not believe that he had remained so near the battlefront. Two days later Saravia moved his headquarters four kilometers behind La Barata.

One night, sitting around the table after dinner, we heard talking on the terrace in front of our house; nighttime silence in that isolated countryside gave those voices—whose words we could not understand—a mysterious fascination. We looked out a large window over the valley toward Montjuich, which cut off our view of Barcelona. The sky through the Badalona gap toward the sea shone with a reflection of fire. Later we saw enemy planes silhouetted by DECA flares. Then came a rain of fire like a fireworks display in the distance, with dull echoes from their payloads. Suddenly I heard him say at my side, in a voice deadened by sorrowful anguish, "Not that, not that! Nothing in the world justifies that horror, that kind of war. Neither the republic nor anything else!"

While it especially troubled him not to participate directly in wartime dangers, my Brother-in-Law insisted that the rest of us should not be exposed to them—those who had no useful military duty to perform or a political duty behind the lines. While he regretted that our government had never found an opportunity for him to visit the front, he also disapproved of Negrín's making a great parade of risking his life by going to the front lines every other day. Sometimes Spain's premier had to throw himself to the ground in a trench during an air attack. Overnight the President decided that my wife and children should leave for the country house we had rented in Collonges-sous-Salève in French Haute-Savoie six kilometers from Geneva, right on the Swiss frontier. They had left La Prasle three months before when he feared that they might get caught up in a war in France. Now that scare had calmed down, but our war had turned so violent that resistance had become impossible, and so we felt they should now take the same evasive action in a reverse direction. I refused to accompany them even to the frontier at Perthus. A few days earlier a friend had expressed his happiness in knowing that my wife and children remained with me, "That will please my mother and sister! If the President's family stays, then things cannot have become so serious as to give up all hope!" I had promised to let him know if our government decided to evacuate the capital. Now I could understand my sister Adela's feelings a year before when she insisted on returning to Madrid from Geneva.

On 31 December 1938 I performed for the first and last time my duties as introducer of ambassadors. M. Jules Henry, the new representative of the Republic of France, presented his credentials. A career diplomat, a financial specialist with particular interest in French markets and industrial investments in Spain, he was also reputed a friend of M. Bonnet, France's minister of foreign affairs. While I waited in the Pedralbes garden, dressed in top hat and cutaway coat, an air raid warning sounded. These aerial attacks always accompanied announced ceremonies in an effort to spoil their effect. A military escort met me at the ambassador's residence to save horses and riders a long, tiring trip from their barracks to the President's official residence. They still had to accompany the ambassador and me back and forth between the French embassy and Pedralbes Palace. This escort also arrived a little late, delayed by the air raid. I found M. Jules Henry waiting for me with M. Fouques-Duparc, my Geneva acquaintance, now an embassy counselor. Neither of them alluded to the bombardment. We started right out for Pedralbes. As we passed, people lined up on both sides of the street cheered us, but more respectfully than enthusiastically. I made the official introductions. The President received the ambassador in a salon hung with magnificent tapestries from our National Patrimony. Despite all our wartime hardships, the republic maintained decorum.

After the customary required speeches and obligatory friendly conversation, I returned to the French embassy with the ambassador's suite. M. Henry seemed genuinely impressed by his informal conversation with the President, more than by the formal speech. Increasingly, these speeches had become a protocolary formula, submitted ahead of time to the Ministry of Foreign Affairs for amendment and correction. Still M. Henry's reaction made me hope that presidential mettle might overcome everything and that his efforts for peace would succeed. My Brother-in-Law later told me that, with due discretion, he had repeated what he had said to M. Labonne. The governments of England and France had only themselves to blame if the USSR seemed to have a certain preponderance as compared with other foreign representation. Even this seemed debatable, though, since nobody had replaced the second Soviet ambassador after his withdrawal; a chargé d'affaires performed his duties. England and France had lessened an unquestionable earlier influence by not reprimanding their ambassadors for shamefully withdrawing to Hendaye. The President hoped for much from the tardy rectification of this situation and from M. Henry's presence. The latter, hardly established, went home to celebrate New Year's Day in Paris, and, coming back to Spain, got only as far as Figueras. By then the republic's ministers and President had left Barcelona.

With our troops in Catalonia in full retreat and General Saravia's headquarters established behind the presidential residence, the premier again insisted that we leave La Barata. My Brother-in-Law finally yielded to the pressure of circumstances, and in two days we evacuated that house; the government turned it over to Tarrasa city officials. With small-town pride, they considered it a museum because of its four or five good modern paintings and the four pieces of crockery displayed in glass cabinets that they called their ceramics collection. After spending a day burning superfluous papers in fireplaces, we went to spend Saturday night in Llavaneras.

The principal house in that town, assigned to the President, was still unready, so they had to requisition a contiguous one in a hurry, dislodging its tenants. Just a few days before, Don Mariano Gómez, chief justice of the Supreme Court, had lived there. We settled down to our dinner with the President in a very bad mood. The house seemed cold to him, and it filled up with smoke when we tried to implement its heating system. Giral came to see my Brother-in-Law after dinner; he and Bolívar undertook to find another refuge farther from Barcelona in case of an attack on the city. We slept badly—the house proved small for so many of us; or to speak more accurately, though the President slept badly some of us managed better. I have always slept soundly, taking each night's rest where I found it. We spent most of the following day in the upper house's garden watching the intense aerial bombardment of Barcelona. I called my wife in Collonges-sous-Salève. Though we had a bad connection, I understood that they had arrived without incident, and she understood that we had left La Barata. The enemy almost caught our servants who had stayed behind to pack. They left Sunday night, and on Tuesday the vanguard of Franco's army occupied that house.

In less than twenty-four hours Giral's goodwill and Bolívar's determination achieved what nobody had succeeded in doing for the past six months.

They returned Sunday night to report to the President that they had arranged a really suitable lodging near Figueras in the Castle of Perelada,
confiscated from Mateu, a well-known Catalonian businessman. A large part
of the Prado Museum's pictorial treasury was stored there for safekeeping.
I recalled to my Brother-in-Law that two years earlier Mateu's chauffeur, a
refugee in Geneva with his employer, had come to our consulate to assure
me of his faithful republicanism, and that his employer had not troubled him
about it. The latter, owner of Perelada, hoped that the President would settle
there to protect it from falling into the hands of some less scrupulous tenant.
I had reported this without paying much attention to it, and as a result the
President had wandered hither and yon following the war's vicissitudes; his
prestige and comfort had suffered. My Brother-in-Law replied that this
move, now unavoidable, would have seemed premature two years before
because of the castle's distance from our government in Valencia and Barcelona and its proximity to the French frontier. We decided to resume our
journey in two days, but things did not work out that way.

The President suggested that Giral stay for dinner, but he would not, and
we settled down to two tables of Russian Bank to pass the time until our
meal. My sister Adela played with our Brother-in-Law, and his wife, Lola,
and I played at a small table next to the dining table. Suddenly an unmistakable explosion and clatter of broken glass interrupted our game. Lola
jumped up at once; I sat glued to my seat. I literally *saw* a broad enclosure
full of cow dung where I was executing a sort of veronica in the face of a
charging bull calf. Thus after thirty-five years the fear surfaced of my first
personal encounter with bulls at my aunt and uncle's, the Cuadrilleros, near
Medina de Rioseco. Now again I did not run.

The President, with that usual serenity and intense paleness that accompanied his indignation, urged us to follow the advise of Santos, who appeared
at the doorway and suggested that we should go outside. Apparently a ship
that we could see had fired a broadside, and its vibrations had broken glass
in an exterior gallery overlooking the road leading up to the Llavaneras
heights. We had to vacate because another shot might hit the building. We
filed out through the kitchen and the back door. We stayed in the garden
less time than seemed prudent because the President got impatient. As on
other similar occasions, he refused to stay outside, despite an autumnal
mildness on that January night.

He wanted to go back inside, but, in spite of his protest, we decided to
go up to the house next-door, available to us but not really ready, lacking
even beds. We gathered in its dining room to sit out the night as at a wake—
someone made that apt comparison. We passed our time telling jokes, forget-
ting the corpse, so to speak. We tried playing poker but soon got bored with
it. After a half hour we learned that the bomb had not come from the ship
but from a seaplane patrolling that coast between Barcelona and Mataró.
When the plane gave us no more trouble, we decided to sleep on some

overstuffed chairs and a sofa, the President uncomfortable and annoyed because our alarm seemed unjustified.

At first light of dawn, however, Santos came in to tell us that we ought to go into an air-raid shelter; a Bengal light from the plane had fallen into the garden of the house where we were staying. We obeyed sleepily, the President in a bad mood. He made them bring along a chair for him, but afterward would not sit in it. Fortunately, we did not have to remain in that refuge. It provided very limited security, anyhow, with its roof uncompleted. Morning light seemed to dispel any serious danger from the plane. We learned later of the destruction during that night of a little house that Negrín had rented at the foot of the hill on which ours stood. It was situated near a railroad line, the enemy plane's apparent objective. We spent that night in Llavaneras surrounded by candelabra and piles of tapestries intended to decorate the presidential residence.

My Brother-in-Law decided that, since they expected him at Perelada, we should go there without further delay, and so we left early in the afternoon. Roads were clogged by people in flight who had stayed to the last minute and suddenly found themselves threatened by an approaching enemy. We traveled in a procession of four or five cars, just the President's assistants, Santos Martínez, and assigned police. My sister Adela and I rode with the President and his wife. The spectacle of those crowded highways depressed us terribly. It took us a whole afternoon to make a trip that should have taken less than two hours. Vehicles blocked each other, and carts and wagons slowed down our Hispano Suiza and Ford. Inhabitants of towns we passed through watched us with sad impassiveness, helpless and resigned to evident defeat. Some people gave us signs of respect; others just watched, disconsolate.

We arrived after dark at the castle, a little beyond Figueras, having had to return to the highway exit to ask for directions. This made the President impatient, as always, when a little carefulness would have save him nuisance. In the courtyard, at the foot of a great stairway, Negrín and Giral stood waiting for us, along with José Giner and Pérez Rubio, assigned guardians of the Prado paintings stored in that castle. They gave us a tour of its main rooms, well furnished by the current owner, Mateu, with tapestries, paintings, and crystal chandeliers. An extensive collection of paintings by Vicente López begun by one of the last counts of Perelada especially surprised us. Among them the President pointed out to me a good portrait of the pretender Don Carlos, whom Carlists call Charles V and liberals call "Charles the Blockhead" (Carlos *Chapa*). Another portrait of a friar—a Catalonian guerrilla judging from his unmistakable expression of exalted violence—showed us clearly how little things had changed since the Carlist Wars, contrary to what we progressives tried to believe.

The premier and Giral, still minister without portfolio, left us. Pepito Giner had dinner with us; we all continued to call him that following the long-standing practice of his family and his friends from the Free Institute of Education. After dinner Pérez Rubio came up to join us. He, Giner, and others attached to the museum, among them Pérez Rubio's sister-in-law, lived on a lower floor of this very large building. My Brother-in-Law took great interest in the fate of those priceless paintings it had cost so much effort to preserve from the fortunes of war. All or most of them had been removed from their frames, rolled up and rescued from the Prado, which insurgents bombed soon afterwards. Trucked to Valencia, they had remained quite safe in the Torres de Serranos fortress. Their transfer to Perelada Castle had proved extremely hazardous. An iron balcony fell on the truck carrying Goya's famous painting *Executions of May 3* and almost destroyed that masterpiece. Passing through Benicarló the truck's vibrations had brought down the balcony already loosened by enemy bombs. When we arrived at the castle experts had begun restoring the torn canvas.

The owner's butler and other servants maintained his household, and we found things in good order, though, as you would expect, domestic arrangements of a Catalonian businessman fell short of real grandeur. In particular, the President immediately noticed the lack of a sufficient heating system, and so did I. He always felt the cold, and the weather had turned chilly and rainy. Lacking anything better, we spent our time blowing on logs burning in fireplaces, and, with those chimneys uncleaned for a long time, we got smoke in our faces and consequent headaches. Each bedroom was furnished in a different style and decorated with tapestries of a different color. Several beds had curtains, and those heavy curtains helped to dispel loneliness in the vast apartments. I got a bed without curtains in a little Empire-style room. A first-rate drawing by David stood on one of the tables as part of my room's decoration. I later regretted not taking it with me. If it happened to disappear after we left, our malicious enemies would certainly blame us for its theft anyhow.

No minister appeared the day following our arrival. That night, listening to the Italian radio network, we heard Mussolini's unpleasant voice announce Barcelona's fall. The next morning my Brother-in-Law sent me to Figueras, only about six kilometers from Perelada. Giral pretended not to know that the rebels had taken Catalonia's capital and went so far as to ask me if I believed lies from Radio Rome. I saw no signs of Negrín but brought Vayo back with me. Earlier he had told me to come and see him when he got back from Geneva; now he had come back precipitately, unable to return to Barcelona. I waited for him, with bombs falling all around, in the Castle of Figueras, where they had set up temporary offices for his Ministry of Foreign Affairs in uncomfortable rooms formerly occupied by the garrison.

Heading back to Perelada, Vayo said to me, "Though we don't need it just now, I have prepared your nomination as our ambassador to Brussels." That dumbfounded me. A minor incident had interrupted our diplomatic relations with Belgium, and its solution included replacement of Mariano Ruiz Funes, our representative at that point. Though this ambassador was a lukewarm republican, I knew that the President felt well-disposed toward him. Thus when I left the Geneva consulate, I wanted to see Ruiz Funes and urge him to return to presidential service. My Brother-in-Law, however, cut short my initiative, refusing to back any effort on my part along these lines because Ruiz Funes had hesitated about returning to Barcelona. He felt that, under the circumstances, initiative toward integration into domestic politics should come from the former ambassador himself. Seeing my surprise, Vayo continued, "I know that this seems inopportune, but its time may well come." Responding to my skeptical smile, he insisted, "Ah! If only we can hold out just one more week! A week from Tuesday war will break out between Italy and France; the general European war will follow, and that means our salvation."

The President spoke to Vayo as frankly as ever, even bluntly because of our situation. He insisted that the minister of foreign affairs look for Negrín. Still, the premier did not turn up that day or the next. In fact, of the cabinet, only Giral and Bernardo Giner came to Perelada. Giner told us that coming from Gerona to Figueras he had found the road jammed by a confusion of cars, carts, and wagons, and had had to walk much of the way. The same thing had happened to Casares, our guest during his last two days in Spain. The President did not take up our friend's ready offer to remain with us until the end. My Brother-in-Law felt that he did not want to leave Spain in the company of this particular man. Martínez Barrio also came to visit, much alarmed by what seemed to him the President's excessive passivity, but my Kinsman felt that he had to wait for cabinet decisions and at least an opportunity to talk with Negrín before making his own arrangements. We heard that the French ambassador was staying in Perpignan, with considerably greater justification than our minister of foreign affairs, who crossed the frontier to sleep every night in France. Knowing that my brother intended a visit to Le Boulou to lodge our unmarried sister with his wife and child who now lived there, the President gave him a letter for M. Henry requesting an interview.

As Negrín failed to come bringing General Rojo to Perelada in response to the presidential request, and given the pressure of events and our need to make essential plans, my Brother-in-Law decided to summon the general alone. Finally, on the twenty-fourth, if I remember correctly, both personages turned up. The three of them talked for a long time. When the President returned to the dining room where I waited, his relieved expression told me that he had achieved what he desired. Without giving me time to ask, he said, with a smile full of emotion, holding the palms of his hands upward in a characteristic gesture, "Peace." Though expected, this news still surprised me.

As soon as General Rojo had entered the office with the premier, he had said, "What are you doing here, Mr. President? Nothing but highway stands between this house and our enemy; they have already reached Arénys de Mar."

"Do you mean, then, that we have lost the war?" When the general did not answer, the President went on, "Do you believe that our central front can, somehow, hold out?"

General Rojo said that he could not perfectly estimate the Madrid front's capacity to resist after the Catalonian front had collapsed, but, as his best estimate, after a hundred thousand more casualties we would have to surrender.

"Well, then, Mr. Premier," said the President, "nothing remains but to obtain the good offices of England and France to arrange a humane peace. We cannot ask for more than that now. Do you gentlemen want me to go to Paris to negotiate this armistice?"

The premier did not believe it useful or opportune to inflict this humili- ation on the President. At least I remember my Brother-in-Law putting it that way. Negrín backed the general, insisting that we abandon our present residence as soon as possible. He said that arrangement of an armistice through representatives of England and France fell more naturally to our minister of foreign affairs. Vayo would have to speak with them anyhow about transfer of the Prado treasures to Geneva.

As he spoke to me, my Brother-in-Law seemed relieved of the tremendous burden of those hopeless days. A humanitarian peace. The republic would surrender, and in return those with no other choice would go into exile. Others conquered by unjust force would be granted clemency and amnesty.

That same afternoon, or the next, Major Parra went to check a nearby town, Massanet, where the president of the Cortes had settled and where they had told us we might find accommodations for the President and at least his closest retinue. Meanwhile, after a terrible bombardment of Figueras, we suffered many air attacks and sought protection under the castle's broad doorway lintels. Planes seemed to come from several airfields that more or less surrounded Perelada. Major Parra returned to say that he would not assume responsibility for the President's taking refuge in the suggested house; discomfort seemed the least of its problems. The village of Massanet, situated at the end of a Pyrenean valley, had no access or exit except a small road leading to the main highway to France.

While all of this was going on, the Cortes had assembled in some unpleas- ant castle with most deputies absent, unwilling to return from France for that kind of sham session. Delegates present agreed to continue our war to the uttermost until we had achieved victory. The premier did not even men- tion to the Cortes his and General Rojo's conversation with the President. Someone later told my Brother-in-Law that one deputy, either from urgent need or as his only comment on these proceedings, had urinated in a corner of that improvised conference hall.

The President particularly wanted to confer with General Saravia. Assigned to Barcelona's defense at the last minute, Saravia had found its garrison disbanded. He himself had to decamp hastily in the middle of dinner at his hotel as Italian troops descended from Montjuich down the Gran Vía Diagonal and the Paseo de Gracia. Then the Council of War made some kind of attempt to judge him and blame him for the collapse, something clearly not his fault. Afterwards, at Perelada, it took my Brother-in-Law considerable effort to convince Saravia that, before all other considerations, he should try to rescue his family from their early refuge, once well behind the lines but now on the battlefront, and get them to safety. Saravia spoke seriously of organizing a guerrilla force under his command; this seemed preposterous to my Kinsman, given our lack of manpower. Events now confirmed the President's judgment months before at that famous council of ministers and syndical representatives which had sacrificed Prieto to the feigned revolutionary and warlike enthusiasm of the Communists. Someone there had spoken of Numantia as our example to follow over the centuries. The President had replied sensibly and courageously, "I don't know about all of that. I do know that the people at Numantia did not have airplanes in which they could escape."

My brother, who had intended to return from Le Boulou in two days, could not do it. Halfway, faced with the impossibility of getting through the jammed highway, bogged down for hours at night in a winter downpour, he had turned back. He sent a message to me that he could not find the French ambassador to let him know of the President's strong desire to speak with him.

Finally, seeing that our own situation kept getting worse without anyone doing anything about it, the President decided that we should set off with minimal hand luggage, leaving the rest of our household at Perelada to finish packing and departure for France. He, his wife, and I left in the afternoon, with only Santos Martínez, his private secretary, Major Parra, and the cook, with four policemen as his guard; we headed for General Headquarters in a nearby town. General Masquelet and those who made up the President's military household waited behind at the castle for orders to leave. Our arrival at Perelada Castle had obliged the general to assume his most fundamental responsibility, but he had tried to avoid it. Showing notable impatience at our arrival, on his own authority he had established his headquarters right on the French frontier some kilometers behind the castle in which he had his post in the President's service.

We arrived at General Headquarters in midafternoon. The expression on the face of the commander of our military forces, looking up and seeing his unexpected Visitor, lies beyond my powers of description. He had established himself in a private house, and we found him in its hall, a place decorated in the worst Catalonian style with garish colored panes in its windows and doors. President and general withdrew for a quick exchange of impressions, and they telephoned to Negrín. In the meantime, my sister, overnight case in hand, stood waiting while Santos Martínez and I leaned against a table in the middle of that large entry hall. Soon after the telephone call, Negrín came in; he went right up to my sister, all smiles.

"What are you doing here, Señora?"

"What should I be doing? Accompanying my Husband."

"You would be much better off in France! Pardon me, but you ladies only get in the way."

"I don't get in the way. I'm little and don't take up much space. Where he goes, there is room enough for me."

"I like to see you always smiling."

"What should I do? Add to everyone's burdens with a sad face? On the outside I always smile."

"Then I will have to teach you how to smile on the inside as well."

"I cannot. What is happening is no laughing matter."

Fortunately the press of business cut that incident short; with each of my sister's replies the conversation had become more abrasive.

General Rojo considered it impossible for the President to remain there. As soon as our enemy discovered his headquarters he would have to move immediately. He offered us his field truck; we could spend that night in it up in the mountains. At least it provided a less dangerous lodging for the moment. We started out, then, in the three cars which had brought us, expecting his truck to follow.

As we drove into La Bajol, Major Parra got out of the car to ask about possibilities of our lodging there. Through the car window, which he had rolled up because of increasing cold, we saw him engaged in a lively discussion with a peasant. We later learned that when this individual, a native, learned the identity of his town's guest, he had asked contemptuously, "And what brings the President of the republic here?" He was an employee of the Treasury Department, and the President had to intervene to prevent Parra from arresting him.

We drove up to the door of a house someone had pointed out to us. Hardly more than a hut for road workers, it marked the town limits; from there on the road seemed to lead up into foothills surrounding the village. Getting out of the car my sister twisted her ankle, and its pain caused her great discomfort in the following days. She saw it as a fulfillment of a prophecy her Husband had made early in the war, "We will leave Spain on foot." It also meant that she became, in fact, an impediment, as Negrín had said.

The President considered a police garrison stationed in La Bajol superfluous for his protection. The Presidential Battalion had that responsibility, and he had repeatedly asked the premier to withdraw the garrison. My Brother-in-Law hoped in this way to lessen friction and suspicion, already present since the police had resisted giving up their barracks to his guardsmen. In fact, the mere police presence also bothered him as a sign of general lack of thoughtfulness; the least annoyance now seemed harassment.

Eventually, after another request, the premier did withdraw the policemen, and the Presidential Battalion assumed their duties.

We did not sleep in General Rojo's truck that night. We settled down in it on the town's outskirts but had hardly finished our dinner when we began to notice a lack of heating needed in those altitudes in early February. They had not sent essential electrical apparatus to heat the truck, and we found the cold increasingly unbearable. We finally stayed in that first house where we had stopped. Its housekeeper, a policeman's wife, received us with complaints and sighs, even when she learned her guest's identity. She feared blame from her masters, the under secretary of the interior, a strong Negrín partisan, and three Army Medical Corps doctors. They had rented that refuge some time before, probably foreseeing the situation in which we now all found ourselves. Among the doctors she spoke of Dr. Pittaluga, my friend Gustavo's brother. When he and his comrades turned up hours later, they proved most obliging. They readily agreed to sleep in the general's truck, leaving to us six or seven beds that the house afforded. Epifanio, our cook, found that he had to prepare chickens for dinner outside on an open fire; the house's cooking fire proved too difficult and too meager.

The next day Don Diego Martínez Barrio, president of the Cortes, and Don Luís Companys, president of the Generalitat, paid us a visit. The former seemed highly circumspect; the latter made it clear that he wanted to leave Spain, if that became necessary, not one minute before or after the republic's President. My Brother-in-Law would not accept this. He readily consented to leave with the president of the Cortes, but even in that last extremity he would not agree to leave with another head of government whose company might signify parity of rank and position with his own.

After we had lived in that hut for two days we went for a look at the last Spanish shelter of the Prado's artistic treasury. Giner and Bolívar accompanied us. They had been going back and forth between Perelada and Perpignan where they safely stored those pictures in the cellar of an old mill under the lee of a mountain pending their transport to Geneva. The safety of those wonderful paintings now meant more to the President than anything else. In his first conversation at Perelada with Pérez Rubio and later talking with Álvarez del Vayo, he had insisted on the primary importance of saving the Museum, so far successful. "Within a hundred years," he had said, "some people will not even recognize Franco's name and mine, but everyone will always know Velázquez and Goya."

On the morning of the third day, our under secretary of foreign affairs called to tell me that the French ambassador and the English chargé d'affaires had expressed amazement that Spain's government had not requested their intervention in its interest, given a virtual flood of refugees crossing the Pyrenees. People kept coming in far larger numbers than anticipated, and this had already created considerable problems. Vayo, then, had done nothing toward the negotiation agreed upon with the President eight days earlier in Perelada Castle. Through that same channel we informed M. Henry and Mr. Stevenson the English chargé that the President urgently wanted to speak with them.

That same afternoon we made an excursion to a nearby farm almost on the French frontier, the lodging place of the Presidential Battalion. My sister, her ankle still bandaged, came with us to try walking again; it relieved her considerably to find that she could manage it with relative ease. Along the way her husband, supporting her by the arm, pointed out the nearby frontier. From our present, thousand-meter height it did not seem so formidable a climb as she had feared.

The battalion received us in formation. We went on into the farmhouse to visit its staff—the pretext of our walk. From a terrace we saw a picturesque party of fugitives searching for an alternate route to cross the frontier; like ourselves they wanted to avoid the main highway. In the kitchen we met a group of Catalans, one a high-ranking Generalitat employee. They greeted us somewhat shamefacedly, just waiting for dismissal so that they could get away.

Coming out again, the President reviewed his troops, his head uncovered. When he reached the center of the formation, he squared his shoulders, "Soldiers, long live the republic!" Unanimously and clamorously, they repeated his words, their echo resounding from the mountains. A boy resolutely broke ranks and cheered the President by name and title. "Hurrah!" the battalion responded. The voice of a lone Catalan added, "Long live Catalonia!" Nobody responded. With knots in our throats and some with tears in our eyes, we turned back. My Brother-in-Law broke the silence. "Did you see that soldier? He must come from my home town." Thus he covered his feelings instinctively with a quip, protecting himself against sentimentality.

Before we got back to our temporary home an emissary came out to meet us; the French ambassador was waiting for the President. We found him inside, and I stayed in the cramped entryway with my old acquaintance, Fouques-Duparc, embassy counselor, while ambassador and President talked in the dining room. M. Henry offered his services in any way that seemed useful.

That night after dinner Negrín, Martínez Barrio, Giral, and Álvarez del Vayo turned up. They had come to advise the President that he should leave national territory. The enemy army had advanced to about twenty kilometers from La Bajol, the last Spanish town in every sense. My Brother-in-Law reminded Negrín of what he had said to him in Perelada and even in Barcelona, that he intended to resign as soon as he crossed the frontier. The premier, in turn, asked him to agree to establish himself as President in our Paris embassy.

For purposes of negotiation the French government had agreed to the concept of an incognito Spanish President within the compass of Spanish territory represented by our embassy; we might gain some advantage through this in our surrender. Now Negrín's cabinet was accepting tardily a proposal my Kinsman made eight days earlier. They agreed, then: the premier would inform Spain's people by radio that their President had left Spain for the Paris embassy; Negrín would meet him there forthwith. Thus my Brother-in-Law agreed to continue in a position he had intended to resign as soon as enemy arms forced him out of Spain. He did it solely because he hoped to save lives that would be doomed by unconditional surrender. When Vayo asked about the possibility of his returning to Spain, the President answered categorically, confirming a decision he had made long before: he would not return to Spain. They called me in to type up copies of a statement required by the French government. I noticed several spoiled versions, evidence that Vayo's nervousness had prevented him from doing that job.

All night long we heard trucks passing, carrying the last Prado paintings into France, heading for safekeeping in Geneva. The following afternoon our automobiles left for the main highway, which was usually jammed; they would wait for us across the Pyrenees in a town called Les Illes. We began our own journey before dawn the next day traveling in other cars until the La Bajol road ended in mountains. Our party was not large. We got out when the first vehicle stuck in mud. Martínez Barrio rode in that one with his wife and sister-in-law; he had not introduced them to us, not even to my sister. Giral, who also accompanied us, excused it as shyness. Negrín came with us to the first French village. Besides police and the Presidential Battalion's commander, who had given its banner to my Kinsman the day before, we also had Major Parra, Major Riaño, Santos Martínez, Epifanio the cook, and Antonio the valet. My wife's brother, Diego, also joined us, rescued at the last minute from Saravia's headquarters where he had served since Teruel's capture. Also, fraternal memory had caused Luis Martínez Díaz to seek refuge in France with us. Brother of the President's nephew who had been killed in Valencia, he had, like him, served our republic as an engineer.

We crossed the frontier in darkness. Border police had orders not to notice anyone who might pass at that hour, but one of them, recognizing the most outstanding fugitive, presented arms to him. My sister did not even realize the point at which we entered foreign territory. At dawn we saw an automobile fallen into a gorge; it seemed incomprehensible in those stretches almost inaccessible on foot. Giral slipped on an icy path and fell, and Martínez Barrio lagged behind, having sprained his ankle as my sister had a few days earlier.

The mayor welcomed us in Les Illes. After we had gotten into the presidential cars, which had gone around by way of Perthus and which we found waiting for us, we headed for Le Boulou, where we made contact with a delegate of the prefect of Pyrénées-Orientales. Negrín parted from the

President, saying that they would meet two days later in Paris. We had more trouble in controlling our emotions in parting with Major López Gómez, whom the President now ordered to dismiss the soldiers of his battalion. We saw many others now who had stumbled over those mountains. My Brother-in-Law also dismissed the police agents at this point. We drove to Perpignan to drop Giral at the railroad station so that he could have a brief reunion with his family before he joined the President, Negrín, and Martínez Barrio in Paris. It was only nine in the morning when we surprised the President's brother-in-law, sister, and nieces; like my brother, mother-in-law, and unmarried sister, they did not expect us so early in Le Boulou.

Our first moment of exile proved one of relief and rest.

45
Resignation in Stages

Temporarily we left my sisters and brother in Le Boulou; my Brother-in-Law and I, with Santos Martínez and Major Parra, left that same afternoon for Collonges-sous-Salève in Haute-Savoie. We had hardly gotten out of Le Boulou when we met a speeding car, and a fat and frenzied Frenchwoman stuck her head out of its window and shouted, "Long live Franco!"

That morning in Perpignan, M. Jules Henry, the French ambassador to Spain's republic, had given me a safe-conduct that instructed all authorities along our route to allow us to travel freely and to provide any assistance we might require. Certainly the French government had not overtaxed itself along these lines. Just a few days before, accompanying a truck loaded with presidential diplomatic baggage—clothing, household goods, and books—to Perpignan, I had suffered all kinds of difficulties perpetrated in the name of the secretary of the Prefecture of Pyrénées-Orientales, though that prefect himself was not involved. They had spared us nothing but the horrors of concentration camps, which indeed even the first Spanish refugees had suffered. Having fled from Franco's Moroccans, they found themselves welcomed by the bayonets of Algerian Zouaves across the frontier.

We had dinner in Montpellier, very late by French provincial standards. Our passage might have gone entirely unnoticed except for the curiosity aroused by the unaccustomed sight of our Mercedes parked in front of the hotel where we ate. The President's chauffeur, Sergeant Benito in his days as Minister of War, had risen to the rank of captain through accelerated promotions during the campaign in which our republic had just perished. We slept in Nîmes and left very early in the morning; welcomed by cold weather and snow to Haute-Savoie, we got home in time for dinner in the early afternoon. I had never seen my Brother-in-Law so inattentive to a passing landscape. He finally laughed to hide his impatience at my efforts to arouse him from his melancholy by pointing out notable sights along our route. On the sidewalk at La Prasle's doorway my three little boys, proudly dressed in their Presidential Guard uniforms, stood at attention as the President got out of his car. He evaded cameras and questions of waiting reporters, and, after a brief exchange of pleasantries with the subprefect of Haute-

Savoie and the town's mayor who had come to welcome him, we withdrew as a family from all curious outsiders.

My wife and I noticed that he did not much like the house we had prepared for him—of course he found it rather crowded. We could never have anticipated that during a certain period more than thirty of us would live there. Besides the family, my Brother-in-Law and sister could not just dismiss service personnel before they had arranged either immigration to America or residence in France. Neither option proved easy.

The President wanted to inform our Paris embassy at once of our imminent arrival, according to his agreement with Negrín. Unlike my Brother-in-Law, I could not hide my surprised indignation when our ambassador, pretending to know nothing about that plan, suggested that the President's Paris visit would have a very bad effect, the French government's approval of his incognito notwithstanding. A few hours later Giral arrived in Paris, and the ambassador phoned to say that he finally understood from talking with him what we intended and that he would expect us the next day.

Though in French territory, our house stood closer to Geneva than to Bellegarde, and we crossed the frontier to take our train that morning from Switzerland's capital. My wife and I crossed that frontier daily after we left the consulate and set up in Collonges. At the station a considerable party of "Friends of the Spanish Republic" saw us off, led by M. Nicole, former cantonal president and head of Geneva's Socialist party. Moments before our train left, China's delegate to the League of Nations, M. Hu, came up to our window and asked me to introduce him to the President so that he could pay his respects. His brother had served as secretary of his country's legation in Madrid and Valencia. Only Major Parra and I accompanied my Brother-in-Law. Santos Martínez stayed with the ladies in Collonges, and General Saravia joined us in Paris after settling his family in Marseilles as well as he could.

Our express train arrived very early at the Lyons Station in Paris, so only the ambassador, a secretary, and my mother-in-law and brother-in-law came to meet us. She had worked for some time in our Paris consulate. We had dropped my brother-in-law, Diego, at the Perpignan railroad station with Giral; thus we had spared him the incarceration in a detention camp that so many others suffered. Also, as a protocolary act of courtesy, a functionary from the Quai d'Orsay came to greet the President for France's minister of foreign affairs.

As soon as we reached the embassy, we noticed Ambassador Marcelino Pascua's discourtesy toward us. According to well-informed sources, his talents as a diplomat mattered less than his abject submission to Negrín, formerly his colleague and now his strong protector. He told us right away that he had room in the embassy for only the President and two other persons. Since the President's military adjutants were his official attendants, I had to lodge at a nearby hotel. A few days later, the ambassador did find room for other guests whom he preferred: Álvarez del Vayo, minister of foreign affairs, and Pablo Azcárate, ambassador to London.

Early that afternoon Pascua left us on our own, merely offering us use of one of his cars in case we wanted to get out for a breath of air. We did this almost every day of our sojourn, but surroundings that had pleased my Brother-in-Law in the past now seemed to me to add to our melancholy. The day after our arrival we visited Saint-Denis and its famous cathedral, pantheon of French kings. The following morning an insidious item on *Le Matin*'s front page reported in these or similar words, "The President of Spain, after burning that country's beautiful churches, amused himself by inspecting ours at Saint-Denis." A police agent charged with our protection felt obliged to explain this by telling me that *Le Matin* had sold out to Germany.

Only one French politician, M. Paul Boncour, visited the Spanish President, leaving his card. My Brother-in-Law instructed me to notify this former premier, whose policies as minister of foreign affairs favoring our side in the war had led to his departure from the Quai d'Orsay, that he would like to greet him personally. "Poor France!" M. Paul Boncour said as he extended his hand. We believed at the time that he was making an excuse, not expressing his actual feelings.

We had spent two or three days in Paris without Negrín appearing or giving any sign of life when Demetrio de Torres former under secretary of the economy showed up at the embassy. This son-in-law of our friend Amós Salvador brought a letter from the premier asking the President to come to Madrid, where he himself had recently flown from southern France. He assured my Brother-in-Law that he had found in Madrid an invincible will to resist to the end. The latter replied predictably. He had no reason to change the decision he had made when General Rojas had accepted our war as lost. Further resistance seemed useless and cruel to him, and in the meantime we were losing an opportunity to negotiate a humanitarian armistice. For that purpose he had come to Paris, and he awaited Negrín's promised appearance.

Every afternoon at our embassy the President met with Don Diego Martínez Barrio, Augusto Barcia, Casares Quiroga, and Don Antonio Lara, a former minister of the Republican Union party assigned early in our war as an adviser for purchasing armaments or something like that. My Brother-in-Law consulted them and also Largo Caballero and Araquistáin, who had recently arrived and came to see him, about what they thought of Negrín's request. He did not intend to change his own position, but he wanted to know. They all agreed on the nonsense of returning to Madrid in present circumstances. Nonetheless Martínez Barrio held that the President should not resign in any case.

A few days later, as I have said, others arrived together at the embassy, Vayo from Madrid and Azcárate from London. The minister of foreign affairs brought an urgent charge, reinforced by his own request, for the President to return to Spain.

"Where is General Rojo?" my Brother-in-Law asked.

The commanding general of the republic's forces remained in France with no intention of again assuming command in Spain under any conditions.

Vayo continued to insist, "What could happen to you, at the worst?"

"Nothing to me," the President answered, serenely ignoring his impertinence, "or to you. I know well enough that finally you and I would have the use of an airplane. But what about those who have to stay behind?"

"All right," the minister responded dramatically, "I will go back and let them cut off my head!"

Only once did Ambassador Pascua have the courtesy to join us at dinner, with Vayo and Azcárate, though we asked him more than once. That meal turned out more a matter of drinking than of eating, given the contrast between the exquisite wines and the carelessness about food. While we ate, the President spoke of the magnitude of our disaster. As he saw it everyone came out looking bad.

Vayo replied, smiling with inane presumption, "I'm sure, Mr. President, that you will agree with me that the admirable Spanish people do not come out of it looking bad."

"Well, if you believe that by saying that you will make me back down, you are mistaken," the President replied. "I find the Spanish people as admirable as you could want, like all other people, after all; but I don't really know what you mean. Spain's people remain a quarry. To make a building or a statue you must shape the rock into something. In Spain we have not yet done that."

One day General Rojo and Colonel Hidalgo de Cisneros unexpectedly turned up at the embassy. In the course of conversation, the President, in Giral's presence, asked General Rojo to put into writing his spoken decision not to return to Spain. At least I understood it that way. Hidalgo de Cisneros left the office abruptly to communicate to Ambassador Pascua his belief that the President's request was unsuitable, even unconstitutional. Pascua agreed and warned the general not to do it. The next day, however, Giral received a letter from Rojo making excuses that stands as sufficient proof that he had said it.

Another supremely sad event epitomized Spain's grief in those unhappy days. The poet Antonio Machado, our special friend, had remained in Barcelona to the last minute, ignoring prudent counsel that urged him to cross the Pyrenees while time remained. He died in a shabby French hotel where he had found shelter in his last, sudden illness after crossing the frontier. As part of a sorrowful caravan of literary men and professors, the enemy army at their heels on Catalonia's crowded highways, he had to sit in a roadside ditch during a required halt and had suffered from weather as inclement as the war and politics. Beyond a doubt that produced the bronchopneumonia and consequent death that took him from us. Proofs of his last writing, an ardent prologue to one of the President's unpublished works, lay buried in our baggage.

After we had waited twenty days with no sign of Negrín, M. Henry called to ask me to meet him, not at the Quai d'Orsay as customary but at a hotel bar near the embassy. Thus we could elude ministry informers who leaked information to newspapers. M. Henry, continuing in his official position as ambassador to the President of the Spanish republic, asked me right away, "Where is M. del Vayo?"

"I don't know," I answered, "presumably in Madrid."

"What? Don't you know that he came to Paris two days ago? M. Bonnet has been waiting for him since the fourteenth." Then he explained to me. On that date the French minister of foreign affairs had asked our minister of foreign affairs how many people our government reckoned would have to leave Spain prior to an armistice. France's government already had M. Léon Bérard, a special envoy, in Burgos to arrange French terms for recognition of General Franco's government, and the English were preparing to take the same step. Now he wanted to arrange evacuation for politicians most directly threatened by reprisals after the victory of the so-called Nationalists. Vayo figured that about ten thousand persons would have to immigrate to France. Henry said that M. Bonnet had answered, "That seems a high figure so late in the game," but, finally, counting on assistance from the English fleet, it had seemed possible to arrange. They needed urgently, however, to draw up lists and get these people collected at ports for embarkation. Now with time running out, the final attack on Madrid imminent, the republic's minister of foreign affairs had not responded to his French colleague's request. He never did.

Vayo excused himself by saying that he had found it impossible to choose those who really needed to leave Spain from among so many, far exceeding the number expected—even the French minister had found his estimate excessive. In the first days of that enormous exodus, Vayo himself had complained about so many people passing into France. "Where will they settle, and what do they fear?" He forgot that our propaganda had tried to bolster weakening Catalonian resistance with radio broadcasts about random shooting of women, children, and old people by the Italian vanguard. In fact the Italians had perpetrated these atrocities in the first towns they occupied.

My Brother-in-Law did not seem at all surprised when I told him what the French ambassador had just told me. He had predicted exactly this situation repeatedly. He had tried to prevent it by working out some kind of compromise with the insurgents, first, to save our republic and, until the last minute, to save lives. He had failed in all of it in the face of obfuscation by Negrín and his ministers—how much of it in good faith? Excepting Giral, we identified with them all the republicans who had accompanied us in our shameful exile and who now proved so remiss in fulfilling what they had agreed to with the President in Figueras and La Bajol. He found himself abandoned in our Paris embassy waiting out the fatal events. During these same days he learned of a telegram sent by Lord Halifax, English minister of foreign affairs, to Negrín offering his services to obtain an honorable peace in Spain. Our premier had answered—I quote exactly, "The Spanish government, knowing its strength, does not believe that the moment has come for foreign intervention in the civil war going on in our country."

Soon after that Ambassador Henry informed me, to pass it on to the President, that France's government, to its great regret, would find itself obliged to recognize General Franco's government in the very near future. Once the British government had taken this action, they would follow suit. The President had made no effort to hide from the French government his intention to resign—indeed, he had come to Paris for that purpose, and they wanted him to do it before they recognized Franco. Otherwise it might appear that France had stabbed Spain's republic in the back. Though the President's refusal seemed certain, I, of course, promised to transmit M. Henry's message. The ambassador had often heard my Brother-in-Law's opinion on this point, and I felt sure that this officious request would not change it. After all, part of the cause of his resignation was lack of assistance from the governments of the French republic and His Britannic Majesty. He would hardly agree to help them now when, under pressure from the reactionary Right on both sides of the Channel, these governments wanted to counteract German and Italian influence on General Franco's government, which owed its victory to those Axis powers.

Nonetheless, my Brother-in-Law believed that if Negrín wanted it, even at that late hour for Spain's republic, we might utilize the good offices of England's government to investigate possibilities of obtaining some strictly humanitarian considerations to save lives. Mr. Halifax's proposal, like M. Bonnet's to Vayo, implied political interest that might prove serviceable if we acted quickly and prudently. While our republic was still resisting in the Levant and Madrid, England and France might approach the Burgos government with an offer to spare Franco the difficulty of a final offensive. In return for simple surrender by the losers, the winners might spare them a predictable, atrocious reprisal. In thus serving both sides the English and French, who had suffered defeat at the hands of the Germans and Italians along with our republic, might yet salvage some influence with the peninsula's new regime.

I had not forgotten my Brother-in-Law's admonition months before about politicians' superficial understanding of historical problems, and not merely politicians who knew nothing at all about history or those with knowledge limited to the encyclopedia article or textbook. He told me, for instance, that Englishmen regularly call our struggle against Napoleon "the Peninsular War" or, maybe, "England's war against the French Empire in the Iberian

Peninsula." We call it our "War of Independence." Besides that, he and I both recalled a recent article by Mr. Winston Churchill, a former volunteer in Cuba against Spain and now a likely candidate for prime minister of the United Kingdom. Before our disastrous defeat, in this article published in *Paris Soir*, to which he regularly contributed, the distinguished Englishman considered the consequences Franco's triumph might have for his country. Quite obviously, he said, Spain's republic had lost viability since it had not succeeded in maintaining order in the country, the essential responsibility of any governmental regime. Of course, General Franco could not have much fondness for Britain, given his affinity for the antidemocratic ideology espoused by governments in Italy and Germany, especially since Fascists and National Socialists had greatly assisted him. Churchill went on to say that he did not know the probabilities of a restoration of Spain's king, as his dynasty lacked the prestige necessary for monarchy. Summing up, however, he felt that Britons might find consolation in the thought that any future Spanish regime would have to reckon with England.

My Brother-in-Law told me that he had quickly informed the French ambassador of the moral impossibility of his resigning his presidency if that in any way contributed to recognition of Franco by France and England. In fact he did not believe that they needed to recognize Franco at all except as a *de facto* government, a procedure that would avoid strengthening his regime through establishment of regular diplomatic relations. In any case, he asked M. Henry to have the kindness to warn us ahead of time so that French recognition of the new regime would not catch us unawares in Paris, with Quiñones de León turning up at our embassy to claim his post and unexpectedly evicting us.

In the midst of all of this, one morning a minor Spanish journalist came to see me; I had known him in Geneva as a partisan of the insurrectionists and in other connections not to his professional credit. He came to ask a question on behalf of the Infanta Eulalia, Alfonso XIII's aged aunt who had thoroughly scandalized Spain's court, from which she had lived almost entirely apart in an exclusive circle of Parisian society. She now resided as a lay boarder, in seclusion, in the famous convent where Mother Loriga had served as superior until her very recent death. This nun, a great intriguer much devoted to Spain's royal family, was the aunt of our very republican friend Major Vidal, now an immigrant like ourselves.

The infanta wanted to know the truth of a rumor she had heard two years before from former minister Chapaprieta that my Brother-in-Law's intercession had enabled her to recover some jewelry. This property, found in a trunk when the Junta of National Patrimony took over the Royal Palace in our republic's first days, had been deposited in the Bank of Spain until its owner claimed it. I asked the President, who answered with further details confirming that rumor's essential truth, though back then he had no more responsibility in either government or Ministry of the Interior than Lerroux or Chapaprieta himself. The journalist later called me on the phone to express Doña Eulalia's thanks; except for her illness, she would have come to thank the President herself. She regarded him as "a Spanish gentleman." My Brother-in-Law judged it unsuitable for me to call on the infanta, something I would have enjoyed, always curious about picturesque personalities and things and preferring anecdotal history to what comes from learned tomes.

Days passed slowly and boringly within the embassy confines, a condition exaggerated by our unpleasant, though distant relationship with the ambassador. He concerned himself far more with his magnificent Siberian husky dog than with us. The nuisance of caring for that animal involved not merely servants but also secretaries, one of whom had as a principal duty taking it out to satisfy its natural functions in the gutter. I have already said that the President went out only for his afternoon ride. He retired early after a brief *tertulia* limited to a few of us. These sessions did not always pass harmoniously because he felt irritated by the worrisome, confined waiting, which also seemed interminable to my wife and sister in Collonges-sous-Salève.

Sometimes, unpleasant incidents occurred in which I became the protagonist because of my habitual impetuousness. One night I denounced Negrín's conduct with a vehemence that caused Giral to get up and leave almost without saying goodbye. That, in turn, aroused my indignation against this prudent friend, with whom I had felt annoyed since our arrival in Paris when he had complained to the President in a friendly way about my wife. Pestered by a reporter during that interim between the announcement of our departure from Spain and our arrival in Haute-Savoie, my wife went so far as to say that my Brother-in-Law would already have made peace if it lay in his power. I had not seen this newspaper story, and my wife had not said anything about it, no doubt considering it unimportant; but the President had reacted far differently to the charge than Giral probably expected. My Kinsman said that in fact he didn't like families making political statements of that sort. On this occasion, however, since others who ought to have spoken out had not, it seemed only fair that my wife should have the pleasure of telling the truth. No doubt she had become infected through my own indiscretion, never harmful and sometimes helpful. After all, her candor had harmed no one and had indeed served him.

One Saturday morning M. Henry called me again to tell me that on Tuesday a deputy would raise the question in the Chamber of Deputies whether to recognize General Franco's government in Spain. In spite of having taken a box at the Opéra-Comique for a concert, the President decided to leave next day. The great [Felix] Weingartner was to conduct the *Pastorale*; this musician's interpretation of Beethoven's nine symphonies remained one of my Kinsman's fondest memories from his first stay in Paris twenty-five years before.

That Saturday Méndez Aspe, treasury minister, turned up at the embassy; until then he had been entirely remiss in reporting to the President. My Brother-in-Law's incognito had saved expenses inherent in a presidential household, but Negrín had still seemed niggardly about his petty expenses. The President had left Spain without even succeeding in converting all of his last salary payment into francs at the Central Office of Money Exchange. They had merely allowed him to convert two hundred fifty thousand francs, which included two thousand francs each to help persons attached to the presidency in their first period of immigration. The president's secretary had a lot of trouble in obtaining even those francs for the pesetas, though that money came from the presidential privy purse.

Méndez Aspe, who, I repeat, had remained entirely aloof during our residence in Paris, now appeared on the eve of our departure with two decrees, and he insisted that the President sign them. One of them turned over to an anonymous society all property, movable and immovable, located abroad and belonging to the Spanish government. The second turned over to the USSR some ships anchored in Russian ports, worth I don't know how many millions and held, I believe, as security for payment for war materiel provided to us. The President made no difficulty about the second decree. If the Russians intended to hold those ships anyhow, we might as well get whatever credit the Government of the People's Commissars would allow toward satisfying our debt.

He considered it nonsense even to propose the first decree. It could only prove ineffectual. Who could believe, for instance, that any French government would accept the transfer of our Paris embassy building one day before France officially recognized General Franco? He saw no precedent in a royal order cited by the minister that Alfonso XIII had signed in Paris during a trip; it made no difference whether that trip was official or unofficial. Above all he felt deeply repelled by any appearance of last minute raiding of national property, belonging to the *de facto* government to which foreign nations now hastened to give legal status, justly or not, and whether we liked it or not. In vain the minister marshaled Sánchez Román's legal opinion. The President also talked with him and remained unconvinced by his arguments, his reputation as a lawyer notwithstanding. Their dispute got to a point where this illustrious jurist felt offended in his professional dignity because the republic's President remained firm in his belief. This tactic also failed to make my Brother-in-Law accept what he regarded as the nonsensical argument that, along with gold transferred abroad—which he did accept as legitimate, these property transfers were essential to pay the expenses of the exiled republican government, established by popular will and inviolable to forcible change. Méndez Aspe had to leave, then, with an agreement only on the decree ceding those ships anchored in Russian ports.

The knotty problem of funds intended to alleviate the hardship of immigrants compounded all of this. No one had foreseen the multitude that left

Spain. The President had indeed thought of this situation at the war's beginning, and he had established a fund deposited in a Geneva bank in my name. He did not intend to provide a sinecure for persons obliged to emigrate, but enough for their first adjustment. He never dreamed then, however, of the actual numbers we now saw in huge concentration camps, with Spanish refugees all lumped together as "Reds" through the French government's inhumanity and the French people's indifference. In fact, though, the noble color of blood did provide the basic color of our tricolor flag.

Not a year had passed since the President had agreed to a request by Giral, acting minister of foreign affairs, to withdraw that first deposit we had made for refugees. Giral had turned it over to Negrín to use in whatever way might best suit any circumstances that might arise. One time in Barcelona Araquistáin had asked me whether I knew anything about Negrín's intentions along these lines. Back in the days when Negrín served as minister of finance in Largo Caballero's cabinet, he had proposed to his friend Araquistáin, then ambassador in Paris, a bank deposit involving himself and a few other government officials who would administer it secretly for greater efficiency. Araquistáin had said then that he opposed this plan. The President of the republic knew nothing at all about it. When he had once spoken to the premier about the eventuality of emigration, which at that point seemed imminent, Negrín had answered benevolently that the President would lack nothing in time of need. This would have sufficed for my Brother-in-Law not to speak of it again, from innate fastidiousness.

On Sunday afternoon, then, my Kinsman, secluded at the back of a very inconspicuous theater box with Saravia, Parra, and myself, turned with melancholy dignity away from our deceptive dreams and surrendered to the delights of Beethoven's symphony. "How white his hair has become," he commented about that great, still energetic German conductor standing before the Opéra-Comique orchestra, baton in hand, acknowledging his public's ovation. Afterward, seeing the President in the crowd, the audience leaving the concert, a Basque recognized him after staring a long time, and he removed his typical national beret—a gesture of respect—as we got into our car. We had only time to pick up our luggage at the embassy and hotel before catching the train.

Giral and Victoria Kent, then an embassy secretary, headed a small party of friends who saw us off; the unpleasant ambassador did not join them. A considerable body of curious spectators did accompany them, as well as a photographer whom we could not avoid. When an agent who punched our tickets at the platform entrance greeted my Brother-in-Law as a good French republican, he could do no less than give him a deferential smile. As our train pulled out in notable silence, M. Lachenal, president of the Canton of Geneva, traveling in a compartment next to ours in the sleeping car, approached me and asked me to introduce him. The President acceded to his request, and we had a short, merely polite conversation. The next morning

M. Lachenal failed in his efforts to direct the attention of Geneva's journalists at Cornavin Station to Spain's President. Foreseeing curiosity about our passing through Switzerland and our departure from Paris, we had instructed Santos Martínez to pick us up by automobile at the frontier Bellegarde Station.

Finance Minister Méndez Aspe had not come with the others to see us off at the Paris-Lyons-Mediterranée Station to have his decree signed. The morning following our return to Collonges-sous-Salève, an embassy courier arrived with it at our house. The President simply signed it. It greatly surprised him when another messenger from the embassy arrived that afternoon with a second envelope, a telegram from Negrín addressed to my Brother-in-Law in Paris. Speaking for the republic's government, he summoned the President to Madrid for a showdown between them. Negrín offered his own resignation if the President thought his replacement opportune. Should the President refuse to come, Negrín would assume no responsibility for anything that might occur. My Kinsman easily discovered from this messenger that he and the other courier had come on the same train. The ambassador had given them explicit orders to present their two envelopes a few hours apart and the decree first.

My Brother-in-Law left us in the living room and went into his office; soon he returned with a paper he gave me to read: "To His Excellency, Don Diego Martínez Barrio, President of the Cortes in Paris. As of this date I resign the presidency of the Spanish republic," and his signature at the bottom. "Does that seem right?" he asked me.

"No. You don't say anything about the reasons that cause you to resign, and you must give them."

"You are right." He left and returned again almost immediately. The new draft telegram said this, more or less: "Having heard the opinion of General Rojo, commander in charge of military operations, in the premier's presence, that we had lost the war, and in view of recognition of General Franco by the governments of France and England, I hereby resign the presidency of the Spanish republic."

When, twenty-four hours afterward, he considered that the addressee must have received this communication, he told me to summon foreign press representatives from Geneva to La Prasle's living room and to read them its text. This action ended my duties as Introducer of Ambassadors, Head of the Diplomatic Household of the Presidency of the Republic. Negrín, speaking for the other ministers, answered with a telegram of respectful acknowledgement.

"Now you will see," my Brother-in-Law said to me, "why Don Diego felt so concerned that I retain the presidency, apart from my determination not to return to Spain under any circumstances. He wanted to avoid the position he now occupies. He won't go to Madrid either, of course, and legally they have no other president than himself until they elect my successor. How will they manage that?" Still, Martínez Barrio's attitude caused the Former President no indignation. On the other hand, he called Negrín's behavior blackmail. Now he understood—though never so well as I did afterward—the premier's passive resistance about exchanging into francs his last presidential salary payment, which he had received in "Negrín notes"—merely colored paper. Now, too, he understood the stinginess about the least expenditure in connection with his incognito presence in Paris. Now, above all, he understood the pressure exerted on him about that decree alienating property of the Spanish state abroad to an anonymous society.

As hard as we tried, and we were not used to manipulating the radio, we failed to find any report indicating that anyone told Spain's people the actual terms of their President's resignation.

46

Farewell to Paris

A few days later a Toulouse newspaper, *La Dépêche*, famous in the annals of French journalism, published without comment General Rojo's challenge to the text of the presidential resignation. Apparently he had unsuccessfully requested that the president of the Cortes make this correction. In the newspaper General Rojo asserted that he "was not and never had been answerable for the war." When the President heard of it from Parra, the general's friend and in direct communication with him, it annoyed him that Rojo should have become upset for no reason. He consented to Parra's making an explanation on his behalf, trying to assuage the grievance without sacrificing presidential dignity. It lay clearly above and beyond the call of duty to speak to someone who had so badly misinterpreted his words. He had not intended to say more or less than he had said: technically, Rojo as commanding general had responsibility for military operations. This did not impute to him any blame whatsoever, certainly no political blame, though I think maybe the President really felt, as I did, that Rojo deserved it. No, he had merely meant that as President of the republic he had based his own opinion about the war on that of his commanding general who expected nothing more from its continuation but terrible destruction. He made no public answer to that inopportune challenge. Later Rojo left for Buenos Aires with his numerous family. He had become reconciled with Negrín, who provided him, at least, with a subsidy to pay for his voyage.

During our stay in Paris, representatives of the French and foreign press had aggressively approached the President seeking provocative statements from him or to publish his *Political Memoirs*. He had turned them all down categorically in spite of the high prices offered by newspapers like *Paris Soir*. At that point he did not feel that he could decently appear before the public making personal judgments about men and events, not with a decision in Spain still pending, however certain the outcome of our war seemed. His resignation changed all that. Once he had finished editing his *Memoirs of War and Politics* and had made a clean copy of *Vigil in Benecarló*, he decided that we should go to Paris to talk with an editor about publication of these books in French translation and to investigate possibilities of Spanish editions. His reading of the *Vigil* to our family circle after dinner at La Prasle made an unprecedented emotional impact on his audience.

Before we left Collonges-sous-Salève, one night a radio broadcast from Madrid surprised us; it reported Negrín's replacement by a Junta for the Defense of Madrid headed by Besteiro and Colonel Casado. We rarely listened to the radio because my Brother-in-Law did not much like it, and furthermore he could not stand the increasingly confused and untrustworthy news coming out of Spain. I tried in vain to ease his concern about this abandonment of power by Negrín's administration to an interim government, as the Junta called itself. I argued that this new regime to a degree and to a point stood for the peace he himself supported. He could not agree that what had happened had much to do with his way of thinking, and, of course, it had absolutely nothing in common with his approach to government. A man of peace, he had addressed Spaniards with "words of peace" when he took over the presidency; he would never have wanted our fatherland's soil bloodied by civil war under his authority—the most horrible and pitiless war in human memory.

He could not understand Besteiro. A few months earlier at La Barata, his old friend had refused to assume the responsibility of government, at that time precisely because he couldn't possibly determine the majority belief not only of our nation but even of his own party. Now he had joined with a military man rebelling against a legal, functioning government, repeating the pattern of Franco's coup d'état. To compound their error they had used Franco's pretext: excessive presence or intolerable pressure of Communists in government. The President also did not believe that Besteiro and Casado would get support from England and France or any other foreign power or that they had any guarantees from the triumphant insurgents. As always in challenging his thinking, I erred in arguing with him about this. He felt sure that Besteiro counted on his own undeniable prestige and aloofness from the civil war as an advantage, but that neither of these considerations would impress the enemy. Colonel Casado's mistake came from counting on a military esprit de corps, but his colleagues would see him as a traitor to the military class. Thus these two had undertaken a risky surrender, believing that Franco's government would at least respect their persons and also those of the many thousands of unwary Spaniards who could believe, as they did, in the possibility of their conqueror's generosity.

"They have achieved nothing," he said to me, "except to provide Negrín and his ministers with a way out of the dead end where they had situated themselves. You will soon see that." The time had passed for settling the war by compromise. Now it had even grown too late to settle it by accepting defeat. They would have done better to follow the premier's pledge to fight to the end. Surrender had become inevitable in any case. At the worst these new insurgents might find themselves in a position of having no constitutional authority to arrange their surrender, no one to make conditions on behalf of the conquered, guaranteed through some stipulated intermediary.

Thus we went to Paris, just the two of us, as we had twenty years earlier, but in a very different mood. Still, we did not feel spiritually defeated; in a way we had resolved to begin again, united again in the great adventure we had shared in literature—and in the theater I had dreamed of. For the first time since their marriage, the President was taking a nonpolitical trip without his wife. This made me believe that one of his purposes was to compensate me with this excursion full of memories for a friendship blighted in the closest sense by pressures of tawdry politics. We did not speak of all that, but our melancholy return together did compensate me for the years of public life in which my Brother-in-Law had wasted his life's secret treasure, sacrificing it as a holocaust to the insatiable monster of the nation. Defeat of his ambition for power, or for service to our inconstant people, had restored my friend to me. Though he was wounded and battered to an extent I did not then realize, his personal dignity remained intact. His courageous spirit had now achieved an insuperable excellence; tempered by adversity, his character had become heightened in its sensitivity to a point of musical perfection, capable of reacting to ethereal vibrations of a subtle and ineffable sort.

No, we did not have to say anything on that train rushing toward Paris with far better accommodations in a sleeping car than in the crowded second-class compartment of our first visit years before. I could sense relief and unburdening in my restored friend; it showed in his joyful, childlike smile, the smile of our country walks, or when he faced a plateful of good French cooking, or when he heard a Mozart symphony. He did not think of liberty as personified by an emblematic matron wrapped in a tricolor flag and wearing a Phrygian cap. No, he identified it with a fixed and limited ambience, measured in the shadows and light, smells and sounds of the world's capital: Paris.

Alas, we could not enjoy the freedom of our youthful excursion. We no sooner got off the train than an unmistakable police agent approached me to offer to M. le Président the protection and attention due a guest of his eminence. Useless to refuse him. He had orders to follow us even if we did not wish simply and openly to accept use of a car that the Police Department placed at our disposal. I had not requested this attention; French police assigned to our house in Haute-Savoie and the Swiss had informed their Paris colleagues about the Spanish President's trip, and French officious solicitude had taken it from there. That same afternoon the police officer who had accompanied us during our embassy stay appeared at our hotel to pay his respects. No doubt the President's generous tip in acknowledgement of that earlier, assigned attention had gratified him. In fact, his appearance turned out useful, and his new offer of service proved opportune.

Avoiding better-known hotels in central Paris, the President had chosen a less ostentatious one, yet still very decent, in a street near the Arc de l'Étoile. He and my sister had visited a diplomat friend there during their excursion to Belgium and Holland four years earlier, and it made a good impression on him. He had chosen it in particular because of its inconspicuousness and because the guests he had seen there caused him to suppose that a Spanish or Spanish American clientele did not frequent it. You could recognize them by their lack of elegance in that fashionable district of Paris. Our police escort dropped us there very early in the morning, establishing us in two comfortable but not particularly luxurious rooms. We had breakfast in the dining room without other guests showing much curiosity about us. We went out for an afternoon walk in the Bois de Boulogne. When we got back, Carlos Esplá and Giral visited us, the only personal friends whom we had informed of our arrival up to then.

We were preparing for dinner, planning to go to bed early, when the manager called me to his office and made a very gratifying offer to exchange our two rooms for four much better rooms in a new annex, completed but unoccupied. To my surprised questions, he finally admitted that his clientele, composed almost entirely of South Americans and Spaniards in comfortable exile from our civil war, had threatened to leave en masse if the former President of the republic continued lodging there. Felipe Rodés, a Catalonian minister under the monarchy, had spoken for them. Apparently they considered the very sight of the President an affront. Merely saying that the President would probably not agree to change rooms in such iniquitous circumstances, I took advantage of the courtesy call of our old police acquaintance to refer this matter to him.

A few minutes later the manager called again to say that I had misunderstood his intention. He had only wanted to accommodate M. le Président more comfortably and to save him any possible annoyance. In any case no guest would behave in such a way as to discomfort us. (The officer had told him that if the President had to leave because of inconvenience the hotel would be shut down. Like all hotels it survived through deliberate police disregard of its failure to observe the laws and regulations that governed its operating license.) We remained there, then, during the ten to twelve days of our last stay in Paris. We suffered no snubs; on the contrary, one guest, apparently owner of a major Buenos Aires daily, asked to be introduced to us. Carlos A. Prato, my friend, whom we ran into when he came to the hotel on some newspaper business, served as intermediary.

We suffered unpleasantness only once in Paris. Wandering along the boulevards with no particular destination as we used to do, on the Capucines, I think, one of two young ladies recognized the former President, turned as we passed, and made some sarcastic remarks. Answering her more courteously than her impertinence deserved, I asked her for the name and address of her husband or protector, so that I could seek formal satisfaction. Stunned, she did not answer, and she allowed her insistent companion to lead her away rather than continue a public argument with me. Apart from this minor incident, he received nothing but continual signs of respect and sympathy, tipping of hats, smiles, and even cheers for the Spanish republic. Especially in recent days newspapers and magazines had made his face very familiar, and Parisians reacted to his presence with curiosity and admiration. Except for that and his noticeable resemblance to the French minister M. Sarrail [Albert Sarraut], he might have gone anywhere unnoticed, as he would have preferred.

The same afternoon as that unpleasant incident, he wanted to sit down with Carlos Esplá, who accompanied us, at a table in front of the Café Napolitain. It was the first he had taken me to on our visit to Paris twenty years before. "Let's see," he said, "how long it takes us to collect a crowd of Spaniards." In fact, we had hardly sat down when the Novais Teixeiras joined us. A very amiable Portuguese and our friend from the Regina *tertulia,* Novais had become a fervid republican during his long residence in Spain. Certainly republicanism had nothing to do with his emigration; he had left Portugal as a *Paivante,* the name given to youthful followers of Paiva Couceiro, predecessor in the peninsula of the Francos (Portugal also had one of them), the Primo de Riveras, and the Oliveira Salazars. Mr. and Mrs. Novais had hardly sat down at our table when other compatriots joined us, so many that they soon had to take nearby tables just as the former President had expected.

We had come to Paris with the principal object—if not the sole object— of making contact with publishers about my Brother-in-Law's *Memoirs of Politics and War* and *Vigil in Benicarló.* Actually we needed to see only our old friend Max Aub, an immigrant like ourselves, but now in his third national incarnation, so to speak. His Spanish naturalization, which had given him a nearly perfect native accent, came from his German father and French mother settling in Valencia at the outbreak of the 1914 war. His father had not wanted to join his compatriots in fighting against his wife's brothers. Max Aub had connections with reputable publishers. Along with our translators, M. Jean Cassou and M. Jean Camp who had done *The Crown* and now agreed to do these other two works, he tried to arrange the best possible terms. Of our political friends, we saw only Giral, Santiago Casares, and Esplá.

At that point we also had hopes of a French stage production of *The Crown.* During our war I had met in Paris a very handsome French girl whom I had known earlier in Madrid as the wife of a rather obscure violinist. He had limited his wife's theatrical activities, agreeing only to her participation in amateur productions organized with considerable artistic flair by a lady much attached to Federico García Lorca. Germaine, as her friends called this young Frenchwoman, had so perfected her Castilian accent that, when she came back to Paris during our war, now separated from her jealous husband, she could appear as a Spanish actress in the Camp-Cassou translation of Lope's *Fuenteovejuna*. She interpolated into it Castilian songs that she sang so impeccably that Parisian critics who hailed the debut of Germaine Montero—the Spanish name she adopted—praised above all else the perfection of her French, saying that it had hardly any Spanish accent.

It seemed to me since she had performed with notable success not only in *Fuenteovejuna* but also as the young lady in García Lorca's *Blood Wedding* in its recent French production, she might prove an excellent interpreter of *The Crown* if I could succeed in presenting it in Paris. I also tacitly agreed to give Casares's daughter—whom veteran actress Colonna Romano had taken on as a protégée because of her talent—the delightful role of a Mussetian maid who has a poetic third act dialogue with a page. I could not guess then that in a very short time María Victoria Casares would emerge as an actress, fulfilling a prediction I made to her parents after seeing her in a child's play in their home years before. During the war's terrible uncertainty, with Germans occupying Paris, she unexpectedly became the heiress of Sarah Bernhardt. The great Bernhardt had died twenty years before without artistic succession, during the peace conference that followed the First World War. When I had introduced Germaine to the President while we were waiting for Negrín at the embassy, he had admired her looks and her Parisian insouciance.

Camp, the more knowledgeable of our translators about staging a play in Paris, introduced me to an old actor-impresario, M. Rosemberg, who seemed almost too eager to undertake the project. He seemed primarily interested, however, in getting me to influence the Author to bear all production costs. I did not quite come to the point of suggesting this to the former President. Though it would undoubtedly have pleased him to see his work presented in French translation in the capital of the theatrical world, he made no protest when I commented that we should not throw money away that we might need later. For the moment he wanted to limit his activities to publication of his two books, and so, without abandoning all thoughts of another production of *The Crown*, we did not pursue the matter.

The editor of *La Nouvelle Revue Française* sent his own son to deal with the former President. They agreed to publish first *La Veillée à Benicarló* in an edition of twenty thousand copies, considering that this admirable dialogue would better suit French readers little versed in Spanish politics. Publication of the *Memoirs* would follow shortly. On the other hand, we had trouble finding anyone in all of Spanish-speaking America to undertake a Castilian edition of either work. The Hachette firm, distributors of almost all French translations in the New World and, of course, publishers of the *Nouvelle Revue*, seemed to have decided in our favor; then they backed off. As we understood it, political pressure had a lot to do with it. Other publishing projects also broke down, for instance, editorial collaboration with some periodical like *Paris-Soir*, which had seemed scandalously eager to get the President's signature just a month earlier. Now they offered very inferior terms, which both failed to compensate him sufficiently and limited his freedom, restricting the professional frankness of which he had always boasted.

We spent our time in the long breaks between these negotiations walking through streets we had known in good times of tranquil carelessness, now so far away. We shared again warm evenings in which the moist spring atmosphere, filled with the first fragrance of acacias, enveloped Paris in that blue haze with which nature copies the impressionist painters (as we commented, plagiarizing Oscar Wilde). Together we walked again from Montmartre to the Eiffel Tower, and we enjoyed a new perspective opened up between two buildings constructed for the 1937 Exposition where the old Trocadero used to stand.

If we did not browse, as before, in bookstalls along the Seine, we did go through boulevards and streets casually looking for a house. My Brother-in-Law preferred something not far from Paris if possible, but not in the city itself, where we would have trouble finding anything suitable for so large a family as ours. He did not even consider immigration to America, which our wives wanted. The weak excuses he gave made it clear to me that he just did not want to go. According to him, Spanish émigrés there would settle down to futile arguments about the past that would entirely wreck any chance of achieving anything in politics. He himself had no wish to test political waters again. Still, he did not remember his time in government with despair, and I believe that his reluctance to immigrate to America involved a resistance against going very far from the thankless soil he had renounced. Besides all that, always and in spite of the restlessness of France's political scene, he took pleasure in the very stones of Paris, not merely the monumental stones of the great buildings he loved to look at but even the paving stones beneath his feet.

We did not go to the theater he used to enjoy so much, but some evenings we did go to movies, where darkness provided a better shelter from curious persons who might interfere with his complete freedom, lost in his years as a public man and which he now sought to recover. Withdrawal of his police guard, once the status of refugee Spanish politicians had been regularized by the bureaucracy, contributed a lot to the feeling of rest he did achieve in that brief period of our farewell to Paris. Though it did not occur to me then, I now believe that in the depths of his soul, unconsciously, he felt it as a farewell. His spirit had now become disposed to that tenderness with which death marks out its own.

One afternoon Diego de Mesa, my wife's little brother, came to our hotel to say goodbye, and his farewell embrace moved the President very much. Diego became the family precursor in our necessary flight to Mexico to try to make a new life there. One might, of course, say that, like many young Spaniards uprooted by our uncivil war, he had not really made a start in Spain. One of our last nights in Paris we read in newspapers of the very sad, though expected entry of Franco's Nationalists into Valencia. Expectation did not lessen our sorrow, and fears about the fate of Leopoldo Menéndez, who commanded the republican army there, increased it. The President wanted to go to a neighborhood theater, but we had to leave before the movie ended.

Of the wretched government overthrown by the Junta of Colonel Casado, Besteiro, and other tardy representatives of the spirit of concession, we knew nothing except that Álvarez del Vayo, Azcárate, and Negrín had already established themselves in Paris. Now Giral, his gorge rising at the thought of Negrín, suggested that this former premier had no other plans but to take the money and run. That brought me up out of my chair in protest. I threatened to go to bed right then if he went on like that. My Brother-in-Law could only laugh at my attitude, remembering Giral's similar reaction to my indignation about Negrín a month earlier in the embassy.

47

Memories of La Prasle

Winter lingers well into spring in Haute-Savoie. Snow and rain kept us inside more than the cold; we hardly ventured even into Geneva in spite of its proximity, and we invited only a few guests to La Prasle. My Brother-in-Law wanted to rest from social obligations, and the first period of our residence proved a real exile. Only my great friend Isidro Fabela, Mexican delegate to the League of Nations, joined us with any frequency; sometimes he brought Pérez Rubio and Pepito Giner. They had instructions to turn over those irreplaceable Prado paintings to the secretary of the League of Nations for storage and safekeeping until their return to Spain. These men got no support at all from the two committees in Paris established to aid Spanish expatriates. At that point the two committees, speaking for antagonistic factions, were contesting which of them officially represented the republican government-in-exile. Mr. Fabela and his wife had rescued two little orphans from the horror suffered by most Spaniards in the first concentration camps, and they bestowed on them every parental attention and kindness. Beside the Mexican diplomat, we sometimes had distinguished Italians like "Baron" A. Prato, the lawyer Reale, and the eminent historian Guglielmo Ferrero. Ferrero had moved to Geneva when Mussolini established his dictatorship in Italy, and I had come to know him well during my consulate. Otherwise, as I said, we had few visitors.

The subprefect of Haute-Savoie, whose capital was nearby Annemasse, and the prefect in Annecy showed the former President certain basic considerations, including establishment of a police patrol for our protection, men regularly assigned to posts on the Swiss frontier. At first these police annoyed us in their efforts to mount guard in our garden and even in our house, too small to lodge police agents without interference with familial arrangements.

Though not entirely, our inaccessible location protected us from hordes of Spanish visitors in the same terrible circumstances as ourselves. Had we lived in Paris or some other important city they would have greatly disturbed our peace. If the former President had the slightest wish to return to active political life, the regrettable attitude of our best-known compatriots would in itself have been enough to cause him to withdraw. At that time Prieto arrived in Paris from America, but he found no time to visit us. That greatly disillusioned my Brother-in-Law about friendships based only on political association.

A year earlier when I had felt like making a scene, as they say, about leaving the Geneva consulate, the President had, as always, used our kinship and friendship to calm me down. "You must understand," he said, "that your ceasing to serve as consul does not call for a confrontation. The occasion will arise very soon for dealing with this situation on a larger scale, so let's not anticipate it." Later I understood that this occasion arose in connection with a proposal attributed to Negrín to send Indalecio Prieto to Mexico as ambassador. The President opposed it, "This must not happen. All the more because Prieto himself does not want it. Ah! This one I will not sign. Let them find a signature where they can. But to leave me without the one man I need in the emergency that will come, that I cannot accept. There are limits."

Negrín, however, proved the most cunning of the three, and he prudently refrained from presenting so unlikely an appointment for signature after word got out that the President would not accept it. The premier allowed time to pass, and in the end he gave Prieto a special mission to Chile and Mexico. The fallen minister accepted this more enthusiastically than the President, who saw himself and our republic thus deprived of needed counsel in any proximate emergency. "Goodbye Prieto," he seems to have said in parting, "until we meet again, wherever that may be." At that point Prieto, despite his pessimism about the war's outcome, hardly supposed that he would not have time to get back to Barcelona. It turned out that way, though. Instead he returned to Paris, as I said, during our residence at La Prasle. He made no effort to visit us. Perhaps he considered it indiscreet at a time when the former President notoriously wanted no involvement in the republic's political liquidation.

I believe, but am not sure, that the Permanent Committee of the Cortes had met in Paris before Prieto's arrival. At that meeting the *Pasionaria* attributed our loss of the war entirely to the President's defection, and no one protested. "After all," he later commented, "the *Pasionaria* merely played out her role." (More than once he had praised that woman to me, though he normally did not like political viragoes.) But Negrín had inexcusably gone along with the statement. And how about our friends? Among others, less important, Carlos Esplá and Fernández Clérigo, vice president of the Cortes, attended that session, and nobody, absolutely nobody, challenged the *Pasionaria*. After his friends had allowed this to happen through cowardly passivity, the President could only show his grievance by absolute disdain for anything his enemies might charge against him in his absence.

A definitive break between Prieto and Negrín came later. The former President heard an account of it that went more or less as follows. Negrín had given Prieto responsibility for depositing in Mexico money and valuables, the famous cargo of the *Vita,* a ship leased by Spain's government. The Mexican president, General Cárdenas, had agreed to admit those properties and securities without onerous customs payments. News of the republic's collapse had surprised Prieto in the United States after his return from Chile. There Fernando de los Ríos, our ambassador in Washington, D.C., had turned over to him some money collected in the United States to buy armament—I think it was an airplane. With this purchase nullified by the cessation of hostilities in our war, Ríos instructed Prieto to turn that money over to the Permanent Committee of the Spanish Cortes. At this point Prieto raised the question of gold deposited abroad by our republican government with the principal purpose of taking care of needy exiles. Negrín then asserted that he alone represented the government; he alone had authority to administer that national treasure. He would provide an accounting of his administration to the Cortes after the republic's restoration.

We heard later that Negrín had afterward proposed a junta or administrative committee to control those funds, with both himself and Prieto serving as members. Prieto, on the other hand, favored a committee on which neither he nor Negrín would serve. Finally they could reach no agreement. Two different juntas emerged in Paris, the SERE (*Servicio de Emigración de Refugiados Españoles* or Immigration Service for Spanish Refugees), or something like that, and the JARE (*Junta de Ayuda a los Republicanos Españoles* or Junta for the Assistance of Spanish Refugees). The worst of all possible solutions, it had inevitable repercussions. The whole discussion split our Popular Front coreligionists into factions according to the many different tendencies of various leaders. In the concentration camps each faction circulated scandal-mongering pamphlets condemning the others. All of this helped our conquerors by discrediting those of us who had left Spain, fleeing from barbaric enemy repression. The mere spectacle of haggling refugees in inhumane camps, however, did not seem the worst of it to the former President. He found far more demoralizing the evidence it provided of our apparent national incapacity even to live together; the anarchistic Spaniard did not seem adaptable to elemental norms of living with others.

Prieto indicated that he wanted my Brother-in-Law to come to Paris to work on this matter with the Permanent Committee of the Cortes. "I told him," the former President explained to me, "that I believe him entirely in the right in his debate with Negrín. I cannot, however, in any way and come what may, presume to decide so basic a disagreement after having resigned all responsibility along with the presidential office." Thus he turned his back on all of it and devoted himself to finishing up his *Memoirs of Politics and War* and the French translation of *Vigil in Benicarló.* Our good friend Jean Camp, who had collaborated with Jean Cassou on the French translation of *The Crown,* also did this book. I took great interest in this work, and it compensated me for so much bitterness and sorrow.

Accommodations at La Prasle, more than ample for my wife, myself, and the children, and which we had judged at least adequate for the interim residence of my Brother-in-Law, became very crowded with all the guests we finally had. Besides my brother, his wife, their little José Manuel, and my unmarried sister, the former President wanted people like Major Parra and Santos Martínez to stay with us until they had suitable employment or immigration arrangements. We had, altogether, thirty or thirty-two persons including kitchen and household staff, office personnel, and chauffeurs. Gradually they departed, heading for America as soon as we could arrange their embarkation. My brother, his wife, and child left with no other arrangements than residence in the so-called Spanish House in Mexico, which the Mexican government set up just before our war ended to assist refugees of some intellectual standing. In Mexico he could practice his profession as an oculist, and he could not in France. My sisters wanted to delay his departure, but it spurred my wife to anticipate our own trip to America. I felt much less convinced than she that we ought to immigrate because of my Brother-in-Law's great reluctance to go far from Spain. He had very good reasons not to even think of going back there. On the other hand, he did not want to go to Mexico, where he predicted with his usual foresight, before any evidence had yet appeared, that quarrels—more personal than anything else—would get worse between our immigrant compatriots.

He had made up his mind to settle in France, to use what funds he had to purchase property there, though we had scarcely enough money to sustain the unemployed extended family surrounding us. His sister and his invalid brother-in-law, with his five nieces and two great-nephews, had moved from Le Boulou to Montpellier where the former President and his wife visited them after they had settled in. He returned from this trip peevish and depressed. It made him unhappy to see his family suffering privations or even discomforts, and he helped them to the extent that he could, though without frills. This obligation he had assumed now became the greatest obstacle to our going to America. My sister had made up her mind to try our fortunes there—for better or for worse, and she felt very much aggrieved.

I could not arouse his interest in seeing Switzerland. Just one time he agreed to drive around Lake Léman. Apparently nature, which he so much enjoyed, had nothing to say to him in an Alpine dialect. He even seemed to resist undertaking the walks we had shared in our good days.

General Leopoldo Menéndez had gone from Valencia to Marseilles in the last days of republican resistance. From there he and a few other Spaniards had gone on to England, where they had stayed in private homes and so had not suffered much during their first days of exile. Menéndez did not have an opportunity to visit us on that journey through France. Now my Brother-in-Law got authorization for him to move into our Collonges house until his wife and daughters could leave Spain and join him to travel to America, as they did in a few months.

Menéndez's arrival renewed the former President's desire to know the full story of that Junta for the Defense of Madrid which had finally surrendered our republic to its enemies. Nothing our friend said changed my Kinsman's overall opinion about the political events that had ended Spain's uncivil war. Rather, Menéndez's account confirmed his opinion about the inefficacy and inexpedience of that tardy move. Menéndez said that he had first learned of the movement from a radio broadcast on March 5. Colonel Casado had telephoned him soon afterward to tell him about it. Our guest was surprised that the former President did not in any way approve of Casado's undertaking, remembering very well his belief that, since we could not win the war, we should settle it by compromise before we lost our opportunity to do even that. Explaining his position to our friend, my Kinsman's political argument proved, as always, irrefutable in its clarity and eloquence. He could not support Casado's decision in favor of another military rising against the government. Still less could he support Besteiro, who a few months earlier had rejected the President's suggestion that he take over in a legal way.

Other things that Menéndez told us about his war experiences moved the former President to ask him, as he kept asking Parra, to write down his memoirs. He later told me that they always answered, "We don't have the facts," as though he wanted a technical report. That kind of accounting seemed less important to my Brother-in-Law for future historians than the chance, anecdotal, eyewitness details that made those conversations so vivid.

When summer finally came, though it was chilly with intermittent showers, my Kinsman resumed his old habit of taking walks. He got tired of the car and the limitations its size imposed on our company. Now we had only his Ford, the gift of friends five years before, which I had used in Geneva. He had divested himself of the two magnificent official cars, the Hispano-Suiza and the Mercedes in which we had left Spain. He knew that owners had practically given away innumerable cars and trucks after they crossed the frontier, and he hoped to dispose of ours otherwise before the expiration of our permit to enter France, which allowed us to use them for transport without paying duty on them.

When the permit expired we had either to pay a very high fee or turn the cars over to France's government. The former President decided on the latter course and communicated his decision to the subprefect of Haute-Savoie. The subprefect, acting for his hierarchical superior, who had, no doubt, consulted the minister of finance and probably the premier, received the cars and informed Spain's consul in Lyons that he should come to take charge of them. In this way the presidential Mercedes and Hispano-Suiza returned, or must have returned, by way of French authorities to Spanish authorities. The subprefect gave me a receipt for their delivery, and in turn he got a receipt from the Spanish consul.

They handled the Prado masterpieces similarly. The League of Nations received them in perfect condition, saved from the horrible bombardments and vandalism of the Nationalists' terrible Cain-like victory. The League exhibited them, taking up the entire Geneva Museum, though Spain's new government did not much like this showing. Now nobody could ever charge that these paintings of Velázquez, Goya, Titian, and Rubens, which deserved their label "imperishable" as never before, had suffered damage at the hands of Reds. They failed to exhibit only one, Goya's painting of the executions of May 3. Rumor had it that authorities did not want to offend the French government, given the anti-Napoleonic feeling *El Sordo* had put into that painting. Ridiculous. They did not show the picture in question to prevent anyone from noticing the necessary restoration of its canvas, damaged by a bombardment as I have explained. M. Gielly, the museum's director, came with his wife to give the former President a special tour. He declined the invitation. After all, neither he nor any of our household wanted to vie with Alfonso XIII's visit to the gallery.

I have already said that the former President lived at this time in retirement from social intercourse. He did respond graciously to Guglielmo Ferrero's friendship and went to visit him in his home in Geneva, and he agreed to have dinner one night at the home of the Italian lawyer Reale who wanted him to meet two young French professors, his friends. We went a few times to A. Prato's house in Annemasse, and two or three times we had a meal with Fabela, Mexico's delegate. Mostly, though, we kept to a strictly family life, part of which included his reading from his *Memoirs* and *Vigil in Benicarló*, a real treat for us.

In our afternoon walks with Santos Martínez, Menéndez, and Parra, my Brother-in-Law talked about events near at hand and far ahead with his usual clear-sightedness. I especially remember his sad comment one day on a typical walk through that supremely peaceful countryside, in which he now felt more relaxed and began to take some pleasure. We spoke of the oxen and large horses they use for all of their field work, and we posed the question of the advantages or disadvantages of our Spanish custom of using mules for this kind of work. He went on, transcending agriculture, to the larger political and social order, excited as we had not seen him for some time. He concluded by adding that in his experience Spain's people themselves seemed like mules, intractable unless you hit them on the head with a stick, but afterward submitting to rougher work on poorer land. This made so painful an impression on those two faithful soldiers that they remained silent, not replying. I had to explain later, to make them understand that the former President's somewhat blunt statement meant neither contempt nor disdain, but a compassionate indignation for the plight of Spain's unfortunate people. On occasions like this he renounced Spaniards like a passionate lover who recognizes the hopelessness of his suit.

Another afternoon Parra had spoken somewhat lightly, though not unfairly, of the French people, saying that fascists surrounded us now as much as they had in Spain. The former President replied by giving a very clear exposition of the history of the French republic and what it meant. He traced through its story from Premier Gambetta's challenge to President MacMahon, "either submit or resign," down to M. Lebrun's recent reelection. If a stenographer had recorded his words, the text of that pleasant digression would have provided an invaluable lesson in contemporary history. He went on to say that our republic had collapsed because our people had lacked sufficient republican spirit to join together against Don Niceto when he dissolved the Cortes in 1933. If popular suffrage had faced Alcalá Zamora with the same Republican-Socialist coalition as before, he, like Mac-Mahon, would have had to submit or resign then, not three years later when he had done so much damage that it came too late. Appositely he quoted Don Amadeo's saying when he left the Spanish throne, "This country is ungovernable."

In August our good friend Carlos Montilla came to visit us. He had married a second time during the war, and after representing our republic in Belgrade and Havana he had returned from America to France intending, among other things, to visit the former President. In requesting this visit he had used as his main pretext the delightful excuse of introducing us to his wife, a charming lady, granddaughter of the famous duke of Rivas. My Brother-in-Law felt resentment toward Montilla; and, though it had somewhat abated, he expressed it to me without excuses or euphemisms. He had not approved of the Junta for the National Artistic Treasury, principally devoted to seizure of private property during our civil war's first months, and Montilla had served as its president. Then, having made sarcastic jokes in a newspaper under the heading "Society Notes" about the more or less open flight of many republicans from their wartime responsibilities at home, he had himself accepted a diplomatic post abroad. Furthermore, he had departed for that post without taking leave of the President, a personal friend who had signed his nomination.

Still, Montilla had an irresistible, delightful exuberance, and my Kinsman gave in even before he saw him again. It also helped that, with great elegance of spirit, Montilla refrained from making his excuses right away. Though he did not go into details, we eventually learned of his absurd mistreatment by the famous Uncontrollables functioning more or less legally as police. His wife and a son of her first marriage had suffered similarly in the war's first days when some people called them fascists merely because they belonged to a family from a social class that, in turn, considered them traitors because they did not support the insurrection.

The couple came to spend a day at La Prasle, and the amiable charm and delightful manners of Conchita Ximénez de Sandoval won us all, combined with her grace, enthusiasm, exquisite wit, and her early autumnal beauty that had conquered Montilla. He proved as expansive as ever and even more typically Navarrese than in better days when he had fervently supported the President as a charter member of Republican Action. My wife and I felt particularly grateful to him for his earlier deferential treatment of my mother-in-law, taking her with him to Belgrade. My brother-in-law, Diego de Mesa, went along and served as the legation's secretary until he and Montilla's stepson returned to Spain to fulfill their military responsibilities.

In an inevitably political conversation, however, along with many amicable comments, our friend got carried away. He went so far as to suggest that the former President might have shirked some of his own political responsibilities in wartime leadership, or, more exactly, in heading our government during the conflict that had ended so disastrously for us. My Brother-in-Law defended himself, first exalted and then irritated to the point of intemperance. A friend and admirer of Prieto, Montilla felt almost as much loyalty to him as to my Brother-in-Law, and the famous Socialist minister was ill-informed about the true course of events because of his absence from Spain. Indeed, the general public in Spain had not always understood governmental developments. Montilla, also ill-informed about the real course of events during our war, blamed Prieto's failure and that of the republic on the President's ill will toward his Socialist colleague. The President took Montilla's complaint, echoing Indalecio Prieto's, as a censure of his own presidential attitudes. My Kinsman had always held to the regime's basic principles, acting as faithful agent of the national will that could express itself only through the voters and was indicated by their representatives in the Cortes.

The former President, as I said, rebutted Montilla by attacking Prieto, though not as Negrín and the Communists had for having lost the war through demoralizing "pessimism"—something finally impossible to prove. Rather, he blamed Prieto chiefly for irresolution in yielding to his Socialist colleagues' senseless veto right after the 1936 elections when, as President of the republic, he had wanted Prieto to become premier. On this point my Brother-in-Law refused to budge an inch, and he spoke of it to me repeatedly both before and after this incident; so in repeating it here I go beyond an episode in my chronicle and set forth his incontrovertible doctrine about good republican politics. He felt that an implicit pact had existed between himself and Prieto. He thought of it as a matter of friendly understanding, though Araquistáin malevolently spread word that there was a formal agreement. The pact ensued from the Socialist leader's proposal of my Brother-in-Law as candidate for the republic's presidency. He would under no circumstances have accepted that nomination without the understanding that Prieto would preside over the cabinet and an indispensable Republican-Socialist coalition. Perhaps Prieto as premier could not have avoided the insurrection; he might even have provoked it. As premier, however, he would have strangled it at birth.

Certainly the Popular Front had not demonstrated any outstanding capacity to govern in the few months between its triumph in February's elections and the presidential election of May 1936. On the other hand, men who called themselves defenders of social order had spent that same period in plotting the events that swept us into war, and they, not the government, bore the terrible guilt for our war's revolutionary chaos. Without their plotting, members of the parliamentary Right would certainly have played a legitimate political role and resisted temptations to resort to dissolving the Cortes in the tradition of Don Niceto's ominous rule. If they had played this role, given the small numerical difference between the two antagonistic parliamentary blocs, we could have experimented with various coalitions toward establishing a cabinet that broke down the rigidity of leftist alliances and rightist groups. Thus we could have established power in the hands of representatives dedicated to compromise between the opposite poles of our national political life.

The former President felt that no man could so effectively as Prieto have headed that kind of Republican cabinet. No principle stood in his way, and, whether he served as premier or not, he would have brought in Socialist ministers. Prieto might have guided opposing factions in the Cortes toward some truly national—Spanish—consensus better than anyone else because the Rightists, with no comparable unifying leader of their own to offer, feared and respected him. Instead, Prieto had held closely to a narrow concept of party discipline, something he could no longer enforce once war had overwhelmed the fragile structure of national unity that our republic had tried to build.

Just as the former President refused to accept major responsibility for our recent past, so he now rejected no less violently Montilla's insistence on his reentering political life in the more or less proximate future. He did not foresee that possibility for a long time. Spain had now retreated into a period comparable to the reactionary era of Ferdinand VII, and he regarded any talk of restoring a constitutional republic as wasted effort. After all, he and his former associates couldn't actually do anything along those lines. Ah, but if some sad day, neither foreseeable nor probable, someone thought of asking him again, he would come to the Pyrenees and shout back "Imbecile!"

This explosion of indignation, the product of his deep sorrow, cleared the charged atmosphere of that heated discussion. Montilla, despite his indomitable optimism and efforts at encouragement, could not even sound the depths of depression that the war's boundless horror had caused in our Friend's spirit. Yet Montilla, by challenging the President's reasoning and his exalted protest, did, somehow, release his spirit that had until then been weighed down by his characteristic dialectical pondering.

A few days after the Montillas' visit, my wife had a sudden appendicitis attack requiring an emergency operation in a Geneva clinic to save her life. In that crisis family feeling overcame the anguish in which we lived. Again,

I felt my Brother-in-Law's inexhaustible generosity in his steadfast companionship sharing my agony.

Once the doctors had saved that precious life, inseparable from my own, and we had returned to our normal routine, the former President began again to think of looking for a house that would better suit our needs and his tastes than La Prasle. We made several trips without finding anything satisfactory. On one of them we found a real palace near Poitiers at not too bad a price, though in very bad condition. It had an extensive garden, woods, and a meadow going down to a river bank. My Brother-in-Law felt more enthusiastic about it than my sister, who saw in its seclusion disadvantages for a person accustomed to city life. The agent, very solicitous at first, backed off afterward; we believed that this resulted from his realizing the buyer's identity. We began to discern something we would never have suspected in our ingenuous admiration for all things French: a disposition to reaction had grown up in France in the past twenty-five years, a national craving for luxury that conflicted with the Revolution's liberal tradition.

Sympathy offered us by an old, retired schoolteacher in Collonges did not suffice to restore our illusions. One day, meeting us in the street, she detained us and spoke very graciously, "Mr. President, allow me to welcome you and thank you for honoring the soil of France with your presence. Are you happy here? I assure you that you have the hearts of all good French people with you." She lived on as a survivor of the last generation of the France of "Liberty, Fraternity, and Equality." She embodied the republican spirit my Kinsman had admired in Paris during his youth and discovered in his reading of Rousseau.

After searching in our environs and writing to a few agents, my Brother-in-Law changed his mind and considered buying La Prasle. Its owner, an able businesswoman with characteristic French bourgeois pedantry—and furthermore she boasted of Parisian origins—succeeded in convincing him in the course of a visit that he would make an excellent deal in this purchase. He had come to the point of signing a contract when the long-expected declaration of war halted these negotiations. The prefect of Haute-Savoie warned us that we ought to leave that region. If Italy invaded France or Germany invaded Switzerland—both foreseen possibilities—the government would evacuate the civilian population. We did not find it easy, though, to start all over looking for the right house. On trips to Limoges and to Guéret I found two or three large country houses, but in the end they did not suit us. The President now found it as hard to change his mind about buying La Prasle as he had originally found it hard to decide in its favor. He continued to think about tearing down and reconstructing that refuge in Collonges he had at first considered unsatisfactory. Undeniably, however, we ran a risk there of finding ourselves dispossessed at any minute.

Though we expected it, war came as a surprise, and it no longer brought compensating hopes of salvation in our own war. *"C'est la guerre!"* Carlitos had boisterously announced coming into the house, repeating what he had just heard outside among French people gathered around a proclamation calling up French soldiers to active duty. Unlike their enthusiasm in 1914 Frenchmen received these orders with a seriousness that seemed intelligent and based on their experience. Mobilization took place without fuss, without vibrant hymns, and, when all is said and done, without ardor. We wondered among ourselves whether these might prove signals of defeat.

The Germans burst into Poland; Warsaw's fall a few days later with hardly any resistance caused Colonel Parra, my sister, and especially me to extol in a fervent posthumous eulogy the people of Madrid's heroism year after year. The President did not refute us, but, typically, he showed greater caution in dithyramb and abuse. We waited for the first French action, and when it appeared that their army had left the Maginot Line to attack the Siegfried Line he did go so far as to prophesy, looking backward, "Let's see whether they will make a classic entrance into Germany through the Palatinate." He anticipated France's declaration of war on Italy, her sending troops through the lower Alps into Austria in the Napoleonic pattern—supposedly General Gamelin's plan.

One afternoon, after our now daily visits to a dentist in Annemasse, we prolonged our trip to call on our friend A. Prato. The President commented to him in passing, concerning the increasingly disturbing news about the USSR, "We will see Russians in Zurich yet. History is repeating itself in many ways."

My wife's mother and sisters had no time to say goodbye except by a letter announcing their unexpected departure for Mexico.

At this point we heard from Montilla. Foreseeing the war, he had moved from Paris to Arcachon, and he wrote to say that another house for rent near his own seemed very suitable for us. The former President decided one fine day that he and I would go to investigate its possibilities. It was now mid-October.

48

The Spell of *Fresdeval*

We did not travel by automobile, for it had become difficult in those days to get gasoline and permission to travel France's highways. Also because of the war, our train had no sleeping cars. We made the trip in two stages, from morning to noon as far as Lyons and overnight from there to Bordeaux and Arcachon. We had enough stopover in Lyons to eat and spend most of an afternoon on a café terrace. Many people passing by recognized my Brother-in-Law, at least with sympathetic curiosity and most of them with obvious respect.

Our nocturnal journey seemed the counterpart to another train trip that we took twenty years before—a long time before—from Paris to Strasbourg. As then, some soldiers invaded our compartment, but, though we again sacrificed our comfort to give them room, these men provided us with considerably less diversion. Circumstances had changed greatly. On that distant occasion we shared a journey of victory with other soldiers, they to mount guard on the Rhine and we to attend the inauguration of the French university in Alsace's capital. Now these soldiers were joining the ranks for a wretched war from which we had already returned, our battle lost. Yet these fledgling combatants did not provide us with the comradeship we deserved as allies against a common enemy. These men came through our compartment door with a hostile insolence far different from the amiability and easy camaraderie of those simple soldiers in the year of victory. At first they hardly paid attention to us. When they realized our Spanish nationality, without ascertaining the position and identity of their traveling companion, they made it manifest that they shared the general feeling of Frenchmen in that deplorable era. They regarded us as intruders who intended to live at their expense.

At daybreak, as twenty years before, I felt a bridge trembling, now as we crossed the Garonne and entered Bordeaux. We had only enough time there to catch our train for the short trip to Arcachon, where we arrived early enough for breakfast. Montilla's eldest stepson met us at the station with a real estate agent who dealt in city properties. The latter said that, as a good Radical Socialist candidate for the council of his municipal district, he felt very sympathetic to our cause and regretted our loss. They took us in his

374

Citroën to Montilla's place in Le Moulleau, a settlement along the highway leading to the famous dunes ten kilometers from Arcachon.

We went at once with the Montillas, just out of bed, to look at the house they had written about and reserved for the former President. Though it entirely conformed to what they had said about it, I later understood that it did not really suit my Brother-in-Law. Also, in talking with the agent we learned that very complicated conditions governed its rental. We had a meal with our friends, and afterwards another compatriot and his wife came for coffee. One of the few career diplomats who had remained entirely true to the republic, he had served as our wartime ambassador to Ankara. His wife offered at once to help Mrs. Montilla and the agent, whose wife proved an efficacious collaborator, in searching for another house. The mild climate charmed us, and the peaceful atmosphere of that fragrant countryside gave us a sense of pleasant restfulness. With its country-style buildings, neat and comfortable, standing separate and surrounded by gardens, the settlement had a most attractive appearance of civilized rusticity. We had a short walk on the extensive beach, and we went to bed soon after dinner. The Montillas did not have room for us in a house barely large enough for them and their three sons, so we stayed in very comfortable lodgings rented by the agent and his wife in their home.

Coming as we had from the early winter of Haute-Savoie, already white with its first snow, Arcachon's autumnal mildness, the waters of its bay reflecting a blue sky, filled our hearts with contentment. We hated to leave the place. Yet, hearing my Brother-in-Law speak of Arcachon's delightful climate, it seemed to me that the company and talk it afforded pleased him more than its light and warmth. Often in Madrid's cloudless winters he had missed the overcast skies of Paris. He became more talkative that first day and during the time we spent there than I had seen him since we left Spain eight months before. Certainly it did seem curious, as he pointed out to me, that for a long time past he had not stayed more than eight months in the same place, and he counted over his life in eight-month spans: Valencia, Barcelona, Collonges.

Though not early, we did get up earlier the next day than we usually did at home. Right after breakfast we went out to walk along a highway that led to the dunes, up and down crossing streets from pine forest to beach and back. About an hour later we turned around as dinnertime approached. After a while we passed a house that stood out from its neighbors and attracted our attention and our desire. We looked at each other, but, at first, repressed the same thought; then we said simultaneously how much we admired it. Unfortunately, it also seemed beyond the former President's means and plans, a far finer residence than he had in mind. On the road we met the diplomat's wife, hurrying to tell us that she had heard of a house that would, beyond a doubt, suit us. She pointed to the one we had just discovered.

Now no other could satisfy him. It was located near the road, halfway between Arcachon and the great sand dune. With pine woods behind, it faced the beach, the bay's mouth, and open sea. If it had a less extensive garden than others nearby, still a sufficient distance separated it from neighboring houses. "Eden," for the house had that name, offered us the worthiest, pleasantest refuge we had seen up to then. Of course, the former President found its name overly paradisiacal. Two old ladies, mother and daughter, lived there as charity guardians, interim mistresses whom the owner allowed to use the lower floor, kitchen, and servants' quarters until his property was sold. Showing us through the house, they made it clear that we could not rent it. They also assured us that a recent government decree prevented their eviction for the war's duration. The agent thought otherwise, and, in view of his Guest's strong interest, he offered to leave for Paris that very night to try to consult the owner about the exact terms of sale.

Casting up his accounts, my Brother-in-Law came to the conclusion that he could not make better use of his francs, given wartime depreciation, than to buy that house. Though he did not hesitate about putting all his money into an estate whose value must increase with time, he did feel concern about venturing everything in one single undertaking, given the uncertain times. I urged him not to hesitate about that; my sister Adelaida would gladly give him what he needed. She would buy Eden. In doing it she would make a good investment of her money, and in providing him and his wife with a suitable place to live she would reciprocate the fraternal familiarity with which they had always treated her.

No sooner said than done. We stayed on a few days longer than we had intended, waiting for the agent's return from Paris. That also gave us time to look for another villa in Arcachon itself for his sister, brother-in-law, and nieces. Thus they could live nearby and still have independence in their own home, something more comfortable for all of us with so large a family. Also, the paralysis that now afflicted his brother-in-law required more time for rest than seemed possible if we all lived together as guests of the former President.

During our days of waiting an old friend, Garciá Miranda, turned up. A career diplomat, he and his very pleasant Argentinean wife had visited us recently in Collonges. Now, influenced like us by Montilla's propagandizing about Arcachon, they had come down from Paris to look for a safe asylum from the first German bombardments. After they went back to Paris, however, they could not return to Arcachon because French officials refused them safe-conducts and travel permits. Franco's ambassador had begun his machinations.

Every day, and sometimes twice a day until the agent returned, my Brother-in-Law and I went through the house from top to bottom. Pleased as a boy with new shoes, he planned how we might arrange things most comfortably.

We would have to give our home a new name; he could not live, he laughed saying it to me, in a house called Eden. Of course, I agreed, and then suggested one that might suit him. Call the house "Fresdeval" because here he would finish the novel he had begun so many years before; I felt determined that he should continue it, as with *The Friars' Garden* twenty years earlier. He protested. Not "Fresdeval." It seemed a bad omen. He did not believe in spells, but no use asking for trouble. I, in turn, protested against his protest. Certainly events had interrupted the writing of *Fresdeval* several times since he began it, but not always unfortunate events. The first interruption came on April 14 when, hearing of the republic's proclamation, he had said to me with a sincerity that had seemed comical in its disproportion to that event, "What a shame! Another month and I would have finished my novel." He had turned to it again when he left the government at the end of 1933. The crisis of autumn 1934 surprised him while absorbed in his writing, and obliged him to abandon his book again. After his release from imprisonment on the ship, he committed himself entirely to political writing—which carried him from the Field of Comillas to the premiership and our republic's presidency.

Resting after many hectic months, he had again taken up *Fresdeval* in La Quinta's restful surroundings at the Pardo when on July 18 the terrible shock of military rebellion and war again altered his literary plans. He put away the novel to work on *Vigil in Benicarló* and his *Political Memoirs*. Certainly he had suffered bad luck in their publication; *Vigil* had appeared in its French edition on the very day when France declared war on Germany, momentarily distracting readers' curiosity about literature. Official censorship aggravated the situation; fearful of the political comment that might appear in connection with reviews of this book the censor prohibited any published commentary. Nevertheless the French edition had sold out in less than a year. "No," he said, "we must find another name. Not 'Fresdeval.' No."

When we returned to La Prasle from Arcachon we began at once to prepare for our move, a major undertaking because of all our baggage—especially books. My Brother-in-Law and sisters went on ahead; my wife, children, and I stayed behind to finish up in Collonges. My wife and I bade farewell to that house with some sadness. After all, its ancient walls had provided us with shelter and some quiet hours in our hectic life during the past few years. What did destiny hold for us in Eden? I highly praised to her the incomparable pleasantness of the Atlantic coast in that region so close to Spain's Bay of Biscay, now calling us with such fatal attraction.

"Well," the former President had said to me, "I don't believe that Franco will come to look for us in Bordeaux." I had picked up on it and made it a joke. It very well suited our conquerors to see us out of the country, and they would lend wings to our departure from Spain rather than have us there as martyrs. It made too much sense to be valid. "I don't know. I don't know," he had said, shaking his head as if in doubt. That indelible village skepticism was one of the deepest roots in his "doubting" character, as he called it, laughing at himself and using the peasant word that expressed it best. I didn't have to urge him long to abandon his foolishness. Of course Franco would come into France looking for us, just like that, and of course the French would let him take us back to Spain!

When we arrived at Eden with the children, I noticed that the former President seemed somewhat fatigued. A lot of it came from the laborious task he had undertaken of single-handedly and one by one arranging all the books of his library. He had not found it much of a chore to shelve those belonging in his office on the first floor. Most of his books, unfortunately, belonged upstairs. Opening box after box and carrying them up wore him out, but he would not let me take over. He had to decide himself how to classify each volume and where to put it on the shelves. This library had its own history of adventures and travels. When he left his calle de Serrano flat, he had stored it in the basement of a friend's bookstore on one of the fashionable streets off the Plaza de Isabel II. By fortunate chance his own books survived a fire in that depository, which did not leave the shopkeeper so well off. After that the President's library had traveled in two or three return trips from Madrid to Valencia in trucks that had brought supplies to members of the presidential staff remaining in the palace to perform duties that could not be transferred. Later my Brother-in-Law moved his books with his household furniture to his sister's home in France, where he picked them up during his exile.

His furniture had an even more extraordinary adventure in the first period of our war. When he left his flat, with no question of moving household goods into the palace, a personal friend, minister of a Central American republic, had offered to store them in the legation. During the minister's absence an indiscreet secretary allowed refugees to move into that building. Against all legal precedents, such persons occupied many of Madrid's embassies. An amazed Santos Martínez, then presidential secretary, discovered these precursors of the Fifth Column sitting on the President's armchairs and lying on his sofas. Santos told me with a grin about his forced invasion of the embassy accompanied by enough moving men to carry away this furniture, actually displacing those interlopers, who never realized its owner's identity. My Brother-in-Law always lamented his loss in that storage, no doubt through theft, of valuable paintings he had bought at an exhibit of Japanese pictures held in Madrid shortly before the war. Little did the former President suspect the futility of his efforts to save books, goods, and chattels from our uncivil war. At the hands of German soldiers and Franco's police this property finally did suffer the fate he had tried to avoid.

Santos Martínez left for Mexico before we had completely settled into our new house. Every day the President kept urging him to go, but the separation cost Santos tears. After all, my kinsman could not ask our friend to sacrifice his youth in the service of someone who could no longer pay a salary. A private secretary, however low his pay, represented a luxury beyond our resources. In any case, except during his terms of government service, he had never needed help to manage his correspondence. Our unforgettable and faithful friend Major Parra also had felt obliged to leave us a little earlier, heading for Argentina. With the official chauffeurs gone, there remained only one chauffeur who drove our own Ford, Epifanio our cook, and an old maidservant who had left her only daughter in Spain and wanted to return as soon as possible.

Santos had come back indignant from a trip to Paris to make arrangements for his journey. He had applied to the assistance agencies as an employee of the Public Works Department. People at both SERE and JARE had told him, "The President can pay for it." Clearly administrators of those offices had no use for anyone even remotely connected with the presidential household—though one of the official chauffeurs did finally get passage money to Chile. General Menéndez got to Colombia through a generous friend who sent money for his voyage from there. Saravia and his large family had a miserable time in a small town near Marseilles where they settled. His son-in-law, a career officer who had served us alongside his father-in-law, had much to fear from returning to Spain in spite of close family connections among the conquerors. Still, he finally preferred to return with his wife and small son rather than to suffer the dreadful hardship of destitution in France with no assistance at all.

Early in February the President had to stay in bed for a day or two suffering from a bad cold. My sister and I attributed it to his insistence on working in his study, reading and writing, without sufficient heat. We found a major disadvantage of our new house in the high cost of heating it, given wartime escalation of the price of coal. He would not agree to call a doctor, and so for several days more he was up and down fighting what we considered a lingering case of flu.

We had recently received copies of *Vigil in Benicarló* published in Buenos Aires in Spanish at the same time the French edition came out in Paris. The publisher sent only two copies by airmail. The Author kept these for himself; others coming by ship he would distribute to friends. He also wanted to establish a depository near the Spanish frontier from which it might be sold. Later a Portuguese bookseller wrote to us to arrange this, but we could not reach an agreement because of increased wartime censorship of international mail. We knew from unfavorable reviews that many friends did not like the book. They felt that the former President had acted prematurely in expressing his judgment so frankly about events connected with the republic's fall. Even dramatized as a dialogue, his statement came through crystal clear. We heard only indirectly of adverse reviews by anarchist writers, but we sometimes talked about them at mealtime.

Antonio Lot, the President's faithful valet, heard these comments. Learning of Antonio's struggles with the French version, which he had bought, my Brother-in-Law offered to lend him one of the Spanish copies. The boy devoured it during his own convalescence from a bad case of flu that had begun to worry us. When I asked whether he liked it, he answered, yes, very much, and so had a Spanish friend in Arcachon, apparently a shoemaker. Emphasizing his point, he said, "And they say some people don't like this book? Those must be ministers." That pleased the President exceedingly.

About this time I heard from Sánchez Albornoz, a fellow member of Republican Action and the republic's last ambassador to Portugal; he wanted to come to pay his respects to his old friend the former President. My Brother-in-Law had criticized him as "the adrift minister" in 1933 because he had accepted a post in Lerroux's first cabinet while en route from Buenos Aires without consulting his own party's leadership. After his embassy in Lisbon, where he had gone in 1936, ended with the first incidents that led to our break in diplomatic relations with Portugal, Sánchez Albornoz had not returned to Spain. Settling in France, he had repeatedly written to the President who had not answered his letters. Writing to a mutual friend, Sánchez Albornoz could think of no better explanation for that silence than some kind of interception or interference with the mail. "That's not it," the President said to Amós Salvador to pass on. "I have nothing to say to people like him who lack the common courtesy and respect for protocol to come and report to me when their embassy ends." In fact, the former ambassador's behavior annoyed my Kinsman for various reasons, and it always bothered him when a Left Republican emigrated. Sánchez Albornoz did finally visit my Brother-in-Law in Valencia when he came back to pick up his last salary payment for his service in Lisbon. Then the President spoke severely to him, and not much enthusiasm remained for maintaining their old friendship.

About the middle of our war Sánchez Albornoz went to Cuba to give a series of lectures at the university as professor of medieval history. His visit coincided with April 14, and he refused to participate in the embassy's commemoration of that republican anniversary organized by Spain's representative in Havana. Carlos Montilla, our chargé d'affaires in Havana at that time, remembered this and confronted the professor with it when he came to visit us in Arcachon. My Brother-in-Law had not wanted to receive him, but Sánchez Albornoz had insisted. After all, he lived in Bordeaux, where the university had granted him a small sinecure, and there seemed no point in perpetuating a quarrel.

The former President did complain, though, when, after his establishment in Eden, Indalecio Prieto failed to come over from Bordeaux to say goodbye before he embarked for Mexico. He merely sent a police commissioner, one of his friends, to make his excuses for not coming in spite of being so close. He explained it by the pressures connected with his journey.

Sánchez Albornoz appeared at our house accompanied by an attractive young woman who drove him in her car. The professor introduced her as his fiancée without further comment. An unpleasant incident soon occurred while my sister served us tea and pastries. The young lady from Bordeaux made a denigrating comment about Spanish emigrés, saying that they had greatly prejudiced French opinion against our republic. She had seen some lower-class women taking out from under their large breasts, ill-concealed by sleeveless blouses, valuable ornaments that they offered for sale very cheap. No doubt they had stolen them. My sister could not contain her indignation and answered our indiscreet visitor justly. She did not deny that some thieves may have come along with many worthy Spaniards like ourselves, forced to settle on French soil. She had, however, seen with her own eyes the spectacle of French policemen plundering unfortunate, frightened Spaniards at the frontier, taking even their watches for a few francs. From a window in her home in Le Boulou, our sister Adela had seen French officials in the concentration camp there burning pitiful bundles belonging to immigrants, against possible contagion.

Our friend proved no more discreet than his companion, and the President replied vigorously, speaking in Spanish with a vehemence we had not heard for a long time. He seemed to forget that the vivacious and importunate young Frenchwoman did not know our language. It pleased the rest of us to see him excited in this way, not just speaking in his usual, calm, resigned tone. "Is it true," Sánchez Albornoz asked him, "that at the start of the war Martínez Barrio resigned right after his nomination as premier because he telephoned to General Mola and the general refused to talk with him?" My Brother-in-Law had heard this rumor before. He asserted that Martínez Barrio had not mentioned it to him at the time and that nobody since then had said anything to convince him that it had happened.

As to General Goded's having approached the President to warn him of what might occur, he roundly denied that, though he had not taken the trouble to make a public denial of an article published in a French periodical by the general's supposed envoy. Through her husband, Enrique de Mesa, my mother-in-law knew this envoy, a Castilian nobleman and well-known journalist. She had facilitated that interview with the President, but once in the presidential office the man had merely indicated that General Goded would like to see him. My Brother-in-Law had answered that Goded could see him whenever he liked. He need only ask for some kind of furlough from his command in Majorca to come to Madrid, using some regular procedure, for instance emergency leave. The President assured the emissary that our minister of war would grant it immediately. Once in Madrid, whatever his pretext, he not only might, but normally ought to call at the presidential office. On the other hand, there seemed no reason to summon him to Madrid in some special way. Perhaps the general, already solicited by his comrades but holding back, intended this approach through an emissary as a kind of trial, insinuating something that he never actually said. In fact, though, nobody had either said or done anything more.

Finally, Sánchez Albornoz suggested the image of the President as prisoner of his own government. That business really got my Brother-in-Law stirred up, especially when someone asserted it openly as Sánchez Albornoz did. "No, my friend, no. I have never been a prisoner except of my duty. I have never shirked that; others with as much responsibility as mine to defend our republic have turned their backs on duty. Did the war bring excesses and crimes that I hated? Certainly, of course. Ah well, but the blame for them in no way falls on me or on republicans; Franco and his accomplices must bear that charge. I had the responsibility, I emphasize that, to remain at my post as long as my presence served any useful purpose. It was not my fault that I believed we had lost the war. We lost it, as you know, because of France and England. You already know my opinion. Time will judge us all."

Days passed, and my Brother-in-Law's cold, persistent and neglected, became worse instead of improving as we had expected. One afternoon he had to come back home as soon as he arrived at the Montillas' house, afflicated by a sudden pain that left him short of breath. This alarmed us very much. Miguel Salvador, Amós's brother, had settled in the region about two months before with his second wife and son. They and the Montillas feared on the basis of those symptoms that he had cancer.

I could not help remembering his obsession. A few days earlier he had enthusiastically read a chapter of *Fresdeval* to Montilla and me. He had begun to work on it again with a strong will and zest.

49

Dr. Monod's Verdict

I used the excuse of Antonio's illness, now abating, to arrange for a doctor to examine the former President. Though my Brother-in-Law agreed to see the doctor, he made excuses for bothering him about something not really serious. I think in the depths of his soul he was afraid and hoped that his pains and difficulties would go away if he ignored them. It particularly alarmed me that he felt soreness in the upper part of his chest, near his neck, when he leaned back in an armchair. At first the doctor seemed overly serious, but he became very friendly after the examination. When my Brother-in-Law learned that Dr. Monod belonged to a famous Huguenot family, he talked with him for a long time, proud and enthusiastic in his familiarity with everything French.

Dr. Monod finished his first call without making any apparent diagnosis. As he left, though, with professional urgency he asked me to come with him in his car, which he drove himself, to fill at the pharmacy a prescription he had just written. I got the impression that he wanted to say something more than he had said to my sister.

"Haven't you noticed any alarming symptoms before?" he asked as soon as the door had shut. Faced with this revelatory question I could only answer with the exculpatory forcefulness that fear gives to people whom misfortune has prepared to face an inescapable surprise. We had noticed nothing until the recent illness that had caused us to call him. On the basis of his preliminary examination with a stethoscope, the doctor judged that my Brother-in-Law had a very serious lesion of the heart. He could diagnose with some assurance a very dilated aorta and heart, probably years in developing. I answered that, until the last few days, he had pursued his usual way of life, including renewal of long walks with me. We had gone the ten kilometers between our house and Arcachon's center, and, if he had tired somewhat, that had not seemed strange, given the long time since we had taken that kind of exercise. Certainly, I now realized that in Collonges he had preferred flat roads to climbing mountains, but, as I shared his preference, it had not seemed strange to me. Doctor Monod put off a final diagnosis until he could consult a specialist friend from the Faculty of Paris, whom he expected soon during the traditional French Easter vacation.

Though he had prescribed the greatest possible quiet, the doctor did allow my Kinsman to travel by car to that consultation. The specialist had prepared for an X-ray in a sanatorium headed by Dr. Monod in a half-century-old villa in the so-called Winter City on heights above Arcachon. Nearby a plaque commemorated an "interview" between Archduchess María Cristina of Hapsburg-Lorraine and King Alfonso XII of Spain, a prelude to the official engagement and marriage that brought to the throne our future queen regent. In spite of our care, my Kinsman got somewhat tired going up and down the few stairs from his bedroom to the hall at Eden and taking a few steps in the gardens of our house and the sanatorium. He did not seem to make much of the consultation; maybe he wanted to believe that just leaving home and going through the X-ray treatment would spare him anything serious, not to say desperate.

The Paris specialist confirmed Dr. Monod's diagnosis, and I found it very hard to hide the truth from the Patient with some pretense that seemed unworthy of our fraternal friendship. That the shadow of death should lie between us without our daring to face it as we had confronted life seemed to me abject surrender to general human cowardice. Refusing to think about life's ending seemed to limit consciousness itself. I spoke plainly to my sister Adelaida and to my wife. The President's wife, "the little one" as my father used to call her, settled down with the same courage she had shown in recent years. She resisted the fatal evidence and turned to nurturing the life that lay in her hands, hiding hopelessness in an attitude of maternal tenderness. In one night I wept out my impotent bitterness and resolved to contribute, at least with strength of spirit, to lessening the imminent danger. Convinced after a few days of the seriousness of his infirmity, the Patient helped us very much. He could hardly misread his fatigue and suffering, as he was unable even to sleep in a completely supine position, or the doctor's strict orders, which he followed exactly by keeping completely quiet in his second-floor bedroom, hardly talking or moving in bed.

Reading helped him to endure the need not to talk. I read aloud to him because it fatigued him even to do that, and in necessary breaks, which we tried to keep brief, Miguel Salvador or Montilla took my place. With the pretext of amusing them, though it afforded him as much or more pleasure than it did our friends, he told me to choose some of his own humorous articles from volumes of *La Pluma*. These even brought a grin to his face. One of them had enjoyed considerable popularity among our friends eighteen years before. He had written, with prodigious foresight, of Don Niceto the Ancient and a great Battle of Carabanchel against Arab invaders. A humorous allusion to Spain's 1921 defeat at Anual—back then it had seemed farcical nonsense. Certainly more than once during his service as minister and premier under that same Don Niceto Alcalá Zamora we had commented on the danger of someone discovering, resurrecting, and republishing it in a magazine. It would have caused embarrassment, to say the least, as that article made specific fun of Don Niceto's garrulous speechifying. We need not have worried. The absolute poverty of Spanish literary life saved us. Publications of a certain intellectual caliber had few readers, so that not many people would remember the article, even in an anecdotal way, to take advantage of that opportunity.

Other times he asked for readings from his favorite books, usually from Cervantes. Sometimes his wife relieved me. It always pleased her to read to him in spite of the occasion. It gratified both her and me to see his tremendous enjoyment right from the beginning of some passage of *Don Quixote* or having me repeat a page from the *Colloquy of Dogs.* Knowing how much he enjoyed everything French, I tried more than once to read from some old favorite or something new in that language, but he always stopped me right away. He did not like hearing French pronounced without the euphonious inflections of the Parisian accent, and I could never really manage that despite my efforts. It seemed somewhat like his later feelings about the theater, which he used to enjoy so much: it could no longer measure up to his ideals.

During recent years, even during our war, he had found delight in reading the volumes of Jules Romains's series, *Men of Good Will,* as they appeared; some of them he reread with enjoyment. He recommended Dr. Axel Munthe's *The Story of San Michele* as having relieved his boredom during his inactive exile in La Pobleta. This famous Swedish doctor, after living many years in Paris, had retired to Capri, where he built a pleasant residence on the ruins of the Roman Emperor Tiberius's palace. Though he enjoyed memoirs—far more than he did the novelized biographies fashionable at that time—he did not like André Gide's *Diaries,* which came out immediately prior to the war. Literary cynicism did not appeal to him.

After a few days Dr. Monod agreed that my Brother-in-Law could see another specialist in Bordeaux, recommended by the oculist to whom I took my third son. This new diagnostician gave us no more comfort than the first doctor or the professor from Paris. On the contrary, he increased our fears. He told us that, though the former President might live a few years longer if no complications arose, we must always avoid emotional upset. That would probably prove fatal.

In Dr. Monod's considered opinion, so serious a lesion could not have developed in a short period of time. Nonetheless, when I went over the unfortunate events of my Brother-in-Law's recent life and above all his terrible anguish over his responsibilities and frustrations, the doctor agreed that in an extremely sensitive man who kept strict control of his feelings, this tormented restraint might do the damage of years in a short period. The President's prediction impressed Dr. Monod, his saying in his first wartime speech in Valencia, "My heart will break, and nobody will every know how much I have suffered for Spain's freedom." The doctor said, "Well, there is no better diagnosis than that. He has exactly that, a broken heart." He had

what the French call a *coeur de boeuf* (literally "bull's heart," a greatly
enlarged heart). Dr. Monod showed me with his hands what the first stereo-
scopic examination and the later X-rays had discovered—how greatly dis-
proportionate a space, compared to normal, his heart occupied in his
thoracic cavity. When I repeated the Spanish saying that a magnanimous
man "has a heart too big for his chest," he said sympathetically, "A very
fitting expression because a man cannot survive when his chest can no
longer contain his heart."

His courage and patience notwithstanding, my Brother-in-Law certainly
realized the seriousness of his illness; his wearisome discomfort made that
perfectly clear. The renal complication and pleurisy, both of which customarily accompany aortic and cardiac conditions, combined to make it terribly
hard for him to bear his physical breakdown. Those of us around him, his
wife especially, tried to help by not acting overly concerned, even acting
exaggeratedly casual and always smiling in his presence, but we could not
fool him. Such rigorous prescriptions of rest and absolute silence could
hardly apply to any malady but the true one. Even if he had lacked self-
awareness or the invalid's typical hypersensitivity, Dr. Monod's young assistant gave it all away. This young man temporarily replaced the doctor, who at
that time lost his twenty-year-old daughter to a hopeless infection. Without
consulting us, this assistant took advantage of the opportunity to ask the
great Spaniard to autograph the first page of a book on cardiac illness. My
Kinsman could not miss the significance. "He wanted to hurry up and get
a souvenir autograph. After I die he can show it off and tell how he studied
this disease in that book and in me." It did not lessen his amusement, I
think it heightened it, to note the fledgling doctor's embarrassment when he
appeared on subsequent visits to give him injections.

When Dr. Monod came again he agreed that we might, with great caution,
move the Patient downstairs. My sister thought that her Husband would
feel more comfortable settled in the anteroom to his study, across the hall
from our dining room. We wanted to carry him in a chair, but he insisted
on walking down and rather fast, horrifying Dr. Monod, who happened to
arrive at that moment. Established in the new room, he sat up in an armchair
during the day, but at night resting upright, supported by pillows, he could
not stretch out in bed. After some time had passed, he could come into the
dining room at noon, wheeled in an armchair to avoid the walk across the
hall from his improvised bedroom. He received our few visitors sitting by
the fireplace with the rest of us. His sister could still not come often because
her husband required her full attention; his nieces sometimes brought little
Manolito, though less frequently now because of his Uncle's illness. My
children also spent less time with him, partly, of course, because we tried
to avoid the fatigue their presence entailed. Mostly, though, the youngsters,
with childhood's egoism, refused to really comprehend what had occurred.
Still, they took great interest in seeing their Uncle given injections, which I

could never stand—and it somewhat frightened them too. Even more than
Manolito, because of her proximity, little Susana enjoyed the prerogatives
of being the youngest. The child always had free entry into her Uncle's
room, though she did not linger there.

When our refugee friends in Paris learned of his illness and its seriousness, they tried to give what little help they could. Among them, Casares
offered, if it seemed a good idea to me, to send down a doctor friend who
had fled from Spain at the beginning of our war. The Montillas favored this
and advised me not to just accept a fatal diagnosis because of the three
doctors who had already seen the Patient. My sister, without venturing to
decide on her own, suggested that her Husband would not accept this offer;
in any case, she believed that we should consult Dr. Monod before we said
anything to the Patient. At my request the doctor himself readily suggested
to my Brother-in-Law that one more examination by someone else might
prove useful. My Kinsman, thanking his doctor for his scrupulousness, expressed satisfaction and confidence in his present treatment. He did not go
on to specify his real reasons for rejecting the suggestion.

He spoke more frankly to us. Did they not have good doctors in France?
Why must we turn to that particular émigré? No, he felt a grievance toward
his old friend [Dr. Teófilo Hernando], not so much political as personal.
The republic, especially cabinets over which he had presided, had shown
deference and respect for that doctor's medical reputation. Then when war
broke out he had run away to France, "caring nothing about either side."
The former President seemed to find this kind of prudence least acceptable
in those who had the greatest obligation to participate in our war effort.
How could he abide someone who had denied the republic, however badly
republicans had behaved? We heard that the doctor excused his flight on the
grounds that he had always avoided politics. That sufficed for my Brother-in-
Law to regret a friendship whose inconstancy again emphasized the self-
denial of thousands and thousands of men who had died and were still
dying, shouting not only "Long live the republic" but also "Long live the
President," even cheering him by name.

He did not take other defections so hard because he had never identified
them with the constancy of imperishable friendship. On the wall of his office
anteroom, now his bedroom, hung a print—"a little print, a curious print,"
as I might put it to parody Azorínian reiteration. It represented a beautiful
young woman dressed in white and wearing a royal crown. Its caption, in
romantic-style letters, read *La Couronne* (The Crown), and at the bottom
was Azorín's dedication. With this gift that illustrious writer and assiduous
explorer of second-hand bookstores had paid an elegant tribute to *The
Crown*'s renowned author about the time of its premiere. Then the wheel of
fortune spun round, changing everything, and the President heard nothing
from Azorín until, fairly well into our war, he wrote concerning the fate of
Antonio Espina. One of our special friends, Espina had been appointed

provincial governor of Majorca—the republic still lacked means of rewarding writers more adequately than with political jobs. He had hardly arrived in Palma when he found himself assaulted by insurgents against established authority, imprisoned like so many others, and on the point of execution. Azorín's letter to the President contained a veiled reproach. No doubt he believed that members of the government who shared Espina's destiny as propitiatory victims could find some better way of helping him in his terrible plight than by merely appealing to those who held him prisoner under threat of execution.

Quite apart from Azorín's letter, Espina's awful situation had always preoccupied the president. He had involved Esplá his under secretary in efforts to secure our governor's deliverance. He also enlisted Giral, who had special responsibility for arranging prisoner exchanges when he served as minister of foreign affairs. My Brother-in-Law arranged to send his friend some money, but learned later that it had not reached him because of a breakdown in transmission. It increased the desperate frustration to learn that this captive had, more than once, reached Barcelona's harbor on the point of freedom and then got sent back to prison on Majorca, threatened with execution as before because of last minute problems about his release. The President feared that Espina might feel abandoned, and, trying to console him, I said that some day the hostage himself would tell us that he had never doubted that the government did everything possible for him—and for others in even greater need, though not with greater right. He never heard those words from his friend, but I did.

In April an unexpected letter came from Don José Giral in Mexico enclosing a manifesto directed to all principal Republican political refugees now dispersed in Spanish America and France. Before circulating it for additional signatures, he wanted them to sign it in their capacities as ministers or under secretaries. Heading that list stood the name of Don Diego Martínez Barrio, president of the Cortes. We learned that a little before or afterwards Martínez Barrio founded an Ateneo in Mexico, a sort of Platonic archetype of a society of free Spaniards to commemorate the republic. He named it for Salmerón, no doubt to prevent anyone from thinking of naming it for my Kinsman, a figure more significant in recent history and whose living person better incorporated the republic's memory. This didn't really bother my Brother-in-Law, though it seemed ridiculous to assign the role of "historic republican" to a stuffed shirt who had lived under the Regency and reign of Alfonso XIII. The former President really minded, however, that his closest collaborators had asked him to sign that manifesto merely as a former minister, apparently a sign of contempt. In another letter, Don José Giral apologized for not having taken into consideration the former President's position; probably he alone did take it into consideration.

Beyond all that, my Kinsman found the manifesto itself completely wrongheaded. He hurried to dictate a letter in response—his last public document.

He wasted no words. He began by applauding the republicans for finally accepting our republic's defeat a year after it happened. Then he went on to explain briefly his reasons for abstaining from signing any such proclamation. He did not believe that our conqueror, who had triumphed over a government established by the national will, would care much for a proclamation drawn up in the name of that government. On the other hand, it seemed premature to try for a restoration of the defeated regime. For republicans to try it alone, without Socialist collaboration, seemed even less feasible. He believed that his own hour had passed, that neither he nor those who had associated with him had anything more to achieve. Having said that, if at any time things changed, in the short run or in the long run—but at a time he could not foresee—then, as in the past, they would find him ready in Bordeaux or in Mestalla. He took this occasion to respond to a letter from a member of Republican Action, the secretary of the Left Republicans and a candidate under their banner in the Popular Front election [Roberto Escribano]. This man had written to the former President about *Vigil in Benicarló,* which he had read in Mexico and apparently not liked. This response paralleled what he had already said to signers of the manifesto.

Afterward he talked to me about it, not budging an inch from what he had written. No, he had nothing to do in Spain. He had failed, and all of the men of our republic along with him. How we all had laughed at those inflexible "beards" of the 1873 republic. Hadn't we of the April 14 minirepublic proved their spiritual heirs in every way, with our debates on the constitution, our controversy over a one-house or two-house legislature, our discussions of constitutional reform, agrarian reform, military reforms, divorce, separation of church and state, and so much else? No, his day had passed, he repeated, whatever happened in Spain. When the current era passed, and it would last longer than those persons believed who did not realize terror's effectiveness, when this era ended, then Spaniards would recognize it and take the steps they had to take. Then Spaniards in Spain would inaugurate the next era, not Spaniards in France—they had already shown their ineptitude—nor in Argentina, nor in Mexico, nor in the United States. Spaniards in Spain.

I could not understand who these Spaniards would be if not those in exile. He had said to me earlier that Franco's government had either killed or imprisoned everyone in Spain on our side. He reasserted his argument, dismissing my reference to liberal émigrés in the nineteenth century because those exiles had done their plotting in a Europe propitious to their activities; today's Europe had become unfriendly to conspirators. "Who knows," he said smiling, "perhaps some unknown functionary in the Registry Office of the Justice Department will become the next leader."

No, his detachment from the power that had once tempted him did not come from disillusion or hopelessness. Rather, illness had purified him. Doctor's orders had reduced his meals drastically, and in a few days this had both much debilitated him and brought some improvement in his condition. Weakness aged him, but it made him more spiritual. Day by day his sickness sharpened and purified his spiritual sensitivity, forcing him, through suffering, to sound depths of understanding that brought him to that perfect sanctity which constitutes the highest state of humanity. (More than once he said to me, "a saint is a perfect man, nothing more.") His dominant intellectualism had always seemed to me the foundation of his character; most people saw this serene decisiveness as unfeeling righteousness. Now his intellectual self-confidence became sublimated in the face of death into voluntary suffering for others. His suffering brought a sense of fulfillment rather than of resignation, a splendor that comes just before an ending, like the dignity a setting sun imparts to thatched roofs, or like the last pages of *Don Quixote* (his Spanish Bible). Seeing him brought tears to my eyes, like seeing the majesty of winds stirring up the sea or a setting sun's last rays through mountains.

One day he felt that he died. Then he became aware that my sister Adelaida, who alternated with his wife when they did not keep watch together, had given him an injection of medicine from a bottle kept in the drawer of a little table by his armchair. Then he recovered enough to ask her whether she had been careful about it; had she injected him with camphor solution? He confronted his approaching death face to face, without fear or surrender. He had always fulfilled his duty, and a man had the obligation to live as long as God chose. When he revived after that first encounter with death had passed, he said to his wife on one side and me on the other, his eyes brimming with tears, "I am going now." My sister wept with him. I tried to hold back. I have never suffered so sharp a pain in my soul. Neither before nor afterward.

No, he didn't die. He remained true to himself to the brink of his grave. Now he is at rest. After that, however, he said to me calmly what my sister did not want to hear, that he wanted to put his worldly affairs in order so that she could live dependent on no one. I interrupted, treating his request as a joke. What did he want me to do? Tell him that he was really terribly ill? Well, I couldn't do it because the doctor didn't believe it. Then I returned to his side, ashamed of my cheap, lying consolations, my childishness. Despite all that, he never made the least allusion to any preparation for a good death in conformity with rituals established by the tradition we call Catholic. Still, he had affirmed on some other occasion that after twenty centuries we have all become more Christian that we believe.

When that crisis passed, our spirits gave something like a sigh of relief in response to his apparent recovery. Then one afternoon Miguel Salvador and his wife came to visit us. She did not seem really close to our political beliefs, but she had shared our anxieties in misfortune and defeat, and now she shared our intimate family feelings about that life we saw slipping away, virtually defenseless against destiny. It please the Invalid to see them, and he particularly appreciated a gift of some kind of jam that Salvador's wife had made herself, precisely because he believed her somewhat remiss politically.

Suddenly the conversation turned dangerous. This involved a lady friend of ours who had come to pick up her son in Pyla, where a philanthropic hostel had been established for uprooted little Spaniards. She challenged the Author of *Vigil in Benicarló* on his opinion about Spanish women as she perceived it. She believed that he had portrayed them unfairly in that dialogue when he represented them by a soprano from the Zarzuela. Of course the Author had not intended, far from it—how crazy—that the soprano in question should represent any particular person, and still less a social class or Spanish women in general. The lady persisted in her argument, proposing that a dialogue must necessarily take place between two persons, no more. It seemed curious to her that with so many persons involved, he had called *Vigil in Benicarló* a dialogue.

When Salvador's wife joined in this discussion, it took a turn more worthy of the Invalid's polemical skills. He suddenly cast aside his weakness, in spite of our efforts to remind him of the importance of remaining calm. She had ventured some opinion that did not seem opportune to the rest of us about crimes committed and the excesses of revolutionary passion aroused by the insurgent soldiers' outrages. The former President got excited without becoming annoyed, always preserving a courtesy he never lost in disputation. His questioner had fallen back on the commonplace about poor little nuns murdered by Reds. He replied that this thorn had pierced his swollen heart, that through the years this kind of irresponsible crime had blemished dawning revolutions with innocuous, if not always innocent, blood. The particular crime to which she referred had caused him more shame, opprobrium, and disgust than anyone else. Crimes by our enemies, however, sickened him a hundred times more, and they bore the additional guilt of their supreme crime of having caused our war.

All of that notwithstanding, he had a fixed opinion about curates, friars, nuns, and especially the lord bishops! "God will not pardon the Catholic Church for what it has done in Spain, and if terrible things have happened to it, even more terrible things will yet come. Future havoc will prove much greater, and none of them will survive to tell about it. Then, too, in their attack on the Church, the people will have what they haven't had during this war: justification for their deeds."

50

Miguel Maura Returns Our Call

The war was going badly. The Germans conquered Poland; then with truly Napoleonic speed they occupied Denmark and Norway, invaded Holland, and launched an explosive attack on Belgium. In France, Reynaud's premiership succeeded that of doleful Daladier whose whining broadcast speeches put the former President in a bad mood. One day on the radio I heard this new premier make an unexpected announcement, "The traitor king of the Belgians has betrayed us." Gamelin, France's commander in chief, flung his best troops into Belgium, and the Germans wiped them out, as they say, in one battle. The English retreated to Dunkirk and returned to their own country. Motorized divisions of Germany's army boldly entered France. My Brother-in-Law began to believe that France might lose the war any time. My sister Lola and my wife insisted on regretting how much better off we would have been if we had left for America when we still had time, and I racked my brains for some kind of argument to justify my decision and my Kinsman's to remain in France. Weygand became commanding general in place of Gamelin.

In spite of all this, through April and May, the President's health began to improve markedly. Dr. Gómez Pallete now came to live with us. My sister Lola had retained great affection for this schoolmate of our brother Ramón, who had died twenty years before at the age of eighteen. When we received Pallete's letter from a concentration camp inquiring about the President's health (he had heard rumors of the illness), we urged him to join us. My invitation found him working in a hospital, but we got permission for him to live with us in Pyla so that the Invalid could have a doctor continuously in attendance. As I had warned him ahead of time, my Brother-in-Law's appearance did not shock Pallete too much. After his first conversation with Dr. Monod, however, because the pain that had first alarmed us persisted in the upper chest, they became concerned about the terrible possibility of cancer of the mediastinum. These fears disappeared after a second, less pessimistic diagnosis. As we continued to see improvements, and fed by Pallete's great optimism, we began to have hopes that in the midst of so much misfortune the former President's condition would mend.

My brother and Santos Martínez wrote urging us to arrange the journey to Mexico that we did not yet dare to make, though my Brother-in-Law now began to favor going as much as he had previously opposed it. We could not possibly think of moving him; traveling even to the nearby port of Bordeaux might bring a fatal relapse. Besides, ships had become very scarce. Then it occurred to the Invalid to solicit from Mr. Bowers, the last United States ambassador to Madrid, the necessary authorization for our inclusion among citizens of that country on a homebound liner. We had seen its proximate arrival announced in the press and a warning to United States citizens that it represented their final chance. Americans who decided to remain in French territory had to realize that they no longer had their government's protection from the war's consequences. I had recently received a letter from Mr. Bowers, sent from Santiago de Chile where he now served as ambassador. He had heard of the former President's illness and inquired about his health. I took advantage of the coincidence, given his interest, to answer Mr. Bowers in the tenor suggested by my Brother-in-Law.

One fine day Sánchez Albornoz called me on the telephone from Bordeaux as he had many times. In spite of his stormy visit some months before, he continued to keep in touch with us, especially after he learned of the serious illness of his Leader and Friend. Right away he announced that he had with him Miguel Maura, who wanted to talk to me about the possibility of a meeting with the former President. I told him that, of course, he could come to our house whenever he liked and without asking beforehand, certain that he would find himself most welcome. Nonetheless Maura insisted that I check with my Brother-in-Law, repeating that he wanted very much to see him, but only if the visit would do him no harm. As I had supposed, the Invalid agreed, "By all means! Yes, let him come. You'll see. His visit has some definite purpose." We agreed, then, that they would come the next afternoon.

To Miguel's question of whether it might upset the President to see him after so long a time and in such critical circumstances, I answered no. Forewarned, he could control his emotions so that the visit would do him no harm. On the other hand, I warned Maura against his own possible upset at finding my Kinsman much changed from the last time he saw him. During all of this, I kept thinking of another urgent telephone call from Maura in another hazardous period, which had led to my first acquaintance with him. He had called my home and asked me to visit him; later he had visited my father's home where my Brother-in-Law was hiding. I especially remembered that August evening in 1931 when the Minister of War felt inspired to drop in on "Maurilla" for a cup of chocolate. After all those years, I mused, Miguel will return our call. That occasion in 1931 had proved more gratifying because of Maura's on-target prediction of his visitor's early accession to the Provisional Government's premiership than for its chocolate and doughnuts. The prediction had shocked its Protagonist who, in turn, had foretold difficulties that position might entail for anyone thrust into it by political contingencies.

The former President received his old friend with a sincere embrace. Despite differences separating them, they had high regard for each other. Though my Brother-in-Law became impatient to the point of irritation over the former justice minister's persistently juvenile capriciousness and inconsistency, he valued Miguel's characteristic cordial spontaneity. I had more experience of this inconsistency than anyone. In the republic's early days he would greet me effusively in the halls of Congress one day and refuse to speak to me another day, depending on the current state of his political relations with my Kinsman.

Moved by the scene of hearty reunion and noting their less than sincere expressions of pleasure at seeing each other looking "so well," I did not at first notice that Sánchez Albornoz had left. Thinking that he had withdrawn from that emotional encounter because of exaggerated discretion, I went to look in the hall and found him seated on a sofa, head in his hands. He apologized for his weakness at the sight of the former President. In four months my Brother-in-Law had become an old man with death's hallmark imprinted on his face. I had to help our friend to find strength to get through that afternoon. For the moment we retreated to the office, where we were all to have some refreshments, leaving my Kinsman and Miguel Maura in the dining room without witnesses. When Miguel Salvador, Montilla, and their wives arrived by special invitation, my sister and Pallete decided to interrupt the Invalid's conversation with his visitor lest he become overly tired.

No hint emerged while we ate of the real reason that had brought Maura from Nice to Pyla. Somehow our conversation turned to Spain's war for independence against Napoleon. The two principal conversants agreed that, while Francophiles were technically correct in praising Napoleon's influence in Spain since he had incarnated the revolutionary spirit, still, all things considered, those persons who blamed him for his imperialism saw him in his true colors. The former President thought that the deputies at the Cortes of Cádiz who opposed Napoleon had acted as true agents of our native tradition combining liberty with national independence, as Spaniards in charge of their own destiny.

Miguel left saying that he would stop by again when he came back from Paris, before returning to Nice. He had no fears about Italy's imminent declaration of war against France in spite of the proximity of his house to the Italian frontier.

After our visitors had gone my Brother-in-Law told me Miguel's real purpose in his visit. Facing an expected Italian declaration of war, M. Delbos, French minister of foreign affairs during most of our civil war, had approached Maura confidentially. His government felt anxious to insure Spain's neutrality, to avoid a Pyrenean war front. On its behalf, M. Delbos had requested that Maura, speaking officially for the French government, seek out the opinions of all refugee Spanish political leaders living in France, including not only republicans and Socialists but also monarchists. Many monarchists, like Maura's close relative the count of the Andes, had settled in Biarritz unwilling to return to Spain before General Franco restored the king. Maura's mission involved a proposal for France's government to intervene with Franco to obtain broad amnesty allowing repatriation of many thousands of refugees now in French concentration camps. In return these refugee party leaders would accept the new order that had triumphed in Spain. They would assure Franco's government that in no case would Spaniards protected by French hospitality take up arms to sustain a new civil war on Spanish soil. This proposal intended to confirm Franco's government in its neutrality, which the government of France feared might change to their disadvantage—even to the point of an attack across the Pyrenees— after Italy declared war.

The former President had answered Maura that anything seemed preferable to renewal of war in Spain. He did not, however, believe that Franco would agree to something that might seem to diminish his victory. In any case, he himself felt more disposed than anyone could possibly believe to act in some way to prevent new victims for the repressive reaction that now dominated Spain. I asked him what more he could possibly do. He said that, in return for Franco's agreement to a general amnesty, he would offer himself as a propitiatory victim to ransom all lives not yet sacrificed in the terrible vengeance that they now called justice in our country.

This plan, which he explained with serenity and determination, seemed absurd to me. Later he also understood that there would be no point in doing such a thing. If Franco had no reason to accept the proposal France's government made through Maura, he would have still less interest in this new scheme. As Franco's government would undoubtedly use my Brother-in-Law's flight to besmirch his reputation with charges of cowardice, they would hardly bolster that reputation by bringing him back to Spain and making a martyr of him. In any case there was no time for any of it to happen.

Maura did not have time to get to Paris. Once Italy declared war on France, and faced with the simultaneous advance of German troops, the French government recalled Marshal Pétain from his embassy in Madrid to become premier. Pétain found himself cruelly called by a fickle destiny to seek an armistice from avengers of the 1918 defeat of imperial Germany. We did not hear again from our friend Miguel.

51

The Debacle

A few days before Pétain's recall, I had received a radiogram from Mr. Bowers, former United States ambassador in Madrid and now in Chile, in response to my letter. He reported that President Roosevelt had ordered Mr. Bullitt, his ambassador in Paris, to facilitate the voyage of the former President and his family to the United States. This radiogram's arrival coincided with a violent German offensive in what remained of independent French territory. The United States ambassador announced that he would remain in Paris. I wrote to my friend Gustavo Pittaluga, supposing that he must have contact with the Americans because he had worked in Spain's Washington, D.C., embassy during the last period of our war. I asked him to make personal contact with Mr. Bullitt. He answered me quickly that I should get in touch with the United States consul in Bordeaux, who had already received the necessary orders.

I went there and with much difficulty succeeded in speaking directly with the secretary and then with the consul. They knew nothing of our situation. When I explained the matter to them, they did not seem much interested in helping me. What could they do? They saw no signs of an American ship. In the present circumstances, they could no longer talk directly with Mr. Bullitt. They saw no use in taking the former President under their protection. Germans did not have to respect the American flag flying over a private house. If I had received a radiogram from Mr. Bowers, then certainly Mr. Bullitt would take up the case with Hitler himself. My alarm somewhat diminished. The consul went on to ask me what the former President could possibly fear. When I pointed to the Austrian premier's terrible death, he replied by emphasizing the differences between the two cases. The Führer had a personal grievance against Dollfuss; his concern to maintain Franco's friendship represented something quite different.

Leaving the consulate, I learned from newspaper headlines that France's government had asked for an armistice. At home the Invalid had not yet heard this news, and we justifiably feared its seriousness might fatally aggravate his condition. We decided that I should tell him sometime before he learned it from the next day's papers; he would not hear it that night as he did not like listening to the radio. Contrary to what we all expected, especially me, he reacted calmly. "Do you know what I think? Now I believe that the English will win this war." Without asking why he felt so sure of this at so critical a moment, I agreed in a very convinced way, beaming with satisfaction to see him react so optimistically, so favorably for his own health, since it showed control over his emotions.

"Yes," he went on, "because now they can go ahead and fight their own war. They will move it away from England; they will take it to the Orient, to Africa, and in due course they will win. Yes, I did not take into account England's traditional perfidy! What a pity that they did not propose to France earlier what they have thought up now!" He spoke of a proposal that the English in their desperation had made government-to-government at the time of France's surrender. Audacious, risky, and undoubtedly somewhat late, like everything the English did in those days to maintain the security of their island, whatever it cost to the security of others. Certainly it was brilliant: military abandonment of French territory in Europe to the German invader, concentration of all French naval forces in English ports, France's army carrying on the war from colonial bases, and establishment of one single government, one Franco-English parliament, to govern their war effort. It represented nothing less than the active nucleus of a great European confederation, and not merely a matter of theory or treaties. It came late.

On the other hand, my Brother-in-Law truly sympathized with Pétain's position. He had admired the marshal as defender of Verdun in the 1914–1918 war and could treat him fairly in spite of his unfortunate embassy to Franco and his disdain toward us. He could never regard Pétain as a traitor, realizing the tremendous sacrifice that the French people themselves called on him to make in accepting responsibility for presiding over their atrocious, incalculable defeat. Twenty years before, the marshal had defended those same French people successfully, contributing as much as Foch to victory by his determined defense of the position entrusted to him, whatever it cost in the lives of his stalwart soldiers. The clever thing, the act of genius, my Brother-in-Law repeated, would have been to accept England's proposal, but that assumed a capacity for resistance that France's people did not have. Couldn't we see their tired resignation in receiving the costly peace settlement? Nobody wanted total occupation of French territory (the immediate consequence of resisting without surrender). We could see how readily the populace accepted German propaganda attacking politicians who called for continuation of the war. It called them men safe in comfortable and profitable exile who wanted only to spill more French blood.

Now my Kinsman refused to accept my complaints, not only against Pétain but against all French politicians, especially members of the Popular Front, for their blameworthy indifference to our cause. I protested against their conceited ignorance in failing to recognize what the former President and all that he had represented in Spain had meant for France. My Brother-in-Law, however, had detached himself from all egoistic considerations and judged persons and events with impressive objectivity. Only a saint in his perfection could treat the world's changing fortunes in this way, with no consideration of his own position. He clearly analyzed Pétain's error, which he took as costly to ourselves, as coming partly from the French people's clear disheartenment and partly from an honest and respectable mistake in judgment. "It all comes from their two million deaths in the other war. They lost a whole generation, the one that would have been between forty and fifty years old today. You can see it. They do not want to have another two million men die."

Not so long before, though, still in Spain, I had heard him speak in his last conversations with Ambassador Labonne with less readiness to accept as inevitable France's resignation from the ranks of great powers, though he did accept it. "What does current French policy mean? They no longer want to serve as Europe's policemen. They have the right to renounce this privilege and its attendant responsibilities. In return, though, they will have to accept the status of a third-rate power and withdraw from their empire and colonies into their patrimonial boundaries."

I returned to Bordeaux another day to see the Mexican consul. In spite of repeated assurances in telegrams from my brother that we had the protection of Mexico's government, their consul gave us no practical assistance. We could not even learn from him the whereabouts of his country's ambassador, who, had left Paris with the rest of the diplomatic corps when German troops entered. I met Casares in Bordeaux with his wife and daughter, the latter despairing because her hopes had collapsed of appearing soon on the Paris stage. She had spent a year preparing for it with a real vocation and assiduous effort. My encounter with these friends moved me deeply.

A few nights later, after dinner with the Montillas, I received a telephone message to return to Eden immediately, though they said that nothing serious had happened. I literally ran the fifteen minutes' distance between those two houses, but Negrín had already left before I arrived. His unexpected visit had prompted the call. They had wanted to inform me so that I could get there in time to see him, but his precipitate departure prevented it. In a few words he had explained his purpose to Gómez Pallete, his friend: he intended nothing less than to take the former President and me to England that same night. Nobody else. He had prepared a small boat in Bordeaux's harbor in which he would also evacuate Lamoneda and Casares; the latter had told him of the former President's condition and our circumstances. Negrín did not have room for the women, but he took it for granted that nothing would happen to them when the Germans came. He had asked to speak with my Brother-in-Law if his colleague the young doctor and my sister thought that a visit would not upset him too much. "A visit from Negrín upset me?" my Kinsman seems to have said when they told him. "No, I'm used to him." And when he saw the former premier coming through the door, responding to his hearty greeting, he said, "Just by coming you have already done more than many friends."

The Patient told me about it smiling. "I said to him that there was no way to move me. Don't you agree that I ought not to go anywhere with Negrín, especially to England?" I agreed, but it took an effort to hide my uncertainty. Pallete had presented the matter to Negrín, in realistic terms: he could see the former President's condition; yet Pallete did not want to assume responsibility for his remaining there. My sister in her distress preferred for her Husband to die on the road rather than have him fall into German hands. I denied the latter possibility but had trouble hiding my fears that it would happen.

Negrín had insistently recommended, in view of the Invalid's refusal to go with him, that I go to Bordeaux still another time and arrange an interview with the United States ambassador to Poland. President Roosevelt had given him interim responsibility for United States representation to France's government (itself adrift) in the zone still free from German occupation. Negrín promised to speak to this ambassador and make clear the former President's difficult position; it would assure me of American help. Things did not turn out that way. The ambassador refused to see me, and after considerable waiting his secretary gave me cold comfort, saying, "After all the Germans have not exactly reached the Pyrenees." Still, they had crossed the Loire and had not answered a French request for an armistice. With the invading troops approaching, I assured the Invalid that the United States ambassador had received me in a very friendly way and that, whatever happened, we could count on the protection of their flag.

Bordeaux now seemed like Figueras a year and a half earlier. Unlike Figueras, though, Bordeaux surrendered after a first, timid aerial bombardment and declared itself an open city.

In the meantime we learned that our neighbor, the writer M. Legrand who had sometimes visited us, had suddenly and surreptitiously embarked for England with all of his family in a boat patrolling the coast to pick up refugees. Others came to visit the former President and urged that we get away from the invasion zone: Dr. Pittaluga, fleeing from Paris; Just, a former minister; and some months earlier our good friend López Gómez, who had commanded the presidential battalion. Others under great pressure or, like Casares, more restricted left without stopping. The police had denied Casares permission to travel even from Bordeaux to Arcachon. The German writer Von Unruh and his wife, also refugees in our vicinity, urged more strongly than anyone that we should not stay. At the war's outbreak French authorities had put him in a concentration camp as a German, though he had a well-known anti-Hitler reputation as a good Social Democrat. The Von Unruhs stressed the terrible danger we all ran in our carelessness about an invasion now coming very close. Not carelessness but helplessness made me assure myself that nothing would happen to the former President, now abandoned by all friendly protection.

A decree appeared prohibiting movement from one French province to another. It assured all persons in territory under German control, including properly documented foreigners, of the protection of French authorities in everything opportune for the occupation's success. German authorities had jurisdiction only over their own soldiers. I calmed down. The police officer assigned to surveillance over foreigners in the Arcachon district seemed very solicitous; hopefully he would keep us informed about changing conditions. For a moment we even hoped that we would escape the Germans altogether because Marshal Pétain's government announced its installation in Bordeaux. Then we learned of the French government's retreat before an unimpeded German advance. Right after that the authorities published armistice terms including in the occupation zone the Department of the Gironde and the coastal region down to Spain's frontier at Hendaye. At this point the police officer communicated to us the prefect's wish—I had seen him more than once without achieving anything—to save the former President any possible annoyance. Because even the sight of Germans might upset his tranquility and delicate health, the prefect both authorized him to leave the zone and provided him with an ambulance.

We decided on his immediate departure for Montauban accompanied by my sister, Dr. Pallete, and Antonio Lot. My Brother-in-Law and my sisters wanted me to go with them; I did not agree. Though it seemed a good thing to spare him even the sight of Germans, it did not seem a good thing to leave our house empty and exposed in those uncertain times. Therefore, though it distressed me not to accompany him, I resisted his urging with some violence. "For once, let me do what I want!" He looked down at the palms of his hands in a characteristic gesture that did not hide his displeasure.

On the morning of their departure he seemed much better, even rejuvenated. He had already settled down in the back of the ambulance while I fiddled around doing one thing and another, undertaking useless errands through which my mind resisted our farewell. He called me over and said with ironic humor, "Well, goodbye. Note that I have said it. I don't want you writing to me from Mexico to tell me that I didn't." This alluded to my resentful complaint, on the point of returning to Spain in 1936, about our farewells before that American voyage. My wife and I had already boarded our express train in Madrid's North Station, ready to leave for La Coruña, New York, and Havana, and some friend interrupted our leave-taking with a confidential message. We almost missed saying goodbye, and my letter complained about that. The message had identified General Sanjurjo as leader of those then plotting a coup d'état. When his ambulance turned onto the highway I could not believe that we would never see each other again.

Quite the contrary, his good spirits when he left fed the optimism that Dr. Pallete had begun to allow us.

We had as guests at that point the Barcelona professor and deputy José Xirau Palau, his wife, and their three children whom they had picked up at the Pyla philanthropic hostel I have mentioned. The Xiraus wanted urgently to get their children back to Lyons where they had settled after leaving Spain, and they did get there two days later. By that time our own travelers had already resumed their trip to Montauban. We knew that they had stayed briefly in a castle on the outskirts of Périgord, delayed by demobilization of French troops who had surrendered.

Meanwhile, the Germans, making a remarkably fast advance even considering the lack of French resistance, took over Arcachon and the Le Moulleau-Le Pyla road as far as the great dune. For twelve days we had no trouble from occupation troops. An officer, with whom my wife spoke in German, came to seek lodging for a general. We agreed, and he chose just one room, not the best but the most private. He advised us that we should not lodge anyone else; we should refer anyone who came seeking lodging to the *Kommandantur.*

I received a magnificent letter from the Invalid, written with a very firm hand and with his old verve and subtle humor. He had not been able to write a letter for a long time. In it he told of their arrival in Périgord; with no place to stay, they had gone to the prefecture. The prefect himself came down to welcome them and arranged accommodations in a castle on the outskirts, the property of a daughter-in-law of Alfred Nobel, the well-known founder of the famous prizes awarded by Sweden's Academy. That lady, French by birth, had at first seemed highly circumspect about her guests. Soon, however, she became very solicitous and ended up vexed when the French government requisitioned her home for other purposes. The government then granted leave for the former President to go on to establish himself in Montauban; his letter came from there. They had found temporary lodging with Spanish friends; Ricardo Gasset, former editor of the *Imparcial,* presided over that household.

Thus we expected things to go as well as possible under the circumstances and relaxed a bit enjoying Atlantic breezes. Then at dawn on July 10 we heard a knock on the door. We thought that it must be the general for whom we had prepared a room. Instead, without quite comprehending, we found ourselves confronting German policemen and obvious Spanish agents masquerading as Germans. Their leader, a Spaniard, began by saying that he only wanted "political documents" inasmuch as the "master of the house," or the man they considered its master, had now gone beyond their reach to Montauban, outside of *our zone.* (Though he spoke in French, he slipped and said *nuestra zona.*) He finished by urging us not to leave any money behind; the Germans would make a thorough search of the house.

They took all of us, including the chauffeur, cook, and my sister's old maid, as detainees to University City in Bordeaux. When we arrived in Bordeaux the Germans searched all of our baggage and confiscated our household money; subsequently they returned a few thousand francs to my wife and sister. A few hours later Carlos Montilla and Miguel Salvador joined us. We men spent that night in prison. The following morning that same bus we had ridden in before picked us up, and we found Teodomiro Menéndez and Francisco Cruz Salido seated inside, arrested at dawn. They drove us to Irún, where German police turned us over to the Spanish agents who had arrested us in Pyla. My wife, my sister Adelaida, the children, and the maid remained confined in University City.

We stayed in the Irún prison for two days. On the morning of July 13, in a very uncomfortable truck, we began our journey to Madrid. At a bend in the road of the Régil grade, a police car following us pulled up alongside; we stopped and the agent who had arrested us got out and made me get out. He took me back a stretch of road, with an Assault Guard behind, and, making me climb up a few meters into the wooded mountain, he warned me that they would shoot me in five minutes unless I told him the bank where my Brother-in-Law kept his money. I told him that he would find all our money in the truck along with all those boxes and bundles of papers that crowded us so much. No doubt he had already discovered it in the suitcase where my sister had put it when we left for Bordeaux.

"Do you expect me to believe that you have no more money than that?" The day before he had exaggerated it as a fortune; apparently he had not counted it. Then I had answered him, "Do you think that a lot for a President to save? He had a salary of a million pesetas." Now I gave him a converse answer, "Yesterday you called it a fortune. Why does it suddenly seem so little today? Well, he couldn't save any more than that." The agent replied that they had only wanted to test me; they knew very well that Negrín had "the gold from the Bank of Spain." I merely responded that he seemed to know more about it than I did.

An hour later we stopped at an inn, and they took just me out to have breakfast with them, those same agents and two others, the Police Department's secretary general and the marquess of Linares's son—as I learned later. Now they seemed really curious about why my Brother-in-Law had not emigrated with his friend Prieto and why he had kept 750,000 "Negrín pesetas" in the suitcase—his last salary payment, whose exchange into francs they had promised him when he left Spain.

As already indicated, on July 13 I entered the Central Police Department, established in the former Ministry of the Interior right on the Puerta del Sol. Three months passed before I heard news of my family. During this period my wife, my children, and my sister Adelaida, returned from Bordeaux, but they remained prisoners of the Germans in Eden, unable to leave for Montauban or to communicate with the former President and our sister.

In mid-August, while briefly out of my cell, I learned that Companys and

Zugazagoitia were in the same prison. I spoke briefly with Companys in passing, but they did not allow me to share with him food my Madrid relatives sent me or clothing and food sent to him by his family through my relatives. One September morning the authorities took him to Barcelona; we learned much later that they had shot him at the Montjuich fortress.

One typically boring day an officer, I think an Assault Guard, opened my cell door halfway and said in a stupid effort to annoy me. "So then, have they caught your Brother-in-Law yet? They are getting them all." That told me that they had not taken him. I did not answer, resigned to getting through that time of gloomy confinement by stoicism and reflection. I did call the officer of the guard to report this breach of my incommunicado. Nobody bothered me after that. Judging, then, that my Kinsman had not died from emotional upset over the culminating disaster of my arrest, I clung to the idea of my imprisonment as a way of working out the adversity of our common destiny. From the day of my incarceration in Madrid, I turned to composing verses, beginning with a series of fourteen sonnets, the first and last dedicated to his living memory. That began my composition of what had amounted by the beginning of October to 4,800 lines of memorized verse, including a dramatic poem in three acts. It provided me with considerable diversion.

52

Peace at Last

My first letter from my sister Lola confirmed the tranquility with which I determined to sustain myself. The Invalid had serenely withstood the terrible shock of my arrest. She wrote that after considerable improvement he had suffered a relapse from which he had, again, recovered. I could not understand what that really meant.

On October 21 they transferred me to the Salesas Prison with Zugazagoitia, Cruz Salido, Teodomiro Menéndez, Carlos Montilla, and Miguel Salvador. Except for Teodomiro—who got off with a thirty-year sentence—the Summary Court judged us and condemned us to pay the supreme penalty. Only one of the public prosecutor's charges made an impression on me: that I had allowed my "noxious" Brother to influence me. At that moment I dedicated to him the best that was in me. The rest of it had no more impact than my humiliating discomfort before the examining board for a career in diplomacy twenty-five years earlier. Now as then, I felt my Brother-in-Law's support, suffering from my sluggishness and then laughing fondly at me afterwards because my usual flippancy, now as then, had turned into diffidence before my examiners. His presence in the depths of my consciousness sustained me sure and firm without anyone knowing it—neither those judges, nor that noisy crowd of onlookers, not even my fellow defendants on trial. The whole procedure seemed nonsense. I never believed that they would kill me.

The same night, before we knew the verdict, they moved us to the Porlier Prison. Perhaps unconsciously, I refused to notice an obvious warning—which my companions did notice: they left us overnight in its chapel. The next day we waited for a while in the prison office for the sentence hanging over our heads. Later they moved us back to the chapel. My cousin Pedro Cuadrillero came to see me. They had commuted his death sentence a year before, but he remained a prisoner. The chaplain also visited us, as did Dr. Roquero and an intern, also prisoners, who removed an annoying boil for Zugazagoitia.

At nightfall on November 5 my cousin Perico came again to the chapel to tell me news he would have preferred not to tell me under any circumstances. Editors of the prison newspaper *Redención* had just learned of the

404

former President's death. They had heard a radio report picked up in Spain that Velao, a former minister, had sent a message of sympathy to my sister. Spanish newspapers had authorization to print a simple notice without commentary the following day. So far as I know they did not then or ever officially announce his death. They left that to chaplains and missionaries, who used this story for purposes of proselytism in prisons. These people did not approach me.

I tried to control my feelings, but Montilla saw my tears. They all shared my grief, but their heavy silence soon gave way to an effusion of homage that better suited my own feelings toward his memory. That night, stretched out on my sleeping pallet, I relied on the discretion of my five companions and gave way to my tears. In spite of everything, I slept, consoled by one thought: now he has his peace.

On the morning of November 9 at nine o'clock Julián Zugazagoitia and Francisco Cruz Salido suffered the sentence to which the court had condemned five of us. Our lawyer, a man otherwise humanely sensitive, chose this terrible moment of farewell to confirm my personal misfortune in my Brother-in-Law's death by saying erroneously, "Yes, it seems certain. The bishop of Toulouse gave him the Last Rites." A little later I was standing in the doorway of the warden's office where the two condemned men waited for their execution. At least at this point they spared us the reactionary horror of the chapel. Don Amancio Tomé, the warden, asked them whether they had agreed to make their confessions. The Reverend Augustinian Father Félix García had helped me in material ways and made himself a friend to my two more unfortunate companions. Now, as he remained silent, Tomé insisted, "What pride in facing God! Well, look around you! I've heard that your Brother-in-Law made his confession." I answered him, "He may even have done it sincerely. He had a church wedding in 1929, and I never heard him renounce his baptismal vows." Father Félix García discreetly interrupted that painful conversation, "Many people who do not seem to practice are actually more Christian than others."

Only months later did I learn the actual circumstances of the former President's death. Quite a while after I arrived at the Puerto de Santa María Prison to serve my sentence, a letter came from my sister, Lola, giving irrefutable, precise details that she later confirmed for me. Only now in the freedom of exile can we reproduce that letter fully and uncensored. She wrote as follows:

"When we got to Montauban, no doubt because we had to renew our trip so soon, our Invalid felt so exhausted that he barely made it up a few stairs and into the house. Once inside, he could not speak to the people waiting for him. After resting a while in an armchair, he went straight to bed. It frightened Pallete and me to see him like that, and we decided that he should have an injection. With that he got a good night's sleep. Soon, daily letters from Adela and you became his best medicine, knowing that you were all right in spite of the occupation. Gradually, after seeing almost nobody those first days, he began to get better again.

"He didn't much like our lodging, but the prefect told us on a visit he made the day after our arrival that they just didn't have other available housing in Montauban. The prefect's notion of moving him into the prefecture seemed unwise because the army was using it as temporary headquarters. Since there was no help for it, he accepted our accommodations without further comment. Certainly everyone had arranged things for us with the best will in the world. Dr. Cabello shared his house with other Spaniards, each paying his own board and room. Ricardo Gasset presided, and the household included an old gentleman, a deputy from Martínez Barrio's party; a young Catalonian lady, a relative of the old gentleman or a family friend; another deputy, a Left Republican who had arrived two or three days before we did; and Santos's cousin, also recently arrived. The young lady had given up her small room for us and moved into a friend's house. She went back and forth, continuing to act as mistress of the household, and she always joined us for meals.

"Alone in our room, our Invalid commented sorrowfully on what we had come to. He only agreed to stay in the house on the basis of our paying for board and room. We were sure that nobody had means beyond his own immediate needs. All in all, in spite of the annoyances and disturbances of living in so small a house with people he did not know well, he began to feel at home. He didn't go outdoors, but he soon settled into something like a normal routine. He would change from his invalid's robe and pajamas into a suit for meals in the dining room. He said that it seemed wrong to act as he would in his own house. He spent his time reading and occasionally writing, but mostly resting as usual.

"Three or four days of not hearing from you upset him. I couldn't explain it as a delay in the mail because other letters kept coming in. His pleasure, almost like a child's, in your and Adela's concern for him, your spoiling him—to the point of each writing separately in case a letter got lost—turned suddenly into an obsession about what had happened to you. From the moment he became convinced that some disaster had occurred, he counted the hours until mail deliveries or radio news broadcasts, living only to find out what had happened. He learned it in a letter from his sister that she had put into an envelope addressed to Dr. Pallete; Pepita was afraid to send a letter in her brother's name from the zone occupied by Germans. He tore it open anyhow, sure that she meant it for him, so we could not prevent his reading it.

"The family at Eden villa had disappeared, and nobody knew what had happened to them. It stunned both of us, sitting there alone in our room. He moved to get out of bed, and, since he would not listen to me, I went to find Dr. Pallete so that he would tell him, as a doctor, to stay quiet in bed for the sake of his health. Our Invalid answered the doctor that he would die in the plaza on his way to the prefecture, if that had to be, but he must inform the French government of what had just happened. In the end he went with Pallete and someone else, but after he got to the prefect's office he could not talk with French officials in Vichy. He could hardly even talk to the prefect. Still, this effort so impressed the prefect that he communicated the President's wishes to the minister [head of the Mexican Legation in Vichy] saying that he had him right there. The minister said that, given the seriousness of this news, he did not want to comment without having exact information. He said that he would go to Bordeaux and promised to send word to us as soon as he found out. That word never came.

"The prefect wanted to save our Invalid feeling obliged to repeat what he had just done, with such danger to his serious condition. Therefore he gave orders that whenever the Invalid wanted to use the prefecture's official telephone line they should connect it with the telephone in our house. After that, though his health rarely permitted him to talk, he kept urging me to use the phone in his name, especially to call the United States and Mexican embassies. When he did once succeed in talking with Herriot [Edouard Herriot, president of the French Chamber of Deputies], Herriot cut their conversation short because he was afraid of monitoring of the telephone lines. In his desperation he talked another day with the chargé d'affaires or secretary of the United States embassy. He informed them of his condition and asked for whatever help they might provide in getting him an embassy car so that he could travel to Vichy. They answered that they had no gasoline.

"He suffered this terrible uncertainty with nobody paying any attention to him for a couple of additional days until a second letter came. This one, from Monod, gave more details. The authorities were holding the women and children incommunicado in the house, and everything in it of value had disappeared, archives and money. As he had heard nothing about you, Monod supposed they had taken you to Spain. 'Well, they really knew how to hurt me! This one thing I cannot stand!' our Invalid commented. Yet he amazed everyone by his tremendous effort to control his feelings in consideration for me. It soon proved too much, and, as he had feared, a very few days later he woke up stammering for words when he tried to speak. This really upset him. I went to find Pallete in his room. He immediately recognized the symptoms of a stroke and did not want to assume full responsibility in that moment of crisis. He and Dr. Cabello decided to inform a Montauban doctor who was to serve as Dr. Monod's replacement. They and this Dr. Pouget, to whom the Invalid took an immediate liking, put him under the same rigorous regime as at the beginning of his illness, and again rest and seclusion brought the beginning of a recovery. He took to reading from his writings to members of the household; Dr. Pallete said that he did it as an exercise in his obsession to recover his pronunciation.

"Things went on like that from the end of July until mid-September. Then

I began to feel concerned about a group of Falangists who had recently come to Montauban from Spain. (Monod had warned in his letter about urgent questions concerning the Invalid's whereabouts at the time of your arrest.) Pressed by the owner of the house to move, I called the Mexican minister in Vichy and succeeded in convincing the Invalid to accept General Cárdenas's invitation to move into their embassy. Minister Rodríguez agreed to come for us in a car with Mr. Castro, the legation's secretary, on the morning of September 15. On the afternoon of the fourteenth, our Invalid, who could not do it himself, thought that I should bid farewell to the prefect and thank him for his first visit and all of their later meetings. (The prefect had also sent two young ladies on a supposed errand to Pyla with the sole purpose of bringing back fuller news about the detainees.) Accompanied by Pallete, I went to the prefect's office, and to my surprise he said that the President could not leave Montauban without specific permission from the French government. I tried to hide my natural annoyance when we returned home so as not to upset the Invalid, and we tried to make him believe that the Mexican minister would certainly bring the required permit. He was hard to fool; he answered right back that I should have no illusions, it would not turn out that way. He now realized that we must stay in Montauban and could not leave no matter how hard we tried.

"On the following morning, still hoping that once the minister arrived in Montauban he could arrange everything, we got ready and settled down to await his arrival. Our Invalid became impatient when the minister did not arrive on time, but they had only been delayed. Our news surprised Mr. Rodríguez, and, though he felt sure that he could resolve everything in a minute with the prefect, his interview proved our Invalid right. Rodríguez could do nothing; we could not leave. Then the minister decided to move us to a hotel, and he himself took us there in his car. He registered our room in the legation's name and arranged for two or three persons to lodge there to look after us: a consul, a secretary, and a military attaché. He would return to Vichy to talk with French authorities. We slept that night in the hotel, and in the morning the minister requested permission to present to us members of the legation who had just arrived and who would remain in our service until he returned. The Invalid felt very pleased and gratified, and he talked quite a while with them, until the minister said goodbye. Then the others went to their rooms, very close to ours. After his earlier great upset at not being able to leave Montauban, the Invalid spent the rest of that morning calmly.

"Though the best hotel in Montauban, it was second or third-class. I suggested some arrangements to make the Invalid more comfortable, especially about his food. Perhaps Antonio, our servant, could handle all that, both its serving and its preparation in the kitchen downstairs. The owners would have cooperated; from the first day to the last we found them perfectly helpful and pleasant, but we could not convince the Invalid. He insisted that we make no effort for anything different from other hotel guests. Determined to show our complete satisfaction, he began by eating everything they brought; then he went back to bed as usual. I sat in a chair by him, reading, and he seemed to go right to sleep. After less than an hour he surprised me by sitting up, and, noticing that he had awakened, I turned toward him and saw him trying to get out of bed, his face terribly contorted, unable to speak. Just then Ricado Gasset happened to enter our room, and recognizing the situation and its effect on me, he signaled to me from the doorway to stay calm. He went to find the two doctors, and they came back with him right away.

"He had had another attack, and this one so severe that they considered recovery impossible. We waited all day expecting the end, and when night came we believed that it would be his last. The minister had only gotten to Toulouse when he learned of this attack, and he came back to stay with me. Contrary to even the doctor's expectations, the Invalid did begin to improve; however, as days passed, I recognized a difference from the other recoveries that we had seen. The minister left again, but the other persons from the legation remained with us; if they served no other purpose, their mere presence contributed greatly to our Invalid's tranquility. He began to walk, but with a cane, unsure of his feet. At first, though his facial paralysis largely disappeared, he had difficulty in talking. Also, his inability to think clearly made me believe that he could not really recover, and a change in his usual facial expression increased this impression. After the first few days, though, when he went back to talking normally, for long intervals I forgot his illness and came to believe that he would recover. I had the illusion that his thinking faculties would return to their normal state.

"One fine day a nun from Montauban turned up asking him to see her. I resisted this on several occasions when she came to the hotel, fearing that she might want to meddle about something that would upset the Invalid. As she insisted, Pallete saw her, and far from what I expected, she had come to us as persons who might put her in touch with the Mexican minister toward assisting some Jewish families who wanted to get out of France. (Nobody could understand their position better than I, she said.) Finally some of them did get out, and another lady, still in Montauban, came to the hotel to thank me for all that we had done for them. In this way I came to know Sister Ignace. She continued to come from time to time to ask about the Invalid and about the rest of you, and he heard so much from Pallete about how nice she was that he said that he would like to meet her. He asked that she come up to his room so that he could thank her for her concern. One day she did come up with Mrs. de Acosta, Altamira's daughter, who had also been assiduous in her inquiries about him. They stayed for only a short time, but the nun's visit made him think how much he would enjoy seeing Father San Sebastián.

"He asked me to inquire when I saw her whether, as a French Basque and friend of Spanish friars who had come into France, as she had said during her visit, she might know that friar and might discover his whereabouts. When I asked the nun, she inquired everywhere, especially since our Invalid became obsessed about it. Though we couldn't find Father San Sebastián, he kept insisting that we keep searching. Pallete, seeing me upset to the point of distraction because I didn't know what more to do, tried to calm me by saying that, without realizing it, our Invalid sometimes went beyond normal rationality and did not know what he said. For that reason, he added, I shouldn't take everything literally. This new sorrow overwhelmed me. His preoccupation about you made him try to think of anyone who might assist you. When his reason or consciousness went, he kept coming back to the same idea and spoke constantly of you all. In the hours before he died, he called for you in a hopeless, awful delirium.

"I never left him. Pallete felt that because of the seriousness of the illness Saravia should come to Montauban, and he did. Apart from him and a half dozen other people, we never had visitors. Still, the Invalid got tired of that same room, and sometimes he would walk from the armchair in his room to one in Saravia's room on the same floor. Other times, obsessed with the idea of going in search of you, he would just walk up and down the corridor with Antonio. When he left our room I would shed a flood of tears because of his hopeless wish to see you all. Pallete was the first person who came into our room, every day at eight-thirty, and was the last to leave at night, after the injection to help our Invalid to sleep. Always the same. Also his regular doctor came twice every day without fail.

"A friend told us that a new bishop had arrived in Montauban. Also we heard a great ringing of bells in the cathedral opposite our hotel at the moment the bishop blessed the people after his consecration. That afternoon our Invalid, feeling quite well, spoke to me about the pretty ceremony in the cathedral, 'too bad we couldn't have seen it!' and in this connection he recalled celebrations in the Escorial church. Days later on one of many occasions when he pondered what else we might do for you and the others, in passing he thought of the bishop. He didn't, however, say more about it. Then on another occasion in the middle of a conversation, he said again that he really would like to see the bishop. He insisted several times, but I resisted doing anything about it, not knowing whether he really meant it. 'I should like someone in France to know that I am not a bandit.' He said that many times, grieving about the little or no respect shown him by French authorities and foreign governments represented in Vichy. We talked about it calmly then, but afterwards this became one of his obsessions when he lost control of his thoughts and got things mixed up without order or connection. His eagerness to see the bishop became so great that one day in Saravia's presence he complained that I paid no attention to what he said. Still, though Saravia said to me that it would be easy to gratify this wish, encouraging me to do it, I did not let him convince me. I remembered Pallete's earlier arguments when he wanted to calm me.

"On the morning of October 15, it surprised both of us, but especially the Invalid, that Pallete did not come into our room as usual. I went to find Antonio so that he could tell him that we were waiting. In the corridor I met Saravia, his face grief-stricken. He said that Pallete had suffered an appendicitis attack so urgent that they had taken him to the hospital, where, because of its seriousness, they hesitated to operate. With this terrible shock I returned to my Invalid's side, not telling him how serious it was. I treated it as something routine, merely saying that Pallete had gone to the hospital with an appendicitis attack. It seemed better to handle it this way because someone might forget and inadvertently mention it. The others, in turn, deceived me all that day. The nun countered my wish to visit Pallete in the hospital by saying that with my Invalid so accustomed to my presence, my own absence would upset him more than anything else could. Early the next morning, leaving my room to find someone to give me news, I found the nun waiting for me. She embraced me weeping and said. 'We can do nothing more for him.' She told me that by Saravia's orders that had hidden Pallete's death from me all those hours. I dried my tears and, again finding strength in weakness, went back to my room as though nothing had happened. The Invalid asked several times for Pallete. I said that he had gone to consult Dr. d'Harcourt in Toulouse, but, no doubt, he understood what had happened. Soon he neither asked about him nor mentioned his name.

[Dr. Pallete committed suicide. Mrs. Azaña repressed this information in earlier editions of this book not sure whether his family knew it.]

"After this new horror, I wanted to leave Montauban, and Dr. Pouget also thought that a move might benefit the Invalid. If we could not expect a real cure, a milder climate and, above all, more pleasant surroundings than that dreary hotel corridor might help his nerves. Thus Dr. Pouget wrote up a certificate informing the authorities of his Patient's needs. Pouget could not leave his other patients, and he thought it would be risky for us to move to Aix (the place that we chose) by ourselves now that we didn't have Pallete; he suggested Dr. Acosta as a substitute. Acosta agreed right away when I inquired through his wife, but we could not make the move. However serious his illness, the government refused to allow the President to leave Montauban. Nevertheless Acosta went on taking very good care of him to the very end, and the Invalid got so accustomed to his new doctor that he was always asking for him. Now our Invalid kept inquiring every day about our journey to Marseilles, but I resigned myself to merely changing to a more cheerful room. He took to looking out onto the plaza from the window of this second room. One day he said that he would like to go out and shake hands with all the Spaniards in Montauban who did not dare to come up to see him. Other times, looking at the cathedral's facade, which he could see better than in our other room, he repeated his sick man's insistence that he wanted to meet the bishop.

"At the end of October, I think on the twenty-eighth, some friend came into Saravia's room and panicked when he saw our Invalid reading a newspaper. He had come to the hotel expressly in case the President had not yet seen the report of your condemnation. He hurried out to get Saravia who came in and literally pulled the newspapers out of our hands. That astonished us, and I went out to ask for an explanation. They said that they had wanted to prevent his reading about Companys's execution, but I couldn't read about it either because the paper had disappeared. I spent another anguished night, sure of some new deception. Saravia told me the truth the first thing next morning, against his better judgment but overruled by the others. A summary court had judged and condemned you to death.

"Without leaving Saravia's room, where they had called me, I began writing cables to friends and enemies all over the world who might help to prevent your execution. Right after that, accompanied by the nun, I went to see the bishop, who received me at once and tried to console and calm me. He dictated two cables, one to Franco and one to Rome. To reassure me, he let me send them myself. The morning after that, concerned because he had not received a reply from Spain, the bishop came to our hotel for news. Once there, he came up to see our Invalid, who knew nothing of what had happened. We just told him that the bishop had come to meet him. Very pleased and smiling, sitting by the fireplace during that short visit, he spoke of you, of the children, of his youth at the University of the Escorial; in short, he spoke of all his concerns, but especially of you all, obsessively. After all, his illness prevented him from saying much. The bishop, no doubt seeing his fatigue, left very soon. We did not ask him to come back.

"The bishop did come again, though, to inquire about you. No doubt he had recognized the Invalid's extreme illness, and this time he brought a Spanish priest, a refugee in France whom I did not know. Though the Invalid no longer understood what was going on, I would not let that priest in. Because he had asked so many times to see the bishop, I did let him come in. Finally I didn't know whether I was doing what he wanted or not, and, tormented that someone might annoy him, I locked our door from the inside. After that hardly anyone came in but Saravia and Antonio whose room connected with ours. That night after ten, with Antonio by my side, I realized that our Invalid was dying. Distressed at staying alone in my grief, I asked Antonio to call Saravia who had some friends in his room. Once Saravia came I sent Antonio to get the nun, who, by my request, brought the bishop with her. Our Invalid died minutes later, and all my strength left me. I knew nothing for some time—maybe hours or maybe seconds—until I woke up stretched out on a bed in the room next door surrounded by friends. I could not return to my own room. On the following morning I wanted to go back for a last time, but, again, had not strength to stay. I could not watch them take him away.

"The Mexican minister and people from the legation attended the burial. He took me to Vichy that same day and arranged for Saravia and Antonio to accompany me. Before leaving Montauban I asked Saravia to come with me to say goodbye to the bishop. Other friends made cemetery arrangements according to my wishes. Just a flat tombstone with two cypresses and a bronze cross and under it the inscription:

Manuel Azaña
1880–1940.

"I hope you agree," my sister wrote in that letter back then, "that I did the right thing." [Mrs. Azaña's concern was about putting a cross on the tombstone.]

You did the right thing.

Now he has what he longer for: *peace.*

Genealogies of the Azaña Díaz, Rivas Cherif, and Ibañez Gallardo Families

Names appearing on more than one tree are in boldface.

AZAÑA DÍAZ

Long established in Alcalá de Henares (Madrid Province) the Azañas had contributed notaries and other civil servants to the city.

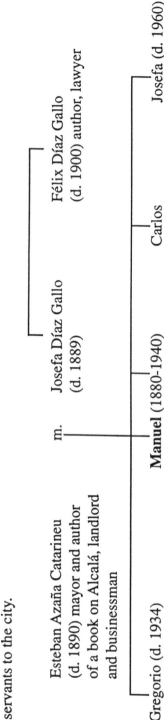

Esteban Azaña Catarineu (d. 1890) mayor and author of a book on Alcalá, landlord and businessman   m.   Josefa Díaz Gallo (d. 1889)

Félix Díaz Gallo (d. 1900) author, lawyer

Gregorio (d. 1934) lawyer, judge, married three times, had six daughters and son, Gregorio, public prosecutor in Córdoba where Nationalists shot him 1936.

Manuel (1880-1940) m. 1929 **Dolores de Rivas Cherif**, no progeny

Carlos died in youth

Josefa (d. 1960) m. Ramón La Guardia army officer, no progeny

A Díaz Gallo cousin married Gen. Ángel García Benítez a prominent Nationalist. They and their sons and daughters appear in this book.

RIVAS CHERIF

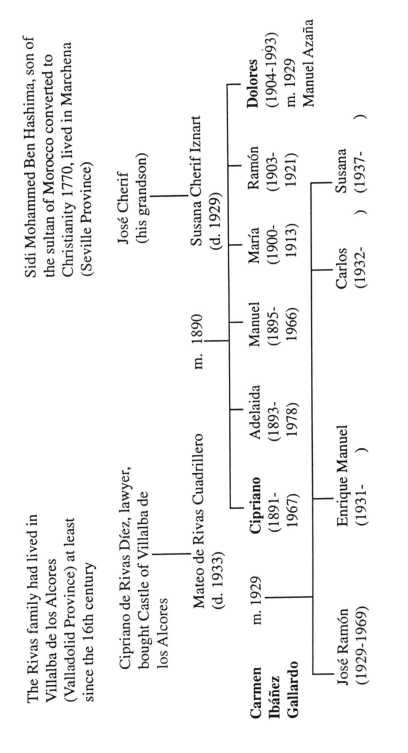

The Rivas family had lived in Villalba de los Alcores (Valladolid Province) at least since the 16th century

Sidi Mohammed Ben Hashima, son of the sultan of Morocco converted to Christianity 1770, lived in Marchena (Seville Province)

José Cherif (his grandson)

Cipriano de Rivas Díez, lawyer, bought Castle of Villalba de los Alcores

Mateo de Rivas Cuadrillero (d. 1933)

m. 1890

Susana Cherif Iznart (d. 1929)

Cipriano (1891-1967)

Adelaida (1893-1978)

Manuel (1895-1966)

María (1900-1913)

Ramón (1903-1921)

Dolores (1904-1993) m. 1929 Manuel Azaña

Carmen Ibáñez Gallardo

m. 1929

Enrique Manuel (1931-   )

Carlos (1932-   )

Susana (1937-   )

José Ramón (1929-1969)

IBÁÑEZ GALLARDO

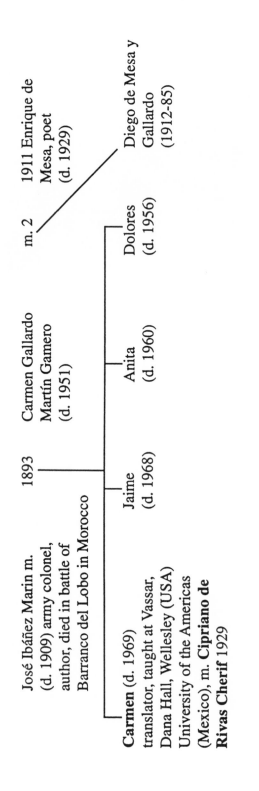

José Ibáñez Marin m.
(d. 1909) army colonel,
author, died in battle of
Barranco del Lobo in Morocco

1893

Carmen Gallardo
Martín Gamero
(d. 1951)

m. 2

1911 Enrique de
Mesa, poet
(d. 1929)

Carmen (d. 1969)
translator, taught at Vassar,
Dana Hall, Wellesley (USA)
University of the Americas
(Mexico), m. **Cipriano de
Rivas Cherif** 1929

Jaime
(d. 1968)

Anita
(d. 1960)

Dolores
(d. 1956)

Diego de Mesa y
Gallardo
(1912-85)

Index